Germans, Jews and the Claims of Modernity

GERMANS, JEWS AND THE CLAIMS OF MODERNITY

Jonathan M. Hess

YALE UNIVERSITY PRESS
NEW HAVEN AND LONDON

Library
University of Texas
at San Antonio

Copyright © 2002 by Yale University

For information about this and other Yale University Press publications please contact:
    US Office: sales.press@yale.edu   www.yale.books.com
    Europe Office: sales@yaleup.co.uk   www.yale.up.co.uk

Designed by Elizabeth Smith
Set in Caslon by SNP Best-set Typesetter Ltd., Hong Kong
Printed in Great Britain

Library of Congress Cataloging-in-Publication Data

Hess, Jonathan M., 1965–
    Germans, Jews and the claims of modernity/Jonathan M. Hess.
      p.   cm.
    Includes index.
      ISBN 0-300-09701-8 (hardcover: alk.paper)
    1. Jews—Emancipation—Germany.   2. Jews—Legal status, laws, etc.—Germany—
      History—18th century.   3. Jews—Legal status, laws, etc.—Germany—History—19th
      century.   4. Antisemitism—Germany—History.   5. Germany—Ethnic relations.
I. Title.
    DS135.G33 H43 2002
    305.892′4043′09033—dc21   200201452

A catalogue record for this book is available from the British Library.

10 9 8 7 6 5 4 3 2 1

For Beth, Rebecca and Lily

CONTENTS

ACKNOWLEDGMENTS

The research and the writing of this book would not have been possible without generous support from a number of foundations and institutions. Stipends from the National Endowment for the Humanities, the German Academic Exchange Service and the Leo Baeck Institute allowed me to spend several months in 1999 working in the extensive collections of the Leo Baeck Institute in New York. Diane Spielmann and Frank Mecklenburg at the Leo Baeck Institute deserve a special word of thanks for making the LBI such a wonderful place to conduct my research. I would also be remiss here if I did not express my gratitude to my mother, Frances A. Hess, for exclusive rights to her guestroom during my stay in New York, and for so many pleasant dinners.

Thanks to a fellowship from the American Council of Learned Societies and an Andrew W. Mellon Foundation grant from the National Humanities Center, I had the privilege of spending the academic year 1999–2000 as a fellow at the National Humanities Center in Research Triangle Park, North Carolina, where I was able to complete much of the research for the book and begin writing in earnest. The librarians at the National Humanities Center, Alan Tuttle, Eliza Robertson and Jean Houston, have left their mark on this book in ways they probably cannot fathom; they continually amazed me in their ability to track down what must have seemed to them extremely obscure essays and reviews in journals that had been out of print for nearly two hundred years. I also need to thank Bob Connor, President and Director of the Humanities Center, Kent Mullikin, the Humanities Center's Deputy Director, and all the fellows in the class of 1999–2000 for creating such a stimulating atmosphere in which to think and write.

Back at my home institution, I was able to spend yet another semester devoted to research and writing at the UNC Institute for the Arts and Humanities in Fall 2000. Lloyd Kramer and John McGowan, directors of that fall's faculty seminar, should be singled out both for creating such a productive forum for intellectual interchange and for their comments on my own work. The University of North Carolina further supported this project through a University Research Council grant that covered the costs of reproductions and paid for a professional indexer. The librarians at the interlibrary borrowing office at Davis Library at UNC, whom I have rarely seen face to face, also deserve special recognition for managing to locate for me just about anything I requested, no matter how obscure.

Germans, Jews and the Claims of Modernity spans several disciplines, and it would be difficult for me to estimate just how much the book owes its present shape and form to formal and informal discussion with friends and colleagues at UNC and elsewhere. It would be impossible to give a list of everyone whose good will and generosity I have taken advantage of, but a few individuals do need to be mentioned here. Susannah Heschel read more of this book in manuscript that anyone should really have had to, and her criticisms, comments and enthusiasm were crucial for me in refining my grasp of the issues at stake here. During the early stages of the project, I profited tremendously from the comments of Martin Davies, Sue Kassouf, Ron Schechter and Allan Arkush on some of my initial essays on Christian Wilhelm Dohm. Tomoko Masuzawa, Karin Schutjer and Jay Geller all made perceptive comments on my work on Michaelis when it had yet to be integrated into a larger whole. Allan Arkush and Matt Erlin read an early draft of the Mendelssohn chapter and made wise suggestions for revisions, and Tony La Vopa provided a helpful sounding board when I was still formulating my ideas about Ascher and Fichte. Throughout my work on this book, Liliane Weissberg proved a valuable resource, and she deserves thanks as well. If the introduction to the book is clear, it is undoubtedly because of the constructive criticism I received from David Brenner, Jeff Grossman, Kathryn Starkey and George Williamson. Sections of the book were presented at the annual meetings of the German Studies Association, the Association for Jewish Studies, the American Society for Eighteenth-Century Studies, and the American Academy of Religion/Society for Biblical Literature, and at a variety of other national and local venues, and the questions and comments of these audiences were instrumental in helping me to clarify my arguments. Twice during the work for this book I had the opportunity to teach a graduate seminar on "Germans, Jews and the Discourse of Enlightenment," and I owe a special debt to my graduate students in this course—and in several others—for allowing me to subject them to my musings on the topic of this book. My chair, Clayton Koelb, and all my departmental colleagues were all extremely supportive of my research, and it with great pleasure that I express my gratitude to them here.

Adam Freudenheim at Yale University Press has been an exemplary editor since we first began to correspond about my project, and I thank him not just for his enthusiasm but for his perceptive comments on fundamental matters of style and substance at all stages of the book. If *Germans, Jews and the Claims of Modernity* reaches the audience it aspires to, it is partly his doing. The three anonymous readers of the manuscript also made extremely helpful comments and criticisms, and the book in its final form owes much to their critiques. Beth Humphries deserves a special word of gratitude for her expert copy-editing, and I am greatly indebted to Margot Levy for preparing the index.

More than anyone else, though, I need to thank my wife Beth for her love, support and good humor (and for reading and commenting on more of the manuscript than she should have been expected to). I dedicate this book to her, and to our two daughters: Rebecca, who was born just as I started my fellowship at the National Humanities Center, and Lily, who came on to the scene just weeks after I sent the final version of the manuscript off to London. In all fairness, I should also mention our resident hound dog, Fookie, for reliable companionship during so many of the solitary hours spent at my computer at home.

*   *   *

An earlier version of Chapter 2 was published as "Johann David Michaelis and the Colonial Imaginary: Orientalism and the Emergence of Racial Antisemitism in Eighteenth-Century Germany," *Jewish Social Studies* 6.2 (2000): 56–101, and I would like to express my gratitude to Indiana University Press for permission to use this material here.

Some of the ideas I present in Chapter 1 were introduced in a much earlier form in a series of essays: "Sugar Island Jews?" *Eighteenth-Century Studies* 32 (1998): 92–100; "Modernity, Violence, and the Jewish Question," in *Progrès et violence au XVIIIe siècle*, ed. Valérie Cossy and Deidre Dawson (Paris: Champion, 2001), 87–116; "Rome, Jerusalem and the Imperial Imagination," in *Monstrous Dreams of Reason: Writing the Body, Self, and Other in the Enlightenment*, ed. Laura Rosenthal and Mita Choudhury (Lewisburg: Bucknell University Press, 2002); and "Memory, History and the Jewish Question," in *The Work of Memory: New Directions in the Study of German Society and Culture*, ed. Alon Confino and Peter Fritzsche (Champaign: University of Illinois Press, 2002). I would like to thank the Johns Hopkins University Press, Éditions Champion, Bucknell University Press and the University of Illinois Press for permission to drawn on this material here.

ABBREVIATIONS

AA   Immanuel Kant, *Gesammelte Schriften, Akademie-Ausgabe* (Berlin: Georg Reimer, 1902–)

D   Christian Wilhelm Dohm, *Ueber die bürgerliche Verbesserung der Juden* (Berlin and Stettin: Friedrich Nicolai, 1781–83), 2 vols.

J   Moses Mendelssohn, *Jerusalem, Or, On Religious Power and Judaism*, trans. Allan Arkush (Hanover: University Press of New England, 1983)

JubA   Moses Mendelssohn, *Gesammelte Schriften, Jubiläumsausgabe*, ed. Felix Bamberger, Alexander Altmann et al. (Stuttgart-Bad Cannstatt: F. Frommann, 1971–)

LBIYB   *Leo Baeck Institute Year Book*

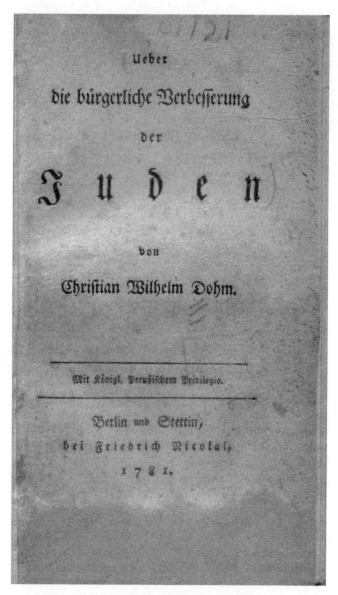

Fig. 1. Title page of Christian Wilhelm Dohm, *Ueber die bürgerliche Verbesserung der Juden* (On the Civic Improvement of the Jews) (Berlin and Stettin, 1781). Courtesy of the Leo Baeck Institute, New York.

INTRODUCTION
Modernity and the Legacy of Enlightenment

In November 1777, Christian Wilhelm Dohm, a twenty-five-year-old pastor's son from the northwest German city of Lemgo, finally managed to secure an audience with Frederick II, King of Prussia. Dohm, a professor of finance and statistics in Cassel who had studied at Leipzig and Göttingen, was a great admirer of both British politics and Frederick the Great's brand of enlightened absolutism. The translator of important travel narratives to India, Persia, Japan and the Middle East, he was an aspiring political writer and the founder and coeditor of the *German Museum*, a prominent political journal that sought to foster among Germans the sort of "public spirit" he found so attractive in Great Britain. Weary of academic life and eager to play a more active role in shaping the political world, Dohm traveled from Cassel to the Prussian capital with high hopes of landing a job as a civil servant. The letter from the Prussian Minister von Schulenburg inviting him to Berlin had made clear that Frederick was interested in him merely as a tutor for his nephew, the future King Frederick William II. Dohm, who had already spent some time in the early 1770s as a tutor for Frederick William's brother Ferdinand, came to the interview expecting to demonstrate to the king that he was a statesman in the making, and not just another private tutor for the prince. Before the much-anticipated meeting, accordingly, he sent Frederick his recently published *History of the English and the French in the East Indies* (1776), along with a memorandum he had written outlining a plan to revitalize the Prussian East Indian trade. He hoped in this way to show the king both his impressive political vision and his commitment to increasing Prussia's standing in the world. For all his best efforts, the meeting was not a success. Frederick explained to the young academic that his proposals, while well intentioned, were simply not appropriate for Prussia, and he arranged for

Dohm to be notified the following day that there was at present no position for him in the government.[1]

Dohm did eventually achieve both his rise to fame and a prominent position in the state, but not as an architect of Prussian colonialism. He began his career as a writer in the 1770s critiquing violent forms of colonial expansion and planning to produce a large-scale work on India that would demonstrate that southern Asia, India and China were the "true fatherland of humanity"—projects that were standard fare for the European Enlightenment.[2] Indeed, his *History of the English and the French in the East Indies* openly acknowledged its debt to the influential critique of colonialism in Raynal's 1770 global history of European expansion. The project to locate the origins of human civilization in India and the Far East that Dohm shared with Voltaire and others was similarly typical of its age, a symptom of both the increasingly global vision made possible by colonial expansion and the skepticism with which many European intellectuals were beginning to approach the literal truths of scripture and the biblical accounts of human origins. By the early 1780s, in any case, both Dohm's interests and his career were beginning to take on more definite shape. Appointed by foreign minister Ewald Friedrich von Hertzberg to a minor position as an archivist and councilor of war in Frederick the Great's department of foreign affairs in 1779, he relocated to Berlin and became active in the circles of Enlightenment intellectuals prominent in the Prussian capital. In this context, he came into contact with Moses Mendelssohn, the Jewish philosopher known across Europe as the "German Socrates," and he began to develop the arguments for granting Jews equal rights that eventually earned him the renown of his contemporaries and the reverence of later generations of German Jews. Since the late Middle Ages, Jews had lived in linguistic, cultural and social isolation almost everywhere they were permitted to reside in Christian Europe, typically subject to strict population control and a multitude of economic and legal restrictions designed to keep them apart from, and under the control of, the Christian majority. Dohm was not a stranger to the political status of this "nation" of "unfortunate Asiatic refugees," as he and others called them. As part of his interest in Asia, he had already conducted extensive research on Jewish history, and one of his earliest published writings was an "Attempt at a Short Characteristic of Some of the Most Famous Peoples of Asia" that looked at the "Hebrews" alongside the Turks and Indians and complained about the oppression Jews had suffered since the onset of Diaspora.[3] It was, however, only when Mendelssohn enlisted his help in drafting a memoir on behalf of Alsatian Jews under attack by a wave of popular Jew-hatred that Dohm took on the issue of Jewish emancipation as his own. For Dohm, as for so many Enlightenment intellectuals in the German lands and elsewhere, it was an accepted fact that Jews were morally, politically and even physically "degenerate," and the late eighteenth century had witnessed the publication of a growing list of scattered works debating possible changes in the Jews' political status and ways to improve their character.[4] Like many of his precursors who argued from a secular perspective, Dohm insisted that the condition of the Jews was entirely a product of their treatment at the hands of Christians in power. But he also developed a systematic political solution to this problem, conjuring up a comprehensive program of state intervention that included granting Jews civil rights, requiring them to perform military service, and moving them away from the "dishonorable" practice of trade— hitherto their chief means of livelihood—to transform them into productive farmers and artisans.

Soon after helping Mendelssohn prepare the memorandum to the French authorities, Dohm presented the public his proposals in *On the Civic Improvement of the Jews* (1781), a short book whose rapid rise to prominence and notoriety surpassed even its ambitious author's wildest expectations. From the moment of its release, Dohm's work met with a level of public attention that was radically incommensurate with either the numbers or the prominence of Germany's Jews, a largely indigent group of merchants, peddlers and itinerants that rarely amounted to more than 1 percent of the population. In 1781, unlike in the period before World War II, Jews were hardly a visible presence in German culture. In Mendelssohn's Berlin and a few other urban locales, to be sure, there was a growing Jewish economic elite increasingly engaged in secular culture, but this was atypical of German Jewry as a whole, the exception rather than the rule. Until the late eighteenth century, German Jews for the most part still spoke Yiddish and had not yet begun to master German.[5] The rhythms of their lives were still determined almost entirely by traditional Judaism, even though this too was beginning to erode in some places. In outlining the civic improvement of the Jews, Dohm was proposing the rehabilitation of a largely poor and seemingly unproductive segment of society, voicing his faith in the power of a progressive state to transform the fabric of its citizenry. This was the aspect of his project that captured the interest of his contemporaries.

Reviewed almost immediately in all the major journals, Dohm's book engendered widespread, often contentious debate from the beginning, prompting one commentator, the prominent Protestant theologian Johann Gottfried Eichhorn, to speak in 1789 of "proposals for improvement that had been echoing from one end of Germany to the other since 1781."[6] Translated into French a year after its German publication, *On the Civic Improvement of the Jews* inspired a number of French treatises in the 1780s and helped set the tone for the drawn-out debates in the aftermath of the French Revolution that resulted in the emancipation of French Jewry in 1791.[7] Germany, of course, had so such revolution and did not even exist as a unified political entity until 1871. For this reason, in Prussia and the more than 300 other states and principalities that eventually became the German Empire, the questions Dohm raised about the conditions under which Jews might be best transformed into productive citizens tended to play an even more striking role in public discourse. Depending on where they lived, nineteenth-century German Jews generally saw a gradual increase in both their rights and government measures to promote their integration, but it was not until unification that they gained complete legal and political equality. The ninety years separating Dohm's treatise from the creation of the German Empire witnessed recurring waves of heated debates over Jewish emancipation. Political writers, theologians, philosophers and lay intellectuals alike produced a seemingly endless mass of pamphlets, books and journal articles that ruminated on the possibility of a moral, political and physical "regeneration" of the Jews and grappled with the question of how participation in a modern, secular state could ever be compatible with the Jews' stubborn adherence to an antiquated, Oriental religion. The meticulous Nazi historian Volkmar Eichstädt documented in his 1938 *Bibliography of the History of the Jewish Question* that more than 3,000 titles dealing with Jews, Judaism and Jewish emancipation had inundated the German book market by 1848—a figure that does not even include the hundreds of essays in the prominent book review journals that helped shape the reading practices of a rapidly growing reading public.[8]

Clearly, Dohm had picked a perfect topic to showcase his skills as a political writer. Taking advantage of the widespread interest in his work on the Jews, he produced a sequel in 1783, a book that reprinted the arguments of many of his critics and offered a further elaboration of what became in subsequent years the classic argument for Jewish emancipation. After the success of *On the Civic Improvement of the Jews*, a 1785 book *On the German Royal Alliance*, an earlier essay on the physiocrats and other major publications, Dohm rose quickly in the Prussian civil service. Ennobled by Frederick William II soon after he assumed the throne in 1786, he spent twenty years in leadership positions as an envoy in Westphalia and Cologne before dying in 1820, hailed by Johann Wolfgang von Goethe and others as a great statesman and political writer. But why was it such a propitious career move to shift his interests from Asia and proposals for nonviolent colonial expansion in the East Indies to the project of regenerating Germany's Jewish population? Why were Jews and Judaism of such enormous interest to the German public during this period? Why was it that the issue of Jewish emancipation was able to attract the attention of a reading public that for the most part had little contact with, or real knowledge about, Jews or Judaism? In his analysis of the debates over Jews in revolutionary France, where Jews made up a considerably smaller percentage of the population than in the German states, Ronald Schechter has argued perceptively that the Jews were chiefly of symbolic significance to the French. Precisely because Jews were universally thought to be the embodiment of civic vice and deception, Schechter points out, they could easily become part of a "thought experiment" about the possibility of moral regeneration of a revolutionary citizenry.[9] Viewed by traditional prejudice as the ultimate anti-citizen, Jews thus offered the perfect test case for revolutionary principles of the moral transformation of both individuals and the French nation as a whole. In this regard, it makes sense that the conditions of Jewish emancipation—particularly the question whether Jews would be eligible to hold public office—proved such a provocative issue for the revolutionaries. In debating the moral and political transformation of the Jews, the French were testing the limits of the very concept of political universalism.

In Germany, the Jews offered up a similar occasion to debate more general political principles, and did so for a much longer period than in France. Dohm, a proponent of reform from above like so many other Germans, was not without a vision of political transformation. He wedded his plea for Jewish emancipation to a novel concept of universal citizenship, invoking a future political order beyond the divisions of estate society in which "the nobleman, the peasant, the scholar, the artisan, the Christian and the Jew" would all conceive of themselves, "more than anything else, as *citizens*" (D1: 26). Dohm viewed this process of political modernization, moreover, as an entirely non-coercive project, contrasting the "humanity" of the Enlightenment and its potential to realize a secular ideal of universal citizenship with the violence and brute force with which medieval states exiled and oppressed foreigners (D1: 86). While some of the ideals espoused by Dohm were realized fairly quickly—in Prussia, the Allgemeines Landrecht of 1794 helped dismantle the corporate state by institutionalizing the principle of the equality of all citizens before the law—the fact that Jews were for the most part excluded from these reforms made the anomaly of their political status all the more striking. For so many of the writers deliberating the pros and cons of Jewish emancipation, it was this distinctly modern and secular ideal of citizenship that was at stake. Some recent historians, breaking with the inherited wisdom that German nationalism came into being largely in reaction to the Napoleonic invasions of 1806, have contended that an aggressive, xenophobic nationalism was already present in the mid-eighteenth century.[10] The early discussions of the civic improvement of the Jews, however, rarely made reference to conceptions of a "German nation," and this may be telling for how we evaluate the prevalence of nationalist ideas in pre-Napoleonic Germany. Particularly in the period prior to 1806, the issue at stake was not how and whether Jews could become "Germans" but how and whether Jews could become *citizens* in a modern, secular state. In debating the ability of the state to bring about the civic improvement of the Jews, German intellectuals may have been less radical than the French, but they too were contemplating the viability of a political order grounded in a concept of secular universalism. The project of Jewish emancipation provided the ultimate test, in practice, of the rational ideals of the Enlightenment, the perfect arena for speculating about translating the lofty premises of Enlightenment universalism into concrete political practice.

The great advantage of emphasizing the function of reflections on Jews and Judaism in the Enlightenment's larger vision of a rational political future is that it opens up the door to a more subtle understanding of the role Jews played in the cultural imagination of the period. Dohm and others arguing for emancipation characterized the present state of Jewry in almost entirely negative terms, speaking nearly without exception of a condition of moral and political degeneracy in need of improvement. In this way, inherited prejudices against Jews obviously played a prominent role in the project of emancipation. There has, indeed, been little scholarly disagreement on the point that emancipation was presented to the Jews as a call to remake themselves in the majority culture's ideal image of itself, and not as an emancipation of Jews as Jews. Some historians, moreover, have gone so far as to locate the origins of modern antisemitism directly in this process. In his influential 1968 book *The French Revolution and the Jews*, Arthur Hertzberg argued that the modern, secular forms of antisemitism that culminated in the Nazi Holocaust were not a right-wing *reaction* to the Enlightenment and the liberal ideals of the French Revolution but a product of the Enlightenment and the Revolution, an outgrowth of the antagonism toward Jews and Judaism so deeply ingrained in the seemingly liberal offer of emancipation.[11] It was not just in France that anti-Judaism played such a significant role in Enlightenment culture. For so many intellectuals concerned with imagining new forms of political community in Germany, Judaism also appeared to offer up the perfect antithesis to the norms of the modern world. Typically cast as a clannish and coercive form of legalism irreconcilable with the Enlightenment's insistence on individual autonomy, freedom of conscience and the very power of reason itself, Judaism seemed to provide the perfect point of contrast for intellectuals wishing to imagine a secular political order grounded in the principles of rationalism and universalism. For precisely this reason, however, it is crucial to focus just as much on what eighteenth- and early nineteenth-century Germans wrote about Jews as on why and in what context they were writing and reading about Jews in the first place.

Negative, even hostile, visions of Judaism were a crucial component of the visions of Enlightenment and modernity we have inherited from philosophers such as Immanuel Kant. This fact alone, however, need not force us to draw a direct line from the Enlightenment to Auschwitz. On the other end of the spectrum, the antagonism toward Jews and Judaism underwriting the visions of regeneration in both Germany and France should certainly make us suspicious of the specter of an antisemitism fundamental to, and even constitutive of, German culture that has recently gained renewed life in the work of Paul Lawrence Rose and Daniel Goldhagen.[12] Particularly before 1806, the debates over the civic improvement of the Jews were participating in a larger, European vision of political modernization. The aim of this book is thus less to study the relationship between antisemitism and nationalism than to explore the tensions in the normative vision of universalism that was formulated, in part, *by* these eighteenth- and early nineteenth-century reflections on Jews and Judaism, a tradition of thinking about universalism that, in all its contradictions, in many ways retains its hold on us today. We shall see that there were Jewish voices at the time who realized that the Enlightenment was producing new, distinctly secular forms of Jew-hatred, and indeed, one of the main objectives of this book is to reconstruct a crucial and often neglected chapter in the history of secular antisemitism. But before we consider the relationship between Enlightenment antisemitism and the disasters of the twentieth century, it may be wise to revisit the role of Jews in Enlightenment culture on a much more dynamic level, to consider the role played by both myths about Judaism and Jews themselves in formulating a view of modernity that is in many ways still with us.

MODERNITY AND THE JEWS: A RECONSIDERATION

"Modernity" and "modernization" have long since been dominant concepts in the writing of Jewish and German history alike. Later in this introduction it will be important to spell out precisely how the term "modernity" was used and understood in the period in question and address the role that both novel concepts of historical time and visions of a "new" or "modern age" played in underwriting Enlightenment visions of political universalism. Before delving into that analysis, it may prove helpful first to clarify the stakes of my project in somewhat broader terms, highlighting the differences between my interest in the contradictions attending the emergence of normative visions of universalism in the Enlightenment and the manner in which the social theorist Zygmunt Bauman has reflected on the relationship between German Jewry and modernity. In his 1991 study *Modernity and Ambivalence*, a sequel of sorts to his 1989 book *Modernity and the Holocaust*, Bauman cast the

German-Jewish experience as paradigmatic of modernity's fundamental inability to tolerate difference in its quest for uniformity and universalism. Part of the project of the modern state, Bauman claimed, has been to transform its culturally heterogeneous population into a homogeneous collective, and this explains the paradoxical position of the Jews, who were called on to assimilate and then rejected as alien once they did. For Bauman, assimilation, as the "trade mark of modern politics," was in effect an impossible project, as Jews by definition were never permitted to advance to the privileged position of those who set the standards.[13] However, particularly in the late nineteenth and early twentieth centuries, Jews began to occupy a place in society that allowed them to view, comprehend and theorize the contradictions of modernity and its assimilatory project; as the first to recognize the dream of uniformity as a nightmare and assault, the Jews emerge as the first to "sample the taste of postmodern existence."[14] In many ways, *Modernity and Ambivalence* echoes Hannah Arendt's critique of assimilation in both *The Origins of Totalitarianism* (1951) and the biography of the German-Jewish *salonière* Rahel Varnhagen she wrote in the 1930s. Bauman celebrates precisely those individuals like Varnhagen whom Arendt labeled "conscious pariahs," that is, Jews who rejected modernity's call to assimilate and insisted, in an heroic act of resistance, on the challenge that their status as Jewish outsiders issued to the homogenizing forces of modern society.[15]

Influenced by Theodor Adorno and Max Horkheimer's *Dialectic of Enlightenment* (1944), Bauman emphasizes the repressive dimensions of the Enlightenment. Bauman's "modernity" is seamlessly hegemonic and hopelessly abstract, a monolithic creator of uniformity that extinguishes all difference, dialogue or debate and provokes little resistance along the way. It leaves us little room to take seriously both the emancipatory dimensions that many Germans and Jews alike found in Enlightenment visions of universalism and the fact that, particularly in the period under examination in this book, there was sustained debate between Germans and Jews about the terms of such universalism. Assimilation may have been modernity's injunction to the Jews, but it was one that was contested from the very beginning. Indeed, from the moment their civic improvement began to be discussed, there were Jews among the intellectual elite who responded to the tenor of public debate in a distinctly subversive manner. Anything but silent victims of the modern state's quest to produce a homogeneous citizenry, Jews often spoke out to challenge the terms of emancipation, questioning the assumption that they were desperately in need of state-sponsored moral regeneration. From Mendelssohn on, Jews also offered up Jewish critiques of modernity. Repeatedly calling attention to those elements of Judaism that Enlightenment culture typically viewed as most antithetical to the spirit of the modern age,

Jews reformulated and reclaimed dominant visions of universalism by grounding them in Judaism's own normative tradition. *Germans, Jews and the Claims of Modernity* thus recovers, from the German-Jewish experience, a vital tradition of opposition to the exclusive nature of Enlightenment universalism. It tells the story of this Jewish claim to modernity and the dominant culture's struggles to contain its potentially subversive impulses. For Germans and Jews alike, there was much more on the agenda than the political status of a religious minority. At stake was a more fundamental question, the ability of emergent visions of political universalism to accommodate difference, resistance and their own subversive appropriation by those whom they sought to emancipate in the name of Enlightenment and progress. The discourse on Jewish emancipation from 1781 to 1806 brings to light, in other words, not Bauman's postmodern critique of modernity but a dynamic tradition of debate *within modernity* about the promise, contradictions and the limits of universalism.

In this sense, *Germans, Jews and the Claims of Modernity* joins a host of contemporary works that seek to displace the concept of "assimilation" from the central position it once held in the writing of German-Jewish history.[16] In the eyes of most recent historians, German Jewry did not passively accept ideas and social norms imposed from outside during the era of emancipation; few German Jews relinquished their Jewishness to become German. Rather, German Jewry actively shaped itself and its own identity, forming what David Sorkin has aptly termed a distinct German-Jewish subculture.[17] For these reasons, the multivolume *German-Jewish History in Modern Times* edited by Michael Meyer, a work created to be the definitive general text for years to come, consistently uses the term "acculturation" rather than assimilation, stressing the productive manner in which German Jewry engaged with its non-Jewish environment.[18] In a recent book, Paul Mendes-Flohr has foregrounded the "hybrid" identity of Germany Jewry, a byproduct of its struggle to live with a plurality of idenitities and cultures.[19] My work similarly emphasizes the agency of Jewish intellectuals seeking to fashion new forms of Jewish identity. In focusing on the attempts of Jews to intervene in a largely non-Jewish debate over the terms of emancipation, however, *Germans, Jews and the Claims of Modernity* also brings to the foreground a *polemical* dimension of the German-Jewish experience that is often overlooked in studies that focus primarily on either the German or the Jewish side of these debates. This is not a book that seeks to reconstruct harmonious moments of German-Jewish dialogue and recuperate the emancipatory potential of Enlightenment ideals of tolerance.[20] It is certainly not my intention to minimize the historical importance of the classic example of such a meeting of minds, the famous collaboration and friendship between Mendelssohn, the Jewish philosopher, and Gotthold Ephraim Lessing, the Enlightenment writer whose drama *Nathan the Wise* (1779) became for so many Germans and Jews alike the standard formulation of the plea for tolerance. The mere fact that Mendelssohn and Lessing could collaborate and become friends obviously signals the perception of a common ground between Christians and Jews that is of enormous significance. Yet stressing dialogue and tolerance, even with an acknowledgment of their historical limits, runs the risk of overlooking the power dynamics permeating such debate, power dynamics that so many German-Jewish intellectuals of the period—such as Mendelssohn himself, as we shall see in Chapter 3—explicitly struggled against in their polemical contributions to the debates over emancipation.

In his often cited 1964 essay "Against the Myth of the German–Jewish Dialogue," Gerschom Scholem bemoaned the fact that discussion with Jews was a peculiar one-way street in Germany. Dialogue with Germans, Scholem complained, was almost universally predicated on the "expressed or unexpressed self-denial of the Jews, on the progressive atomization of the Jews as a *community* in a state of dissolution, from which in the best case only the *individuals* could be received, be it as bearers of pure humanity, or be it even as bearers of a heritage that had in the meantime become historical."[21] Debunking the myth of the "German-Jewish symbiosis" in this manner, Scholem indicted both Germans and Jews, who were themselves, he claimed, all too ready to perform the "liquidation of the Jewish substance" that the majority culture expected of them.[22] The problem with Scholem's analysis is not just that it depends on the now dated category of assimilation, censuring Jews for their willingness to assimilate at the same time as it charges Germans with having required that they do so. As Bauman has noted, it also reads at times like a lament of unrequited love.[23] Scholem may argue against the idealization of German–Jewish relations—and this was an important argument to make in the immediate postwar period—but he nevertheless retains the *expectation* of dialogue between Germans and Jews, measuring the historical record against a model of crosscultural communication that is as idealistic as it is anachronistic. The notion that Germans and Jews might have entered into dialogue in some neutral social space where all power relations were suspended assumes that there could have been at least some basic level of formal equality between participants. For Jews intervening in the emancipation debates, it was precisely the absence of this possibility that was so striking. The problem here was not that Jews cast themselves, in Scholem's words, as either "bearers of a pure humanity" or "bearers of a heritage that had in the meantime become historical." Acknowledging that they were speaking from positions of political powerlessness, Jews spoke out as Jews for whom Judaism was not simply historical. Challenging the dominant vision of modernity and its claims to universalism by the very act of staking out a place for Judaism within it, they put forth an alternative conception of the modern world, one that would indeed have been able to accommodate a dialogue with Jews and Judaism. Ultimately, this attempt to make a Jewish claim to modernity amounted to the sort of "cry into the void" lamented by Scholem. The mere fact of this failure, however, should not lead us to misread the radical nature of much German-Jewish thought of this period. The distinctly Jewish visions of universalism and modernity that emerged in this period never came to dislodge those of the dominant culture, but they did open up debate and provoke responses from their Christian peers. It is this debate and its underlying power struggle that is the subject of this book.

DYNAMICS OF INTERNAL COLONIALISM: CHRISTIANITY, MODERNITY AND THE JEWS

Both the nature of this power struggle about the terms of universalism and the fact that Jews were at the center of controversy make little sense if approached from a narrowly political perspective. From the beginning, indeed, the debates over emancipation were as much about theology as about the politics of universal citizenship. In considering the integration of Jews into a modern state, Germans were necessarily dealing with the legacy of Christian universalism, with Christianity's claim to normative status in the modern world. In this context, it should not be surprising that Protestant theologians were among the most vocal participants in the debates over regenerating the Jews. It was not just the unanimity of inherited prejudice against their religion and character that made the Jews appear ideally suited to be part of a thought experiment about universal citizenship. They were also representatives of a religion that was an important part of Christianity's own history, and during the entire period in which the issue of Jewish emancipation was up for debate, theologians themselves were struggling with defining and delimiting the exact nature of Christianity's historical derivation from Judaism. The basic issue of Christian origins, of course, was hardly new; from the early Church on, the notion of Christianity's "supersession" of Judaism had been one of the central mechanisms by which Christianity legitimized itself and its universalist message. In the aftermath of the Protestant Reformation, the denigration of Judaism that had been so central to Christianity's early polemics with its parent religion had ushered in an even more intense vilification of the "dead letter" of Old Testament "legalism" in contrast to the Lutheran emphasis on the liberating "spirit" of Christian "faith." The form in which theologians typically posed the question of Christian origins, however, underwent a significant shift in the eighteenth and nineteenth centuries. This is due in large part to the rise of historical theology and historical biblical

criticism, novel approaches to scripture that had their roots in both the
renewed attention to the text of the Bible brought in by the Reformation and
the budding interest in history that was such a distinctive feature of Enlightenment culture in Germany.[24]

Confronted with the radical suspicion of the text of scripture inaugurated
by Baruch Spinoza in the late seventeenth century, Protestant theologians
in Germany typically refrained from treating the Bible just like any other
profane text from antiquity. They did, however, begin to develop historical
forms of biblical and textual criticism and an interest in the historical Jesus,
and by the mid-nineteenth century, Germans had become the world's
acknowledged leaders in the burgeoning field of historical critical biblical
scholarship. As German scholars subjected the Bible to historical critique,
approaching it as an artifact that reflected its time and place of origin and its
various human authors, they found themselves facing the task of salvaging
Christianity for the modern world. They had to demonstrate, that is, not just
the historical dimensions of scripture but also how Christianity *transcended* its
concrete, historical origins. The typical corollary of this project was a vision
of Judaism as the historical religion *par excellence*, a religion that made little
sense outside the historical framework that originally gave rise to it. Starting
in the eighteenth century, pioneering Orientalists such as Johann David
Michaelis (1717–91), Johann Gottfried Herder (1744–1803) and Johann
Gottfried Eichhorn (1752–1827) began reading the Hebrew Bible as a product
of ancient Israelite culture in its historical and geographical specificity.
Judaism came to be viewed not just as the antiquated religion long since
superseded by Christianity but as an essentially "Oriental" legal system, one
that may have had value in its time but was now radically out of sync with
both Jesus's Christianity and the spirit of the modern age. One of the fundamental gestures by which Protestant theologians revived the original spirit of
Jesus's Christianity for modernity, accordingly, was the divorcing of Jesus from
his historical Jewish context, emphasizing the opposition between the universalism and continued relevance of Christianity and the narrow, parochial
and legalistic national existence fostered by ancient Judaism and Mosaic law.
When Kant commented that Jesus was essentially a "Greek" figure whose
genius consisted of cloaking Occidental wisdom in Oriental dress—an issue
we will explore in Chapter 4—he was only conceding the more general anxieties about the role of Judaism in the formation of Western civilization
that were so central to the rising discipline of historical biblical criticism.[25]
From Mendelssohn on, Jews intervening in the emancipation debates
routinely defended Judaism by stressing its normative role in the genesis
of Christianity, Enlightenment and modernity—a position that mounted an

obvious challenge to Christianity's insistence on its originality and unique status as the true beacon of universalism. The very notion of granting Jews entry to the modern world as Jews thus raised serious questions about both the hegemony of Christianity over its antiquated Oriental parent religion and the claims of Christianity to be a determining force in the modern world. For generations of Jews and non-Jews alike, the question of Jesus's relation to Judaism provided the symbolic battleground for debates that were as much about history and theology as about contemporary politics and the proper shape of the modern world.

In many ways, this book uncovers a prehistory to the vital challenge to Protestant theology that Susannah Heschel has located in the work of Abraham Geiger (1810–74), nineteenth-century Germany's leading ideologue of Reform Judaism.[26] In her 1998 book *Abraham Geiger and the Jewish Jesus*, Heschel challenged the understanding of Reform Judaism as a form of assimilation by zoning in on the novel visions of Christian origins that were so central to Geiger's understanding of Judaism's essential modernity. Focusing on Geiger's attempt to write the history of Christianity in such a way as to foreground Jesus's Jewishness, she found in Geiger an early form of "postcolonial" writing; the value of Geiger's work for Heschel, that is, lies in its attempt to unsettle the hegemony of Christian theology with its characteristic denigration of Judaism and rewrite the history of the West from a distinctly Jewish perspective. Appropriating the tools and methods of Protestant biblical criticism, Geiger cast Jesus not as the founder of a new religion that displaced Judaism but as a Jew seeking to reform Judaism from within, a Jew who bequeathed to modernity the essentially Jewish characteristic of enlightened, critical thinking. Heschel does not simply use the language of postcolonial criticism to cast Geiger's work as an act of subaltern resistance, an intellectual revolt on the part of a minority lacking political stature whose religion had traditionally been "colonized" by Christianity. She also offers a crucial revision of the study that launched the field of postcolonial studies, Edward Said's *Orientalism* (1978).[27] In *Orientalism* Said outlined a tradition of Western discourse that, in staking out its intellectual authority over the "Orient," implicitly expressed and justified European colonial power over the East. For Said, "knowledge" is rarely as disinterested and neutral as it usually claims to be; instead, it tends to feed into and on power, with Europe's intellectual domination of the Orient inextricable from the progress of empire. For Heschel, Said's analysis of the European quest for intellectual authority over the Orient needs to be supplemented by studying an analogous form of Orientalism, one that is internal to the West: the attempt, central to the rise of historical theology in the late eighteenth and nineteenth centuries, to control and contain Christianity's historical relation to Judaism. It is in this context that she likens Geiger's Jewish account of Christian origins to a form of postcolonial writing.

The cases of Jewish oppositional writing I consider in this book bring to light an even more explicit connection between power and knowledge— between the political project of regeneration and the question of political rights, on the one hand, and the question of who had the right to speak authoritatively about Judaism, on the other—than Geiger's theological polemics. Indeed, the debates in the period I examine lay bare dynamic connections between Orientalism, visions of empire and the reflections on the terms on which the Jews' political status might be changed. In many ways, it is more than an accident of biography that it was through a consideration of colonial expansion and Europe's encounters with the cultures of the East that Dohm migrated toward an interest in Central Europe's "unfortunate Asiatic refugees." In speaking about Jews, eighteenth- and nineteenth-century German intellectuals were inevitably reflecting on Germany's own position in a world whose contours were increasingly determined by European colonialism. Critics of *Orientalism* have not failed to note that the German case seems to offer an obvious exception to Said's reflections on the relationship between power and knowledge. By 1830, the Germans had emerged as the preeminent Orientalist scholars in Europe—the leading Semiticists, biblical critics and Indologists—and they did so in the absence of any colonial holdings in the Near East, or anywhere else, for that matter. Himself aware of this problem, Said argued that the German search for intellectual authority over the Orient was thus largely a scholarly concern without direct political import; unlike French and British myths about the Orient, the vision of the Orient constructed and sustained by Germans tended to lack any direct connection to the power dynamics of imperial expansion. As Sheldon Pollock, James Pasto and I myself have contended, however, Orientalism in Germany often tended to be directed inward as well as outward,[28] and the case of the Jews offers in many ways the perfect arena for testing this hypothesis. Judaism was not just an object of Orientalist scholarship alongside Islam and the East in the nineteenth century. Both the academic study of Arabic and the field of comparative Semitic languages trace their origins to eighteenth-century innovations in historical approaches to the Hebrew Bible. In the eighteenth century, Orientalists were by and large Old Testament scholars interested in studying the Bible as a product of its original historical context.[29] As we shall see in Chapter 2, the first major scholarly expedition to the Arab world—the journey to Yemen that Michaelis directed from his chair at the University of Göttingen in the 1760s—was launched in order to find traces of the culture and language of the ancient Israelites. The authority Michaelis gained from this expedition later proved instrumental in mounting arguments against Jewish emancipation. In a telling moment of rhetorical excess in an influential critique of Dohm in his *Oriental and Exegetical Library*, Michaelis contended that since this degenerate "southern race" would never have the proper bodily stature to perform military service, the ideal solution would be to acquire German West Indian sugar islands where one might send Jews to work alongside African slaves.

Susanne Zantop has argued persuasively that the fact that Germans had no colonies until the late nineteenth century did not mean that Germany lacked an indigenous tradition of colonial discourse; indeed, from 1770 on, German culture was permeated by what she terms colonial fantasies, visions of colonial conquest and cultural hegemony in which Germans typically appeared as "good" colonists far more benevolent that the British, French or Dutch.[30] Concentrating on the longstanding German preoccupation with South America, Zantop focuses almost entirely on visions of external colonial expansion. She obscures the heated discussions over the assimilation and regeneration of a subject people on the domestic front, thus perpetuating the distinction between colony and metropolitan center that so much postcolonial scholarship has sought to question.[31] In Germany, Orientalist discourse was neither an apolitical body of scholarship nor an abstract colonial fantasy, although at times it certainly may have functioned in each of these capacities. At key junctures, it also helped set the terms for the emancipation of Germany's Jewish minority, a group whose regeneration was often discussed with reference to experiments undertaken with subject peoples of French and British colonialism. We shall see in Chapter 1 that Dohm and other proponents of civic improvement explicitly introduced Jewish emancipation within the framework of a project of "internal colonization," arguing that regenerated Jews might serve as the equivalents of foreign "colonists" to boost Prussian economic productivity and help settle its newly claimed Eastern regions and other uncultivated areas. One anonymous author responding to Dohm even suggested that emancipating the Jews would function as the symbolic equivalent of a Prussian colony in the New World. The question around which such debates usually revolved was not whether Jews had the right to emancipation but whether such a degenerate people could ever be regenerated and made productive, that is, whether there was such a thing, in Dohm's words, as an "unimproveable race of humans" (D2: 23). The contested concept of "regeneration" that propelled the debates over civic improvement was not just an invention of political discourse. It fed directly into—and on—controversies raging in Enlightenment anthropology over the permanence of racial "degeneration," an issue that gained prominence both through the scientific works of Kant, Johann Friedrich Blumenbach

(1752–1840) and lesser known eighteenth-century anthropologists writing on the novel concept of "race," and through more popular travel literature describing real-life encounters with "degenerate" peoples in Africa and the New World. In this sense, the controversy over Jewish emancipation contributed to the emergent discourse on race central to precolonial Germany's colonial imaginary, marking one of the first explicitly political discussions of a category that would become so crucial in the late nineteenth century.[32]

Part of the reason why the issue of Jewish emancipation aroused such widespread public interest lies undoubtedly in the multifaceted concerns that came together in public deliberations on how best to deal with Germany's Jewish population. Depending on the author and audience, civic improvement was as much about anthropology as about politics, as much about theology as about philosophy, and as much about citizenship in a modern, secular state as about competing visions of the ancient world and grand narratives about the genesis of Western civilization. It is only against this backdrop, moreover, that one can fully appreciate the Jewish interventions in the debate, many of which took the form of proposals for religious reform. As a major institutional presence, Reform Judaism is a product of a somewhat later era than that under consideration in this book. Practical reforms in synagogue worship were first instituted in the late 1790s in French-controlled Holland and in the first years of the nineteenth century in French-occupied Westphalia, a kingdom that in 1807 was the first German state to grant full equality to the Jews. In 1810, Israel Jacobson (1768–1828), the leader of the Westphalian reform efforts, opened the first modern Jewish "temple," complete with an organ and services conducted partly in German. Once the French were ousted from Westphalia in 1814, Jacobson relocated to Berlin, where he played an important role disseminating the spirit of reform in the Jewish community there. In the aftermath of the emancipation decrees of 1812, which granted Prussian Jews many of the rights accorded their Christian peers, elite Jews in Berlin were eager for practical experiments with religious reform. The decade from 1814 to 1823 witnessed both the establishment of reform services in Berlin, first in Jacobson's home and then in the home of Jacob Herz Beer, as well as intense ideological debate within the community about the status of reform. In 1823, however, Prussian authorities fearing that a modernized Judaism might weaken missionary efforts to convert Jews to Christianity put an end to all such reform efforts. Apart from the Hamburg Temple established in 1817, Jewish worship in the 1820s and 1830s remained largely unaffected by reform. In was only with the emergence of a new generation of university-trained Jewish leaders like Geiger in mid-century that one can speak of a distinct reform movement exercising widespread influence on Jewish life in Germany and beyond.

Both this story and the story of the leading role played by German Jewry in the Reform movement have been told elsewhere.[33] My interest here lies less in the institutional development of reform than in the relationship between the concerns of the emancipation debates and the beginnings of an ideology of reform as it emerged in the 1780s and 1790s. Clearly, one cannot study the intellectual and social origins of Reform Judaism apart from the specific experiences of the German-Jewish community's struggles for equal rights during this period. But as Michael Meyer stresses in his magisterial history of the Reform movement, for the most part Jewish reformists "refused to allow political considerations, however important to them, to dominate their religious thinking."[34] The Jews' quest for equal rights may have been part of the picture, in other words, but it never became a *determining* force in the massive reconceptualization of Judaism that marks the modern era. For most historians of German Jewry, as David Sorkin has observed, the relationship of reform to emancipation has been an extremely delicate subject.[35] Concentrating on the political aspirations that may have helped frame the way modern Jewish thinkers reconceptualized Judaism runs the risk of robbing reform of its integrity. Viewing religious reform as resulting from a desire to make Judaism more "palatable" to the majority culture undermines the agency of such thinkers. For this reason, both Meyer and Sorkin have stressed the ways reform marks a creative encounter with modernity, one that had significant roots in internal Jewish developments that predated the emancipation debates.[36]

There is a distinctly political dimension to the early ideology of reform that needs to be stressed as well. Jews issuing proposals for religious reform inevitably insisted on Judaism's essential compatibility with modernity, and given the atmosphere in which they were writing, the very project of reform articulated in these terms was a highly political act. In the case studies of Jewish interventions in the emancipation debates I consider in Chapters 3, 4 and 5, accordingly, the question of the political ambitions and potential political consequences of reform appear paramount. In each of these cases, proposals for the "purification" of Judaism—the term "reform" was not yet used widely during this period—are presented in explicit connection with both the ambitions of citizenship and the Protestant denigration of Judaism as a stagnant, Oriental religion. Religious reform was the avenue Jews often chose in which to seize political agency for themselves, reclaiming the Jewish tradition as their own in such a way as to issue fundamental challenges to Protestant Orientalism and the politics of civic improvement alike. In this sense, religion and politics were by necessity closely interrelated in the Jews' quest to find a place for themselves in a modern, secular state. *Germans, Jews and the Claims of Modernity* thus reclaims a politically charged vision of reform that cannot be equated with either assimilation or a recasting of Judaism from within—a vision of religious reform that recuperates Judaism for modernity at the same time as it issues a challenge to emergent concepts of political universalism whose links to the Christian legacy were in desperate need of clarification.

Each of the five chapters that follow focuses on a pivotal moment in the controversy over emancipation, highlighting the dynamic rhythm of debate, and not simply the arguments of major figures. Rather, say, than devoting a chapter to Kant's denigration of Judaism as a "collection of mere statutory laws" devoid of moral value, I consider this vision of Judaism and its position within Kant's thought as they impacted the emancipation debates. My concern in the chapter devoted to Mendelssohn, similarly, is less with the philosophical unity of his thought—although this is certainly important as well—than with the series of polemical challenges he issued to the Protestant denigration of Judaism, and, subsequently, with the way his challenges were received, ignored and disposed of by a host of writers, many of whom have been long since forgotten. Indeed, throughout the book, the task of reconstructing the culture of debate has necessitated resurrecting those whose names rarely appear in the annals of German-Jewish history. I thus contextualize the writings of major figures like Mendelssohn much more intensely than is often done. It is only by opening up the complexity of the period's dominant visions of Jews and Judaism that we can gain a more complete sense of what Jews were struggling with and against as they sought to stake out a place for Judaism within the modern world. Jewish historians have traditionally been reluctant to view the interventions of Jewish intellectuals from the perspective of the Christian majority, and this has often resulted in a caricatured image of many Jewish attempts to offer fundamental critiques of modernity; the perfect example here, we shall see in Chapter 5, is the case of David Friedländer, the intellectual leader of the Berlin Jewish community notorious for his desperate proposals of mass baptism in 1799. Friedländer, of course, hardly offers a model for Jewish action, but there is a highly subversive element to his thought that his contemporaries responded to and that warrants serious attention on our part as well. Regardless of the particulars of their positions on emancipation and religious reform, nearly all the participants in the debates—whether Jewish or Christian, whether political writers, theologians, philosophers or lay intellectuals—shared a concern with outlining more general norms for a new and modern world. Before we can open our discussion of the debates themselves, it will be necessary to say a few more words about the concept of "modernity" that propelled so much of the discussion over emancipation.

JEWS, JUDAISM AND THE INVENTION OF MODERNITY

Modernity is hardly a new term in German-Jewish history or Jewish studies, where it is generally taken to mean the emergence of the Jews from the relative isolation that had characterized their existence since the late Middle Ages and their entrance into the non-Jewish world and its increasingly secular concerns. Whether conceived of as a distinct period or a more general process, modernity inevitably meant a life for Jews where Jewish identity emerged as a problem, something they needed to define and redefine in relation to themselves, their history and their non-Jewish environment. Jewish historians have usually linked the onset of modernity in this sense to the Enlightenment and emancipation, often casting the acculturation of German Jewry in the late eighteenth and nineteenth centuries as paradigmatic of the Jewish modernization process in general.[37] In an often cited 1975 essay entitled "German Jewry as Mirror of Modernity," Gerson Cohen claimed that "virtually every characteristic associated with the Jews of Germany has its analogue and parallel in the history of the Jews of Central and Eastern Europe: enlightenment, assimilation, conversion, religious reform, nationalism, social mobility, rediscovery of the Jewish past, articulation of Jewish culture in modern terms and so on endlessly."[38] Recent scholarship has tended to break with the Germanocentric focus inherited from the nineteenth century. It has both highlighted crucial dimensions of the German-Jewish subculture that were not reproduced among other Jewries—such as its peculiar relation to the protracted emancipation process—and brought to light important models of modern Jewish life that make little sense when viewed through the lens of the German-Jewish experience.[39] Despite its obvious lack of national specificity, however, the term "modernity" has tended to endure, albeit often with a twist. Both a 1994 anthology and a recent book by Shulamit Volkov call for renewed attention to German Jews' encounters with "modernity," proposing that we study the Jews' participation in the more general processes of social, political and economic modernization alongside a consideration of how German Jews produced their own distinctly Jewish version of modernity in the nineteenth century.[40]

In general German historiography dealing with the period Jewish historians treat as "modernity," interestingly enough, both modernity and modernization have often been highly contested terms. In their effort to understand the collapse of the Weimar Republic and the rise of Nazism, postwar historians of Germany often looked at the nineteenth century to see where the path of German history went awry. The result, frequently, was an inversion of prewar conceptions of the "peculiar course" or *Sonderweg* of German history.

Early twentieth-century German historians often praised nineteenth-century Germany for its unique combination of a strong monarchy, a powerful military and rapid industrialization, stressing the superiority of the German system and its "spiritual" values to both the ideals of the French Revolution and the materialism of British culture. In the postwar period, in contrast, such German exceptionalism has generally been seen as a problem, an aberration from the "normal" course of Western political development represented by the triumph of bourgeois liberalism in France and Great Britain. In this framework—and the failure of the 1848 revolution is generally the prime example here—nineteenth-century Germany deviated from the proper path of "modernization," failing to coordinate economic, social and political developments so as to produce the sort of thoroughly "modern" society found in Britain and France. As David Blackbourn and Geoff Eley demonstrated almost twenty years ago, this use of modernity as a standard against which to measure the German nineteenth century runs the risk of obscuring more than it illuminates.[41] Emphasizing how Germany deviated from a proper modernization process not only reduces the nineteenth century, in hindsight, to an abnormality that led almost necessarily to the catastrophes of the mid-twentieth century. It also relies on an abstract, normative and dated notion of "modernity" against which the British and French cases would also have to be judged as abnormalities. As Blackbourn and Eley claim in their effort to debunk what they call the "myth of a benign and painless 'western modernization,'" Germany may in fact have been "much more the intensified version of the norm than the exception."[42]

In its full implications, the problem of the exceptionalism of German history in its relation to "modernity" is an issue that lies outside the scope of this book. Rather than measuring the concerns that emerge in the debates over Jewish emancipation against an abstract norm, I attempt to reconstruct what modernity meant for the writers debating emancipation and what function it assumed in their thought. The term "modernity" is important here, in other words, not as a tool of analysis but as an object of study. I seek to understand, that is, what role these reflections on Jews and Judaism played in *constructing* modernity as a normative category to begin with. Whatever the peculiarities of German political developments in the later nineteenth century may have been, eighteenth- and early nineteenth-century intellectuals were very much concerned with delineating universal norms for development toward a rational political future, and despite obvious differences in political cultures, they were participating in a larger European project. "Modernity," understood in this sense, is not simply a period or a process. It is not merely something the Jews were subjected to nor can it be grasped as a process of social, economic or political transformation whose conformity to an abstract standard might be quantified. It is, rather, a *discourse*, a mode of envisioning a new and secular world that claimed its legitimacy not with reference to the various traditions and legacies of the past it sought to overcome but solely in relation to itself, to the break it performed with tradition to insist on its right to institute and follow its own norms.

As Jürgen Habermas, Hans Robert Jauss and Hans Ulrich Gumbrecht have demonstrated, this notion of modernity as a "new age" that insists on the right to produce its own norms first surfaced in the realm of aesthetic criticism.[43] In the late seventeenth and early eighteenth centuries, much cultural debate in France was dominated by the famous "quarrel between the ancients and moderns," that is, the question, central to French classicism, of the extent to which modern art might create its own norms and standards rather than simply taking classical art as an eternal model for imitation. In the aftermath of Johann Joachim Winckelmann's influential 1755 *Thoughts on the Imitation of Greek Works*, German intellectuals inaugurated their own phase of the quarrel. As Peter Szondi has argued, Winckelmann's relation to classical antiquity was marked by a fundamental contradiction.[44] On the one hand, Winckelmann insisted that the sculpture of ancient Greece represented an eternal standard of good taste, a universal model for the production of all art. He linked his idealization of the Greeks to a vision of history in decline, assigning modernity the task of recuperating the lost greatness of the ancients. At the same time, however, Winckelmann also sought to understand Greek art in its historical specificity, as a product of the culture and climate of ancient Greece, and for this reason, he is often seen as the first art historian. For many eighteenth-century intellectuals engaged in the debates over the legitimacy of modern art, it was precisely this tension in Winckelmann's injunction to imitate the ancients that proved so fruitful. Winckelmann's successors too sought to bring about a renaissance in German culture, but most did so by stressing modernity's independence from the legacy of ancient art and poetics, its right to follow not the model of the ancients but their example of creating great art for themselves according to their own norms. Modernity had to create its art in a manner appropriate to its own historical situation, and it was only by doing so that it could release itself from the burdens of the ancients. With his essays on "modern literature" and his celebration of the genius as the divinely inspired human being who gives rules to himself and brings the entirety of a culture's developments to a focal point in the work of art, Herder is generally seen as a key figure in this development.[45]

One of the reasons why these aesthetic concerns with modernity were so influential is that they were not just about art. Indeed, it was not until the very end of the eighteenth century that art began to be conceived as a domain separate from morality, politics, religion and the sciences. Even the emergent concept of an autonomous aesthetic domain—a sphere where art would exist and be valued on its own terms—was in its inception closely linked to the Enlightenment's search for new forms of political community.[46] In Germany in particular, from the mid-eighteenth century on, reflections on art and aesthetics provided the forum for a wide variety of deliberations on politics, cultural renewal and the shape of the modern world. It was through this avenue that the discourse on ancients and moderns opened up the door for more general debates over the "legitimacy" of modernity, a term Hans Blumenberg has used to stress the modern age's claim to radical independence from the burdens of antiquity and Christianity alike.[47] Whatever form it took, the quest to defend the legitimacy of modernity tended to be inextricable from a novel concept of both history and historical time. While the term "modern" dates back to the medieval period, it was, as Reinhart Koselleck has demonstrated, only in the course of the eighteenth century that it began to be used to refer to an age or period thoroughly distinct from that of the "Middle Ages," a designation that rose to prominence during this period as well.[48] Dohm himself routinely contrasted the Enlightenment and its vision of progress with the stagnant prejudices of the "dark centuries," and he was hardly alone here. Indeed, for many eighteenth-century intellectuals, three key events roughly around 1500—the discovery of the New World, the Renaissance and the Reformation—were perceived to have ushered in an epochal shift that gave rise to a "new" or "modern age" (*neue Zeit*, later *Neuzeit*) radically distinct from the past. It was characteristic of this new age of which they themselves were a part that it was overwhelmingly concerned with envisioning its own future. And the "new" or "modern age" that insisted it was producing its own norms did so, importantly, not in a vacuum but through historical reflections on the past. As Koselleck notes,

> History stood revealed in its current truth. The "new age" lent the whole of the past a world-historical quality. With this, the novelty of a history in emergence, reflected as new, assumed a progressively growing claim to the whole of history. . . . [I]t was precisely along the plane of progress that the specificity of the epoch had to be expressed. Hence, diagnosis of the new age and analysis of the past eras corresponded to each other.[49]

"Modernity" made sense, in other words, only in relation to the past, in relation to a specific conception of the past and its relation to the present. In its claim to radical novelty, the discourse of modernity had to negotiate its relation to the historical past and secure its position as the heir to the entirety of history itself. In this framework, of course, it was not just antiquity, Christianity and the medieval legacy that needed to be reckoned with but Judaism and the question of Christian origins. The "new age" that so many of the writers debating the question of Jewish emancipation were trying to bring about desperately needed both clarification and historical grounding. One of the fundamental tasks of *Germans, Jews and the Claims of Modernity* is to lay bare the way both representations of Judaism and Jews themselves participated in launching this massive conceptual reorganization of the world that in many ways remains with us today. For Jews, the entry into modernity may indeed have represented what Habermas has called a "leap into a foreign history."[50] Concepts of a radical new, secular age obviously represented a challenge to traditional Judaism with its understanding of exile and its expectation of messianic redemption. But Jews also played an active role in *shaping* this emergent vision of modernity, and they did so not merely by appropriating its concerns and embracing its claim to universalism as something alien to Judaism. Jews sought to articulate both distinctly Jewish theories of modernity and distinctly modern theories of Judaism, and they did so *both* for their fellow Jews *and* for the dominant culture as a whole. They were not just staking out a place for themselves in a modern world that had, at best, an ambivalent relation to Judaism. They were also launching a provocation to modernity and its emancipatory project that should still be of immense interest to us today.

Dohm is important here not simply because he offered the initial provocation for the debates over Jewish emancipation. His work itself put forth a vision of modernity—and of the leading role that a thoroughly secularized Prussia would play in delivering the modern age from the burdens of its medieval past—that deserves our careful attention. It is thus to Dohm that we will turn in Chapter 1, studying the origins and functions of his treatise *On the Civic Improvement of the Jews* as a means of setting the stage for our discussions of the culture of debate unleashed by the political quandary of Jewish emancipation.

I

ROME, JERUSALEM AND THE TRIUMPH OF MODERNITY
Christian Wilhelm Dohm and the Regeneration of the Jews

THAT LEVANTINE DRINK, A TRUE POLITICAL EVIL:
INTERNAL COLONIZATION AND THE JEWS

In the August 1777 issue of the *German Museum*, the political periodical Dohm launched with his friend Heinrich Christian Boie in 1776, there appeared an essay by Dohm that ventured a solution to one of the burning political problems of the day. Voicing his support for the "rights of man" and the "natural equality of human beings at all levels of society," Dohm encouraged Prussia and the other German states to emulate Great Britain, the world's model of "political Enlightenment," by developing political systems in which the "voices of all estates would be heard, and the interests of all classes of citizens would be weighed against each other."[1] In many ways, these comments were typical of the pages of the *German Museum*, a journal that sought to promote British-style "public spirit" among Dohm's compatriots and "make Germany better acquainted with itself and its own national affairs."[2] In this case, however, these remarks were not occasioned by an abstract admiration for British politics or for the American colonists, whose struggles for independence he supported elsewhere in the *Museum*.[3] Dohm here was writing about a novel form of sensual pleasure that had recently taken Germany by storm, a commodity that Germans at all levels of the social spectrum were beginning to regard as necessary staple of daily life: coffee.

The late seventeenth century had witnessed an explosion in coffeehouses, first in London, then on the continent, where they became key institutions of sociability and served as central places for the exchange of information, the conduct of business and discussions about politics, art and literature.[4] Indigenous to the Middle East, coffee was largely unknown in Europe until

1650. By 1700, however, imports from Arabia no longer sufficed to meet rising European demands for this novel beverage, and coffee increasingly became a colonial good, a product of Dutch and French plantations in the East and West Indies. For Germans, who had no colonies and had to purchase such goods through middlemen, the consumption of coffee was a double-edged affair. Coffee's appeal lay not merely in its flavor, its value as a stimulant or even its widely hailed medicinal properties. It also represented, on a symbolic level, the power and urbanity Germans typically associated with international players such as England, France and Holland. As Wolfgang Schivelbusch has argued, drinking coffee gave Germans a chance to partake "in a level of Western urbanity" they had not yet achieved for themselves,[5] and in practice, this symbolic boost to Germans' self-image had the effect of undermining rather than bolstering the international stature of the German lands. The increasingly prevalent consumption of coffee meant huge amounts of money leaving Germany to end up in the coffers of colonial planters, and to stem this problem, Prussia and other German states drafted a series of restrictive "coffee laws" and promoted high taxes on this import. Intellectuals like Dohm were generally supportive of such efforts to foster Germany's economic self-sufficiency and promote a healthy balance of trade. August Ludwig von Schlözer (1735–1809), Dohm's former professor in Göttingen and a well-known historian and political journalist, routinely reprinted coffee laws and accompanied them with supportive commentary in his *Correspondence, Mostly of a Historical and Political Nature*, an influential organ of public opinion. Since "Germany neither grows coffee nor possesses West Indian coffee islands," Schlözer pointed out, following a common line of argument, "all the money that coffee costs us is thus completely lost for Germany."[6] In his article in the *German Museum*, Dohm made a similar plea for national self-sufficiency. Calling coffee a "true political evil," he deplored the loss of German money to Dutch, French and American planters and issued systematic proposals for developing home-grown coffee surrogates such as chicory and encouraging Germans to support local beverage industries by consuming wine and beer rather than this newly popular "Levantine drink."[7]

In order to work effectively, Dohm argued, such economic regulation would have to be geared at promoting patriotism and public spirit, and indeed, much of what caused the coffee question to pique his interest were the opportunities it opened up for promoting an enlightened political culture. It was crucial to Dohm that coffee legislation not be perceived as arbitrary or despotic, as this would only encourage Germans to savor their coffee "with the proud thought that they are vindicating the rights of man."[8] Particularly because coffee consumption cut across class divisions, restrictions would have to respect the "natural equality of human beings at all levels of society." To avoid a perceived intervention into human rights, Dohm wanted change to proceed slowly, with governments first subsidizing the efforts of domestic beverage industries to create popular substitutes for coffee. Only then would it be possible to raise coffee prices gradually, over a long period of time, expending considerable effort along the way to educate the public about the evils of a colonial product it would eventually lose interest in. In this way, he claimed, the German public would not just reeducate its palate to embrace the products of local industry. It would also learn to reason about the process of law-making and the true interests of its fatherland in a manner that approached the marvels of the English political system. In this scenario, Germany would compensate for its lack of coffee-producing colonies by strengthening its domestic industry and its political culture alike, ultimately coming to rival that nation Dohm celebrates as the "happy fatherland of the most noble liberty." The essay on coffee legislation in the *German Museum* concludes, not surprisingly, by hailing Frederick the Great's Prussia as the model for all legislative wisdom.[9]

Making a virtue out of necessity, Dohm transformed Germany's lack of colonies into an opportunity for political growth, the springboard for the emergence of Prussia as a political order second to none in its claims to embody the principles of freedom and enlightenment. In this sense, his essay on coffee legislation would seem to offer a corrective to Susanne Zantop's vision of German Enlightenment culture as being dominated by fantasies of colonial expansion.[10] For rather than indulging in dreams of empire, Dohm sought here to *compensate* Prussia for its lack of colonial holdings by channeling his energies into internal consolidation, working to bolster Prussia's stature in the world from within rather than without. In an important sense, indeed, Dohm's economic principles are opposed to any form of colonial rule. As he wrote four years later in *On the Civic Improvement of the Jews*, one of the most important tasks facing every state should be to maximize economic self-sufficiency by "excluding products of foreign industry, cutting itself off from all others like an island and working toward producing its complete internal consumption within its borders" (D1: 7).[11] *On the Civic Improvement of the Jews* obviously dealt with human beings rather than their beverage choices, but Dohm's proposals for Jewish emancipation drew their rationale from the same logic of national consolidation that marked his reflections on coffee and human rights. Prussia under Frederick the Great pursued an aggressive policy of "internal colonization" and managed population growth, subsidizing foreign "colonists," primarily farmers and artisans, to settle in the country, particularly its eastern regions, and contribute to economic growth. By the mid-1780s, one sixth of the Prussian population consisted of such colonists, a figure that surpassed that of all other European states.[12] Jews, of course, were never invited in as settlers, and the domestic Jewish population was closely controlled so as to be kept to a minimum. In the areas of West Prussia gained in the 1772 partition of Poland, in fact, 4,000 Jews were removed from their homes in order to make room for foreign colonists.[13] Dohm began his treatise by noting this apparent contradiction in Prussian colonial policy. Casting population growth as the "final purpose" and "most reliable barometer" of a state's prosperity, he insisted that it hardly made sense to continue the policy of limiting the Jews' population and economic productivity while expending such large funds to attract colonists. He introduced the "civic improvement of the Jews" thus as a challenge to Prussian colonial policy, presenting the regeneration of these "Asiatic refugees" already residing within Germany as an effective substitute for the practice of subsidizing foreign settlers (D1: 6–8, 89–94).

Obviously, there are differences between developing surrogates for a Levantine drink that had to be imported from the West Indies and transforming Jews into productive citizens. Yet in one regard these substitutes for colonial goods and for foreign colonists were part of the same project: each was intended to promote Prussia's economic self-sufficiency while translating the universalist principles of the Enlightenment into political practice, calling on the powers-that-be to transform Prussia into an exemplar of the modern state. Like the essay on coffee legislation, Dohm's proposals for Jewish emancipation also envisioned a new political order, in which individuals' identification with the state would override all religious and class differences. The "great and noble business of government," he wrote, is to weaken "the exclusive principles of all the various societies" and "dissolve them in the great harmony of the state" (D1: 26). Unlike so many of his contemporaries, Dohm had no fundamental problems with Judaism as a religion; he found nothing in Judaism to be incompatible with citizenship and was willing to let Jews retain Jewish law, Rabbinic courts and other forms of Jewish self-governance. He promised, however, that granting Jews rights and transforming them into farmers, artisans and soldiers would make them into something more than members of the "Jewish nation": they would be building blocks of a political order in which "the nobleman, the peasant, the scholar, the artisan, the Christian and the Jew" would all conceive of themselves, "more than anything else, as *citizens*" (D1: 26). Arguing self-consciously from the perspective of an enlightened present, Dohm declared the political status of contemporary Jewry to be an anachronistic remnant of "inhuman and unpolitical prejudices of the darkest centuries" (D1: iii), the "result of fanatic religious hatred that is unworthy of the Enlightenment of our times and that should have long since been eradicated by such Enlightenment" (D1: 39). Much to the embarrassment of Enlightenment intellectuals, the prejudices of the Middle Ages were apparently continuing to exert power over the contemporary world, and for Dohm it was the task of the state to eradicate their lingering influence and destroy this affront to modernity. Civic improvement had thus less to do with the Jews than with creating a state true to the secular ideal of universal citizenship, a political order that would emancipate *itself* from the burdens of the medieval period. It was, Dohm explained, the Jews' persecution by Christians and their political status that was responsible for their "moral corruption" and all their other faults, and he trusted that citizenship would bring about a radical transformation in Jewish identity. As both he and his earliest reviewers frequently noted, emancipated Jews would cease to be "Jews, properly speaking" (D2: 174, 176–77).[14] They would emerge from civic improvement with a modified character and a modernized religion entirely compatible with the goals of a consolidated Prussia.

As Dohm stated in the second volume of his treatise in 1783, his goal was not to defend contemporary Jews and their obvious defects but to promote the causes of humanity and the interests of the state; it was for this reason, after all, that he stressed improvement in the title of his work (D2: 151–52). For the generations that followed, accordingly, Dohm's treatise became synonymous with an unbridled faith in the power of the state to promote human perfectibility. Before we begin exploring some of the tensions in this vision of state power, we should note that the dominant response to Dohm was, from the beginning, to reject his call for immediate emancipation as a much too risky experiment. Anton Friedrich Büsching (1724–93), a prominent theologian, geographer and historian who was a school director in Berlin and a friend of Dohm, noted in an early review that agreeing with these proposals for improving the Jews would force readers to overcome "prejudices that are older and more deeply rooted than the oldest oaks and cedars."[15] Indeed, in his insistence that Jews be given rights immediately, we shall see in later chapters, Dohm was among the most radical of the ideologues of civic improvement, most of whom wanted Jews first to regenerate themselves and demonstrate their suitability for citizenship. Many others were against emancipation altogether, insisting that the Jews were simply not capable of the sort of moral and political transformation Dohm expected citizenship eventually to produce. According to his own statements, Dohm was promoting political "principles that contradicted those followed by entire nations for centuries" (D1: 151), and as the statistician and economist August Wilhelm Crome (1753–1833) commented in a sympathetic review in 1782, the victory of truth and Enlightenment over medieval prejudice was bound to be a long battle.[16] In this context, it makes sense that Mendelssohn would inaugurate the official Jewish reception of *On the Civic Improvement of the Jews* in 1782 by casting Dohm's treatise as a vindication of "reason" and "humanity," or that a group of prominent Berlin Jews once honored Dohm by presenting him with a birthday gift of a set of silver cutlery.[17] During his lifetime, indeed, he received numerous expressions of gratitude from Jews in Germany and abroad, even from places as far away as Surinam. Most historians too, not surprisingly, have classified this work as an honorable attempt to include Jews in the promise of political universalism, a grand defense of the emancipatory project of Enlightenment.[18]

There is nevertheless a flip side to civic improvement that deserves our attention as well. As we noted in the introduction, Dohm's vision of emancipation hinged in crucial ways on a commonly accepted negative image of contemporary Jewry, and there have been historians who have commented on this anti-Jewish tendency, some, like Paul Lawrence Rose, even going so far as to link Dohm to the rise of modern antisemitism.[19] Critical approaches to civic improvement, however, are hardly a twentieth-century invention. From the beginning, there were Jewish voices who took note of the power dynamics of the project to use the state to "regenerate" the character of its Jewish population. Mendelssohn himself, for instance, praised Dohm at the same time as he strategically recast his project, speaking of "civic admission" rather than "civic improvement."[20] In *Jerusalem* and other works from the early 1780s, as we shall see in Chapter 3, he challenged both Dohm's vision of regeneration and the triumphalism of so many Enlightenment concepts of modernity. Saul Ascher (1767–1822), a Berlin writer who was a similarly enthusiastic proponent of Dohm's proposals, sought to shift the direction of the debates to foreground the Jews' "natural rights." In an anonymous pamphlet published in 1788 in response to the Austrian Emperor Joseph II's decision to use Jewish recruits in his war against the Turks, Ascher stressed the potential dark side of civic improvement, the possibility that a state eager to transform Jews into useful subjects might violate the Jews' human rights, essentially turning them into slaves rather than citizens.[21] For Dohm himself, of course, "humanity" and "genuine politics" were "one and the same" (D2: 71n), and there was no dark side to an emancipation undertaken in the interests of the state. The regeneration of Jews as potential colonists to promote Prussia's internal expansion was an integral part of the state's more general charge to promote the ideal humanity of its subjects, and Dohm frequently contrasted the "humanity" of the Enlightenment's ideal of universal citizenship with the violence and brute force with which medieval states exiled and oppressed foreigners (D1: 26, 86).

What needs to be explored here, then, is the peculiar alliance between "humanity" and state power in Dohm, the way he rooted his vision of emancipation in an explicit defense of the right and need of the modern state to "improve" its Jews in the name of reason and progress. As he stated in his preface, his ambition was to "encourage state governments to increase their number of *good* citizens by no longer causing the Jews to be *bad* ones," and he sought to persuade his readership of the viability of this project largely through a *historical* argument, one that demonstrated that the "Jews are only corrupt as human beings and citizens because they have been denied the rights of both" (D1: iii–iv). As he noted at the outset of his treatise, this project had its origins in an earlier plan to study the "history of the Jewish nation since the destruction of its own state" (D1: i), and indeed, Jewish history was central to both Dohm's understanding of the predicament of contemporary Jews and his more general vision of modernity. His treatise closely follows the wanderings of the Jews from the institution of Mosaic law to the present, offering an account of Jewish history carefully crafted to bolster his argument for civic improvement. Jewish history was not interesting to Dohm on its own terms. His goal was not to understand the Jews the way they understood themselves and communicate to his German audience a distinctly Jewish vision of history. The fact that his initial interest only went back as far as the destruction of the ancient Jewish commonwealth by the Romans is telling here. What drew Dohm to Jewish history was not the grandeur of ancient Israel but the political experience of Jews in Diaspora, first under Roman rule and then in the "dark centuries" of the Christian Middle Ages. Jewish history was useful, that is, as a record of the Jews' experience in exile, a key to understanding both the roots of their civic degeneration and the more general problems the Enlightenment had to confront in emancipating itself from the legacy of an era that had failed to recognize the proper distinction between church and state. In Dohm's rendition, not surprisingly, this history culminates not in messianic redemption and national restoration but in the process of civic improvement, in the incorporation of Jews into a secular political order in which they would cease to be "Jews, properly speaking."

On the Civic Improvement of the Jews offers a master-narrative of Jewish history that is also a master-narrative for the modern state, and it is crucial for Dohm's argument that history offers a precedent for the secular project of civic improvement. Jewish emancipation has a model for Dohm, and its model is the Roman Empire, the political order that conquered Jerusalem and destroyed the second Jewish commonwealth in 70 CE. Dohm authorized his project to recast the Jews' character and stage their homecoming into the modern state by finding a model for civic virtue in Imperial Rome's victory over Jerusalem; the rhetoric of empire was crucial to his vision of regeneration and national consolidation. In the late nineteenth century, once a unified Germany had overseas colonies, it was not uncommon to regard eighteenth-century programs of internal colonization as an anticipation of later German colonial undertakings.[22] In the case of the civic improvement of the Jews, however, internal colonization had little to do with paving the way for colonial expansion abroad. Visions of imperial power clearly play a role in

Dohm's blueprint for a state that would embody the supreme principles of the Enlightenment, but just as in his essay on coffee legislation, here too we are not dealing with direct fantasies of colonial expansion. As in his reflections on coffee, Dohm here also sought to boost Prussia's standing in a world whose contours were increasingly determined by the progress of empire. He did so in this case not by promoting domestic substitutes for colonial products but by domesticating the *rhetoric* of empire, transforming visions of imperial domination into a project of internal colonization that promised to transform Prussia into the ultimate exemplar of the modern state, the symbolic heir to the grandeur of Imperial Rome.

ROME VERSUS JERUSALEM, OR RELIGION, POLITICS AND THE
CHALLENGE OF MODERNITY

The sketch of Jewish history that organizes Dohm's treatise is in many ways unoriginal. Indeed, *On the Civic Improvement of the Jews* is full of footnotes referencing widely read German and French works such as Johann David Michaelis's *Mosaic Law* (1770–75), a monumental historical treatment of ancient Judaism by Germany's leading Orientalist scholar, his friend Büsching's *History of the Jewish Religion* (1779), Baron de Montesquieu's *Spirit of the Laws* (1748) and Jacques Basnage's *History of the Jews* (1706). Dohm also drew liberally from Josephus and other classical sources dealing with the status of the Jews in the ancient world, and he made use of scores of Latin and German legal records and historical chronicles. What was novel about his vision of Jewish history were not its particulars but the overarching framework in which he studied the Jewish experience, the unified perspective from which he summarized the Jews' relation to the political world both before and after the onset of Diaspora.

Dohm began his narrative with a discussion of Mosaic Judaism. In an argument drawn from Michaelis, he defended ancient Judaism against the charge of barbarism that had been common fodder among Voltaire and the English deists, stressing that the laws of Moses were in fact perfectly suited for a nation at a relatively primitive stage of cultural development. Like Spinoza in the seventeenth century, Michaelis conceived of Judaism essentially as a politics, a legal system, and Dohm followed in his footsteps. "Mosaic law," he explained, contained "the most proper principles of morality, justice and order that one would expect of a nation that was just beginning to cultivate itself and had recently escaped from slavery" (D1: 18). Moses's goal, after all, was to create an independent state and a separate nation that would not mix with idolaters, and in this context it made sense that the ancient Israelites had such pride and fancied themselves the "chosen people" (D1: 19–20). Precisely because it was a political order well suited for a primitive nation, however,

Mosaic Judaism was fundamentally flawed. As a theocracy, it was devoid of the universalism and tolerance so crucial to more enlightened forms of politics. As time went on, therefore, and particularly "in the later periods of their own state, the Jews' feelings of superiority gradually became feelings of hatred and enmity toward other human beings, and their noble pride degenerated into an unsociable separation from the rest of the human race" (D1: 20–21). For Michaelis, it was Jesus who intervened here to pronounce an end to Mosaic law and institute a universalist religion. As a political writer who had abandoned the study of theology early on in his student days in Leipzig, Dohm did not even find the question of Jesus's relation to Judaism worth mentioning in this context, and this is telling. He claimed, in fact, that "every religion tears apart the natural bonds of humanity" (D1: 24); the hostility toward the rest of humanity characteristic of the ancient Jewish commonwealth was but an extreme manifestation of a tendency common to all religions—and thus part of the rationale for a political order that would keep such exclusivity in check. In his historical narrative, accordingly, it was not Christianity that dislodged the degenerate politics of ancient Judaism. It was the Roman Empire.

In his account of the struggle between Rome and Jerusalem, Dohm's sympathies did not lie with the Jews, whose enmity toward the rest of the human race apparently caused them to "stubbornly defend their freedom and capital city" and fight against the Roman "destroyers of Jerusalem" with "raging national-hatred" (D1: 40). He narrated the destruction of the ancient Jewish commonwealth entirely from the perspective of the victors, presenting Rome as the desirable antithesis of the theocratic politics of Jerusalem, a political order grounded in a tolerance of religious difference and a presciently modern separation of church and state. The Romans, he noted, recognized the proper distinction between religious and political societies, and in the centuries before Christianity became a state religion, the "wise and mild politics" of the Roman Empire did not just not punish the Jews for their insurrection; the Romans gave the Jews an unprecedented opportunity for participation in civic life, allowing them to enjoy all the rights and duties of citizens (D1: 40, 45). Rome served for Dohm as a model for both Jewish civic virtue and civic virtue *per se*, a crucial historical precedent for the modern project of civic improvement. Dohm's archetype for the modern, secular state was the conquering power that destroyed Jerusalem and initiated the final Jewish Diaspora, and the symbolic significance of this identification with imperial power cannot be underestimated: in its emancipation of the Jews, civic improvement sought to reenact the fall of Jerusalem.[23]

There was more at stake here than a naive call to imitate the ancients. Like so many of his peers who participated in the quarrel between the ancients and moderns unleashed by Winckelmann's injunction to imitate the eternal model of Greek art, Dohm sought to outline how modernity might *surpass* classical antiquity. Like the ancient Jewish commonwealth, the Roman Empire was prone to degeneration, and Dohm narrated the fall of Rome in such a way as to issue a warning to modernity about securing the proper subordination of religion to politics. In his account, Rome was not destroyed from without but from within, by a violation of the boundaries between politics and religion reminiscent of ancient Israel. The exclusion of the Jews from politics that Dohm marked as a "remnant of the barbarism of past centuries" has a precise date of inception here. It begins with the declaration of Christianity as the official religion of the Roman Empire, a move that represents for Dohm both the "abandonment of the wise principle of Roman government" (D1: 45) and a betrayal of the spirit of Christianity, which was originally opposed to all forms of political authority (D2: 200). In the fifth century, he explained, "fanatical fathers of the church misled weak monarchs to suspend the wise ordinances of their precursors and to regard it as proof of their zeal for the religion of love to treat those who thought differently in an unloving manner" (D1: 45). Establishing Christianity as a state religion transformed the "religion of love" into its antithesis, creating a politicized religion of hatred that ate away at the boundaries between the religious and political realms. Persecution of Jews was a political phenomenon of enormous significance, an improper entry of religion into politics that marked the beginning of the end of the Roman Empire.

Christian Rome represents thus a regression to a lower level of political culture, a return to the religiously motivated political enmity toward foreigners that characterized the ancient Jewish state. Implicitly invoking a long tradition that saw the anti-Jewish elements in Christianity as part of its Jewish heritage,[24] Dohm presented the emergence of political Jew-hatred as a revival of ancient Israel's exclusiveness, an outgrowth of the politics of Jerusalem. The final descent of Rome into "barbarism," accordingly, does not need to be presented as a moment in which Rome was conquered from without. Rather, the "barbarian invaders" only completed the process of degeneration initiated by a weakening state's alliance with a church eager to overstep its proper domain. These conquerors, who "knew no virtue other than that of war," treated free-born Romans practically like slaves, and they subjected the Jews—a people Christian Rome had long since excluded from the military— to even harsher treatment. The final desiccation of the wisdom of Roman politics came with the barbarians' conversion to Christianity, for "the only way the victors knew how to express their zeal for this religion was to persecute the unfortunate nation that steadfastly refused to take on a faith that Goths, Vandals and Franks so easily exchanged with that of their fathers" (D1: 50–51). In this scenario, the fall of Rome coincides with the complete transformation of the nonpolitical "religion of love" into a politics of religious hatred. This final dissolution of the emancipatory promise of Roman politics solidifies the Jews' exclusion from the political world, giving rise to an enduring legacy of the "darkest centuries" which modernity can only eradicate by reviving the Roman principles of separation of church and state, by symbolically reenacting the victory of republican Rome over theocratic Jerusalem.

Recast in this manner, Jewish history contains a blueprint for the construction of a secular state that would liberate itself once and for all from the political burdens of religious exclusiveness. Modernity needs to create a political order that will recapture and surpass the grandeur of Rome, an enlightened state that will put religion in its proper place and never again fall prey to the theocratic politics of Jerusalem. Dohm clearly realized that this vision of history was potentially at odds with the way Jews might perceive their own past. He supported his proposals for granting Jews rights, in fact, by voicing the expectation that emancipated Jews would naturally come to reconceptualize their religion in the terms of his own vision of modernity. Unlike many other voices who entered the debates, Dohm did not want to make emancipation contingent on religious reform. Departing from the views of so many of his contemporaries, he contended that Judaism was at its core a rational religion and that a "transformation of the religious system of the Jews" would simply be an inevitable consequence of granting Jews rights (D2: 178–80). In this sense, he expressed a relative tolerance of Judaism that was rare, surpassed perhaps only by that of his contemporary Heinrich Diez (1751–1817), a Prussian official who suggested in an open letter to Dohm in 1783 that the first step in civic improvement would have to be granting Judaism, as a religion, complete equal rights in the state. Diez, a harsher critic of historical religion than Dohm, argued that Jews would certainly be able to transform Judaism into a religion of reason more quickly than Christians, who have needed 1,800 years to put their house in order.[25]

How exactly did Dohm envision this reform of Judaism taking place? Religion, he claimed, has always had to adjust to the advantages of the state, and he argued that the subordination of religion to true political interests invariably has positive effects for religion as well (D2: 188, 213). But how does this work for Judaism, a religion that in its original form apparently knew no distinction between religion and the state, between the theological and the political—a religion that represented the antithesis of a universalist politics? Dohm answered this question by yet another foray into Jewish history, one that sought to explain how it was that the Rabbis came to corrupt Mosaic Judaism and create a religion characterized by an "anxious spirit of ceremonies and minutiae" (D1: 143). In many ways, Dohm's vision of a

degenerate Rabbinic Judaism was a staple of Enlightenment theological discourse, a commonplace he inherited from Michaelis and Büsching, and from
works such as Lessing's *Education of the Human Race* (1777) and the *German
Encyclopedia* (1778).[26] Lessing, for instance, argued that the "hair-splitting"
practices of Rabbinic interpretation "inserted" into the Bible "more than was
really in it" and "extracted from it more than it could contain," "squeezing
allegories too closely, interpreting examples too circumstantially, and pressing
too much upon words."[27] For Lessing—and I quote this passage because it is
so typical—this scenario set the stage for Christianity's triumph over Judaism,
for the emergence of Jesus as the rightful heir to Old Testament Judaism.
Dohm, not surprisingly, framed the issue in different terms, casting the interpretive practices of the Rabbis as a political problem. Situating the origins
of Rabbinic Judaism several centuries later than Lessing (and most of his
other contemporaries), he saw the deficits of Rabbinic exegesis as the fault of
Christian persecution, a symptom of the Jews' exclusion from politics in the
later years of the Roman Empire. It was from this perspective—and this
remarkable passage deserves to be quoted at length—that he outlined the
expected path of Jewish reform:

> Certainly, the unnatural oppression in which the Jews have lived for so
> many centuries has contributed not just to their moral corruption, but to
> the degeneration of their religious laws from their original goodness and
> utility. Moses wanted to found a lasting, flourishing state, and his law
> contains nothing that would contradict this goal. In the observation of
> this law, this state too had its golden age, and until well into the fifth
> century the Jews were good citizens in the Roman Empire. It was only
> afterward, when all civil societies of the earth excluded them, that they
> forgot how their religious doctrine related to civil societies. The singular
> occupation of trade gave them pleasure and also an inclination toward
> hair-splitting speculations. For the lack of anything better to do they then
> tampered with their religious prescripts, anxiously observing certain
> customs and times in an effort to achieve exquisite holiness and greater
> rights to heaven—all of this because civic virtue was forbidden to them,
> because their participation in the happiness of this earth was so limited.
> This anxious spirit of ceremonies and minutiae that has crept into the
> Jewish religion will certainly disappear again as soon as the Jews receive
> a greater sphere of activity. Once they become members of political
> society, the Jews will be permitted to make its interest into their own.
> They will then also rework their religious constitution and its laws
> accordingly; they will return to the freer and nobler ancient Mosaic con-
> stitution and will even find in their *Talmud* the authorization to apply this
> constitution according to the changed times and circumstances. (D1:
> 142–44)

Strategically conflating the ancient Jewish polity founded by Mosaic law with the "golden age" of the Jewish nation under Roman rule, Dohm finds the process of Jewish civic degeneration reflected in a lack of Jewish memory. Disregarding his earlier discussion of the deterioration of the Jewish commonwealth into a political order that perpetuated enmity toward non-Jews, he now insists that Jews have simply forgotten the proper relationship between Judaism and political power, between Judaism and civic virtue. Excluded from political society and forced into trade, the Jews simply "had nothing better to do" than pay excessive attention to their ceremonial law, creating in this way a perverted religious constitution that now stands in the way of civic reintegration. In the next section we will deal more explicitly with Dohm's views on trade. For now, we should note that he casts Rabbinic Judaism here as a compensatory phenomenon, an anxious attempt to produce a canon of religious laws that would take the place of the political sphere of activity the Jews lose once Christianity becomes the official religion of the Roman Empire. In this scenario, Judaism as it currently exists is but a substitute for politics, and a rather poor one at that.

Regeneration in this case means "restoring" Jewish memory of civic virtue by wresting the Jews out from under the authority of Rabbinic interpretation and returning them to their golden age under Roman rule. The Jews' perverted religious constitution standing in the way of civic integration betrays the true spirit of Mosaic law, and it undermines itself as well, allowing Dohm to find in the Talmud an authority for the incorporation of Jews into a non-Jewish state. In reenacting the victory of Rome over Jerusalem, civic improvement thus claims to be restoring the true spirit of Mosaic law, and to be doing so with the authority of Talmudic interpretation. Like the original conquest it seeks to reenact, this triumph of Rome over Jerusalem claims to liberate its victims, granting them possibilities for the "participation in the happiness of this earth" that Dohm marks as the ultimate purpose of Mosaic law. In resurrecting the Roman distinction between church and state, Dohm's goal is not to secure freedom of conscience for the Jews. Rather, he intervenes directly into the realm of conscience here, "restoring" Jewish memory of civic virtue in such a way as to celebrate the Roman victory over Jerusalem as the completion of Mosaic law. In *Jerusalem*, as we shall see in Chapter 3, Mendelssohn will argue for the compatibility of traditional Jewish ceremonial law with the modern, secular state, casting Jerusalem rather than Rome as the model for modernity. Dohm here, however, expects that giving Jews rights will lead to a reformulation of Jewish law, a modernization of Judaism that will make the law compatible with the modern state and also represent a "return to the freer and nobler ancient Mosaic constitution."[28] For the Jews who emerge from this project of civic regeneration, the memory of Rome displaces the memory of Jerusalem. In its intended effects, civic improvement dispenses with Rabbinic Judaism and gives Jews a new form of commemorating the Jewish past: it transforms the fabric of Jewish memory to celebrate the victory of Rome over Jerusalem as a primal moment of Jewish emancipation and modernity itself.[29]

HUMANIZING THE JEWS: PRACTICES OF CIVIC IMPROVEMENT

It is from this perspective that Dohm legitimizes civic improvement, and in subsequent years his invocation of Imperial Rome as a model for the modern state often served as a focal point in debates over emancipation, Judaism and modernity. Mendelssohn for example, blatantly challenged Dohm's uncritical celebration of Roman imperialism, speaking instead of Roman "conquerors of Jerusalem" who "plundered the Temple" and "saw everything with the eyes of barbarians" (*J* 114; *JubA* 8: 180). In an 1802 essay "Conversion of the Jews," on the other hand—and this is more typical—the philosopher Johann Gottfried Herder (1744–1803) reinforced Dohm's opposition of Rome and Jerusalem. Herder outlined a program of political rather than religious conversion, encouraging this "Asiatic people foreign to our part of the world" to abandon their fixation on the "naked mountains of Palestine, that cramped, devastated land" so as to contribute to the collective culture of humanity, which he represented, tellingly, with the figure of the Roman Colosseum.[30] Christian Ludwig Paalzow (1753–1824) and Friedrich Buchholz (1768–1843), anti-Jewish polemicists writing at the turn of the century whom we shall encounter in Chapter 5, often invoked Dohm's distinction between Rome and Jerusalem, using a glorified vision of the Roman Empire to propose programs of civic improvement far more coercive than anything in Dohm.

Rome was more for Dohm, however, than an abstract model for the modernization of Prussia. His vision of history also provided the framework for his practical proposals to transform Jews into soldiers, artisans and farmers that provoked so much attention in the years to come. Reminding his readers that Jews were valiant soldiers in ancient Israel and initially in the Roman Empire as well, he proposed abolishing the current system of having Jews pay special taxes to be exempt from military service, and he also argued for governmental incentives to move Jews away from trade, banking and peddling into the more "honorable" professions of agriculture and the crafts. On one level, his concerns here were strictly economic. Voicing a distrust of trade shared by many of his contemporaries, he simply wanted to transform Jews into productive citizens who would be of use to the state, and he wanted them to do their part for the national defense so as not to be an unfair burden to non-Jewish citizens. When it came to addressing the particulars of these proposals for national consolidation, however, he involved himself once again in a discussion of the role of state power in molding the Jews' character. The pressing task for the state after giving Jews rights was not to transform their religious and historical consciousness; Dohm promised his readers that Jews would reform Judaism on their own, as a direct result of emancipation. In keeping with his principles of economic productivity, the immediate objective of civic improvement had to be regenerating the Jews on a more physical level, subjecting them to a program of bodily discipline that would both revitalize the Jewish body and transform the Jewish spirit.

The parameters for Dohm's program of physical and spiritual regeneration derived directly from his vision of Jewish history. In his account, the Jews' exclusion from politics did not merely give rise to the perversions of Rabbinic Judaism. Excluded from military service by the establishment of Christianity as a state religion, the Jewish body also reflected the more general degeneration of civic virtue. The Jews were a "nation disaccustomed to war for the last 1,500 years" that obviously lacked the "warlike courage and the bodily strength necessary for military service" (D 1: 145). Beginning with Michaelis in 1782, many of Dohm's detractors perceived the incompatibility of the Jewish body with military service to be a major impediment to emancipation; others argued that Jewish law clearly forbade fighting on the Sabbath, which Dohm refuted, or that Jews would simply never be able to become patriotic soldiers for a non-Jewish state.[31] For Dohm, these sorts of doubts were the most serious questions raised by his critics, and in the second volume of his treatise he reiterated his conviction that the Jews could make no claim to equal rights until they proved themselves both willing and able to perform military service (D 2: 223). With his belief in the malleability of human nature and the ability of religion to adjust to political circumstances, Dohm did not find any of the objections raised by his critics to be insurmountable, at least in the long run. From the beginning, his response to this problem was to propose a massive program of discipline that sought to undo these 1,500 years of bodily degeneration and restore the Jewish body the natural strength it had during the Jews' golden age under Roman rule. On one level, both "stronger nourishment" and the "mechanical labor" Jews would perform as farmers and artisans would help here, and indeed, the "same discipline and methods by which we daily see the clumsiest young peasants become useful soldiers will surely have to be able to bring about the same transformation in the Jews" (D 1: 145). But here as well there was more at stake than simply imitating the ancients. Dohm explained that the great advantage of the modern military was that "adroit skill, strict subordination and a gradually forming feeling of honor have replaced patriotic zeal," and this has made the ancient virtue of "personal courage" no longer necessary (D 1: 145–46). Rendering the Roman "virtue of war" irrelevant, Dohm insisted that modern soldiers can and must be made.[32] Jews would simply have to be trained to become good soldiers, subjected to a process of bodily discipline that would *produce* an internal "feeling of honor" that would stand in for Roman patriotic zeal and bind them to the non-Jewish body politic.

Dohm's exaltation of the power of military discipline is hardly unusual for eighteenth-century Prussia, a state known throughout Europe at the time for its strong military. Kant, indeed, concluded his 1784 essay "What is Enlightenment?" by praising Frederick the Great for maintaining a large, well-disciplined army to ensure public safety (*AA* 8: 41–42). In his *Journeys of a German in England in 1782*, a widely read travelogue that was translated into English and Russian, Karl Philipp Moritz (1756–93), a contemporary of Dohm in Berlin, noted the awe British citizens felt for the Prussian military, whose frequent demonstrations in Berlin he himself compared, unfavorably, to the exhilarating joys of the British Parliament.[33] Dohm, of course, was hardly a critic of the military, and indeed, the form of bodily discipline he saw as necessary for the transformation of Jews into soldiers lay very much at the heart of his proposals for Jewish occupational restructuring as well. He preferred agriculture and the crafts to trade not simply because they would make Jews productive members of the national economy but because they were forms of mechanical physical labor that, like military discipline, would help reshape the Jewish spirit. Arguing that it is trade that has ruined the moral and political character of the Jews, he celebrated mechanical labor as the best means of promoting the "peace of mind" he saw as the desirable antithesis of the shifty, overexerted "roving spirit" and "merchant nature" of the Jews:

> Hard work makes him [the craftsman] healthy, and the uniformity of this work brings a certain silent peacefulness into his spirit. . . . The silent, sitting way of life and the peaceful diligence required by the crafts is the very opposite of the restless roving around of the trading Jew. The craftsman's peaceful enjoyment of the present and his satisfaction with little is the antithesis of the trading Jew's hopes for the future, desire for profit and calculations of continually fluctuating percentages. The hard labor and coarser and stronger nourishment of the craftsman will also have an advantageous effect on the Jew's physical constitution; the mechanical skills will lead to the development of new abilities; the monotonous labor and the moderate prosperity will make the Hebrew become more like our respectable citizen and city dwellers. (D 1: 100, 111–12)

The discipline of manual labor, indeed, gives the Jews "enjoyment of the present," severing the Jews from the fixation on the future fostered by trade—

the same occupation, we remember, that encouraged Jews to pervert their religion to focus on achieving "greater rights to heaven" at the expense of participation in the worldly joys of civic life. In his panegyric to the wonders of mechanical labor here, Dohm implicitly links the Jews' longings for messianic salvation with the their anticipation of future profits. He proposes a program of bodily labor that seeks to put an end to *all* Jewish hopes for the future and cause Jews to focus their attention on the here and now of their new role in the modern state.

Conceived in this manner, civic improvement will clearly take time, and while Dohm never expressed doubts about the prospects of regenerating the Jews, he did expect the process of civic improvement to span several generations. It was for this reason that he argued that for the time being Jews should not be encouraged to seek public office. "The still too merchant-like spirit of most Jews," he explained, "will be better broken by hard bodily labors than by the silent, sitting labor of the public servant; and it will be better for both the state and for the Jew in most cases if he works more in the workshop and behind the plow than in the chancellery" (D 1: 119). Dohm was, to be sure, not categorically against Jews becoming civil servants like himself and occupying positions in the state. But he felt that putting Jews in positions of responsibility before their character had been reformed would ultimately pose a political risk. He suggested that if a qualified Jew and an equally qualified Christian should apply for the same position, the position should be given to the Christian. He defended this policy as an "entirely just right of the more numerous nation" that should remain in effect until the work of civic improvement had been completed, that is, until "a wiser treatment of the Jews has transformed them into completely equal citizens and grinded down all their differences" (D 1: 120). In a fitting conclusion to his reflections on the right of the state to improve the Jews in the name of reason and progress, Dohm here underscored the need of the state to safeguard itself and its purchase on an impartial universality against the threat of Jewish difference. "The Jew," he wrote, "is even more a human being than he is a Jew" (D 1: 28). It was the task of the state, accordingly, to ensure that Jews live up to their human potential, to create a political order that would transform the Jew into the archetype of the productive citizen.

THE AMERICAN PRESIDENT

By a fortunate coincidence, the publication of *On the Civic Improvement of the Jews* coincided with Joseph II's Edict of Tolerance, a set of legal measures geared at incorporating Jews more integrally into the fabric of the Habsburg Empire, and in the second volume of his treatise Dohm noted that his proposals would never have captured the degree of public attention they did without such auspicious timing (D 2: 4). In subsequent decades, Dohm's vision of civic improvement did more than provoke heated public debate. In many instances, it also set the terms for concrete legal reforms and state-sponsored programs to encourage Jews to become artisans and farmers.[34] The German lands, unlike France, tended not to heed Dohm's call for immediate emancipation, but many state officials arguing for reform echoed his language and arguments, transforming his link between emancipation and regeneration into what David Sorkin has called a quid pro quo, an exchange of rights for regeneration.[35] The enormous interest the public showed in this project obviously cannot be explained solely with reference to these concrete proposals for regenerating the Jews. For Dohm himself, after all, civic improvement was as much or more about the process of political modernization than about the Jews themselves. Even within the framework of his treatise, the Jews were viewed as important potential manpower for national consolidation, but they also had a symbolic significance that far surpassed their predicted contributions to economic prosperity. More than malleable material for crafting a new body politic, the Jews resided within Prussia bearing their alien history with them, giving Dohm powerful symbolic material for imagining new forms of political community. As a lingering remnant of the victory of a perverted and barbaric Christianity over the wisdom of ancient Roman politics, the contemporary Jewish condition served Dohm as a reminder of both the perils of the Middle Ages and the grandeur of Imperial Rome. As potential colonists for internal expansion, the Jews also supplied Dohm with a history *he* could colonize as a master-narrative for the modern state, a history he could rewrite to cast the Jews' transformation into loyal Roman subjects as the model for a political order grounded in secular ideals of universal citizenship.

Dohm's invocation of Imperial Rome had little to do with direct visions of colonial expansion. But given his sustained interest in promoting Prussia's international stature—one of the ways he originally sought to launch his political career, we remember, was by encouraging Frederick the Great to revitalize the Prussian East India Company—we should pay attention to his use of visions of ancient empire. Particularly against the backdrop of a colonial world in which the German lands lacked a prominent role, staking out a claim to the grandeur of Imperial Rome served as a sort of substitute for empire, and in this sense, Dohm's vision of Jewish emancipation converges once again with his reflections on coffee legislation. Dohm, moreover, was hardly alone in framing the issue of Jewish emancipation in relation to real or imagined modes of empire. In his influential critique of Dohm in 1782, Michaelis argued that it would be easiest to make Jews useful and productive if Germans had wealth-producing "sugar islands" where they might put

Jews to work—an obvious inversion (and perversion) of Dohm's proposals to use the Jews as the equivalent of foreign colonists on the domestic front.[36] An anonymous reviewer in a prominent journal offered up a similar proposal in 1782, but one that retained a greater faith in regeneration than Michaelis, who felt it unlikely that Jews would ever be productive citizens. Wary of Jews mixing with non-Jews before the time was right, this author suggested a concerted effort of European nations to deport Jews to one place in the globe.[37] An essay in the journal later that year, presumably by the same author, elaborated this plan further, proposing that European nations transplant their Jews to an island in the Atlantic that might serve as a colony where the Jews could be effectively regenerated.[38] The Kantian philosopher Johann Gottlieb Fichte (1762–1814) noted in his polemics of 1793 that the best way for Europeans to protect themselves from Jews would be to "conquer the holy land for them and send them all there."[39] And in "Conversion of the Jews," Herder, a much stauncher believer in "humanizing" the Jews than Fichte, imagined a scenario in which Napoleon might act as the Jewish Messiah to set up a European Jewish colony in Palestine.[40]

These four authors obviously differed in their estimation of the pros and cons of civic improvement, but like Dohm, they all articulated their position on regeneration with the vocabulary of empire and domination. So it should hardly come as a surprise that starting with an anonymous 1774 work that purported to have knowledge of a pre-Columbian Jewish colony on the Ohio river, the topic of Jewish colonies was debated widely in the German press, with no fewer than forty proposals for resettlement published by 1819, and many more thereafter.[41] Many of the authors interested in Jewish colonies followed the authors above to propose overseas resettlement, deportation to places like Botany Bay, Australia, unnamed desolate coastal regions or Palestine.[42] Others—and this was clearly part of the same debate—recommended internal Jewish colonies in Prussia, typically agricultural settlements in desolate, previously uncultivated regions where the work of civic improvement might be carried out in relative isolation, much like an experiment in social engineering on an island in the middle of the Atlantic. The proposals for Jewish colonies and Jewish villages, moreover, usually did not come from those like Michaelis or Fichte who felt Jews could not be effectively regenerated. Often they were the products of ideologues of civic improvement, liberal-minded government officials, and, in one case, the Prussian Jewish community itself.[43] Dohm himself, we should note, tended to be ambivalent on the question of internal Jewish colonies. At times, he argued against such proposals, claiming they would only reinforce Jewish difference (D 1: 115–16), but at other points, he tended to be less critical, granting implicit consent to those who argued that civic improvement could best be achieved by creating separate Jewish settlements.[44] Some of these proposals, incidentally, did leave the drafting table. From 1785 to 1789, Joseph II set up numerous agricultural Jewish colonies in Galicia and Bukovina, one of which carried the name "New Jerusalem." Of these settlements, none received the capital and technical support given to other foreign colonists, largely because the authorities feared Jews would use such funds to engage in trade; as a result, none of the Jewish colonies survived.[45] On one level, the proposals to set up domestic Jewish colonies were simply variations on common practices of internal colonization that had little to do with anything going on outside Germany. Given the role that the rhetoric of empire played in Dohm's own proposals for regeneration, however, it makes sense to consider the symbolic connections between these visions of internal expansion and the concern with Prussia's international stature that was such an important part of Dohm's career. Before we conclude this chapter, accordingly, let us consider one further text in some detail, a piece that responded to Dohm in such a way as to foreground how internal colonization could function symbolically as a form of surrogate colonialism.

In 1783, the *German Museum* published a "Letter of a German Jew, to the President of the Congress of the United States of America," which the poet Leopold Friedrich Günther von Goeckingk (1748–1828) claimed to have received from an unnamed Jew he met on a trip.[46] Goeckingk, a Prussian official serving in Ellrich, was a well-known sentimental poet and writer who had edited the *Göttingen Almanac of the Muses* in the 1770s and recently founded the *Journal of and for Germany*.[47] A frequent contributor to the *Museum*, Goeckingk was a close friend of Friedrich Nicolai, the publisher of Dohm's treatise, and a familiar face in the circles of Berlin intellectuals in which Dohm traveled. Given the periodical in which it was published, it is hardly surprising that this letter closely echoes Dohm's argument about political and economic restrictions contributing to the "depravity" of the Jews' character. Rather than proposing that regenerated Jews function as the equivalent of foreign colonists, however, this letter asks the president of the Continental Congress to allow 2,000 Jewish families to immigrate to America and set up a Jewish colony there. This figure is quite astonishing if one considers that Prussia proper, for instance, contained only about 1,600 Jewish families at this time.[48] This letter, importantly, is not a plea for naturalization or citizenship. Indeed, at the time it was published, the Congress was still debating the "General Assessment Bill for Support of Christian denominations," a bill that would have declared Christianity a state religion, and the German public was very much aware of these developments.[49] Noting that the United States already "tolerates" Jews, the author casts the Jewish immigrants as potential colonists who, if granted the proper privileges, will help promote American wealth and prosperity:

> The peace treaty between the distinguished American states and England has led many of us to conclude, with great interest, that you now possess large stretches of practically uninhabited land. It may take more than a century for the inhabitants of the thirteen united provinces to increase to such an extent that they would be in a position to populate and cultivate the land they already possess (much like, for instance, the Duchy of Württemberg is populated and cultivated). Should these stretches of land lie desolate during these hundred years, or become a too large hunting ground for a few roaming savages? ... You have the legislative power in your hands, and we demand nothing more than to become subjects of the thirteen provinces. We will gladly contribute twice as much in taxes toward the good of these provinces if we only receive the permission and financial support to set up colonies and engage in agriculture, trade, arts and sciences.[50]

The vision of the United States that emerges from this letter looks uncannily similar to eighteenth-century Prussia. Now that the former colonies have thrown off the yoke of colonial rule, the thirteen provinces are perceived to be in a perfect position to engage in their own project of internal colonization, subsidizing foreign settlers to cultivate their "practically uninhabited" land and help increase their population. Like Prussia, the US pursues its current policy of internal colonization in the face of a segment of the domestic population that it cannot assimilate, a group of "roaming savages" analogous to German Jews in constituting an exception to the principles of economic productivity and population growth.

The neat symmetry the letter constructs between Prussia and the US is not a result of its allegedly Jewish author's lack of sophistication in political matters. The "Letter of a German Jew" blatantly undermines its claim to authenticity at all turns, clearly presenting itself to the public as a work of fiction. There is, needless to say, no record of this letter having been received by any branch of the US government, nor was there ever any discussion in the Jewish community of these plans to relocate 2,000 families to America.[51] When the letter was reprinted as a separate pamphlet in 1787, moreover, it was addressed to the "American President O ..."—an obvious fabrication— and listed as being "edited" by Moses Mendelssohn (who had died the year before and whose name it misspelled).[52] Whether written by Goeckingk or someone else—and the authorship of the letter seems to be obscure[53]—this letter to the American President functions as a veiled plea to the German reading public. Presenting Jews as desirable colonists for the US had the obvious function of marking them as domestic resources the German states were in a position to *lose* to the US. It is telling that the letter opens by setting up a peculiar relationship between the American President and the King of Prussia. "Honorable Mr. President," the letter begins:

> You will give me special forgiveness if I do not give you the proper title, since this is not known to me. You are the leader of a united state that has waged war with the most powerful monarchy in the world and has won even more than what it fought for. In this capacity alone, you would be justified to demand from every European court (and even more so from a Jew!) the title "Your Supreme Highness," a title you deserve more than many of our royalty. . . . A man like yourself is certainly just as little concerned with complete forms of address as the King of Prussia, who has forbidden people to use his entire form of address, or even a tenth of it. Even if you were simply a well-honored lord in the Dutch style, you would nevertheless not stop being a more important person for Europe than most members of the royal families of Germany; just as that great king would have shone forth above all the kings of Europe even if his grandfather had not assumed the throne.[54]

The war of independence has apparently won the former colonies more than the right to govern themselves. Indeed, in winning a war waged against the most powerful monarchy in the world, the US has gained an almost unprecedented international stature that makes it difficult for anyone, particularly the allegedly Jewish writer of this letter, to address its President by the proper title. In this context, importantly, the letter does not just compare the American President with Frederick the Great—a monarch, we are to think, who has similarly demonstrated his superiority over England. In arguing that the American President is superior to German royal families much in the same way as Frederick the Great shines forth above all the kings of Europe, the letter makes the US seem like a version of Prussia in miniature, a microcosm of Prussia on the other side of the Atlantic.

In congratulating the President of the US Congress on winning his war against England, then, this letter sees its destination as a satellite of Prussia, a country that apparently deserves to be congratulated as the major European power. This letter does much more than conflate Prussia and the US. It casts its destination as a dislocated Prussian colony of sorts, a country much like Prussia but with no economic or political connection to the Prussian fatherland. What the former British colonies have won in their war of independence, it seems, is the right to be like Prussia. England's loss has become Prussia's gain. The proposal to set up a Jewish colony in America targets Frederick the Great as much as the American authorities. As an appeal to the

"American President," this letter contributes to Prussia's own expansion and establishment as a great power, symbolically constructing Prussia as the premier European state. Jews, it seems, are not merely potential resources for population growth and economic expansion which the various German states may be in a position to lose to the US: they are crucial to *Prussia's* own program of internal and external expansion.

How would this work in practice? On the one hand following Dohm, the letter contends that the "degenerate" character of the Jews needs to be overcome by a program of civic improvement, by what it calls a "revolution in our entire way of living and thinking." The only way to achieve this revolution in Jewish moral character, however, is by a strange form of international cooperation between Germany and the overseas Prussian satellite:

> The physical well-being of my brethren concerns me, Mr. Lord President, but their moral well-being concerns me far more. It would be foolishness to want to improve their moral well-being in their present condition. On the contrary, the [Jewish] nation will only get worse and worse. The wise men of our country, who understand very well that this worsening will cause the Christians themselves to suffer along with us, desire a revolution in our entire way of living and thinking, a revolution that no one but you, gracious Mr. President, can bring about. We hope, therefore, that you might deign to present a petition on our behalf to your most praiseworthy Congress. Granting this petition would honor humanity as a whole.[55]

Here the interests of "humanity as a whole" coincide with the interests of both Germany as a whole and the newly independent Prussian satellite. In subsidizing 2,000 Jewish families to become its colonial subjects, the US will not just be promoting growth and economic prosperity. By guaranteeing the physical conditions for the moral regeneration of the Jewish nation, the American President will also be saving the German states from the threat of general moral depravity their unreconstructed Jewish population is threatening to spread. Given the threat of general moral depravity the letter invokes, moreover, the interests of "humanity as a whole" would be better served by a much more radical solution, by a colony of *all* German Jews that would allow the entire Jewish nation to undergo civic improvement. Regenerating the Jews in this manner would certainly make them more useful to the state. It would do so, however, in such a way as to deplete the German states of potential resources, depopulating Germany so as to bolster the economic prosperity of a country that has no explicit link to the German states. It would certainly protect the German states from the threat of moral degeneration but it might upset the balance of power between Prussia and the United States, giving the US a boost in economic productivity and population growth that might make Prussia look like *its* dislocated colony.

Given the implicit threat that mass Jewish immigration might enable the US to prove itself superior not just to England but to Prussia as well, it becomes clear who the ideal person is to bring about the desired revolution: not the American president who is superior to all German royalty but that King who already "shines forth over all the kings of Europe," a king a sixth of whose subjects already consisted of such foreign colonists. The logical solution to the problem the letter poses is not an overseas Jewish colony but a Prussian invitation to German Jews to set up a colony that would both produce the necessary "revolution" in their "entire way of living and thinking" *and* contribute to Prussian colonial expansion. Confronting its German readers with the possibility of a mass population loss to a country that it rhetorically— and only rhetorically—appropriates as a displaced microcosm of Prussia, the "Letter of a German Jew" points toward an obvious alternative: the use of Jews to promote Prussian internal expansion. In inviting in Jews as foreign colonists, moreover, Prussia would be pursuing a politics of internal colonization and would also be engaging, on a symbolic level, in a program of external expansion, an attempt to capture those potential resources that might otherwise become the property of its overseas satellite. Emancipating the Jews would not merely act as a substitute for the practice of inviting in foreign colonists to settle Prussia. Civic improvement would also function as a symbolic substitute for a foreign colony.

In this extreme formulation, the letter to the American President brings to the foreground the link between regeneration and state power so crucial to Dohm's proposals for emancipation, stressing once again the symbolic importance of civic improvement for imagining Prussia's place in the international world. The emancipatory universalism that so many contemporaries found in Dohm is inextricable from the power dynamics of civic improvement, and these power dynamics were directed both inward and outward; they sought to transform the Jews into exemplars of such universalism while simultaneously boosting Prussia's stature in relation to a colonial world to which it lacked any direct connection. By the time he published the second volume of his treatise in 1783, it had become overwhelmingly clear to Dohm that the main opponents he had to contend with in promoting this vision of colonial regeneration were those who insisted that the Jews simply could not be part of his vision of emancipatory universalism. Singling out a skeptical 1781 review of his treatise in the *Göttingen Reports of Learned Matters*, a periodical published by the Göttingen Royal Society of Sciences that was one of the most distinguished review journals of its age, Dohm lambasted those who argued that a "completely unimproveable human race" was possible, a proposition he felt contradicted not just the laws of psychology but the entirety of human history and experience (D 2: 23–24). The review in the *Göttingen Reports* was published anonymously, but Dohm knew very well who the author was: the respected Göttingen philosophy professor Michael Hißmann (1752–84).[56] In his review, Hißmann had linked the moral corruption of modern Jews to that of the ancient Israelites and their longing for the "flesh pots of Egypt," arguing that Jews simply could not be productive colonists, and that emancipation would be far too dangerous.[57] Hißmann, who reprinted his review in pamphlet form the following year, is important here because he came out so strongly against Dohm's vision of regeneration as an academic, writing for a journal that was linked to one of eighteenth-century Germany's most progressive universities, a university where Dohm himself had studied in the 1770s. In his review, however—and this is striking—Hißmann himself never actually used the word "race," a loaded term that had entered German philosophical discourse only with Immanuel Kant's essay "On the Different Human Races" in 1775.[58] Indeed, among the early respondents to Dohm, only one had explicitly used the term race, and this was not Hißmann but Hißmann's colleague, the renowned Göttingen Orientalist whom Dohm himself had frequently hailed in his treatise as an "astute" expert on ancient Judaism: Johann David Michaelis.[59] It is Michaelis to whom we will turn now, tracing how his skepticism about Dohm's proposals participated in a complex matrix of broader reflections on contemporary colonialism, the practices of historical biblical criticism and eighteenth-century visions of race.

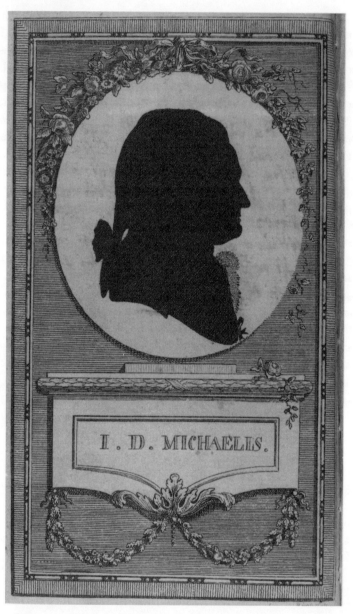

Fig. 2. Silhouette of Johann David Michaelis. From Johann David Michaelis, *Lebensbeschreibung von ihm selbst abgefaßt* (Leipzig, 1793). Courtesy of the Duke University Rare Book, Manuscript, & Special Collections Library.

2

ORIENTALISM AND THE COLONIAL IMAGINARY

Johann David Michaelis and the Specter of Racial Antisemitism

When the term "antisemitism" was first introduced in Germany in the late 1870s, in the aftermath of Jews gaining complete political and legal equality, those who used it did so in order to stress the radical difference between their own "antisemitism" and earlier forms of antagonism toward Jews and Judaism. In contrast to religiously motivated Jew-hatred, anti-semitism introduced itself as a distinctly secular doctrine, a political ideology that took the alleged biological otherness of the "Jewish race" as the basis for a complete worldview.[1] The irony in this assertion of a radical break with religious anti-Judaism is that the concept of antisemitism as it was used in the late nineteenth century was itself indebted to developments within Christian theology. Indeed, the concept of an alien "Jewish race" that anti-semites introduced as their innovation did not derive solely from nineteenth-century pseudo-science. It also had its roots in that "Orientalist" branch of theological scholarship that from the late eighteenth century on had con-cerned itself with "Semitic" languages, "Semitic" peoples and the "Semitic" race.

The terms "Semite" and "Semitic" were coined in the late eighteenth century by the Göttingen historian August Ludwig von Schlözer (1735–1809), who used the terms as early as 1771 to designate both a family of languages and a related group of peoples.[2] Once introduced by Schlözer, these terms quickly gained prominence in theological scholarship, particularly among the growing group of Orientalists eager to read the Hebrew Bible as a product of ancient Israel in its historical specificity. Two of the most influential such works of the 1780s, Johann Gottfried Eichhorn's *Introduction to the Old Testament* (1780–83) and Johann Gottfried Herder's *On the Spirit of Hebrew Poetry* (1782–83), frequently referred to "Semites," "Semitic languages" and

"Semitic tribes."³ Once accepted into historical-theological and philological discourse, these terms began to be used widely, often set in opposition to "Indo-European," "Indo-Germanic" or "Aryan," and linked, particularly in the nineteenth century, to emergent concepts of race. In this context, the inevitably inferior "Semitic race" was often cast as the foil for the triumph of Western, Christian civilization. As an allegedly stagnant people impervious to history and progress, the "Semites" needed to be superseded by the victory of Aryan, Indo-European culture, often embodied in the figure of Jesus, as was the case in the work of the influential French Orientalist Ernest Renan.⁴ When the term "antisemitism" was introduced in the late 1870s as a designation for a secular, political ideology grounded in an antagonism toward the Jewish race, it very consciously gestured toward this tradition.

The specific link between theological antagonism toward Judaism and a racially conceived, politically charged antisemitism, however, is not entirely a nineteenth-century innovation. This connection was forged as early as the 1780s, in the context of the initial discussions over Jewish emancipation and at a point at which modern concepts of race were in the process of being formulated. Johann David Michaelis (1717–91), the Orientalist who trained Schlözer and Eichhorn in Göttingen, was not just the author of the standard eighteenth-century work on Jewish law, the six-volume *Mosaic Law* (1770–75). As one of the Enlightenment's foremost authorities on—and admirers of— ancient Judaism, he also took an engaged role in the early debates on the issue of whether to grant contemporary Jews civil rights, vehemently arguing against Dohm's proposals for civic improvement. In 1782, Michaelis devoted the lead article of his *Oriental and Exegetical Library*, one of the major organs of biblical scholarship at the time, to a forty-page critique of Dohm's treatise. Echoing arguments formulated in *Mosaic Law*, he insisted that Jewish law was designed to preserve separatism and would thus stand in the way of integrating the Jews into a modern, secular state. "Do the laws of Moses," he asked, "contain anything that would make it impossible or difficult for the Jews to be completely naturalized and melt together with other peoples? One should think so! Their intention is to preserve the Jews as a people separated from all other peoples, . . . and as long as the Jews retain the laws of Moses, as long as they for example do not dine with us . . . they will never melt together with us—like the Catholic and Lutheran, the German, Wend and Frenchman, who all live in a single state."⁵ In *Mosaic Law*, Michaelis followed Montesquieu in emphasizing the role of "climate" in shaping law and legal institutions. In his polemics against Dohm, he went further, claiming that modern Jews were themselves products of the "southern" climate of ancient Israel and as such unable to be assimilated into a German state. Invoking the discussions on the concept of race initiated by both Immanuel Kant and

Michaelis's Göttingen colleague Johann Friedrich Blumenbach (1752–1840) in the mid-1770s, Michaelis argued that Jews constituted an "unmixed race of a more southern people" that "even in ten generations" would never have the proper bodily strength to perform military service for a German state (D 2: 51, 63). Throughout his article, Michaelis enumerated many different points of opposition to Dohm. He began his argument, for instance, with statistics that sought to prove Jews' inclinations toward criminal activities. Ultimately, however, it was because of the unfitness of the Jewish body for military service that he came out against any improvements in their legal and political status.

Concepts of innate Jewish bodily differences, of course, have a long history that predates both the debates on Jewish emancipation and the emergence of modern racial theory.[6] What matters here, accordingly, is not simply that Michaelis insisted on the Jews' physical difference but the value and function he assigned this difference in his political antisemitism, the way in which he domesticated the emergent discourse on race. Highlighting the ubiquitous eighteenth-century link between "race" and "climate," he adapted Dohm's plan to make Jews more useful to the state and proposed a solution of his own to the problem Dohm sought to tackle: "Such a people can perhaps become useful to us in agriculture and manufacturing, if one manages them in the proper manner. They would become even more useful if we had sugar islands which from time to time could depopulate the European fatherland, sugar islands which, with the wealth they produce, nevertheless have an unhealthy climate" (D 2: 40–41). The ideal—if not the most practical—solution to the Jewish question, Michaelis suggested, lies in colonial expansion, in relocating the "southern" Jewish race to a climate that would enable Jews to become economically productive, to "colonies . . . where one might send malefactors and degenerates" (D 2: 56). As a "southern race" descended from the ancient Israelites, the Jewish Diaspora apparently needs to be displaced once again, sent to a Caribbean climate analogous to its place of origin where Jews might become colonial subjects promoting the wealth of the European fatherland. Dohm's central goal—the integration of Jews into the German economic and political order—can best be achieved, Michaelis implies, by deportation to a German Jamaica or Haiti, by a model of colonial expansion that would both serve Germany and put the Jewish "race" in its proper place.

Historians have not failed to note that these polemics against Jewish emancipation anticipate arguments that came to prominence a century later.[7] My objective in tracing this genealogy of racial anti-Jewish prejudice back to Michaelis, however, is not to claim his diatribes as the defining moment of modern antisemitism. Rather than reducing his polemics to a foreboding premonition of doctrines that emerged in the 1870s, we need to explore his intervention in the debates over emancipation in its various eighteenth-century contexts. Indeed, we recall from the previous chapter that proposals for colonial deportation were hardly unusual responses to Dohm's vision of national consolidation. Michaelis's vision is important because it came from the pen of such a prominent expert, a respected Orientalist whose *Mosaic Law* was central to Dohm's own understanding of ancient Judaism. In the second volume of *On the Civic Improvement of the Jews*, Dohm reprinted Michaelis's critique in its entirety, introducing his readers to an "astute" and "scholarly" essay that he felt lay unjustly buried in the pages of a specialized publication geared toward Orientalists (D 2: 18–19). Dohm, like so many others, clearly disagreed with Michaelis; indeed, as we noted earlier, his complaints about those who viewed the Jews as a "completely unimproveable human race" seemed to be directed more at Michaelis than at the anonymous review in the *Göttingen Reports of Learned Matters*. Just pages before mentioning Michaelis, moreover, he made yet another implicit jab at the Göttingen Orientalist, equating those who were unwilling to contemplate the emancipation of the Jews with West Indian plantation owners who are "unable to imagine a society in which there are not some people, who, regardless of their humanity, are owned as slaves and treated like cattle by others" (D 2: 5–6). All this criticism aside, however, Dohm thought it worthwhile to broadcast Michaelis's views to a broader public, and he was eminently successful in this campaign. The *Universal German Library*, a prominent review journal edited by Friedrich Nicolai, a friend of Mendelssohn and the publisher of *On the Civic Improvement of the Jews*, noted in a review of the second volume of Dohm's treatise that Michaelis's critique was "an essay written with diligence that, through its calm and modest tone, betrays a nonpartisan man even in his partisan indictment of the Jews."[8] Michaelis's contemporaries, indeed, rarely viewed him as a marginal figure out of sync with his times, and in subsequent years, his arguments against Dohm were cited again and again in debates over emancipation. In a 1835 essay on the "battle of Christian theologians against equal rights for Jews," a young Abraham Geiger presented Michaelis as the first of many Protestant theologians who had used both their official position and their professional expertise to argue against Jewish emancipation.[9] Michaelis's racial conception of the Jews is significant because, like the nineteenth-century doctrine of secular antisemitism it is often seen to anticipate, it was very much a hybrid creation, and one that was deeply enmeshed in its times. This "antisemitism" was as much a theological as a political phenomenon, as much a product of developments in biblical criticism and Oriental studies as an intervention in Enlightenment political debates and a creative appropriation of the emergent discourse on race. Michaelis's fantasy of colonial deportation was far more than a perverse symptom of a deep-seated

Jew-hatred. It epitomized a mode of colonialist thinking that was central to his scholarly work in the emergent field of Oriental studies, his use of contemporary race thinking and the debates over the civic improvement of the Jews.

Scholarship on Michaelis has typically remained within distinct disciplinary boundaries. Historians of antisemitism routinely make note of his polemics against Jewish emancipation but generally do so without studying them in relation to his biblical criticism. Biblical scholars, on the other hand, concentrate on his work on ancient Judaism, usually celebrating Michaelis without qualification as a crucial transitional figure in the rise of historical theology, one of the fathers of modern critical-historical approaches to the Bible. Before exploring how Michaelis's reflections on colonialism unify his biblical criticism and his racial antisemitism, it will be wise to rehearse the image of Michaelis that prevails in that discipline he helped create: the field of modern historical scholarship on the Hebrew Bible.[10] Rejecting the conception of Hebrew as the Adamic language that he had held in his younger years, Michaelis came to stress the close relationship between Hebrew, Arabic and other "Oriental" languages; he was one of the first scholars to use knowledge of Arabic, Aramaic and Syriac to illuminate the Hebrew Bible. In his interpretation of scripture, he made liberal use of contemporary empirical sciences, drawing on geographical, historical and archaeological writings to read the Bible much as one would approach profane texts from antiquity. Influenced by Robert Lowth, whom he had heard lecture in Oxford and whose influential *De sacra poesi Hebraeorum* (On the Sacred Poetry of the Hebrews) he published along with his own commentary, Michaelis sought to study the Hebrew Bible on its own terms, as an historical document of ancient Israel; for the most part, he refrained from stressing its anticipation of the New Testament. In *Mosaic Law*, Michaelis departed from views of biblical Judaism as barbaric that had been common among Voltaire and the English deists. Inspired by Montesquieu, he presented Moses as an enlightened legislator whose legal system needed to be studied as a humane code of laws created to govern the ancient Israelites. For all his attempts to understand scripture in historical terms, nevertheless, Michaelis never issued any challenges to doctrinal orthodoxy. To the contrary, he consistently used his critical-historical methods to *uphold* traditional Protestant understandings of revelation. On the level of textual criticism, Michaelis was similarly nonrevolutionary; for him, Moses was still the sole author of the Pentateuch, speaking alternatively as historian and law-giver. Michaelis's work was both popular and extremely influential in his day; his works were translated into English, French, Dutch and Danish and reprinted in Germany well into the nineteenth century. Particularly *Mosaic Law*, his multi-volume *German Translation of the Old Testament with Annotations for the Uneducated* (1769–85) and his similarly conceived translation of the New Testament (1788–92) reached a wide audience of academic and nonacademic readers, supplementing traditional views of revealed religion with a wealth of historical information about the ancient Near East.

In a recent monograph, Anna-Ruth Löwenbrück chips away at this canonical image of Michaelis, giving a comprehensive overview of both his biblical scholarship and his polemics against contemporary Jews.[11] When it comes to *explaining* his racial Jew-hatred, however, she shies away from establishing a fundamental link between his diatribes against Jewish emancipation and his biblical criticism, noting only that both derive from a basic social conservatism. For Löwenbrück, Michaelis "knew" he could not fight Dohm's enlightened arguments for Jewish emancipation with theology; as a result, she contends, he gravitated toward "scientific" concepts of race and ethnology, thus giving his contemporaries the possibility of using the vocabulary of the Enlightenment to perpetuate traditional forms of Christian Jew-hatred.[12] Löwenbrück is right to stress the link between theological and political antisemitism in Michaelis. Explaining the latter as a displaced continuation of the former, however, fails to account for what is radically new in Michaelis. Rather than attempting to isolate the novelty of his racial antisemitism as it might relate to his own Orientalist scholarship, to Enlightenment thinking about race and to eighteenth-century models of colonialism, Löwenbrück posits an unbroken continuum of antisemitic sentiment that simply gets expressed in a new vocabulary, thus perpetuating the myth of an eternal antisemitism that was so central to the work of Léon Poliakov and others.[13] Casting Michaelis's antisemitism as the antithesis of Dohm's approach toward Jewish emancipation, moreover, conceals the common ground between them: both perceive contemporary Jews as "degenerate," and both solve the Jewish problem by recourse to visions of colonial expansion, albeit very different ones.

In what follows, I explore how Michaelis's biblical scholarship and his racial polemics against Jewish emancipation articulate a very particular version of what Edward Said has called "Orientalism," that is, Western discourse that, in staking out its intellectual authority over the "Orient," implicitly expresses and justifies European hegemony and colonial power over the East.[14] For many, the most characteristic feature of Michaelis's innovation in the field of biblical studies was his use of travel narratives, often contemporary European travel literature on the modern Near East, as a means of understanding the Hebrew Bible in historical terms. He not only published a Latin translation of a description of Egypt by the medieval Arabic writer Abulseda (1273–1331).[15] He also managed to convince King Frederick V of Denmark to launch a scholarly expedition to modern-day Yemen to research the language and customs of the modern Near East in order to gain insight into the culture of the ancient Israelites. Michaelis served as the official "director" of the 1761–67 expedition to "Arabia Felix," formulating questions for the travelers, training them in Arabic and advising them on how best to collect the desired information. Guided by Michaelis, Carsten Niebuhr (1733–1815), the sole survivor of the expedition, published two travel narratives that were translated into a number of European languages and that are often considered to mark the beginning of modern European travel literature on the Near East.[16] I begin my analysis by interrogating the vision of Oriental studies as it emerges from both Michaelis's *Mosaic Law* and his promotion and directorship of the expedition to "Arabia Felix."

The Orientalism we will encounter in Michaelis differs in crucial ways from the nineteenth-century development Said describes. Michaelis is, if anything, more Eurocentric than his nineteenth-century successors in Semitic studies, concerned more with ancient Israelites and modern Jews than with Arabs, whom he reduces to sources of potential data for the historical study of the Hebrew Bible. Islam is of little concern to him. The Orient in which Michaelis specializes is largely the historical birthplace of Judaism and Christianity. Michaelis's approach to the Hebrew Bible hinges on an historiography that uses "knowledge" of the Near East mediated by modern travel to establish his authority over the ancient Israelites. It does so, moreover, alongside polemics against *both* imperial expansion *and* the contemporary Jews who claim to be the legitimate descendants of his objects of study. For Michaelis— and this is crucial—the quest for scholarly authority over the Orient marks the antithesis of modern colonialism. There is, however, more at stake here than what Mary Louise Pratt has called the ideology of the "anti-conquest," a strategy that, like Said's Orientalism, asserts an "innocent" form of European intellectual hegemony that can implicitly justify imperial expansion.[17] For when it comes to modern Jews, Michaelis's anti-imperialist rhetoric betrays itself. The hegemony that his Orientalism ultimately expresses and produces is not merely an intellectual authority over the modern Arab world but also a form of inner European colonialism, a colonial authority over the Jews that uses the modern Near East in order to put both the ancient Israelites and contemporary European Jews in their proper places. In this sense, Michaelis's biblical scholarship will prove to be closely related to the appropriation of eighteenth-century race theory and the proposals for Jewish colonial deportation he articulates in his polemics against Dohm. We will explore this connection by positioning Michaelis's Orientalist scholarship and vision of sugar island Jews alongside both the theories of racial "degeneration" of his Göttingen colleague Johann Friedrich Blumenbach and writings by his colleague August Ludwig Schlözer and other German contemporaries on sugar, sugar islands and the West Indies.

Especially in view of the ever-increasing knowledge of the languages, it was very natural for such sentiments and convictions to lead to the kind of study that involves closer examination of Oriental localities, nationalities, natural products, and phenomena and tries in this way to visualize those ancient times. Michaelis brought the whole force of his talent and knowledge to this endeavor. Travel reports became an effective auxiliary to the interpretation of Holy Scripture, and modern travelers were supplied with many questions to which they were supposed to find answers and thus give testimony for the prophets and apostles.[18]
     —Johann Wolfgang von Goethe, *Poetry and Truth* (1811–14)

Not all Michaelis's contemporaries shared Goethe's enthusiasm for Michaelis's gifts for bringing ancient times to life. In an influential 1772 review of the first two volumes of *Mosaic Law*, Johann Gottfried Herder (1744–1803) complained that Michaelis was representing the past without the necessary degree of critical reflection:

The entire work is supposed to be nothing less than an *Esprit des loix juives*—since everything in our century seems to be concerned with drafting laws or helping with legislation—and in all seriousness, the author spends sixty pages announcing himself as the Jewish Montesquieu. This will cause many to laugh before they read the book, and many more to be angry after they have read it. . . . For Michaelis explains nothing in terms of the Oriental spirit of the time, people and customs. Rather, he merely scatters all over his presentation of Jewish law flowers of a semi-Oriental, good European *common sense* which will satisfy neither the serious researcher, nor the true skeptic, least of all the Oriental who feels the veins of his tribe.[19]

What Michaelis lacks, Herder suggests, is a clear understanding of historical method, a perception of the difference between subject and object that needs to be bridged by the act of historical understanding. Michaelis's attempt to become the "Jewish Montesquieu" makes *Mosaic Law* more a product of eighteenth-century Europe than an authentic account of the ancient Near East. Rather than grasping ancient Israel in its historical and cultural specificity, he gives rise to a strange, uncritical hybrid: a sampling of "flowers" that marks a confused mix of Orient and Occident, ancient and modern.

Much like in his seminal writings on the philosophy of history, Herder here regards historical representation as a means of understanding an alien culture by "feeling oneself" across the bridge dividing the historian from his or her object of study.[20] Michaelis, Herder complains, lacks a sense of precisely those temporal and geographical differences that structure history and make its act of empathy possible, and it is telling whom Herder chooses to consider Michaelis's harshest critic. The critical historiography the passage above calls for claims its legitimacy, interestingly enough, by reference to an "Oriental who feels the veins of his tribe"—a figure who lacks all historical and geographical specificity. It is unclear, and apparently unimportant, from which particular "tribe" this Oriental might derive, whether he is a Jew, Muslim or Christian, where exactly he resides, when he lived or lives and, not least of all, how Herder has access to his wholesale rejection of Michaelis's account of ancient Judaism. What Michaelis lacks, Herder implies, is a vision of the essential Oriental that would organize his thinking and give him a sense of the rigorous oppositions between ancient and modern, Orient and Occident that would enable him to stage the proper meeting between East and West.

On one level, Herder was right. Michaelis's goal was not to gain empathy with the ancient Israelites. *Mosaic Law* consistently expresses great admiration for ancient Judaism. As he explains in those sixty pages where he announces his rationale for studying the Hebrew Bible "with the eye of Montesquieu,"[21] however, his objective for writing the work was to grasp the "foreign" and "Asiatic" laws of Moses in order to enable Europeans to *gain distance* from their Oriental heritage. The clear-cut difference between Orient and Occident is not a given for Michaelis, as it is for Herder; it is precisely the distinction which Michaelis wants to establish:

> The knowledge of Mosaic law is useful if one wants to philosophize about laws as such in the manner of Montesquieu.
> Although the Mosaic laws are no longer binding for us, they deserve a more exact investigation than has been given them. They and their entire context are not of interest merely to the philologist who concerns himself with Oriental languages and treats them as part of Hebrew antiquities. They are also relevant to others—the theologian, the jurist, the philosopher of jurisprudence—and do not deserve to remain so foreign and Asiatic as they have been thus far. They are worthy of our attention simply if one regards them as laws of a very distant land, and as remnants of the oldest legislative wisdom of all. . . . [W]hoever wants to consider laws with the eye of Montesquieu cannot avoid knowing the legal systems of other peoples; the more distant they are in time and climate, the better. . . . The knowledge of the laws of Moses serves to convince

us even further that they are not binding to us: this knowledge is also necessary for the legal scholar, because some Mosaic laws are still thought to be valid in our courts today. (1: 1–2, 5)

Michaelis's primary goal is not to empathize with the ancient Israelites but to intervene in contemporary politics. By putting the laws of Moses in their proper historical context and demonstrating that "according to God's will they were supposed to be binding to no other people than the Israelite" (1: 6), he wants to destroy their lingering hold on the present, purging the contemporary judicial system of traces of its Oriental heritage. In this sense, Michaelis engages in a project of political supersessionism, a supplement to the Pauline pronouncement on Jewish law that accomplishes for the realm of jurisprudence what early Christianity did for the realm of religion. Like Herder, Michaelis seeks to bridge the gap between the ancient Orient and the modern Occident. His reasons for doing so are to liberate the European present from the power of its Oriental past and reduce Mosaic law to what it should be: a legal system of strictly historical importance, relevant merely as an occasion for philosophical reflection on law as such.

Michaelis, then, does not merely write about the ancient Orient. He tries to de-Orientalize the present by relegating Mosaic law to ancient Jewish history. Rather than following Herder's cue and staging a meeting between East and West, Michaelis wants to contain his object of study and stress its lack of direct relevance for contemporary Europeans. When he published *Mosaic Law* in the 1770s, Mosaic law still had subsidiary importance in many European states as a *jus divinum*. Indeed, Michaelis dedicated his work to Olaus Rabenius, a professor of law at the University of Uppsala who had been sent to study with Michaelis with the goal of drafting a new Swedish legal code that would put Mosaic law in its proper place. As a contribution to historical scholarship on the Hebrew Bible, *Mosaic Law* sought to influence the contemporary European court system and make way for more enlightened penal codes; particularly in the last two volumes, Michaelis articulates his own theory of punishment, offering up a secular model of preventive punishment as a substitute for the retributive modes of justice he found in the Hebrew Bible.[22] In this respect, as Friedrich Schaffstein has argued, Michaelis needs to be seen as a precursor of nineteenth-century penal reforms. After his groundbreaking work, Mosaic law was never again granted primary or secondary authority as a *jus divinum* in legal proceedings.[23]

Herder's charge that Michaelis lacks a vision of the essential Oriental thus fails to come to terms with the particular function that the Oriental assumes in his view of modernity. Michaelis simply has a different understanding of what Herder calls "Oriental spirit":

Mosaic law is the most ancient law that has been transmitted to us in such entirety, and it is noteworthy for this reason as well. For in Moses's day many things were still closer to their origin, things which have since changed due to the manifold arts of politics—some fortunate, some unfortunate—and because of changes in customs, misuses and age itself, as it were. Between his laws and other ancient laws of newly budding peoples there is a recognizable similarity in those matters in which they differ from our laws. It seems, therefore, that when it comes to the beginning and origin of peoples the human race naturally falls into certain prescripts, which it must change later, when the people, luxury, trade and chicanery have reached their age of maturity. As long as one does not know this most ancient legal system of the childhood of peoples, the genealogy of our laws is imperfect, as it were. The mere jurist may be able to be consoled over this lack, but the philosopher wishes to see it remedied. (1: 3)

Rather than simply staging an encounter between Orient and Occident, Michaelis positions the ancient laws of Moses within a teleology of historical development. Mosaic law begins to lose its specificity here, becoming an example of primitive "prescripts" the human race "naturally" falls into in its age of "childhood," prescripts that have now been superseded, just as naturally, by the human race's age of modern European "maturity." The ancient Orient is significant because of its alleged proximity to the origins of historical development, and Michaelis frequently sought to compare the ancient Israelites with other allegedly childlike peoples; in his correspondence with Sir John Pringle, George III's physician and a friend of Benjamin Franklin, he asked Pringle to put questions to Franklin about property law among native Americans in the hope of finding illuminating parallels that he might use in *Mosaic Law*.[24]

As Michaelis defines it, however, history is not an entirely natural maturation process. Europe, after all, has not yet been entirely de-Orientalized. Its courts still make reference to legal systems inherited from antiquity; Michaelis still has to convince his contemporaries that Mosaic law was designed to be binding only to the ancient Israelites. In order to reach adulthood once and for all, it seems, Europe needs to write the perfect genealogy of its laws and overcome the deficits in its historical understanding of its Oriental, Jewish childhood. Michaelis claims an enormous importance for his own work, casting *Mosaic Law* as the intervention necessary to help history realize its goal of allowing modern Europe to arrive at definitive adulthood. Michaelis's work is thus as much a performative as a descriptive project, a key moment in the process by which contemporary Europe enters into maturity.

How exactly does Michaelis go about "remedying" this "lack," and what are the gaps he seeks to fill in order to help his fellow Europeans arrive at maturity? Without wanting to diminish Moses's divine inspiration, Michaelis draws on the long Christian tradition of contending that Moses was "instructed in all the wisdom of the Egyptians" (Acts 7: 22) and claims that his legislative wisdom was largely Egyptian in origin. In his adaptation of this tradition, which underwent a renaissance in eighteenth-century Britain and Germany, Michaelis argues that the genius of Mosaic law lay in its superimposition of ancient Egyptian jurisprudence onto an older *jus consuetudinarium*, an even more ancient customary law, that the Israelites had transmitted orally. According to Michaelis, Moses sought to "transform the ancient customs of the nomadic Israelites into laws" (1: 15), and in doing so he borrowed nearly all the key elements of Mosaic law from Egypt. Michaelis argues that the notion of transforming nomads into farmers, the concept of permanent ownership of fields, the plan for a great and powerful state that would be self-sufficient and not need to engage in foreign trade—all these aspects of Mosaic law were Egyptian in spirit (1: 15). What is more, they had to be introduced in the face of a large degree of Israelite opposition. "One must not think," he insists, "that I am describing the actual customs of the Israelites in *Mosaic Law*, for even the ten commandments never became a universal custom of this people" (1: 47). Indeed, the basic "disobedience of the Israelites" made it difficult to put many of Moses's laws into practice (1: 46–47).

As Jan Assmann has argued in his 1997 book *Moses the Egyptian: The Memory of Egypt in Western Monotheism*, contemporaries of Michaelis such as Karl Leonhard Reinhold (1757–1825), Friedrich Schiller (1759–1805) and Friedrich Heinrich Jacobi (1743–1819) were drawn to the radical potential of the figure of Moses the Egyptian; Reinhold, Schiller and Jacobi invoked the Egyptian origins of Mosaic Judaism to unsettle the rigid opposition between monotheism and polytheism so central to monotheism's self-legitimation.[25] Michaelis, however, less interested in polytheism than in questions of legislation and statecraft, drew on this tradition to make Mosaic law appear a mere imitation of Egyptian jurisprudence, and his vision of the Egyptian spirit of Mosaic law was not without its followers. In his *Ideas on the Philosophy of the History of Humankind* (1784–91), Herder too spoke of the role of Moses's Egyptian "statesmanship" in transforming the Israelite "herd of nomads" into a "cultivated nation," and Eichhorn made explicit reference to Michaelis on this point in his *Introduction to the Old Testament*.[26]

For Michaelis, viewing Mosaic law as essentially Egyptian in spirit raised a crucial historical problem: how can the modern world gain access to the ancient *jus consuetudinarium* that Moses "confirmed," "improved" and "invalidated" with his Egyptian-inspired legal code (1: 10)? For the Israelites, he argues, this customary law was common knowledge, so Moses rarely referred to it specifically. Except for the book of Job, which Michaelis insists is older than Mosaic law, and the "short history of the more ancient times, which Moses composed himself" (1: 10), scripture offers few clues. Luckily, there is one other possibility for the historian who wants to fill these "lacunae" (1: 11):

> Without assuming Moses's laws, I can find precisely this unwritten ancient law in those peoples who are most closely related to the Israelites, when I encounter blood feuds (*Tair*), with all their damaging consequences, among Arabs, when they have to let their revenge rest at certain more holy sites. Their customs elucidate the ancient law that Moses sought to amend. If we did not have these customs of the Arabs, we would very rarely be able to elucidate the laws of Moses in reference to an older customary law. The ancient customs have been preserved in this people, who have been cut off from the world and who have seldom been brought under a foreign yoke. Indeed, when reading a description of the nomadic Arabs one believes oneself to be in Abraham's hut. Travel descriptions of Arabia, and of neighboring Syria, will be of much greater help for us than one might dare to think given the great distance of time at stake here. (1: 12–13)

Like Herder, Michaelis has access to an essential Oriental who lives outside of history. The nomadic Arabs, conveniently enough, have apparently remained trapped in the state of childhood Michaelis saw as characteristic of the ancient Israelites. As an isolated people that has seldom been conquered, the Arabs have been immune to impulses for change from either within or without. Travel descriptions of contemporary Arabs can thus easily stand in for the work of the historian, giving modern Europeans easy access to that world they need to understand in order to enter into maturity and gain dominance over their Oriental childhood.

What matters here is not whether there are in fact certain Arab customs that manifest the continuity Michaelis posits but the crucial role he assigns this overwhelming continuity, its position within his concept of Oriental studies. In the passage cited above—and we will encounter the same logic when we discuss his promotion of the expedition to Arabia—Michaelis depicts the Arabs as a stagnant people unable to make steps toward "maturity," a people impervious to the historical progress that is so central to his own scholarship. Contemporary Arabs are of value to Michaelis not on their own terms but solely as a window into the customs of the ancient Israelites— an issue that is made poignantly clear in his near total disregard of the way in which Islam, for one, might serve to disrupt this image of the absolute continuity of Arab life since Abraham's time.[27] The project Michaelis undertakes to enable modern Europe to arrive at "maturity" by purging itself of remnants of Mosaic law hinges on a conception of the Arabs as a people outside of history in perennial childhood, and a conception of the Orient as a realm of the globe that is of value because it retains traces of the childhood Christian Europe needs to recover and supersede in order to reach adulthood.

It is the Arabs' isolation, their almost never having been conquered, that makes them so valuable to the European Orientalist. Indeed, it is character-istic of Michaelis's thinking that he carefully coordinates his search to estab-lish intellectual authority over the Orient with an explicit critique of imperial politics. Let us consider, for instance, what exactly Michaelis's Moses found so exemplary in Egypt:

> When I take a closer look at the legal innovations introduced by Moses without precedent in Israelite customs—particularly those which contain the most remarkable examples of a very fine legislative wisdom—it all seems very Egyptian to me: for example, the decision to base the state on agriculture, a form of livelihood alien to the nomadic herdsmen; the concept of permanent ownership of fields; the plan for a great and pow-erful state without foreign trade, which the Egyptians detested (this is one of the most difficult tasks in politics); the means by which the Israelites would be cut off from all other peoples, etc. What can be more fathomable than that Moses made use of the good in the laws of a people under whom the Israelites had lived, and in whose learning and sciences he himself had been raised? Indeed, Egyptian politics aimed not at con-quering foreign lands but at cultivating and making use of its own land. What ancient people do we know whose politics is more sublime than that of the Egyptians? . . . If we only knew more of the highly developed legislative wisdom of this people, perhaps our modern politics could learn from it, as it too is concerned with cultivating the land and peacefully enlarging its power over its interiors. For those who are concerned with desolating other lands, of course, the ancient kings of Egypt are children compared to the Romans, who have bequeathed to us a perfect exemplar of the wisdom governing a predatory state. (1: 15–16)

Michaelis sees Egypt here not as the nation that keeps Israel in slavery but as the model for the peaceful expansion of domestic power, a politics of economic self-sufficiency he juxtaposes here to the Roman Empire, and elsewhere to the unhealthy obsession with international trade he sees as characteristic of eighteenth-century British and French colonialism (1: 238–42). Unlike contemporary Arabs and the ancient Israelites, then, the Egyptians appear not as Oriental "children" but as precocious adolescents with a "highly developed legislative wisdom" worthy of being imitated by modern Europeans. Contemporary Europe, Michaelis argues, is so "enchanted" by the "mere word *trade*" that it has lost sight of the ideal of national self-sufficiency Moses encountered in Egypt; the "disadvantageous East Indian trade," for example, "dries up every year our silver and, when conducted via sea routes, eats up a large number of people [through disease] and thus prevents marriages" (1: 242). In its attention to cultivating and developing its domestic resources, ancient Egypt offers Europe a corrective to the politics of colonial expansion, a vision of national consolidation that sounds very much like the core ideas of Dohm's political writings.

If we remember that this celebration of Egyptian self-sufficiency is located in a book on ancient Judaism, these apparent diatribes against imperialism need some qualification. It is telling that Michaelis never seems troubled that the Egyptian model he glorifies was predicated on Israelite slavery. In *Mosaic Law*, Moses leads the Israelites out of Egypt not in the effort to liberate them from Egyptian bondage but in order to move a step further away from childhood by imitating the legislative wisdom of their former masters. For Michaelis, the political liberation of the Israelites is a victory for Egyptian jurisprudence. His account of the genesis of Mosaic law symbolically reenacts the subjection of the "disobedient" Israelites to Egyptian rule, constructing ancient Israel as an imperfect imitation of the jurisprudence of its oppressors. In following Egypt's example and privileging domestic expansion over foreign trade (1: 239), Moses perverts the Egyptian model of national self-sufficiency, legislating dietary restrictions and a lifestyle of rituals that serve to prevent the Israelites, as much as possible, from having any contact whatsoever with other peoples (1: 230). These dietary restrictions, Michaelis emphasizes elsewhere, are not Egyptian in origin but derive from the Israelites' "national habits" (4: 193). Unlike the highly developed legislative wisdom it imitated, Mosaic law runs in this regard counter to contemporary European jurisprudence. As well suited as it may have been to the ancient Israelites, this radical insistence on national isolation represents the antithesis of contemporary Europeans' efforts to increase the population of their states by "inviting in foreigners" (1: 231). In his polemics against Dohm's proposal that one view the Jews as the equivalent of such foreign colonists, we recall, Michaelis envisioned a multiconfessional, multinational political order that would naturalize and "melt together" its subjects, and he saw this model of the state as the antithesis of the national homogeneity fostered by Mosaic law. The ultimate victory of Egyptian jurisprudence, then, belongs to a future non-imperialist Europe, to the model of national self-sufficiency Michaelis aspires to for his peers, and not to the ancient Israelites.

Michaelis's critique of imperialism fuels his attempt to establish intellectual authority over the Orient. His anti-imperialist rhetoric puts forth an argument for national self-sufficiency at the same time as it legitimizes the intellectual power of Egypt over Israel—and of the European Orientalist over the ancient Israelites and contemporary Arabs he studies. In his analysis of Mosaic law, Michaelis never feels the need to propose strategies for filling in the acknowledged lacks in his understanding of Egypt's "highly developed legislative wisdom." The assertion of Egypt's nonimperialist politics authorizes the Orientalist's hegemony over his object of study. Intellectual authority, it seems, has nothing to do with power relations; it simply represents a "natural" process of European adults gaining ascendancy over their Oriental childhood, a natural process of proving Egypt's superiority to Israel.

As neat as this distinction between imperial power and the Orientalist's quest for knowledge may be, it nevertheless breaks down at a key moment in Michaelis's introduction. In his effort to relegate Mosaic law to the childhood of humanity and demonstrate its irrelevance for contemporary Europe, Michaelis has to concede that there are those in his midst who still consider the laws of Moses to be binding. Michaelis makes relatively few references to contemporary Jews in *Mosaic Law*, and indeed he noted proudly in a letter to Mendelssohn that his "philosophical" defense of Mosaic law was devoid of polemics against the Jewish religion.[28] He closes his introduction, however, with a drawn-out diatribe against nearly all forms of Jewish biblical interpretation, setting up his project in explicit opposition to Jewish exegetical practices. The struggle for intellectual control of the ancient Orient apparently requires that one particular group of potential opponents be forcefully removed from the playing field:

> Indeed, I often do not know this [most ancient customary law], and in such cases I take the liberty of indicating the lacuna myself—unlike those who claim to know everything and would fill such lacunae with fictions that pass as scholarly investigations, or with Talmudic legends and Rabbinic decisions.... The Talmud, which consists of oral traditions of somewhat ignorant Rabbis, can tell us much about the common law of the Jews at the time these men lived, not, however, about the meaning of Mosaic law. Indeed, Moses's laws would make a very strange figure if one were to understand them in the manner of the Pharisees, whose interpretation was, according to Christ's own pronouncement, often the direct opposite of that which Moses commanded.... Anyone who believes to encounter a *Talmudic Law* here will be very much mistaken. I do not even deign to mention the names of those men whose sayings are collected in the Talmud, and I do not deal at all with the Rabbis. Whoever regards laws with the eye of a Montesquieu will not be angered by this: for the period of ancient Jewish history prior to the Babylonian Captivity, the Talmud is at least as impure a source as Bartolus is for the Romans. Even more, this very comparison is flattery for the Talmud. I will grant it its merits for the Second Temple period, although here too it contains many untruths: but a book that was written so late—and one

that relies solely on oral traditions at that—can tell us nothing credible about the customs under the First Temple, certainly nothing about the age of Moses. (1: 56–58).

The Talmud is thus useless for the proper historical study of Mosaic law. As the product of "somewhat ignorant Rabbis," this collection of fictions, legends and unreliable oral traditions is indelibly marred by its belatedness, lacking the rigorous historiography Michaelis claims for his own project. Whereas Michaelis captures the spirit of Mosaic law, contemporary Jews lack the proper historical understanding of their Oriental origins. Indeed, they often interpret Mosaic law as "the direct opposite of that which Moses commanded," thus perpetuating precisely the sort of Judaism that Jesus rightfully sought to destroy. After the Babylonian Captivity, the Israelites sought only to "fulfill the letter of the laws of Moses," losing sight of their "soul" (1: 238), that is, the spirit of Mosaic law Michaelis reconstructs for his modern European readers. Contemporary Jews constitute an anachronism, out of sync with modernity in their adherence to an antiquated legal tradition and in the blatantly ahistorical manner in which they interpret this tradition. A "Jewish Montesquieu," in other words, is a contradiction in terms.

Herder, in his reflections on Jewish history, explicitly identifies modern Jews with biblical Judaism, stressing what one might call in contemporary terms the continuity of Jewish memory; for Herder, "the religion of the Jews is, as they say themselves, an inheritance of their lineage, their inalienable heritage."[29] Michaelis, in contrast, insists on a radical discontinuity between Mosaic law and nearly all forms of Judaism following the destruction of the First Temple. Judaism for Michaelis shows no historical development. The only aspect of their ancient Oriental heritage that contemporary Jews have retained, it seems, is the "disobedience" of the Israelites—with the essential difference that Jews now disobey Mosaic law while believing they uphold it. For Michaelis, modern Arabs are the only legitimate descendants of the ancient Israelites—a notion which resurfaces at key junctures throughout Michaelis's *oeuvre*. In his autobiography, for instance, he comments that Carsten Niebuhr made one fatal error in his Near Eastern voyage. Without the advantage of having learned Hebrew from Michaelis, Niebuhr failed to grasp "that in seeking to answer my questions one should not have made inquiries to Jews and Rabbis but only to native and full-blooded Arabs; for we in Europe know better what scholarly Jews say about many such things, and those Asian Jews who are scholars get their information from European Rabbis."[30]

Michaelis's effort to secure hegemony over the Orient, then, also establishes him as an expect on the exegetical practices of his potential Jewish opponents, whose arguments he invalidates a priori in the passage above with

the authorization of Jesus himself, thereby severing any connection whatsoever between Judaism and Christianity. As we noted in the previous chapter,
negative visions of Rabbinic Judaism were a staple of Enlightenment theological discourse. But Michaelis goes much further than simply seeing the
Rabbis as corrupting the original spirit of Mosaic law. He presents contemporary Jews as a dispersed group that fundamentally lacks a sense of its own
history. Bound together only by a far-reaching network of Rabbinic perversions of Mosaic law, contemporary Jews are neither authentically Oriental
nor truly European, neither trustworthy remnants of ancient Judaism nor
connected to the modern world. Like the childlike Arabs, they too reside in
a realm seemingly immune to historical progress, but they lack both the innocence and the geographical situatedness of contemporary Arabs, emerging
instead as a group of shabby scholars based in Europe who lack the requisite
intellectual acumen to understand Mosaic law.

It makes sense that Michaelis introduces these impassioned polemics
at such a key juncture in the work. For described in this manner, Jews and
Jewish interpretive practices mark the very antithesis of Michaelis's scholarship, a grotesque alter ego to *Mosaic Law*. The continued existence of Jews
disrupts nearly all the distinctions that are central to his project—the differences between Orient and Occident, ancient and modern, childhood and
adulthood. In order for Michaelis to establish his intellectual authority over
the ancient Orient, he must do more than relegate contemporary Arabs to the
position of Oriental children. Contemporary Jews, too, must be put in their
proper place, yet given the visions of Europe and the Orient we have seen
emerging here, it is unclear what and where this place would be. Michaelis's
mission to help Europe rid itself of lingering remnants of Mosaic law looks
less and less here like a quest for disinterested knowledge; it also involves
contemporary Europe's *political* power over the Jews who reside in its interior. This shift from intellectual hegemony to political power implicit in
Mosaic Law becomes explicit in his polemics against Dohm's proposals to use
the Jews as the equivalents of colonists to help Prussia's internal economic
expansion. There is, it seems, one further lesson to be learned from ancient
Egypt:

> The Jews will always view the state as a temporary dwelling, which, if
> they are lucky, they will be able to leave so as to return to Palestine,
> almost in the way in which their forefathers were suspect to the Egyp-
> tians. . . . A people that has such hopes will never become completely
> native. They will, at least, always lack the proper patriotic love for the
> paternal fields. If they live among themselves—for one would have to
> grant Jewish agricultural colonists villages of their own, and not put them
> among Christians—they are in danger of being stirred up by an enthusi-

ast, or being led astray by the Pied Piper of Hamelin [*vom Hamelschen Rattenfänger in die Irre geführt*]. (D 2: 42–43)[31]

The Egyptians did not merely have a "highly developed legislative wisdom" that sought to "peacefully enlarge its power over its interiors" and build a strong, independent state. They also were rightly suspicious of Jewish longings for such political independence. They issue a warning to modernity when it comes to proposals for further integrating Jews into the political and economic life of Europe. Lacking any connection to German soil, Jews are easy prey for enthusiasts who will lead them astray much in the same way as their childlike ancestors left Egypt. When it comes to giving examples here, moreover, Michaelis does not cite the obvious choice, Sabbatei Sevi and seventeenth-century messianic movements. He makes his argument against Jewish emancipation by invoking a figure from German folklore, the Pied Piper of Hamelin—known in German as a "rat-catcher"—who earned his fame by punishing the town of Hamelin by luring away its children. For contemporary Jews, it seems, legendary German rat-catchers now hold the position once thought to be the property of their future Messiah, threatening to lead Jews *in die Irre*, to a place that is no place at all.

Michaelis's project to de-Orientalize Christian Europe's legal system relegates Mosaic law to the distant past and polemicizes against Jewish exegesis. His Orientalism also puts forth an Egyptian-inspired politics of national self-sufficiency that leaves no place in Europe for the integration of contemporary Jews. Before further interrogating his polemics against Jewish emancipation, however, it will be wise to dwell a bit longer on his understanding of the function of Oriental studies. Continuing to explore the shift from intellectual hegemony to political power in his biblical scholarship will enable us better to appreciate both the place—or the lack of place—contemporary Jews occupy in Michaelis's geographical imagination, and the vision of colonial deportation to imaginary German sugar island colonies he offers up in response to Dohm's proposals for Jewish emancipation.

ARABIA FELIX

Coming among them [the Arabs], one can hardly help fancying one's self suddenly carried backwards to the ages which succeeded immediately after the flood. We are here tempted to imagine ourselves among the old patriarchs, with whose adventures we have been so much amused in our infant days. The language, which has been spoken for time immemorial, and which so nearly resembles that which we have been accustomed to regard as of the most distant antiquity, completes the illusion which the

analogy of manners began. . . . Having never been conquered, Arabia has scarcely known any changes, but those produced by the hand of nature.[32]
                        —Carsten Niebuhr, *Description of Arabia* (1772)

Michaelis's vision of the Arab world as a stagnant realm of the globe representing Christian Europe's Oriental childhood was not a product of armchair fantasies of European intellectual hegemony. It was firmly grounded in "experience," in the large-scale scholarly expedition to the Near East he directed for the Danish crown in the 1760s.[33] The initiative for the expedition came entirely from Michaelis, who first approached the Danish minister Baron Johann Hartwig Ernst von Bernstorff with his proposals in 1756. As he explained in a letter to von Bernstorff—a friend of the German poet Friedrich Gottlieb Klopstock and the uncle of the von Bernstorff who later became Schiller's patron—a journey to the Near East would be of incomparable value for the progress of Oriental studies:

> The purpose of the trip would be:
> (1) to make better known to Europeans the plants and fossils of Arabia Felix. Of particular interest here will be those plants and fossils mentioned in the Bible which we know only by name. It is highly probable, in some cases certain, that these carry the same names today in Arabia. For Hebrew and Arabic are but different dialects of one and the same language, and despite the great interval of time that has passed, the language spoken in Arabia now (or the language of the *Koran* if one pronounces it as it is really spoken, without the arbitrary additions of the grammarians) is not further removed—indeed, not even as far removed— from the Hebrew of Moses as Upper Saxon is from Lower Saxon. . . .
> (2) to give an entertaining and useful account of the customs, buildings, etc. of Arabia Felix. One will hardly find a people that has kept its customs the same for so long as the Arabs; which is a result of their never having been brought under the yoke of other peoples. Everything we know about these customs coincides so exactly with the most ancient customs of the Israelites and thus gives the richest and most beautiful elucidations to the Bible. In contrast, the customs of the Jews themselves among the Persians, Greeks and Romans, and since their European Diaspora, have changed so much that one can no longer see in them the descendants of the people of whom the Bible speaks.[34]

It would also be necessary, Michaelis continued, to map out the interiors of Arabia and gather more precise geographical information about the Near East. Observing the Red Sea's tides, ebbs and flows, for instance, would finally help solve the mystery of the Israelites' flight from Egypt. The expedition, he proposed, would need to observe Oriental forms of animal life as well, copy or

Fig. 3. "Mount Sinai and the Convent of St. Catherine." From Carsten Niebuhr,
Travels through Arabia, and other Countries in the East, trans. Robert Heron
(Edinburgh, 1792).
Courtesy of the Duke University Rare Book, Manuscript, & Special
Collections Library.

purchase Arabic books and, most importantly, "answer questions of several scholars who know what our Oriental philology is lacking."[35] Because of this, Michaelis was insistent that the travelers be scholars rather than missionaries or clergymen.[36] The goal was not to convert the Arabs but to study their customs in such a way as to promote European scholarship on the ancient Orient.

Michaelis must have made a convincing case. Eager to secure Denmark the reputation of supporting the progress of science, King Frederick V approved the expedition almost immediately, and Michaelis set to work selecting the members of the journey in consultation with von Bernstorff, training many of them in Arabic and assembling his questions. The group that sailed from Copenhagen in 1761 consisted of five men, each responsible for a different aspect of the expedition: Christian von Haven, a Danish linguist familiar with Oriental languages; Peter Forsskål, a Swedish botanist and expert in natural history who had studied with Linnaeus; Carsten Niebuhr, the German Göttingen-trained mathematician and engineer responsible for the physical descriptions of Arabia; Georg Wilhelm Baurenfeind, a German painter and engraver; and Christian Carl Cramer, a Danish physician. Rather than following the common trade route and traveling around the tip of Africa, the group journeyed by ship to Egypt and then entered Arabia by land, sailing from there to Bombay and eventually returning to Europe by land.

From the beginning, the expedition met with high hopes all over Europe and was frequently reported on in the press, in journals geared toward scholars and more popularly oriented newspapers as well. Ultimately, however, the expedition was hardly the success Michaelis and others had hoped for. Except for Niebuhr, who paid Michaelis a visit on his way back to Denmark in 1767, all the members of the expedition died within the first three years of the journey, and the promised questions reached the travelers too late to be of much use. There were some clear accomplishments, however. Forsskål's Latin descriptions of Near Eastern flora and fauna were published posthumously by Niebuhr in 1775.[37] And Niebuhr's transcriptions of cuneiform inscriptions at Persepolis eventually provided the basis for deciphering cuneiform script in the nineteenth century.[38] But many of the key tasks remained unmet. Von Haven and Niebuhr did indeed journey to Djebel el-Mokateb on the Sinai peninsula, whose rock faces Moses himself had allegedly covered with inscriptions during the flight from Egypt. Much to their disappointment, however, they found Egyptian hieroglyphics with human and animal forms rather than ancient Mosaic inscriptions. Another task prescribed by Michaelis—to inspect the collection of ancient Hebrew manuscripts allegedly collected in St. Catherine's monastery at the foot of Mount Sinai—met with failure for more mundane reasons; von Haven and Niebuhr lacked the proper letter of introduction to be admitted into the monastery.

As the excerpt from Niebuhr's travel narrative I quote above indicates, the expedition had a greater degree of success when it came to following Michaelis's general instructions. Niebuhr apparently found it easy to "imagine ourselves among the old patriarchs, with whose adventures we have been so much amused in our infant days." Despite—and in part because of—all its difficulties, the voyage decisively shaped Europeans' vision of the Arab world in the latter half of the eighteenth century. Michaelis's almost 400 pages of questions, published in book form in both German (1762) and French (1763), circulated widely among intellectuals in Western Europe and were taken along on other scientific expeditions; Michaelis's English friend John Pringle, for instance, forwarded many of the questions on to James Bruce during his journeys through Egypt and Abyssinia in the late 1760s and early 1770s.[39] The travel narratives Niebuhr compiled upon his return, *Description of Arabia: From His own Observations and News Collected in the Land* (1772) and *Travel Description of Arabia and Other Surrounding Lands* (1774–78), were translated into Dutch (1774, 1776), French (1773, 1774, 1776, 1779), Danish (1779) and English (1792) and were widely read and routinely cited as authorities on the Near East in the late eighteenth century. Both Kant and Blumenbach quote Niebuhr in their anthropological writings; Niebuhr makes frequent appearances in Herder's philosophy of history as well.[40]

When read alongside our discussion of *Mosaic Law*, the passages quoted above from Niebuhr's travelogue and Michaelis's correspondence with von Bernstorff bring to the foreground what is perhaps the most remarkable aspect of the expedition: its capacity to subsume experience of the Near East into Michaelis's categories, its uncanny ability to sustain the worldview that launched it. Several of the particulars in Michaelis's understanding of the Orient were obviously challenged. Niebuhr, for example, realized rather quickly that "the Arabic spoken and written by Mahomet may now be regarded as a dead language";[41] needless to say, viewing the relationship between modern Arabic and biblical Hebrew as analogous to that between Upper and Lower Saxon was not common among Michaelis's successors. The basic vision of the Orient as stagnant, childlike and immune to the progress characteristic of Europe, however, was perpetuated by the seven years of travel. Michaelis's view of modern Arabs as the key to a proper understanding of ancient Israelite culture remained unchanged in the programmatic introduction of *Mosaic Law*. But there is more at stake here than continuity. In popularizing the worldview underwriting Michaelis's vision of Oriental studies, the expedition fleshed out what we have seen to be a crucial element of Michaelis's Orientalism: the careful coordination of a

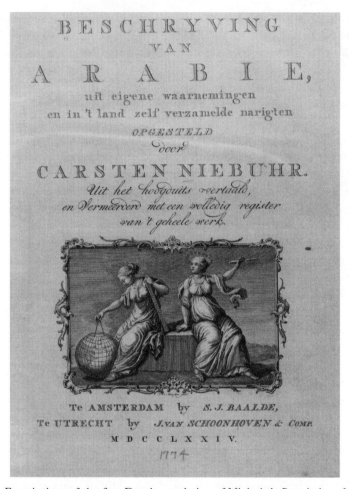

Fig. 4. Frontispiece of the first Dutch translation of Niebuhr's *Description of Arabia*. Courtesy of the Duke University Rare Book, Manuscript, & Special Collections Library.

critique of imperialism with the project to gain intellectual hegemony over the Orient.

In his autobiography, Michaelis notes that the expedition's novel idea of reaching Arabia from Egypt via the Red Sea was subsequently taken advantage of by English and French merchants traveling between Egypt and India,[42] that is, by precisely that "disadvantageous East Indian trade" *Mosaic Law* insisted was depleting Europe of its domestic resources. This allusion to international trade routes is not an isolated occurrence: nearly all the eighteenth-century literature dealing with the expedition mentions its

Fig. 5. "Arabia Felix." Niebuhr's Map of Yemen. From Carsten Niebuhr, *Travels through Arabia, and other Countries in the East*, trans. Robert Heron (Edinburgh, 1792). Courtesy of the Duke University Rare Book, Manuscript, & Special Collections Library.

"scientific" aims in relation to the goals of imperialist expansion, generally juxtaposing the two as mutually exclusive.[43] A Danish official writing to Michaelis expressed his joy at the plans to "use such voyages to tear away lands out of their fable-like condition and darkness," noting that Dutch and English trading companies were concerned only with wealth and would thus never be able to "discover such lands properly" and explore their interiors.[44] John Pringle, whose correspondence with Michaelis includes lengthy reports on other scientific voyages of the 1760s and 1770s—Bruce's travels in Egypt and Abyssinia, Banks and Solander's voyage around the world, Captain Cook's journeys, Phipps's attempt at a polar voyage, and many more—makes similar comments to Michaelis, juxtaposing the high ambitions of science to the "political knowledge" that might directly promote trade.[45] Much in the same way as Michaelis's admiration for ancient Egypt's nonimperial politics fueled his attempt to establish his intellectual authority over the Orient, these critiques of imperialism also serve to legitimize the project of European scientific travel. The scientific expedition to the Orient was not just defined as a nonimperialist quest for knowledge; it was explicitly conceived as the antithesis of imperialist expansion.

The term used in the planning of the voyage plays a role here as well. Michaelis, von Bernstorff and their correspondents consistently label their destination "Arabia Felix" or "Arabia the happy." This term for modern-day Yemen—traditionally set in opposition to the more northern region of "Arabia the desolate"—derives from Alexander the Great, who called the region "Eudaimon Arabia" because he never managed to conquer it.[46] In his 1772 travelogue, Niebuhr rejects this name, pointing out that it is not actually in use in "Arabia Felix" proper. In doing so, he sets up the expedition's quest for scientific knowledge in a very particular relation to imperialist expansion:

Having never been conquered, Arabia has scarcely known any changes, but those produced by the hand of nature; it bears none of the impressions of human fury, which appear in so many other places. With all these circumstances, so naturally calculated to engage curiosity, Arabia has been hitherto but very little known. The ancients, who made their discoveries of countries by conquering them, remained ignorant of the state and history of a region, into which their arms could never penetrate. What Greek and Latin authors mention concerning Arabia, proves, by its obscurity, their ignorance of almost every thing respecting the Arabs. Prejudices relative to the inconveniences and dangers of traveling in Arabia, have hitherto kept the moderns in equal ignorance. . . . In the East there are no libraries, and no men of deep erudition, resources which a traveler might find with great facility in Europe. Yet there are ancient Arabic historians; but the copies of their works are very rare, as I learned at Kahira and Mokha.[47]

Scientific travel is not just the antithesis of imperialist expansion. It also enters into a realm that has "never been conquered," a virgin territory not

Fig. 6. "An Arab on Horseback." From Carsten Niebuhr, *Travels through Arabia, and other Countries in the East*, trans. Robert Heron (Edinburgh, 1792).
Courtesy of the Duke University Rare Book, Manuscript, & Special
Collections Library.

"penetrated" by the ancients which is thus "naturally calculated" to engage
modern European "curiosity." In this sense, scientific expeditions accomplish
precisely what ancient imperialism could not. Arabia emerges as the ultimate
object of imperialist desire, a "natural" region immune to "human fury" that

can best be "conquered" by the scientific invasion of the European traveler. Not surprisingly, Arabia also seems to need its European visitors. In overcoming the "ignorance" of the ancients, the knowledge Niebuhr and his fellow travelers acquire of Arabia also remedies the Arabs' own relative lack of erudition, their inability to know themselves.

In this account of penetrating a realm untouched by trade and imperialism, Niebuhr's travelogue exemplifies what Mary Louise Pratt, in her analysis of eighteenth-century scientific voyages, calls the ideology of the "anti-conquest."[48] Niebuhr and his colleagues obviously position their expedition in a realm altogether different from that of imperial expansion. In Niebuhr's account, however, the Eurocentric gaze that guides the scientific invasion of "Arabia Felix" is not without concrete effects for its objects of study. Over and over again, Niebuhr celebrates Arabia's impenetrability to foreign expansion. The interior realms of Arabia, he points out, have independent princes and sheiks "who have never been subdued, but [who] continue to harass the Turks, and to drive them towards the coasts."[49] "A nation of this character," he continues, "cannot readily sink into a servile subjection to arbitrary power"; their "genius," "customs, and even their religion" are "all inimical to the progress of despotism."[50] It is, moreover, precisely this imperviousness to external domination that has preserved ancient Israelite ways of life. Ultimately, however, his travel narrative disrupts this vision of a stagnant people immune to European-style progress:

> The poverty of the wandering Arabs is plainly voluntary. They prefer liberty to wealth, pastoral simplicity to a life of constraint and toil, which might procure them a greater variety of gratifications. . . . One general cause of the impoverishment of Arabia is, no doubt, its having ceased to be the channel of the trade with India, since the discovery of the passage by the Cape of Good Hope. Yet, if the lands were better cultivated, this country might, without the aid of foreign trade, afford sufficient resources to supply all its inhabitants with abundance of the necessaries and common conveniences of life. . . . The Arabs settled in cities, and especially those in the sea-port towns, have lost their distinctive national manners, by their intercourse with strangers; but the Bedouins, who live in tents, and in separate tribes, have still retained the customs and manners of their earliest ancestors. They are the genuine Arabs, and exhibit, in the aggregate, all those characteristics which are distributed respectively among the other branches of their nation.[51]

Bedouin poverty, interestingly enough, is both "plainly voluntary" and the result of a shift in European trade routes. By reaching India via the tip of Africa, European merchants have left Arabia untouched and are themselves thus partially responsible for the idyllic manner in which contemporary Arabs—"genuine Arabs"—perpetuate the pastoral customs of the ancient Israelites. Here as well, the scientific traveler does what imperial expansion could not. Without wishing to disturb the Arabs' natural imperviousness to external domination, Niebuhr the European nevertheless issues a plan for the modernization of Arabia. The model of nonimperial expansion he puts forth here—a politics that would cultivate interiors and renounce foreign trade—is of course not unfamiliar to us. What the modern Arabs need to do, it seems, is to imitate the behavior of their Israelite ancestors: they need to leave behind their "voluntary" poverty and nomadic lifestyle and take a step closer to adulthood by adopting the principles of jurisprudence that Michaelis, the director of the expedition, insists Moses found in ancient Egypt.

Extending Michaelis's account of Mosaic law as the triumph of Egyptian jurisprudence over Israelite culture, Niebuhr's travelogue seeks to remake Arabia in the image of ancient Egypt. And the vision of Egypt sustained here, importantly, is one contemporary Arabs can have access to only through the European Orientalist. It is not just among the Bedouins that there are no "men of erudition." "The Arabs of Egypt," von Haven writes, "do not know the history of their ancestors before Mohammed. Everything they do know of ancient times consists of corrupted and dismembered stories of events recounted in Holy Scripture."[52] Equipped with the worldview of European Orientalist scholarship, the scientific traveler does not seek to conquer Arabia or open it up to foreign trade. Niebuhr here only wants to promote the "geniune" Arabs' self-sufficiency, yet his plans for doing so obviously run counter to precisely that lifestyle he claims is entirely voluntary. The expedition to Arabia seeks to advance the maturing process of its stagnant object of study, to modernize Arabia with the authorization of a European critique of imperialist expansion. This scientific expedition has a dual function: it seeks both to de-Orientalize European jurisprudence by gaining a better understanding of the historical specificity of Mosaic law, and to remake the modern Orient in the image European Orientalist scholarship constructs of ancient Egypt.

SUGAR ISLANDS AND THE POLITICS OF RACE

Agriculture, the first and most important of all arts, is not in a very thriving condition here [in Egypt]; at least, if we compare the present produce of the lands with what a country of such natural fertility might be brought, by cultivation, to produce.... Egypt, although so greatly declined from its ancient grandeur, still affords many productions which are capital articles in commerce. By its situation too, it is well fitted to be an emporium for foreign merchandise. . . . There is even sugar produced here, the canes growing in Upper Egypt; but it is so ill prepared, that it is just as expensive to buy here as American sugars are in Europe. Were the trade in rice under no restraint, a considerable quantity might be exported. But, for the exportation of this article, the ports of Egypt are shut, and therefore the Europeans dare not carry off any of it, unless by Damietta. The Americans are even said to have brought rice hither, for some time, from Carolina. And if this be so, there can be no better proof of the astonishing decline of agriculture in Egypt.[53]

—Niebuhr, *Travel Description of Arabia and*
Other Surrounding Lands (1774)

Michaelis's celebration of the radical model of national self-sufficiency he locates in ancient Egypt was of course a blatant anachronism by the time he published *Mosaic Law* in the 1770s, an outright denial of the extent to which, particularly when it came to commodities like sugar and rice, tea, coffee and tobacco, the economies of the German states were *already* inextricably dependent on international trade and imperial expansion. In the 1770s and 1780s, moreover, this dependency on foreign trade for such luxury items had increasingly come into the public eye, not least of all, we remember from the previous chapter, due to the restrictive "coffee laws" Prussia, Hanover and other German states introduced to limit coffee consumption and combat the depletion of domestic resources that were flowing to European states with coffee-producing colonies. Michaelis's colleague August Ludwig von Schlözer was, like Dohm, a staunch supporter of legislation geared at promoting the self-sufficiency of the German states. In his *Correspondence, Mostly of a Historical and Political Nature*, an influential political journal, he routinely reprinted coffee laws and accompanied them with supportive commentary.[54] Since "Germany neither grows coffee nor possesses West Indian coffee islands," he pointed out in 1781, following a common line of argument, "all the money that coffee costs us is thus completely lost for Germany."[55] Seen against this backdrop, the alternative Michaelis proposes to Dohm's proposals for the civic improvement of the Jews—the deportation of Jews to German "sugar islands which, with the wealth they produce, nevertheless have an unhealthy climate"—does not necessarily represent an exception to the polemics against imperialism we encountered in his Orientalist scholarship. It marks, rather, a concession of the importance of imperial expansion for the "peaceful expansion of interior power," a wish that Germans might have sugar islands of their own so that they would not be dependent on colonial powers like England and France for such precious commodities. A sugar island colony populated by Jewish subjects would not constitute imperialism at all but—following the logic of Michaelis's Orientalist scholarship—would simply be an obligatory step to help the German states achieve economic self-sufficiency and lessen their dependency on foreign trade. For Michaelis it is the Orientalist's model of ancient Egyptian economic autonomy that provides the archetype for a nonimperialist Europe; in the case of sugar, it seems, the Egyptian model can only be introduced with the help of colonial expansion. In this regard, ironically, the rhetoric of anti-imperialism helps legitimize German colonialism, arguing for the necessity of foreign colonies to promote the internal development of the German economy.

Michaelis's choice of sugar islands is not fortuitous. The eighteenth century witnessed an enormous increase in sugar consumption. No longer the privilege of the wealthier classes, sugar began to be used in large amounts by nearly all segments of European society. A crop unknown in ancient times and never mentioned in the Bible, sugarcane is native to the Near East, to regions like Egypt, and was—like coffee—used widely by Arabs before modern Europeans began to cultivate it.[56] As Niebuhr does not fail to notice in the passage above, the Near East played a minimal role in the eighteenth-century sugar trade. Eighteenth-century Europe imported its sugar almost entirely from the West Indies, mostly from French sugar islands like Saint Domingue but also from Jamaica, Barbados and other Caribbean colonies. By 1792, sugar had become such a necessary staple that huge crowds rioted in Paris to protest against its rising costs.[57] In the German states, the situation was not much different. A 1778 piece in a prominent weekly journal noted that "since the advent of the use of tea, coffee, chocolate, punch and the sweet wines in almost all of Europe, the sale of sugarcane has increased so enormously that one today has to regard sugar as one of the greatest articles of trade."[58] A 1781 article on "Dietary Revolutions in Europe" published in Schlözer's *Correspondence* described sugar as a commodity that is now brought "by the mountain" from the West Indies to Europe, "whose inhabitants soon accustomed themselves to this seductive salt to such an extent that they believe themselves unable to live without it."[59] Schlözer, the Göttingen historian who had been both a student of Michaelis and a professor of Dohm, theorized that this type of shift in dietary habits had brought about "just as large, or even larger, revolutions in our part of the world than the defeat of the unconquerable fleet, the War of the Spanish Succession, the Peace of Paris, etc."[60]

This "revolution in our part of the world" brought about by new commodities like sugar was of course intimately related to the slave trade. Sugar islands were by and large slave colonies. Eighteenth-century Germans, moreover, did not just consume sugar. Descriptions of the political and economic conditions of sugar production were also a recurrent topic in periodical literature of the period. Schlözer's *Correspondence*, a journal with which Michaelis was familiar, included frequent articles, tables of information and statistics on British and French colonies and international trading. In 1781 Schlözer published figures on sugar and rum exports from Jamaica along with statistics on the numbers of negroes and cattle on the island, and a chart borrowed from Edward Long's 1774 *The History of Jamaica* detailing the proportions of negroes to white inhabitants among the population (166, 904 to 17,000 in 1768).[61] In 1779, the journal had published a series of "Confidential Letters from Jamaica" that described the sugar plantations in great detail and depicted Jamaica as an agricultural paradise full of tropical fruits and inexpensive sugar and coffee. The only problem with the island, as the author of the letters repeats time and time again, is its "cruel heat," a climate for which a "German body is not made."[62] Or, as a contemporary wrote in 1780, also referring to the "unbearable heat" and its effects on Europeans' health: "Jamaica, this considerable part of the New World, has little similarity with the Old World. Nature has given it many advantages: but she deals with the Europeans who have settled there as a true stepmother."[63]

It is in this context that we need to consider Michaelis's suggestion that Jews might "become useful to us in agriculture and manufacturing, if one manages them in the proper manner, . . . even more useful if we had sugar islands which from time to time could depopulate the European fatherland, sugar islands which, with the wealth they produce, nevertheless have an unhealthy climate." Michaelis's fantasy of Jewish deportation may indeed be a symptom of deep-rooted anti-Jewish prejudice, and as such it can certainly be seen as linked to both traditional forms of Jew-hatred and more modern discourses on antisemitism. On a less general level, however, it also ensues directly from the ethnological mapping out of the world central to his Orientalist scholarship and his directorship of the expedition to "Arabia Felix." In this regard, it differs fundamentally from pre-Enlightenment forms of anti-Judaism. It is the worldview of Michaelis's biblical scholarship, the specific form of its quest for hegemony over the Orient, that makes it possible to envision this particular deportation of his Jewish contemporaries. Unlike other "foreigners" one might invite in as colonists, Michaelis argues, Jews will never "melt together" with other Europeans; with their radical insistence on national homogeneity and mistaken messianic hopes, they cannot be accommodated in modern European states. Bound together by an ahistorical perversion of Mosaic law, contemporary Jews are for Michaelis similarly out of place in their original Oriental climate, a region that belongs—or should belong—only to the true descendants of the ancient Israelites, the "genuine Arabs." For Michaelis, the only positive source of identity for the Jewish Diaspora is what Jews have inherited from their Oriental climate of origin: their cohesion as an "unmixed race of a more southern people," their "national temperament, which remains unchanged, because they never mix with others" and physical deficiencies that make it unlikely that Jews will ever—"even in ten generations"—have the proper bodily stature to perform military service for a German state (D 2: 51, 36, 63). Jews for Michaelis are the products of the climate of the ancient Orient, and it makes sense that he should envision their deportation to an analogous "southern" and "unhealthy" climate, a region of "cruel heat" that supplies modern Europe with large amounts of a necessary staple that is indigenous to the Jews' region of origin. Unable to be fully integrated into a German political order, the unmixed southern race appears uniquely suited to work on sugar plantations in the West Indies.

The concept of the Jews as the "unmixed race of a more southern people" that emerges from Michaelis's Orientalist scholarship sets up a relationship between "race" and "climate" that supports his quest for European hegemony at the same time as it justifies the slave economy of the sugar islands. The fact that Jews already played an important role in the sugar trade—or that, in places like Surinam, Jews were prominent plantation and slave owners— seems not to fit into Michaelis's thinking. Contemporary German literature on the sugar industry made little reference to Jewish involvement, and Dohm himself, a much better student of international economics than Michaelis, seems to have been unaware of this as well; when a group of Jews in Surinam wrote Dohm an enthusiastic letter after reading the French translation of *On the Civic Improvement of the Jews*, he wrote back asking a series of questions, one of which was whether Jews were even allowed to be complete owners of plantations.[64] Dohm himself equated the reluctance of Enlightenment intellectuals like Michaelis to contemplate emancipation with the West Indian plantation owners' support for slavery. Rooted in both eighteenth-century race thinking and his own biblical scholarship, Michaelis's colonial imagination sees Jews not as planters or traders but as the modern equivalent of Israelite slaves, a subject people well suited to toil alongside African slaves in the West Indies. *Mosaic Law*, we remember, never saw Israelite slavery as a problem. In his glorification of the Egyptian politics of economic self-sufficiency, his account of the genesis of Mosaic law symbolically reenacted the subjection of the ancient Israelites to Egyptian jurisprudence, envisioning a scenario in which Moses sought to impose the "highly developed legislative wisdom" of the Egyptians onto the childlike customs of the "disobedient" Israelites. Michaelis's polemics against Dohm take a similar approach, conceiving of modern Jews as sugar island slaves serving a contemporary European state that he wants to see modeled, not surprisingly, on ancient Egypt. Michaelis, then, finds a place for his unwanted Jewish contemporaries: his geographical imagination puts them in their "proper" place; in this topography, the physical descendants of the ancient Israelites follow the path of sugar, becoming the slaves of a European power that models itself on ancient Egypt. Following the mind-set of Michaelis's Orientalist scholarship, moreover, this program of colonial deportation also considers itself the antithesis of imperial expansion. Unlike the "disadvantageous East Indian trade," which allegedly dries up European resources, German sugar islands in the West Indies would follow the model of ancient Egyptian jurisprudence and simply promote German national self-sufficiency.

In his insistence that the degenerate character of the Jews cannot be eradicated and his accompanying proposal for Jewish deportation to a sugar-producing "colony" of "malefactors and degenerates" situated in an appropriate southern climate, Michaelis challenges Dohm's proposals for regeneration at their most basic level, inaugurating a new paradigm of discourse on the Jewish question. In later years, Michaelis was not alone in his racial and colonial conception of Jews as the equivalent of Africans, a group many eighteenth-century anthropologists considered similarly "degenerate" and well suited for slave labor. Karl Wilhelm Friedrich Grattenauer (1773–1838), a court official in Berlin who also proposed deportation, argued in 1791 that attempts to regenerate Jewish character by baptism or other means would be as effective "as trying to wash a blackamoor white"; like Michaelis, not surprisingly, Grattenauer also conceived of modern Jews as potential slaves who might "improve roads, dry out swamps and lay bricks—like they did in Egypt—thereby promoting the culture of the land."[65] In his later, much more popular writings of 1803, which we will discuss in detail in Chapter 5, Grattenauer characterized the Jews as an "Oriental foreign people" that historians and anthropologists alike agreed were a distinct "race."[66] By the time Grattenauer made these claims, visions of Jewish racial inferiority were hardly a novelty. Indeed, in an influential essay *On the Nature of the African Negro* of 1790, Christoph Meiners (1747–1810), a philosopher colleague of Michaelis in Göttingen who wrote widely on issues of race, forcefully equated the permanently degenerate nature of blacks with that of Jews, arguing in one fell swoop against both the liberation of slaves and the emancipation of the Jews.[67] By the late 1790s, visions of race had very much entered the mainstream of debates over civic improvement, prompting the theologian Gottlob Benjamin Gerlach to complain explicitly, with reference to Meiners, about the use of philosophical visions of race to justify the slave trade in England and the continued oppression of Jews in Germany. Like Dohm and Michaelis, Gerlach also drew an explicit parallel between the plantation economy of West Indian slavery and Germans who opposed regenerating the Jews.[68]

During this entire period, nevertheless, race was anything but a fixed and stable concept.[69] The term had only entered German philosophical vocabulary with Kant's essay "On the Different Human Races," a 1775 piece that sought to salvage the monogenic theory of human origins under attack by Enlightenment thinkers who argued for polygenesis, that is, the use of multiple genealogies of descent to explain the radical differences between human beings. In viewing the Jews as an "unmixed race of a more southern people," Michaelis was not appropriating a concept whose meaning was unequivocal. His vision of the Jews made a very particular contribution to Enlightenment racial science, and this is what needs to be elaborated. By the time Michaelis published his polemics against Dohm, Johann Friedrich Blumenbach, Michaelis's colleague in Göttingen and a figure often said to be the father of physical anthropology, had already made "degeneration" the key feature in his thinking on race. In his influential *De generis humani varietate nativa* (On the Natural Varieties of Mankind, 1775, 1781, 1795), Blumenbach drew on Maupertius and Buffon to present the concept of "degeneration" as a tool one might use to salvage the monogenic theory of human origins and to dispute Kant's insistence that human beings could indeed be rigorously classified into distinct races. Blumenbach thus divides up human beings into five "varieties"—Caucasian, Mongolian, Ethiopian, American and Malay—stressing the imperceptible transitions between these varieties and the great difficulties of determining where one begins and the other ends.[70] The term "Caucasian" is Blumenbach's innovation, and from its inception, it is inextricable from his understanding of the process of "degeneration":

> *Caucasian variety.* I have taken the name of this variety from Mount Caucasus, both because its neighborhood, and especially its southern slope, produces the most beautiful race of men, I mean, the Georgian; and because all physiological reasons converge to this, that in that region, if anywhere, it seems we ought with the greatest probability to place the autochthones of mankind. For in the first place, that stock displays, as we have seen, the most beautiful form of the skull, from which, as from a mean and primeval type, the others diverge by most easy gradations on both sides to the two ultimate extremes (that is, on the one side the Mongolian, on the other the Ethiopian). Besides, it is white in colour, which we may fairly assume to have been the primitive colour of mankind, since, as we have shown above, it is very easy for that to degenerate into brown, but very much more difficult for dark to become white, when the secretion and precipitation of this carbonaceous pigment has once deeply struck root.[71]

The Caucasian, then, is the original variety of human beings from which all others have degenerated. As in so many other eighteenth-century racial typologies, scientific and aesthetic categories coincide here. Indeed, the Caucasian is "a mean and primeval type" in part *because* it is the "most beautiful race of men," or, as Blumenbach states elsewhere, the "most handsome and becoming" variety of human beings.[72] Under the influence of climate and other environmental factors, humans have degenerated from their original state of natural beauty, yielding the "extremes" of the Mongolian and the Ethiopian and the intermediary varieties of the American and the Malay, all of which lack the proper sense of proportion Blumenbach claims for his white Caucasians.

Blumenbach thus puts forth a typology of "varieties" that is obviously anything but value-neutral—even if, in his schema, whites can become blacks, if subjected to the proper conditions for a series of generations, and blacks can even become whites, albeit it seems with somewhat greater difficulty. Once articulated, this type of hierarchical conception of human "varieties" lent itself to a variety of uses. Blumenbach's intention, needless to say, was to salvage a universalist view of humankind. Nevertheless, his notion of the aesthetic and physiological superiority of the Caucasian—and this aspect of his argument is hardly atypical of Enlightenment discourses on race—obviously could be used to legitimize, among other things, the conquering of the New World and the slave trade.[73] When it comes to the Jews, Blumenbach's logic of de- and regeneration seems to break down. Like other eighteenth-century anthropologists, Blumenbach classifies Jews, like Arabs, as Caucasians, as white. His famous skull collection in Göttingen even used a skull of a Jewish infant girl as an example of the Caucasian *norma verticalis*.[74] But Jews constitute a very specific subcategory within the Caucasian variety. The 1775 edition of *De generis humani varietate nativa* speaks of Jews as having a particular physiognomy: "[T]he Jewish race ... can easily be recognized everywhere by their eyes alone, which breathe of the East."[75] The 1795 edition makes an even stronger case for Jewish racial peculiarity: "[T]he nation of the Jews ... , under every climate, remain the same as far as the fundamental configuration of the face goes, [they are] remarkable for a racial character almost universal, which can be distinguished at first glance even by those little skilled in physiognomy, although it is difficult to limit and express by words."[76]

As a particular variety of Caucasians, then, Blumenbach's Jews continue to bear the indelible marks of the racial character inherited from their ancient Near Eastern climate of origin, and they do so despite the various climates and conditions they have lived in since the onset of Diaspora. In this they manifest a racial character that is "almost universal" and thus distinct from all other human varieties. Unlike the "Ethiopians," who under the proper conditions might be able to become white and return to the "mean and primeval" beauty of the Caucasian type, Jews have somehow become impervious to environmental influences, a degenerate variety of Caucasian with no pos-

sibility of regeneration. Jews explode the categories of Blumenbach's physical anthropology, exhibiting a permanence of racial type that unsettles his
system of near imperceptible transitions between varieties in diverse states
of degeneration. The passage cited above, moreover, explicitly reflects on
the disruption Jews cause to Blumenbach's system. The permanent racial
character of the Jews, immediately legible in their Jewish eyes and face,
nevertheless eludes the gaze of the scientific anthropologist: unlike everything else Blumenbach describes, categorizes and systematizes in his treatise,
the Jewish racial character "is difficult to limit and express by words."

Michaelis, in conceiving of the Jews as an "unmixed race of a more southern people" that will never have the proper physical stature to perform military service for a German state, takes Blumenbach's understanding of Jewish
racial character one step further. Like Blumenbach, Michaelis marks Jews as
an alien race that blatantly defies the logic of regeneration, but he also sets
them, as a more southern race, in explicit opposition to Europeans, speaking
frequently, as Mendelssohn complained, of "Jews" and "Germans" rather
than "Jews" and "Christians" (D 2: 76). "Germans" for Michaelis, we remember, apparently include a variety of northern Europeans—the "Catholic and
Lutheran, the German, Wend and Frenchman"—all of whom, unlike the
degenerate "southern" Jews, can gain the necessary bodily stature to perform
military service. Like Dohm, interestingly enough, Michaelis envisions a multiconfessional, multinational state that will "naturalize" and "melt together"
its subjects. He defines his vision of a universalist political order, however,
entirely in opposition to the permanently degenerate southern Jewish race.
Germany emerges here as an amalgamation of northern peoples entitled to
colonial control over the southern Jewish race, an imperial power that, once
equipped with sugar island colonies and Jewish slaves, will no longer be
dependent on foreign trade for sugar and other precious commodities from
the New World.

Michaelis's use of racial theory links his polemics against Dohm once again
to the concerns we encountered in his biblical scholarship. Michaelis's vision
of a degenerate southern Jewish race clearly supports his more general project
to de-Orientalize modern Europe, his effort to purge European jurisprudence
of the traces of its Oriental heritage. For in both Blumenbach's account of the
origins of humanity and Michaelis's racial hierarchy of "northern" Europeans
over "southern" Jews, the ancient Hebrews have to cede once and for all the
privileged position they occupied in biblical history as the origin of humanity. For Blumenbach, Jews mark an irreversible aberration from the original
human variety that inhabited the southern slope of Mount Caucasus.
Michaelis's adaptation of this scenario similarly leaves no doubt as to the
superiority of the "northern" Europeans. With its hegemony over the Orient

secured in this manner, Christian Europe can safely lose all anxiety about the
power and influence of its Oriental origins in religion and jurisprudence.
Racial theory secures for Michaelis precisely that which *Mosaic Law* strove for:
a vision of Europe as *already* de-Orientalized. Seeing the Jews as racial degenerates one might deport to German sugar islands does not merely envision
German as a self-sufficient colonial power much like England or France. It
also emancipates Christian Europe once and for all from the burdens of its
Oriental heritage, allowing Michaelis's northern European peers to gain complete ascendancy over their Oriental Jewish childhood. The quest for intellectual domination of the Orient is no longer distinguishable from colonial
power and the progress of imperialism. Michaelis's Orientalism finds its
ultimate expression here in the colonial enslavement and deportation of
his racially degenerate Jewish contemporaries.

ORIENTALIST ANTISEMITISM

In his seminal 1978 book *Orientalism*, Edward Said argued that the German
search for intellectual authority over the Orient was exclusively a scholarly
concern, one without direct political import. By 1830, the Germans had clearly
become the preeminent Orientalists in Europe, but they did so, of course, in
the absence of any colonial holdings in the Near East. Unlike French and
British myths about the Orient, Said concludes, the vision of the Orient constructed and sustained by Germans like Michaelis, Eichhorn, Herder, Goethe
and Friedrich Schlegel tended to lack any direct connection to the power
dynamics of imperial expansion.[77] What Said's view of German Orientalist
scholarship systematically obscures, as Susannah Heschel has argued, is the
politics of theological discourse within the German academy. Modern German
scholarship on Islam, for instance, Heschel points out, was inaugurated by
Jews and was introduced as a strategic form of counterhistory, an attempt to
reconfigure the relations between the three major Western religions in such
a way as to unsettle the unchallenged hegemony of Christian theology.[78] In
this context, Heschel suggests, Said's analysis of the European quest for intellectual authority over the Orient needs to be supplemented by studying an
analogous form of "Orientalism," one that is internal to the West: the attempt,
central to the rise of historical theology in the nineteenth century, to control
and contain Christianity's historical relation to Judaism.[79]

Michaelis is often cited as the eighteenth-century Orientalist who helps
pave the way for the full-fledged emergence of historical-critical biblical
scholarship in the nineteenth century. In his attempt to historicize Mosaic law,
he also contributes directly to modern Christian theological discourse on
Judaism, inaugurating a form of historical-critical scholarship on the Hebrew

Bible that has to mark contemporary Jews as an anachronism, out of sync with modernity both in their adherence to an antiquated legal tradition and in the blatantly ahistorical manner in which they interpret this tradition. Writing at the historical moment that witnessed the first wave of widespread debates on the question of Jewish emancipation, moreover, Michaelis systematically links this historical-theological containment of Judaism to the question of modern Europe's colonial authority over contemporary Jews. In articulating his views on Jews, Judaism and the Orient in explicit relation to the logic of modern colonialism, Michaelis forces us to reject Said's account. Certainly, the lack of German colonial activity in the Near East left its mark on German Orientalist scholarship; when it comes to the Near East, German Orientalism may indeed be much more ephemeral than its French and British equivalents, concerned almost exclusively with its *intellectual* authority over the East. When it comes to Jews and the Jewish question, however, Michaelis's Orientalist concerns are hardly academic. With his invention of a racially charged, colonialist antisemitism, his Orientalism intervenes directly into the contemporary German political scene, creating a fantasy of Germany as an imperial power supported by the slave labor of its racially degenerate Jews.

In this confluence of Orientalism and antisemitism, Michaelis forces us to rethink yet another of Said's premises: his understanding of Orientalism as a "secret sharer of Western antisemitism."[80] For in the case of Michaelis, there is nothing "secret" in the relationship between Europe's attempt to gain hegemony over the Orient and its position *vis-à-vis* the Jews who reside in its midst. Indeed, Said's vision of German Orientalism's relative isolation from the rise of imperialism obscures the extent to which Orientalism and modern antisemitism come onto the scene as interrelated inflections of Enlightenment colonialist discourse. If one considers the "Asiatic refugees" prominently residing in Germany with a Near Eastern "racial character" that apparently can be "distinguished by first glance even by those little skilled in physiognomy," it becomes difficult to regard Michaelis's contribution to the discipline of Oriental studies as an exclusively scholarly endeavor. For with his vision of sugar island Jews, Michaelis articulates a racial antisemitism that marks the ultimate embodiment of German Orientalist fantasies of both intellectual hegemony *and* colonialist power.

Fig. 7. Engraving honoring Moses Mendelssohn published one year after
Mendelssohn's death in the *Berlinische Monatsschrift*, one of the leading journals of
the German Enlightenment. The Greek caption from the New Testament reads
"Behold, an Israelite indeed, in whom is no guile" (John 1:47).
Courtesy of the Rare Book Collection, The University of North Carolina at
Chapel Hill.

3

MENDELSSOHN'S JESUS

The Frustrations of Jewish Resistance

It is a disgrace that we should reproach Socrates and Plato because they were pagans! Was this a flaw in their morals? And Jesus a Jew?—And what if, as I believe, he never wanted to give up Judaism? One can only imagine where this remark would lead me. (*JubA* 7: 59)
—Mendelssohn, unpublished note (March 1770)

MENDELSSOHN AND THE PYGMIES

When Dohm reprinted Michaelis's essay from the *Oriental and Exegetical Library* in the second volume of *On the Civic Improvement of the Jews* in 1783, he appended to it a letter he had received from Mendelssohn immediately after the Jewish philosopher first encountered Michaelis's arguments against emancipation. In this private correspondence, which was not originally intended for publication, Mendelssohn used an acerbic irony unusual for his well-tempered philosophical style, prompting a reviewer in Nicolai's *Universal German Library* to note that he "surely would have altered his tone had he meant this piece of writing for the public."[1] In the passage of the letter where his polemics came to a head, Mendelssohn directed his anger at Michaelis's doubts about Jews' ability to perform military service:

Laws should pay no attention to particular convictions. They should proceed along their way incessantly, prescribing what is beneficial to the common good. Whoever finds a conflict between his particular convictions and the laws may sit back and determine how to resolve it. If the fatherland has to be defended, then everyone whose calling it is to defend it will have to hurry up and do so. In such cases human beings know how to modify their convictions in accordance with their civic duty. One should only try not to make this contradiction too obvious. In several centuries the problem will resolve itself or be forgotten. In this way

> Christians, despite the doctrine of their founder, have become world con-
> querors, oppressors and slave traders. Jews can thus certainly be made fit
> for military service—obviously, they will have to have the proper stature,
> as Herr M. wisely reminds us, unless one would want to use them merely
> against an army of enemy pygmies or [other] Jews. (D 2: 76–77)

As unusual as they may be for Mendelssohn's *oeuvre*, pygmies at the time were
not just the stuff of legends and Homeric lore. The distinguished Swedish
naturalist Carolus Linnaeus (1707–78) had included the pygmy in a scientific
typology of aberrant human varieties in his 1760 *Anthropomorpha*, and Louis-
Antoine de Bougainville's circumnavigation in 1766–69 had produced sight-
ings of a warlike pygmy nation of "Negro dwarfs" on Madagascar.[2] Others,
such as Georg Forster (1754–94), the famous German anthropologist who had
sailed with Captain Cook, tended to be more skeptical, reviving the position
of Edward Tyson (1650–1708) that pygmies were the products of fable
and fairy tale—probably monkeys or small apes travelers had mistaken for
humans.[3] By putting Michaelis's vision of Jews' physical deficiencies on
the same level as the half-scientific, half-fantastic figure of the pygmy,
Mendelssohn here parodies Michaelis's conception of Jews as a degenerate
"southern race." In his work on ancient Judaism, Michaelis severed any
connection between the "Oriental" laws of Moses and Jesus's Christianity.
Turning the tables on his Christian opponent, Mendelssohn now presents
Michaelis's response to Dohm—his rhetorical suggestion that this southern
race should be deported to sugar island colonies—as a betrayal of Jesus's
original doctrine. The only issue at stake, he insists, is the subordination of
religious convictions to the rule of law, and in this regard, ironically, modern
colonialism's transgression of Jesus's teachings can serve as a model for Jewish
emancipation. If so-called Christians can conquer and populate West Indian
sugar islands with African slave labor, then Jews can certainly help out with
national defense. Casting himself as an authority on Jesus, colonialism and
the slave trade, Mendelssohn undermines Michaelis's expertise on matters
relating to Jews and Judaism, making his fantasy of German sugar islands
populated by southern Jewish slave labor yield up its absurd antithesis: the
threat that an army of African pygmies or Jewish dwarfs might suddenly move
northward and invade German soil.

I open this chapter with this polemic because, even though it was cited
over and over again in the ensuing decades of debate, it may still strike us
today, as it struck the reviewer in the *Universal German Library* more than
200 years ago, as atypical of Mendelssohn's public persona. Indeed, colonial
expansion, the slave trade and thinking about race were hardly Mendelssohn's
chief concerns; engaging in diatribes over questions of Christian doctrine

occupied an even lower position on his list of philosophical priorities. Mendelssohn is known in the annals of German-Jewish history less for his polemics than for his symbolic role as a temperate mediator between Judaism and the secular world of the European Enlightenment.[4] This image, moreover, is not entirely inaccurate. Born in Dessau in 1729, Mendelssohn grew up in an entirely Jewish milieu without significant exposure to secular knowledge, without even speaking German as his native language. After coming to Berlin at age fourteen to continue his Talmudic studies, however, he began to acquaint himself with the world of European letters. Starting with his entry onto the philosophical scene with his *Philosophical Dialogues* (1754), the *Letters on the Sensations* (1755), his *Philosophical Writings* (1761) and a 1763 prize-winning essay for the Berlin academy on the use of evidence in metaphysics, he quickly rose to prominence as one of the preeminent voices of the German Enlightenment. His most widely read work, *Phaedon, Or on the Immortality of the Soul* (1767), was translated into Dutch, French, Danish, Italian and Russian during his lifetime and earned him fame across Europe as the "German Socrates." By the time of his death in 1786, he had emerged as the most prominent Jewish intellectual in Europe, a decidedly uncontroversial figure who would come to exemplify the promise of Jewish emancipation for many Jews and non-Jews alike.

As David Sorkin has demonstrated, Mendelssohn's nineteenth-century heirs could fashion him as the archetypal "German Jew" only by disregarding the nature of his dual commitment to Judaism and secular philosophy, overlooking the particular way in which he used the philosophy of the Enlightenment to uphold the orthodox observance of Jewish ritual law.[5] In this regard, nineteenth-century Jews fell into a similar trap as did many of Mendelssohn's German contemporaries. For in his works written for the general public prior to the initial emancipation debates of the 1780s, Mendelssohn rarely reflected on his efforts to unite Judaism with the philosophy of the Enlightenment. Indeed, for most of his life he scrupulously avoided polemics on Judaism, Christianity and the political situation of the Jews in Christian Europe. A major figure in the Haskalah, the Jewish Enlightenment, he did write widely in Hebrew in a variety of fields: on medieval Jewish philosophy, particularly Maimonides, on questions of biblical exegesis, and on issues in secular philosophy similar to those dealt with in his German works. With the exception of Orientalists like Michaelis, however, few of Mendelssohn's German contemporaries were aware of his prolific Hebrew authorship and the extent of his philosophical and religious commitment to Judaism. For many of his readers, the German Socrates's continued adherence to the "antiquated" laws of Moses remained an enigma. By the time Dohm's treatise appeared in 1781, Mendelssohn had published only one significant piece in German that dealt with Judaism, his brief and somewhat evasive 1770 response to the challenge by the Swiss theologian Johann Caspar Lavater (1741–1801) to refute Charles Bonnet's proofs for Christianity or renounce Judaism and convert.[6]

Yet when examined in greater detail, Mendelssohn's reluctance to engage in polemics is hardly evidence of a temperate character, and in this regard the image we have inherited from the nineteenth century needs to be revisited as well. In public statements, to be sure, he repeatedly expressed his distaste for polemics, particularly in matters of religion. He was, he insisted in the midst of the Lavater dispute, simply not made to be a "moral" or "spiritual athlete," and he had little "gift for polemical writing," as he confessed in a letter to Bonnet from the same period.[7] In a letter to his cousin Elkan Herz toward the end of the Lavater affair, he expressed rather different sentiments:

> You ask why I engaged in dispute? I only wish I had been more engaged.
> . . . If, God willing, I were only to have another such opportunity, I would
> do it all over again. Some have thought it necessary to respond with
> silence; I am not of this belief. When I consider what one is obligated to
> do to sanctify the divine name, I cannot at all grasp why so many of our
> people are always screaming out that I should for heaven's sake not write
> about all this any more. Indeed, God knows that it was not easy for me
> to make myself withdraw from the dispute; my own will receded when
> countered with the will of others. If it had depended on me alone, I
> would have wanted to give an entirely different response.[8]

Mendelssohn's moderation, it seems, is less an essential personality trait than a product of rigorous self-discipline, a necessary tactical response to both the Christian domination of public discourse on religion and a Jewish community hesitant to upset its precarious political position *vis-à-vis* the Christian authorities. As in his letter to Dohm, Mendelssohn here seems quite the eager polemicist, one who even after a full-fledged war of wills with his opponents will only reluctantly resume the dictated position of silence. Certainly, he often *appeared* an unpolemical, uncontroversial figure, but this appearance needs to be seen as an appearance, a function of his powerlessness in political and theological discourse.

It is in this context that we need to understand the cautious manner in which Mendelssohn entered the debates on Jewish emancipation. When Cerf Beer approached him to write a memorandum on behalf of the Jews of Alsace, Mendelssohn turned to Dohm, ultimately convincing him to write and publish *On the Civic Improvement of the Jews*. Eager to keep the public contemplating the prospects of granting Jews rights, he then published in 1782

what he marked as a mere "appendix" to Dohm's book, a preface to a translation of Manasseh ben Israel's *Vindication of the Jews* by his contemporary, the
German-Jewish physician Marcus Herz (1747–1803).[9] The text Mendelssohn
introduced here—a distinguished seventeenth-century Dutch Rabbi's plea to
admit Jews to Cromwell's England—was tame compared to Dohm's vision of
an all-encompassing transformation of the sociopolitical order. Mendelssohn's
remarks, nevertheless, immediately put him at the center of controversy.
Toward the end of his preface, he challenged the contemporary Christian
vision of Judaism as a system of coercive laws, claiming that Mosaic law was
in its purest form devoid of coercive force. Provoked by this counterintuitive
presentation of Judaism, the Berlin writer August Friedrich Cranz published
an anonymous pamphlet that challenged Mendelssohn's commitment to his
religion and renewed Lavater's call for conversion.[10] It was in response to this
pamphlet—and to an open letter by Daniel Ernst Mörschel insisting that
Mendelssohn questioned all revealed religion and was thus nothing but a
deist—that he finally published, in 1783, his only major German work on
Judaism, *Jerusalem, Or on Religious Power and Judaism.*

Jerusalem stands out in Mendelssohn's *oeuvre* as a highly polemical work.
Here Mendelssohn forcefully argues for freedom of conscience and separation of church and state, articulating a normative concept of religion as incompatible with any form of temporal power. It is here that he gives his famous
definition of Judaism as a noncoercive system of "revealed legislation"
without religious dogma, contending that Judaism is more rational than
Christianity and actually better suited to exist alongside a secular political
order constructed according to the principles of modern natural law. As Sorkin
has illustrated, the vision of Judaism Mendelssohn presents to his German
public here contains little that had not already been articulated in his Hebrew
writings or his private correspondence.[11] What matters most about *Jerusalem*,
I shall contend, is thus less its conception of Judaism *per se* than its polemical intent *vis-à-vis* Christianity. Allan Arkush has argued that Mendelssohn's
defense of Judaism is in many ways more rhetorical than real, designed more
to deflect than to refute the fundamental philosophical challenges posed to
biblical revelation by Spinoza, Reimarus, Lessing and others.[12] It is precisely
this rhetorical-polemical aspect of Mendelssohn's thought that is at stake
here. Unlike Arkush, I am concerned less with the philosophical inadequacy
of Mendelssohn's defense of Judaism as a "revealed legislation" than with
the polemical unity of his argument, the way he systematically confronts,
subverts and reformulates the positions of his opponents. In seeking to
defend Judaism against its denigration at the hands of Christian writers like
Cranz and Mörschel, Mendelssohn turns the tables on his opponents to insist
on the coercive nature of Christianity's religious and political power in the

modern world, ultimately using a critique of Christianity's global aspirations as the basis for his distinction between the legitimately coercive power of the state and true religion's lack of temporal authority.

Mendelssohn's invocation, in his response to Michaelis, of Christian "world conquerors, oppressors and slave traders" betraying the doctrine of Jesus may indeed be atypical of his *oeuvre* as a whole; one would be hard pressed to find similar statements in *Phaedon*. This particular critique of Christian imperialism, however, highlights a central aspect of *Jerusalem*. Here Mendelssohn also sets himself up as an authority on the origins of Christianity, recasting the historical relationship between Judaism and Christianity in such a way as to divest Christianity of any legitimate form of temporal power. In a move destined to provoke his opponents, he appropriates Jesus as a Jewish Rabbi who preaches the timeless value of Mosaic law, characterizing Jesus as both a critic of Christian imperialism and a polemicist for Jewish emancipation. Published during a period that witnessed the beginnings of theological interest in the historical Jesus—Mendelssohn's friend Lessing had published the controversial Reimarus fragments in 1774–78—*Jerusalem* intervenes into Protestant theological discourse, articulating a vision of the Jewish Jesus that challenges celebratory accounts of the origins of Christianity and their practical uses in support of European imperialism. This is the framework in which Mendelssohn presents his argument for emancipation.[13]

As Susannah Heschel has argued, Judaism as a "religion" is a distinctly modern invention developed in mimicry of Christianity; premodern Jewish texts typically speak of Torah and *mitzvot* but rarely present Judaism as a religion in any way similar to Christianity.[14] *Jerusalem*, of course, helps produce this modern understanding, envisioning Judaism as a "confession" that will serve for Jews roughly the same function as Christianity might perform for Christians in a secular state. As countless commentators have noted, Mendelssohn has little interest in the "political" or "national" dimensions of Judaism. His sketch of Jewish history in *Jerusalem* glosses over the loss of the ancient Jewish commonwealth as incidental to Judaism's mission of promoting monotheism, and his normative vision of Judaism as devoid of coercive power plainly seeks to dismantle the corporate autonomy of Jews in contemporary European states; any conception of Judaism as a politics belongs to the distant past. For Mendelssohn, modern Jews have a valid role to play in the cultural and civic life of Europe, and *Jerusalem* clearly legitimizes Diaspora in a manner that is almost unprecedented in the entirety of previous Jewish thought.[15] The problem in stressing how Mendelssohn depoliticizes or denationalizes Judaism in order to conceive of a religion that might be palatable to modernity is that it obscures the theological and political context in which he came to present Judaism in this manner. When we understand Mendelssohn in this framework, *Jerusalem* will look less like an apologetic and more like a polemic, a text that subverts governing paradigms of late eighteenth-century Protestant theology, a text that negotiates a place for Jews in the modern state by contesting Christianity's dominant self-representations. Judaism may indeed be constructed as a religion in mimicry of Christianity, but this act of mimicry is a subversive one *vis-à-vis* its object, one that in form—if not in content—foreshadows the Jewish challenges to Christianity Heschel has identified in nineteenth-century Jewish theologians like Abraham Geiger.[16]

Anything but an assimilationist apologetic, Mendelssohn's legitimation of Diaspora rewrites the terms in which his contemporaries framed the question of Jewish emancipation. This is apparent, on one level, in his continued polemics against Michaelis, a figure whom *Jerusalem* never even mentions. This failure to acknowledge the work of Germany's leading Christian authority on Judaism is telling in itself, particularly since Mendelssohn had read *Mosaic Law* and other works by Michaelis and intermittently maintained a friendly correspondence with him—that is, up until the publication of his critique of Dohm.[17] Michaelis's presentation of Judaism as an "Oriental" legal system, nevertheless, clearly lurks in the background of *Jerusalem*, ultimately providing the antithesis of Mendelssohn's vision of Diaspora. Judaism for Mendelssohn is neither "Oriental" nor European; as the religion of Jesus, it is neither simply the product of the climate and culture of ancient Israel nor does it aspire to the type of universality he critiques in Christianity. Mendelssohn conceives of a Judaism that eludes the historicism of Michaelis's Orientalist scholarship, and in doing so, he rewrites Dohm's program for civic regeneration as well. Rejecting Dohm's link between regeneration and citizenship, he presents a vision of Judaism as compatible with the modern state that challenges Dohm's assumption that Jews will inevitably reform Judaism to assimilate it to his own Rome-identified vision of modernity. For Mendelssohn, indeed, contemporary Jews are not just not in need of improvement: it is ultimately Jerusalem and its resistance to the Roman Empire that provides the model for his vision of modernity.

THE LAVATER AFFAIR AND THE POLITICS OF RELIGIOUS DISCOURSE

The polemical stance toward Christianity that surfaced in *Jerusalem* began rearing its head in response to Lavater's provocation, and the delicate manner in which Mendelssohn issued his later polemics makes little sense without an understanding of the pressures he encountered during the Lavater affair. Johann Caspar Lavater was a theologian and deacon in Zurich known for his attempts to convert prominent intellectuals like Goethe and Karl Wilhelm

Ramler to his mystical brand of Christianity. In August 1769, he published a partial translation of Charles Bonnet's *Philosophical Palingenesis*, a French work released earlier that year that challenged Mendelssohn's philosophical argument for the immortality of the soul in *Phaedon* and insisted on the necessity of the revealed truths of Christianity; for most Enlightenment intellectuals, it was a given that Judaism lacked any concept of the immortality of the soul. Encouraged by private conversations in 1763–64 in which Mendelssohn had expressed respect and admiration for Jesus's moral character, Lavater thus dedicated his translation to the German Socrates, challenging him either to publicly refute Bonnet's work or "to do what Socrates would have done had he read this work and found it irrefutable," that is, convert to Christianity.[18] Lavater's hope was that Mendelssohn's acceptance of Christianity would precipitate a large-scale Jewish conversion that would usher in the messianic age. For the most part, this provocation did not meet with sympathy among Enlightenment intellectuals, many of whom saw Lavater's actions as a gross indiscretion, a breach of the rules of philosophical etiquette. Embarrassed by the use to which his work was put, Bonnet himself censured Lavater for forcing Mendelssohn into a public debate that was so obviously grounded in conditions of political inequality. "In truth," he apologized to Mendelssohn, "I do not believe that it is possible to find in the republic of letters two men who are greater enemies of polemics than the modern *Phaedon* and the *Palingenesist.* . . . But apart from all these considerations, how can a Christian and an equitable friend of peace resolve to publicly enter the lists against a Jew as long as the Jew lives under the protection of Christians? The only way to reestablish equality here would be to transport the scene among the Troglodytes or to the Austral lands."[19]

For Bonnet, Lavater's appropriation of his work against Mendelssohn marks a transgression of the rules governing peaceful public conduct. Lavater's dedication may have been theological in intent, but its effect was distinctly political, an effort to promote the dominant religion that took advantage of Mendelssohn's position of political powerlessness; as long as Jews remain under Christian rule without political equality, there can be no true theological dialogue. Talk of granting Jews rights was still a long way off in 1770, and the only solution Bonnet offered was to conduct such theological controversy outside the sphere of direct European rule, either among the Troglodytes—cave-dwellers in Africa whom Linnaeus classified alongside the pygmy in his *Anthropomorpha*—or in the South Seas, that area of the globe currently being explored by Bougainville and Captain Cook. Given that Lavater and Mendelssohn were located not at the colonial frontier but in the heart of Europe, it would be wisest, Bonnet concluded, not to pretend that the republic of letters offers a public forum where theological issues might be debated in an impartial manner. When it comes to Jews defending their religion against Christianity, the realm of print is irreparably permeated by relations of political domination.

On one level, Mendelssohn's response offered similar reflections on the circumstances in which Lavater forced him to speak out. The open letter to Lavater he published in early 1770 identified the "position assigned to my coreligionists in civic life" as incompatible with the *"free* exercise of the mind" and thus ultimately at odds with the "rights of humanity" (*JubA* 7: 8). As a Jew, Mendelssohn complained, he lacked freedom of speech and other basic human rights, and in this sense, his civic position went hand in hand with his philosophical commitment to "avoid all religious controversy and speak in public writings only of those truths that are necessarily of equal importance to all religions" (*JubA* 7: 10). The notion that philosophy should only address truths common to all religions was typical of Enlightenment theology. But Mendelssohn invoked this imperative for a particular purpose, using it both to call attention to his own political position and to unsettle Christianity's claim to universalism. Rather than following Bonnet and taking refuge in a fantasy of colonial escapism, Mendelssohn sought to transgress the limits of theological discourse, to open up a public forum in Europe for precisely that defense of Judaism and Jewish critique of Christianity that Bonnet assumed a Christian-dominated public sphere could not accommodate.

In his open letter to Lavater, Mendelssohn issued an explicit challenge to Christianity, juxtaposing the global aspirations of its universalist revelation to the self-consciously exclusive nature of Jewish law. As in *Jerusalem*, he presented Judaism here as a system of revealed legislation designed only for Jews that was, unlike Christianity, not in any way at odds with the religious beliefs of other peoples. Reworking Maimonides's account of the function of the laws given to the sons of Noah, Mendelssohn explained to Lavater that Jews believed that non-Jews were bound simply to obey the law of nature and the religion of the patriarchs. Indeed, Jewish tradition regards Gentiles who follow the "laws of this religion of nature and reason" as the "righteous men of other nations," as "children of eternal salvation" (*JubA* 7: 10). Conceived of in these terms—and this marks an important innovation within Jewish tradition[20]—Judaism represents the epitome of religious tolerance and, as such, a challenge to any Christian claims to universalism. Unlike Judaism, Christianity refuses to recognize the fundamental universality of natural or rational religion, "sending missions" to the East and West Indies and to Greenland to spread its particular revelation to "distant peoples" (*JubA* 7: 12). In his unpublished "Counterreflections" on Bonnet's *Palingenesis* written during the same period, Mendelssohn critiqued Christianity's global expansion in similar terms: "If the human race is necessarily corrupt and miserable without revelation, why, then, does the greatest part of the human race live without the *true revelation*? Why do both Indies have to wait until it pleases the Europeans to send them clerics to bring them a gospel without which they could not live virtuously or blissfully? To bring them a gospel which, according to their circumstances and the level of their knowledge, they can neither understand nor make use of?" (*JubA* 7: 73). For Mendelssohn, then, the very existence of such a wide spectrum of human religions is itself a refutation of the specific form of universalism Christianity wants to realize through missionary expansion. Understood in this framework, Judaism preaches tolerance, and does so in the face of a globally expansive Christianity that seeks to replace the manifold forms of native religion with *its* exclusive form of revealed religion.

Arguing in this manner, Mendelssohn justifies his general problems with religious polemics at the same time as he legitimizes his arguments against Christianity. In his published response to Mendelssohn's letter, not surprisingly, Lavater took issue with this challenge, pointing out simply that Christianity "is *supposed* to be, according to its nature, a *universal* religion equally suited for all the nations" (*JubA* 7: 34). For Mendelssohn, however, what Christians might *think* of Judaism is only part of the problem. The more pressing matter to be addressed is what Christians *do* to Jews. The universalist zeal that sends missionaries to Christianize the East and West Indies has political consequences on the domestic front, putting the Jews in an even worse position than the inhabitants of the non-European world. Indeed, part of the reason why Mendelssohn avoids religious disputes, he claims in his open letter, is that he is a "member of an oppressed people that has to seek protection from the good will of the dominant nation. . . . Freedoms that are granted to every other human being are denied to my coreligionists, who have to be satisfied with being merely tolerated and protected. They have to regard the nation that takes them in under endurable conditions as performing no small favor, as there are several states in which they are not even permitted to *reside*" (*JubA* 7: 14–15). Forced into a position of gratitude toward their Christian oppressors, Jews lack the freedom of peoples at the periphery of European rule. For Mendelssohn, then, Christianity secures its claims to universality not simply by accompanying colonial expansion with missionary work but by making it impossible for European Jews to challenge Christian doctrine; Christianity's ill-conceived universalism causes the Jews' political oppression and their silence in theological debates.

By calling attention to this, of course, Mendelssohn already begins to break out of this position of powerlessness. What is conspicuously absent from the open letter to Lavater, however, is any explanation of the occasion for Lavater's provocation; nowhere does he publicly account for the respect that he as a Jew professes for Jesus's moral character, a position he had requested Lavater keep private when he revealed it to him in 1763–64. As the passage I quote at the beginning of this chapter shows, Mendelssohn clearly knew at the time that his view of Jesus as an exemplary moral Jew who never wanted to renounce Judaism would be explosive, a challenge to Christianity that public discourse might be unable to accommodate and that might not be approved by Prussian censors.[21] Viewing the founder of Christianity as a Jew, to be sure, was not an entirely novel position. The notion that Jesus never sought to abolish Mosaic law had been promoted much earlier in the eighteenth century by English deists such as John Toland (1670–1722), writers with whose work Mendelssohn was familiar.[22] The prominent German Rabbi Jacob Emden (1698–1776), with whom Mendelssohn frequently corresponded, made similar claims in his Hebrew writings.[23] Mendelssohn, however, claimed Jesus for Judaism in such a way as to challenge Christianity's political power, and it is telling that he did so only in private notes and correspondence. Particularly because this view of Jesus surfaces in both the final, unpublished letter he sent Lavater in early 1771 and in *Jerusalem*, it makes sense to interrupt our discussion of Mendelssohn's public polemics to consider what he felt could *not* be said openly within the contours of this discussion.

In a unpublished statement from 1770, Mendelssohn linked his defense of Judaism and its tolerance to a much harsher critique of Christian universalism. Judaism, he wrote, needs no justification, as

> Jesus of Nazareth and the apostles themselves did not liberate us from the law. Why all these refutations of Judaism, since after all every pupil knows that we are entirely destroyed? Should we convert! We are, indeed, unrepentant, maliciously unrepentant villains who see the truth and do not want to recognize it. . . . A rational man cannot comprehend how I could maliciously not want to want to recognize a truth that would liberate me from disgrace and oppression. But why does a rational person need to comprehend this? (*JubA* 7: 64)

Jesus and his apostles emerge here not as the founders of a new religion but as authorities for the perpetuation of Jewish law. Jesus, Mendelssohn argued in his "Counterreflections," was merely a Jewish reformer, a "prophet" who worked within Judaism to "restore the pure natural religion its proper rights" (*JubA* 7: 100). In this framework, the universal and "rational" "truths" of Christianity that Jews fail to recognize are clearly at odds with both the message of Jesus and the conception of universality and global tolerance Mendelssohn—and Jesus—claim for Judaism. Authorized in this way by Jesus himself, Judaism's continued existence forms a threat to contemporary

Christianity's vision of itself, a challenge Christians try to overcome by refuting Judaism *ad infinitum* and by conceiving of Jews as "maliciously unrepentant villains" who warrant the appropriate political treatment.

Unable to confront Jesus's defense of Judaism, Christians perpetuate the religion they have constructed around Jesus by gaining theological and political domination over Jews, and it is in this context that Mendelssohn understands Lavater's provocation to him. In a letter to the sympathetic pastor Otto Julius Basilius Hesse written during the same period, Mendelssohn elaborates this link between theology and politics, expressing his amazement that Christians continue to use theological explanations to explain and legitimize contemporary Jews' "civic misery": "This mode of argument seems to me not merely unphilosophical but contrary to the spirit of the Gospel. What did Jesus and the apostles seek to impress on people more than that one should not infer the eternal from the temporal. . . . The most remarkable thing is that Christians do everything possible to keep this sort of argument alive. We are carefully kept under pressure so as to be refuted all the more victoriously" (*JubA* 7: 360–1). Christians, Mendelssohn suggests, need to oppress Jews in order to refute Judaism and justify Christianity, which they do in a manner that openly betrays the teachings of that Jew whom they claim as their founder.

The private letter Mendelssohn wrote Lavater to put an end to the conflict toned down this polemic but it did offer a similar explanation of his relation to Jesus. Rather than using Jesus's Jewishness to challenge Christianity's self-representations, he reflected here on why Christians need to think that Jews continually debase Christianity and slander its Jewish founder. Particularly since we shall see many of these ideas resurface in *Jerusalem*, it makes sense to quote this letter at length:

> It is a deep-rooted prejudice of your coreligionists that all Jews continually slander the Christian religion and its founder; this prejudice rather conveniently allows much to be explained in dogmatics, just as it justifies much in common life that is as irreligious as it is irrational. But it is not proper for you, most worthy friend of humanity, even to appear to encourage such prejudices, which are remnants of the old barbarism, and to awaken, even with mere figures of speech, the religious hatred that we should now more and more be putting to sleep. . . . When the more powerful spilled blood for the sake of religion, the weaker had no other means of retaliation than underhand tricks such as slandering the religion of their opponents behind closed doors. . . . The case is the same with the wrong done by the Sadducees and the Pharisees to the person of Jesus. It seems, though, that one still wants us to account for this! How should I know whether my ancestors made just or unjust judgments 1700

or 1800 years ago in Jerusalem? I would be very embarrassed if I were held responsible, for instance, for the judgments of the Royal High Court here, during my lifetime. We possess, incidentally, for our part no reliable information about that great event, no documents, no reports that we might oppose to yours. The infamous *Toledoth Yeshu* is a monstrosity from the ages of legend fit for such an age—and my brethren regard it as such. In the Talmud there are traces of information here and there, but it is still uncertain whether they concern the same event, and they are certainly not sufficient to make a judgment. . . . All my coreligionists who approach the matter properly withhold judgment. . . . I also know several who, like myself, go even further. Drawing from the statements of Christian sources (for I repeat, we have no reliable Jewish ones), we recognize the innocence of that religious founder and the moral goodness of his character. We presuppose, however, the expressed limitations: 1) that he never sought to set himself up as equal to the father; 2) that he never presented himself as a person of divinity; 3) that he subsequently never claimed for himself the honor of being worshiped; 4) that he did not want to subvert the religion of his fathers, and that in many cases he apparently seemed to proclaim the very opposite.[24]

At certain points in history, Mendelssohn concedes here, Jews have indeed slandered Jesus, but these anti-Christian sentiments need to be understood in part as products of Christian power, forms of "retaliation" to which oppressed Jews had to take recourse. The image of Jesus as a deceiver, trickster and magician in the medieval *Toledoth Yeshu*—a popular and widely circulated Jewish version of the gospels—needs to be regarded thus not just as a "monstrosity" of a more primitive era. It also served a purpose, giving Jews a discursive means of compensation for the violence of religious persecution. Premodern Jewish attitudes toward Jesus thus often functioned as internalized responses to Christian oppression. What matters most here, Mendelssohn stresses, is that whereas Lavater is still promoting the "religious hatred that we should now more and more be putting to sleep," contemporary Jews have already moved far beyond the anti-Christian prejudices of the age of "barbarism." Those in the vanguard of Enlightenment like Mendelssohn, moreover, clearly recognize Jesus's exemplary moral character, and they do so by examining Christian sources. Referring here most likely to Emden's Hebrew writings on Christianity, Mendelssohn presents Jews as doing what Christian theologians do not. Jews try to read Christian sources fairly and judiciously. They also appear to be at the forefront of historically oriented biblical criticism, and the result of this endeavor is a vision of Jesus as a Jew that authorizes the continued existence of Judaism in a Christian-dominated world at the same time as it issues a challenge to Christian universalism.

It was only in letters to more sympathetic correspondents that Mendelssohn would expand on these views of historical biblical criticism. In the midst of the Lavater affair, the Crown Prince of Braunschweig-Wolfenbüttel had written to Mendelssohn asking how a Jew could accept the Old Testament while rejecting the New Testament. Reiterating his vision of Jesus as a Jew, Mendelssohn noted in his response to the prince that he found the trinity and other aspects of Christian doctrine unacceptable because they were at odds with reason; Judaism, unlike Christianity, he claimed, never required its adherents to believe anything that would contradict reason. To a certain extent, of course, this insistence on Judaism's lack of dogma and its absolute compatibility with rational religion—a view he would present in more detail in *Jerusalem*—might seem to leave little room or purpose for historical investigation, and indeed, Mendelssohn is known for conceiving of Judaism in ahistorical terms, for lacking the interest in historical method so typical of nineteenth-century German-Jewish theologians and many of his Christian contemporaries. In this particular letter, nevertheless, Mendelssohn engages explicitly with trends in contemporary biblical scholarship. He claims Jesus as a Jew by confronting head on the strategies of Protestant Orientalist scholarship, stressing how ridiculous it would be if "the eternal felicity of the entire human race had to depend on the exegesis of obscure passages in a book that was written in time immemorial in a foreign, now dead language for a particular people in Asia!" (*JubA* 7: 304). Claiming Hebrew as his "second mother tongue . . . a language he understands as well as any modern person" (ibid.), he presents himself as the expert, the modern Oriental, able to see and correct the shortcomings of Christian Orientalist scholarship. Self-consciously highlighting those aspects of Judaism that such scholarship sets in opposition to the universalist message of Jesus, Mendelssohn challenges the way Christians legitimize Christianity by debasing Judaism. For Mendelssohn, it is precisely the national and geographical specificity of the Old Testament—its having been written for a "particular people in Asia"—that mitigates against its appropriation in the service of Christian universalism. "More recent" Christian exegetes, he continues, thinking perhaps of Michaelis, who sought to understand the Old Testament primarily on its own terms and later explicitly rejected Christological readings of Daniel, have abandoned the "forced" and "arbitrary" exercise of allegorizing the Hebrew Bible into an anticipation of the New Testament (*JubA* 7: 304). For the most part, however, Orientalists have not given up these "games" (ibid.), which provide Mendelssohn great amusement: portrayed in this manner, indeed, Christians—not Talmudic Jews—are the scholars with a forced and arbitrary relation to the letter of scripture. Mendelssohn was clearly aware how explosive it would be here to claim Jesus for Judaism and point once again to the role the political oppression of contemporary Jews plays in maintaining Christianity's supersession of Judaism: he begged the prince to destroy this letter immediately after reading it.

The stress of the Lavater affair left Mendelssohn with an aggravated nervous condition that made it difficult for him to engage in sustained philosophical reflection. In the years immediately following, not surprisingly, he retreated somewhat from the German public sphere, concentrating instead on his translation of the Pentateuch, on Hebrew writings that sought to develop Jewish forms of biblical criticism, and on other works geared specifically toward Jews. Mendelssohn's work of this period is not unmarked by polemic. His celebrated edition of the Bible placed the Hebrew original alongside a German translation printed in Hebrew letters, and for this reason it has traditionally been credited with helping promote mastery of High German among Central European Jewry. More than a tool for linguistic assimilation, Mendelssohn's Pentateuch also sought to raise the level of Hebrew learning among his coreligionists, and it aimed to create an authoritative edition of the Hebrew Bible reflecting Rabbinic tradition, a translation Jews might turn to rather than consult Protestant works such as Michaelis's 1769–85 translation of the Old Testament.[25] Mendelssohn continued to produce minor writings in German during this period, but it was only with his preface to Manasseh ben Israel's *Vindication of the Jews*, the text he issued in 1782 as an "appendix" to Dohm's treatise, that he again assumed a position of prominence in the German public eye. This preface, which signaled his official entry into the sphere of political discourse, avoided all explicit mention of Jesus, but it did offer an elaboration of the polemical position he developed in his response to Lavater. The particular way Mendelssohn subverted dominant views of Jews and Judaism here *without* reference to Jesus, moreover, provoked his contemporaries to challenge him to clarify his relation to Jesus once again, and this inaugurated the public controversy that led to the publication of *Jerusalem*.

According to a letter he wrote to his friend Friedrich Nicolai, the publisher of both Dohm's book and his edition of *Vindication of the Jews*, Mendelssohn produced this text in order to keep alive the debates on Jewish emancipation and prevent the public from losing interest in Dohm's proposals.[26] In the preface itself, however, he hardly limited himself to the role of mediator. He explicitly reformulated Dohm's vision of emancipation, positioning it within an analysis of the new forms of anti-Jewish sentiment he had seen come to light in the wake of Dohm's book. Commenting that religious antagonism toward Jews had certainly not disappeared, Mendelssohn focused his attention here on the emergence of novel secular biases against Jews, moral and cultural attitudes that Jews were innately ill equipped for the duties and responsibilities of citizenship. On one level, he challenged these views by echoing Dohm, arguing that the only reason that Jews may seem unfit for citizenship is that they have for so long been excluded from participating in the common good: "They bind our hands and then reproach us for not using them" (*JubA* 8: 6). But he also issued a subtle critique of Dohm, arguing for the "civic admission" of the Jews rather than their "civic improvement";[27] in insisting that Jews were in need of fundamental moral improvement, Dohm had unwittingly perpetuated the secular prejudices Mendelssohn wanted to combat. Mendelssohn questioned Dohm's view of contemporary Jewry in other respects as well, challenging his distrust of trade and its effects on the Jews' moral character. Entering into a passionate apology for the "middle-men" who keep the economy running, Mendelssohn defended not just the "merchant proper" but also the "most common peddler and buyer" and "the most insignificant wandering Jew" as "benefactors of the state and of the human race" (*JubA* 8: 14–15). Jews, he suggested, were already productive members of civil society and not in need of the occupational restructuring Dohm proposed to improve their character and eradicate their "merchant nature."

Proponents of "reason" and "humanity" like Dohm (*JubA* 8: 4), how-ever, were hardly the enemy here. Anti-Jewish feelings have survived, Mendelssohn indicated, because they are not just about modern Jews, or even about contemporary Europe's relation to modern Jews. In its recently secu-larized form, anti-Jewish prejudice was a crucial component of modern Orientalist scholarship, central to the way in which Europeans had recently come to conceive of the Jews' Oriental heritage. Mendelssohn made this argu-ment in his preface in response to the same anonymous 1781 critique of Dohm in the *Göttingen Reports of Learned Matters* that we discussed briefly in Chapter 1. The author of this essay, the Göttingen philosophy professor Michael Hißmann (1752–84), argued against civic improvement by linking the moral corruption of modern Jews to that of the ancient Israelites and their longing for the "flesh pots of Egypt." Following Michaelis, Hißmann stressed the excessive "national pride" and "religious hatred" fostered by Mosaic law yet argued that these features of ancient Judaism were "wise . . . in that early era of the limitations of social feelings and suitable for a horde of humans that was supposed to become a nation that had to detest the horrors of idolatry." With their continual longings for the "flesh pots" of Egypt, nevertheless, modern Jews have failed to progress beyond the crude morals and primitive social feelings of their Oriental ancestors. Not surprisingly, the Rabbinic tradition is partially responsible for the Jews' retarded maturation, as its excessive concern with the letter of the law has made it difficult for Jews to arrive at the rational, Christian understanding of the higher importance of their ancient religion, that is, "the more proper estimation of the true content of the Mosaic laws as it has been discovered by reason and our Christian teachers."[28]

Mendelssohn responds to Hißmann much as we saw him respond to the Crown Prince of Braunschweig-Wolfenbüttel. Speaking as the object of Orientalist scholarship, he forces Orientalist scholars to reflect back on themselves, using in public the same sort of tone we encountered in his private response to Michaelis:

> He [the reviewer] has no scruples reproaching and blaming us modern Israelites for the bad habits of which our forefathers in the desert were guilty, and he does so without considering that, regardless of all the vices for which he reprimands us, the law-giving God of our fathers—or, as the current fashion would have us say, the legislator Moses—nevertheless found it possible to transform this crude mass into a respectable flourishing nation that has sublime laws and constitution, wise sovereigns, army commanders and judges, and happy citizens to show for itself. Indeed, the author never reflects back on himself to consider the sort of culture his own forefathers in northern wastelands had at the same time—ancestors of those who in our day publish reviews in the *Göttingen Reports*. In a word, reason and humanity raise their voice in vain, for aged prejudice is clearly deaf. (*JubA* 8: 10).

Hißmann is not the sole target of Mendelssohn's attack here. Michaelis, the Göttingen Orientalist responsible for popularizing the "current fashion" of speaking of the "legislator Moses," also published in the *Göttingen Reports* and, indeed, edited the journal from 1753 to 1770 during his tenure as secretary and then director of the Göttingen Royal Society of Sciences. In 1754, more to the point, the *Reports* published Michaelis's review of Lessing's *The Jews*, a one-act comedy he critiqued, in secular terms, for its utterly implausible presentation of a Jew as a "noble" character; one of Mendelssohn's earliest published writings was a letter that expressed amazement at encountering such views in a scholar and accused Michaelis of using his review and his professional position to further "degrade our oppressed nation."[29] When it comes to modernizing "aged prejudice" and promoting secular Jew-hatred, Michaelis and the *Göttingen Reports* have consistently been in the vanguard of innovation. The question that needs to be raised here, Mendelssohn comments ironically, is thus not whether Jews and ancient Israelites but whether Göttingen academics and their ancestors might be innately ill suited for citizenship. Challenging Michaelis's historicist account of the genesis of Mosaic law, Mendelssohn stresses here the divine election and exemplary moral education of ancient Israel, juxtaposing the achievements of the ancient Orient to the primitive prehistory of northern Europeans. In this scenario, it is no longer the modern Occident that debates the regeneration of the descendants of the Israelites. It is the Orient that judges the prejudiced Occident, indicting *it* for its lack of reason and humanity. Anything but a primitive legal system that can be relegated to an Oriental past, ancient Israel emerges here as a normative position from which to judge the German past and present. With its dramatic transformation into a flourishing nation, ancient Israel becomes a timeless model for "civic improvement," one that Germans might do well to imitate.

This is, of course, an ironic passage that seeks to unsettle dominant Christian views of Jews and Judaism; Mendelssohn's goal in the preface is to argue for the "civic admission" of the "modern Israelites," not to establish the political system of their ancient ancestors as an ideal to be imitated in modernity. Indeed, he maintains in *Jerusalem* that the ancient "Mosaic constitution," founded as it was on divine legislation, was absolutely distinct from any form of government that human beings themselves might ever institute (*J* 131; *JubA* 8: 196); Judaism as a politics belongs to the irretrievable past. What matters in the context of the emancipation debates is how Jews—and Christians—conceive of the legacy of Judaism as a religion. It is in this respect that he issues his most forceful revision of Dohm in the preface, putting forth a call for freedom of conscience that far surpasses Dohm's treatise. Anticipating an argument he will flesh out in *Jerusalem*, Mendelssohn insists here that "true, divine religion" is incompatible with "power over opinions and judgments . . . and needs neither arms nor fingers for its use; it is pure spirit and heart" (*JubA* 8: 18). Dohm, we remember, was willing to let Jews retain their corporate autonomy and the right to punish and excommunicate, a move that was due to his understandable mistake of "taking things more as they are than as they should be" (*JubA* 8: 21). Addressing this deficiency, Mendelssohn prescribes a religious-political reform that will *make* contemporary Judaism entirely compatible with freedom of conscience and divest it of all coercive power. Rather than touting the superiority of the politics of ancient Israel, Mendelssohn seeks to reclaim his ancient "Oriental" religion for the Occidental present, and he does so in such a way as to claim agency for Jews in the process of their political emancipation.

The religious reform Mendelssohn calls for here does not represent a compromise with modernity but an attempt to "purify" his ancient religion and restore it to its original form. The outer trappings of contemporary Judaism, characterized as they are by the "iron power" of excommunication, he explains, are less an essential aspect of Judaism than an internalization of

Christian intolerance and persecution: "O, my brothers! You have felt the oppressive yoke of intolerance much too severely up until now and have perhaps believed you find a certain satisfaction in subjecting those subordinate to you to an equally severe yoke" (*JubA* 8: 25). Jews, then, are not just victims of oppression. Their political position has also transformed them into eager perpetrators, making them fall prey to the grand "delusion" of the majority culture that religion needs persecution, oppression and coercion to sustain itself. Jewish communities that allow excommunication and temporal punishment of Jews thus perpetuate prejudices absorbed from their Christian environment that have deformed the original purpose and function of Judaism as a religion. In making the Jews partially responsible for the perversion of their religion into an oppressive political system, Mendelssohn also secures for them the possibility of acting otherwise. Jews need to reform Judaism and purify it of these alien elements, and for Mendelssohn, as for so many Jewish writers who followed him, the purification of Judaism figures as a political act, a way for Jews to participate in their "civic admission." In making reform a part of emancipation, Mendelssohn does not sacrifice Judaism to the majority culture and call for assimilation. He may call on his fellow Jews to imitate the "virtues of the nations" (*JubA* 8: 25), but his goal in doing so is to strip Judaism of its alien Christian elements so as to restore a religion of "tolerance," "mercy" and "love" (ibid.)—a normative vision of Judaism that runs counter to the coercive system of Mosaic law one encounters in Christian scholarship of the period. By seeking to reclaim ancient Judaism as a distinctly modern religion, Mendelssohn disrupts the rigid distinction between Orient and Occident, making the radical claim that Judaism in its original purity is perfectly compatible with the European present. Calling on Jews to practice tolerance among themselves so that they might be tolerated by others, Mendelssohn entreats his coreligionists to serve as an example to the modern world that religion can and must do without the power of coercion. By renouncing temporal power, the Jews will not just give the Christian world, in Judaism, the perfect example of a true religion; they will also be demonstrating the need for freedom of conscience, and the need for a secular state that might admit Jews without subjecting them, as Jews, to civic improvement.

Presented in this manner, Judaism is no longer the political system Orientalists relegate to the historical past but a religion whose purification by Jews can serve as a model for the modern distinction between church and state. No longer the primitive, superseded origin of the West, the Orient apparently contains an archetype for liberty of conscience that needs to become the foundation stone for the politics of modernity. An argument like this was clearly destined to provoke opposition, not least of all because Mendelssohn's vision of Judaism as a religion of love devoid of temporal authority sounded to many of his contemporaries more like Christianity than anything they were ready to identify with biblical or Rabbinic Judaism. Indeed, when August Friedrich Cranz openly challenged Mendelssohn in his anonymous 1782 pamphlet *The Searching for Light and Right*, he zoned in on precisely this aspect of his argument. Judaism, Cranz insisted, was at its core a system of "armed ecclesiastical law" (quoted in *JubA* 8: 80) that could never be purified or modernized to become compatible with freedom of conscience. Expressing pleasure that Mendelssohn seemed ready to destroy the "cornerstone" of Judaism's "theocratic form of government" and abandon the coercive system of "Jewish ecclesiastical law," Cranz claimed that Mendelssohn's desire to "purify" Judaism amounted to a decisive step toward Christianity (*JubA* 8: 77–78).

The subversive elements of Mendelssohn's preface could thus easily be misread as a step toward Christian universalism; from the beginning, Mendelssohn's act of resistance allowed itself to be neutralized by precisely that view of Judaism it sought to combat. In his open letter to Mendelssohn, not surprisingly, Cranz renewed Lavater's call for conversion, assuming that Mendelssohn was already leaving behind the Orient to embrace the emancipatory message of Jesus:

> Is it possible that the remarkable step you have now taken could actually be a step toward the fulfillment of the wishes which Lavater formerly addressed to you? After that appeal, you must undoubtedly have reflected further on the subject of Christianity, and, with your sharp spirit of examination and the impartiality of an incorruptible searcher after truth, weighed more exactly the value of the Christian systems of religion which lie before your eyes in manifold forms and modifications. Perhaps you have now come closer to the faith of the Christians, having torn yourself from the servitude of iron churchly bonds, and having commenced teaching the liberal system of a more rational worship of God, which constitutes the true character of the Christian religion, thanks to which we have escaped coercion and burdensome ceremonies, and thanks to which we no longer link the true worship of God either to Samaria or Jerusalem, but see the essence of religion, in the words of our teacher, wherever the true adorers of God pray in spirit and in truth. (*JubA* 8: 81)[30]

Cranz responds to Mendelssohn's purification of Judaism, then, by positioning Mosaic law within a familiar account of Christian origins. In this scenario, Christianity emancipates itself from the "servitude" of Judaism's "iron churchly bonds," instituting a "liberal" and "more rational" worship of God that marks the antithesis of Judaism's geographical fixation on Jerusalem and the ancient Orient. Quoting John 4: 23, Cranz casts Jesus not as a Jew but as the teacher who emancipates human beings from the bondage of Mosaic law to inaugurate a rational, liberal and universal religion for the world. Viewed in this framework, Mendelssohn's call for the purification of Judaism *has* to mark a step toward Christianity, for in preaching a religion of love and freedom that overcomes the rigid legal system Orientalists find in Judaism, Mendelssohn is doing nothing less than following the example of the founder of Christianity. It is not Judaism but Jesus's emancipation from Judaism that gives the modern state its model for freedom of conscience.

In *Jerusalem*, Mendelssohn explicitly engages with the way in which Cranz neutralizes and coopts his vision of a purified Judaism, and it is here that he deals once again with the issue of Jesus, ultimately appropriating the founder of Christianity as an exemplary Jewish reformer, a polemicist for Jewish emancipation and a critic of Christianity's religious and political power. Before moving into our discussion of *Jerusalem*, however, we need to consider one further aspect of Cranz's polemics, the way he himself forces Mendelssohn into the position of Jesus. Toward the beginning of his pamphlet he makes an explicit parallel between Moses Mendelssohn and his biblical namesake:

Moses—the law-giver of the Jews and of the Christian Church that derives from this oldest of all faiths—once spoke to his people with a veiled countenance because, according to tradition, the children of Israel could not bear the brilliance of his face. In the epoch of the so-called new covenant the Christians believed they saw Moses with an uncovered countenance. This figurative mode of presentation means nothing more than that there was a time when the eyes of still unenlightened nations could not yet bear the complete pure truth, and that another time came when one dared to gaze more sharply into the sun and believed one was strong enough to deal with language more purely, to throw off the cover and teach in an unmasked manner what one earlier clothed in hieroglyphics and veiled more than halfway in figurative modes of presentation.

When the indiscreet Lavater misused what you told him in private in order to bring you to a confession of your true heartfelt opinions about Christianity, which he thought you were favoring, you also held a cover before your countenance and answered him from behind a curtain that did not allow us to see you entirely. . . . The situation is different now. You yourself have publicly given great occasion for us rightfully to expect and even demand more thorough explanations from you. You yourself stepped forth from behind the curtain without a mask for one moment with a brilliant gaze of truth. . . . In your previous response to Lavater you claimed, always in very general and thus indefinite expressions, your devotion to the faith of your fathers. At the time you did not explain to us what you actually understood by the faith of your fathers. The essence of the Christian religion is also the faith of your fathers, passed on to us, purified of the statutes of burdensome Rabbis, and augmented by new elements which are all derived from the faith of your fathers and are explained as the fulfillment of Old Testament prophecies. (*JubA* 8: 75–77)

The tradition Cranz invokes here—the figure, in 2 Corinthians 3: 12–18, of Jesus lifting the "veil" of Moses alluded to in Exodus 34: 33—is of course one of the prominent ways in which the New Testament constructs itself as prefigured in the Old, one of the tools by which Christianity has traditionally argued for its supersession of Judaism. The problem with Jews, according to this tradition, is that they continue to understand scripture literally, mistaking Moses's veil for what it concealed and thus blocking themselves off from the truth and brilliance of Jesus. Cranz here does not merely equate this process of illumination with Enlightenment. He also forces Mendelssohn, one of the preeminent philosophers of the Enlightenment, into the positions of both Moses and Jesus, entreating him to reenact Christianity's original supersession of Mosaic law and forgo the "unenlightened" Judaism he seems to profess. In contrast to Lavater, Cranz feels justified in putting Mendelssohn on the spot, as Mendelssohn himself has already begun to speak in "veils" and publicly play Moses, as it were, using deliberately ambivalent language that reveals moments of Christ-like "brilliance" at the same time as it seems to vindicate an "unenlightened" adherence to the antiquated laws of Moses. The task Cranz assigns Mendelssohn, accordingly, is merely to complete the work of enlightenment, to cast off obscure figurative language to embrace Jesus's purification, abrogation and fulfillment of Mosaic law. It is, we shall see, precisely this challenge Mendelssohn answers in his *Jerusalem*.

REIMARUS, JESUS AND THE THREAT OF "JEWISH" HISTORICISM

Dohm may have made little mention of Jesus in *On the Civic Improvement of the Jews*, but the debates unleashed by his treatise ultimately forced Mendelssohn to clarify his relationship to Jesus once again. Cranz's renewal of Lavater's challenge, nevertheless, differed considerably from the controversy of 1769–71. Unfolding within political debates over granting Jews rights, Mendelssohn's *Jerusalem* would bring to the foreground the political ramifications of his strategy of appropriating Jesus as a Jew—precisely that which his public writings during the Lavater affair had tended to gloss over. Even more fundamental, however, was the shift in the theological atmosphere in the decade between Mendelssohn's final letter to Lavater and the appearance of Cranz's pamphlet. The publication of Michaelis's *Mosaic Law* in 1770–75 helped launch, legitimize and popularize historically oriented scholarship on the Hebrew Bible and transform Old Testament criticism into an investigation into the politics and culture of ancient Israel. At the time of Lavater's provocation, the New Testament had yet to be subjected to the same level of historical-critical scrutiny. It was one thing to regard Judaism as a legal system bound to the Oriental past, another thing entirely to reflect on the extent to which Christianity might be a product of such local historical circumstances. Since the late seventeenth century, to be sure, there had been a long tradition among deists and their followers of challenging the credibility of scripture and reconceptualizing Christianity as a rational religion stripped of supernatural elements such as Jesus's divinity and resurrection. A historical-critical approach to the New Testament with an interest in reconstructing the life of the historical Jesus, however, did not emerge in Germany until much later, not until the controversial piece "On the Purpose of Jesus and His Disciples" that Lessing published in 1778 as the last of the excerpts from a work whose authorship he kept a careful secret: Reimarus's *Apology for the Rational Worshippers of God.*[31]

Hermann Samuel Reimarus (1694–1768) was a professor of Oriental languages at a Hamburg *Gymnasium* best known during his lifetime for *The Most Eminent Truths of Natural Religion* (1754), an influential defense of rational religion that was translated into Dutch, English and French and underwent several printings in German in the eighteenth century.[32] In this work, Reimarus insisted on the compatibility of rational religion with Christianity, putting forth a vision of reason's harmonious coexistence with revealed religion that the 4,000 intentionally unpublished pages of his *Apology* brazenly dismantled at almost every turn. Inheriting the suspicion toward the text of scripture inaugurated by Spinoza and the radical deists, Reimarus subjected both the Old and New Testaments to rigorous scrutiny with the aim of discrediting their claims to contain a coherent revealed religion and a reliable account of the historical record. In the section of the *Apology* dedicated to Jesus and his disciples, Reimarus critiqued the teachings of the apostles about the life and purpose of Christ by juxtaposing them to his historical reconstruction of the life of Jesus. It was this methodological move that distinguished his work from the arguments of his deist precursors. Jesus was, Reimarus claimed, not the founder of a new religion but a Jew preaching within Judaism who never wanted to abolish the law, a Jewish messenger of rationalist morality and tolerance. In presenting himself as the son of God and announcing the imminent kingdom of God, for instance, Jesus was not proclaiming a universalist revelation or making any sort of metaphysical claims.

He was speaking to a Jewish audience, who understood his message within the context of first-century messianic movements as a mission to seek deliverance from political oppression and establish a worldly kingdom for the Jews. Early Christianity, Reimarus contended, had its origins thus not in Jesus but in the work of his disciples, more specifically in the underhand and disingenuous tactics they resorted to when confronted with his unexpected death and crucifixion. Jesus himself never spoke about suffering and dying, so his death caught his followers by surprise. Suddenly finding themselves without a leader, his disciples stole and hid his body so as to invent the myth of resurrection and predict his return, all of which was made possible by the Jewish apocalyptic traditions of the day. Viewed in this context, Christianity and Christian dogma mark an obvious betrayal of Jesus, a fraudulent tradition rooted in internal conflicts in first-century Judaism.

Reimarus's goal in insisting on Jesus's Jewishness, of course, was not to promote Judaism but to attack Christianity and pave the way for pure rational religion, and Lessing's publication of the *Anonymous Fragments* from 1774 to 1778 unleashed an enormous controversy among theologians and state authorities. After the release of the fragment on Jesus and his disciples, indeed, Lessing was forced to turn in the complete manuscript of the *Apology* to the authorities and submit all his further writings on religion to close censorship. A complete discussion of this controversy and its reception in nineteenth-century New Testament scholarship lies beyond the scope of this book; tracing the role the shock of the Reimarus fragments played in launching the Protestant interest in the historical Jesus would take us too far afield.[33] There are, however, two contemporary responses to Reimarus's historical critique of Christianity that need to be explored here, as they provide a crucial context for *Jerusalem*'s presentation of Jesus. The first of these, a piece seminal for the development of "liberal theology," is Johann Salomo Semler's *Reply to the Anonymous Fragments, particularly that on the Purpose of Jesus and His Disciples* (1779).[34] Semler (1725–91), a distinguished theologian at the University of Halle, followed Reimarus's attempt to position Jesus within first-century messianism; like Reimarus, Semler stressed Jesus's Jewish context and offered an historical reconstruction of Jesus's life. At the same time, he also set limits to Reimarus's historicism. Emphasizing Jesus's break with the Jews' narrow nationalism and his investment of the law with transcendent spirituality, he rigorously separated the historical Jesus from the divinity of Christ. What ultimately mattered for Semler was the transcendent "spiritual power," not Jesus's historical relation to Judaism, and the latter became significant only insofar as it could be used to demonstrate the former.

Lessing offered a different response to Reimarus but one that similarly qualified his profane treatment of Christian origins. Lessing's goal in publishing the fragments was not to give unequivocal support to Reimarus but to lay the ground for his own attempt to salvage the concept of revelation apart from the question of its historical foundation as transmitted by scripture—a position that the Lutheran orthodoxy of the day found equally unacceptable. Lessing, importantly, did not challenge Reimarus's account of the historical record. He did, however, shift the emphasis of the debate away from the question of the historical credibility of the Bible. In *The Education of the Human Race* (1780), the first section of which he published in 1777 as a rejoinder to Reimarus's diatribes against the Old Testament, Lessing redefined revelation as a human capacity for religion that needed to be understood historically, as part of humanity's progressive development toward pure, rational religion. Rather than conceiving of rational religion and revelation as potentially or necessarily at odds with each other, Lessing viewed them as interrelated over time. "Revelation," he claimed, "gives the human race nothing that human reason would not discover if left to itself: but it gave and gives humanity the most important of these things only earlier."[35] In this way, he both justified revealed religion and limited its claims to absolute truth, displacing the very question of its credibility. Indeed, Lessing had as little interest in "who the person of this Christ was" as in the resurrection and miracles ascribed to him;[36] Jesus's Jewishness and other aspects of his historical existence were irrelevant in this context. Jesus was important neither as a Jew nor as the divine Christ but as the "first reliable practical teacher of the immortality of the soul," a human being who gave the Jews and eventually the rest of humanity a religious doctrine that far surpassed the "primer" of the Old Testament.[37] Unlike Reimarus, Lessing had no need to denigrate Judaism and Christianity and reject their truth claims. Proposing a philosophy of history in place of Reimarus's historicism, he interpreted Judaism and Christianity as successive stages in the education of the human race, with Christianity able to be overcome by pure rational religion just as it had once superseded the primitive and childlike understanding of God characteristic of ancient Judaism.

In his 1779 drama *Nathan the Wise*, Lessing presented Judaism, Christianity and Islam as having potentially equal access to the truths of rational religion, articulating a static view of the relationship between Judaism, Christianity and rational religion that his progressivist philosophy of history clearly repudiated. In *Jerusalem*, not surprisingly, Mendelssohn—the model for the title figure of *Nathan*—critiqued the triumphalism of Lessing's recasting of Christian supersessionism in *The Education of the Human Race*, arguing against such historical master-narratives that inevitably situated Judaism in the primitive past: "I, for my part, cannot conceive of the education of the human race as my late friend Lessing imagined it under the influence of I-don't-know-which historian of mankind. One pictures the collective entity of the human race as an individual person and believes that Providence sent it to school here on earth, in order to raise it from childhood to manhood. In reality, the human race is—if the metaphor is appropriate—in almost every century, child, adult, and old man at the same time, though in different places and regions of the world" (*J* 95–96; *JubA* 8: 162). Rejecting Lessing's global philosophy of progress in favor of an appreciation of the individuality of particular cultures and religions—a position reminiscent of his writings during the Lavater affair—Mendelssohn issued a challenge to the prominent tendency in eighteenth-century thought to dissolve historical particularity in teleological views of history that inevitably celebrated the European Enlightenment. Rather than a thinker who lacked an appreciation of the eighteenth century's nascent interest in history, Mendelssohn thus needs to be seen, as Edward Breuer has suggested, as a significant critic of the "epistemological implications of progressive historicism" and the often "self-serving triumphalism of the Enlightenment."[38]

This frequently quoted critique of Lessing is not the only section of *Jerusalem* that engages with the issues brought up by the controversy over the Reimarus fragments. In his defense of Judaism as a "revealed legislation," to be sure, there is little that reflects Remarus's skepticism toward tradition. Mendelssohn deals with the question of the reliability of historical transmission cursorily here, claiming that the "credibility" of the "narrator" of the "historical truth" of the revelation at Sinai is simply beyond dispute (*J* 93; *JubA* 8: 160). In this respect, as Arkush has demonstrated, Mendelssohn dodges rather than engages with the issues raised by Reimarus, most obviously his claim that the Old Testament was never intended to reveal a religion.[39] Here and elsewhere, Sorkin has argued, Mendelssohn is "historical without being historicist: he acknowledges history in the Pentateuch rather than the Pentateuch as a product of history."[40] Mendelssohn resists the historicism of his peers, Sorkin points out, by taking refuge in arguments typical of the religious enlightenment of the 1730s and 1740s; there is nothing in Mendelssohn's *oeuvre* that approaches the type of textual criticism being propagated at the time by Johann Gottfried Eichhorn's *Introduction to the Old Testament* (1780–83).[41] Eichhorn, an Orientalist trained by Michaelis, stressed the corruption of the original biblical text and the need for historical reconstruction and correction, a position diametrically opposed to Mendelssohn's refusal to challenge the authority of Jewish oral traditions. For Mendelssohn, the credibility of the Hebrew Bible and its account of the revelation at Sinai simply stand beyond question; history can be used to support this revelation but not to challenge it.

For Mendelssohn's contemporaries, however, it was Reimarus's devastating critique of the New Testament that posed the most immediate affront to their religious sensibilities; disparaging views of the Old Testament were nothing new in the 1770s. If we approach *Jerusalem* as a work that deals not just with Judaism but with the role of Jesus in delimiting the relationship between Judaism and Christianity, Mendelssohn's involvement with the theological concerns of his Christian peers comes more clearly into focus. In many ways, *Jerusalem*'s vision of Jesus as a Jew who never intended to abolish the law clearly derives from a variety of Christian and Jewish sources that all were available to Mendelssohn during and before the Lavater affair: the writings of the English deists, who were of great importance to Reimarus as well, the work of Jacob Emden, and, of course, Mendelssohn's own reading of the New Testament. *Jerusalem*, indeed, never refers explicitly to "On the Purpose of Jesus," other of the Reimarus fragments or Semler's attempt to rehabilitate the divinity of Christ; the critique of Lessing's philosophy of history is the only passage that expressly alludes to the Reimarus controversy. Appearing in the aftermath of the uproar over the fragment on Jesus and his disciples, however, Mendelssohn's appropriation of Jesus as a Jew inevitably participated in the larger controversy over the historical Jesus raging in Protestant theological discourse of the period, and it needs to be understood in this context as well.

From the beginning of the turmoil caused by the fragments, Mendelssohn was never far from the center of controversy. He was one of the few contemporaries to have the opportunity to read Reimarus's *Apology* in its entirety; Lessing showed him the text in Wolfenbüttel in October 1770—four years before any of it was published—and he allowed him at that point to take the *Apology* back to Berlin with him to read through at his convenience.[42] In the minds of many of his contemporaries, even more significantly, the challenge of historicism that the fragments issued to orthodox Christianity constituted a "Jewish" attempt to slander Christianity and its founder, and this put Mendelssohn, Lessing's friend and the foremost Jewish figure of his generation, once again in a conspicuously vulnerable predicament. One view circulating through the rumor mill, in fact, held that the Jewish community of Amsterdam had paid Lessing 1,000 ducats to publish these slanderous fragments.[43] In his prominent polemics against Lessing, the orthodox Hamburg pastor Johann Melchior Goeze argued on a different level but supported a similar view of the "Jewish" function of the fragments. Goeze sought to dismiss the fragment on Jesus and his disciples by representing Reimarus's historicist critique of the New Testament as a continuation of medieval traditions of Jewish rewritings of the Gospels. "The Jews," he wrote, "will welcome the last fragment in particular. By confirming them in their unbelief and hostility toward Jesus and his religion, it will be more useful to them than even their *Toledoth Yeshu*."[44] In a move reminiscent of the Lavater affair, Goeze here claims Jesus as the founder of Christianity by denigrating Jews, and by branding Reimarus's historicism as a "Jewish" rebellion against Christian doctrine. There was, not surprisingly, one Jewish writer whose name frequently came up in the widespread speculations over the authorship of this modern-day *Toledoth Yeshu*: Mendelssohn.[45]

Appearing in this atmosphere, *Jerusalem* clearly does more than respond to Cranz's challenge to embrace Jesus's abrogation and fulfillment of the law. It also negotiates a position for Mendelssohn in the debates on the historical Jesus, staking out a Jewish appropriation of Jesus that speaks to the more general theological and political challenges of the day. Building on the attention Reimarus and Semler gave Jesus's Jewish historical context, Mendelssohn claims for Jesus a position of prominence in *Jewish* history, ultimately assigning him the task of that purification of Judaism alluded to in the preface to *Vindication of the Jews*. In this way, he neutralizes some of the more explosive claims made by Reimarus at the same time as he confronts contemporary Christian resistance toward Reimarus's "Jewish" appropriation of Jesus, thereby challenging the attempts of Semler, Lessing and Cranz to reinstate traditional scenarios of Jesus's supersession of Judaism. Like Reimarus, for instance, Mendelssohn stresses the disparity between Jesus's teachings and those of his disciples, who "without his authority . . . believed they could release from the law also those Jews who accepted their teachings" (*J* 134; *JubA* 8: 199). Mendelssohn's Jesus, however, is hardly the messianic revolutionary of the Reimarus fragments. He emerges instead, as we shall see, as a quiet reformer, a theorist of the proper relationship between church and state who restores Judaism to its original purity and secures it its proper place within—and ultimately as a model for—modernity.

DE-ORIENTALIZING JUDAISM

Cranz's interpretation of Mendelssohn's call for the purification of Judaism as a gesture toward Jesus's invalidation of the law did not go unnoticed. Mendelssohn challenged Cranz directly in *Jerusalem*, presenting Judaism as the antithesis of the primitive legal system of "iron churchly bonds" whose historical mission was exhausted by its prefiguration of Jesus's emancipatory universalist message. Quoting Cranz back to himself, he argued that Judaism constitutes the indispensable foundation for Christianity, and as such, its status in modernity has to be more than that of a historical curiosity. Judaism has enduring value of its own, and its continued existence is actually essential to Christianity:

> If it be true that the cornerstones of my house are dislodged, and the structure threatens to collapse, do I act wisely if I remove my belongings

from the lower to the upper floor for safety? Am I more secure there?
Now Christianity, as you know, is built upon Judaism, and if the latter
falls, it must necessarily collapse with it into *one* heap of ruins. You say
that my conclusions undermine the foundation of Judaism, and you offer
me the safety of your upper floor; must I not suppose that you mock me?
(*J* 87; *JubA* 8: 154)

In arguing against ecclesiastical law and for liberty of conscience in his
preface, then, Mendelssohn was not merely laying forth the spirit of Judaism
is its original pristine form. He was also presenting his vision of a purified
Judaism as central to Christianity, stressing the extent to which Christianity
is itself historically and essentially derived from Judaism. Challenging Cranz,
who celebrated Jesus's emancipation from Judaism as a primal moment
of modernity, Mendelssohn presents Christianity as a mere addendum to
Judaism.

But what exactly does Christianity build upon its Jewish foundation?
Echoing an argument made in his open letter to Lavater, Mendelssohn insists
that Judaism is not a revealed religion but a revealed "legislation" entirely
compatible with rational religion, and it is precisely this harmonious coexistence of revelation and reason that Christianity *betrays* in its doctrinal departure from its parent religion. Indeed, the "characteristic difference" between
Judaism and Christianity is that whereas the revealed legislation of Judaism
lays forth rules of conduct—"laws, commandments, ordinances, rules of life,
instruction in the will of God as to how they should conduct themselves in
order to attain temporal and eternal felicity"—Christianity prescribes doctrines, truths or dogmas necessarily for salvation (*J* 89–90; *JubA* 8: 156–57).
Unlike Christianity, Judaism allows Jews and human beings all over the globe
to arrive at the eternal truths of religion through the power of reason. "According to the concepts of true Judaism, all the inhabitants of the earth are destined to felicity; and the means of attaining it are as widespread as mankind
itself" (*J* 94; *JubA* 8: 161). With its insistence on the universality of the original revelation it ascribes to Jesus, however, Christianity betrays the tolerance
that is its Jewish heritage, instituting religious dogma that seeks to displace
both the diverse manifestations of global religion and the universality of
rational religion. It is, Mendelssohn implies, not Judaism but Christianity that
uses "iron churchly bonds," prescribing beliefs and dogmas that stand in the
way of human beings' natural proclivity toward rational religious inquiry. As
a supplement to Judaism, Christianity always seeks to supplant Judaism and
all other religions, and it does so here, as in the Lavater affair, by sending missionaries to the "two Indies" to bring them a "gospel without which they can
. . . live neither virtuously nor happily," to "bring them a message which, in

their circumstances and state of knowledge, they can neither rightly comprehend nor properly utilize" (*J* 94; *JubA* 8: 161).

Presented in this manner, it makes sense that Christianity should seek to
discredit that religion that is its historical foundation. Indeed, denigration of
Judaism seems in this context just as natural as colonial expansion. Both are
means of realizing Christianity's universality and underlining its originality;
both serve to establish its absolute priority over Judaism and all other religions. For Christianity, the question of its historical relation to Judaism is
always potentially explosive, one Mendelssohn deals with in the remainder
of *Jerusalem* by repositioning the issue of Christian origins within a sketch of
Jewish history. Let us consider, for instance, how Mendelssohn presents what
he calls the "basic outlines of ancient, original Judaism":

> Although the divine book that we received through Moses is, strictly
> speaking, meant to be a book of laws containing ordinances, rules of life
> and prescriptions, it also includes, as is well known, an inexhaustible
> treasure of rational truths and religious doctrines which are so intimately
> connected with the laws that they form but one entity. All laws refer to,
> or are based upon, eternal truths of reason, or remind us of them, and
> rouse us to ponder them. Hence, our rabbis rightly say: the laws and doc-
> trines are related to each other, like body and soul. . . . The experience
> of many centuries also teaches that this divine law book has become, for
> a large part of the human race, a source of insight from which it draws
> new ideas, or according to which it corrects old ones. . . . [L]aws cannot
> be abridged. In them everything is fundamental; and in this regard we
> may rightly say: to us, all words of Scripture, all of God's commandments
> and prohibitions are fundamental. Should you, nevertheless, want to
> obtain their quintessence, listen to how that greater teacher of the nation,
> Hillel the Elder, who lived before the destruction of the second Temple,
> conducted himself in this matter. A heathen said: "Rabbi, teach me the
> entire law while I am standing on one foot!" Shammai, whom he had
> previously approached with the same unreasonable request, had dis-
> missed him contemptuously; but Hillel, renowned for his imperturbable
> composure and gentleness, said: "Son, *love thy neighbor as thyself.* This is
> the text of the law; all the rest is commentary." (*J* 99–102; *JubA* 8:
> 165–68).

This passage rehearses Mendelssohn's well-known argument that Mosaic law
helps lead Jews—and others—toward the truths of rational religion, truths
which are resistant to codification in "symbolic books" or "articles of faith"
as practiced by Christianity (*J* 100; *JubA* 8: 167). But Mendelssohn also claims
for Mosaic law a special position in the history of religion here, highlighting
once again the way in which Judaism serves as the foundation for

Christianity. Undermining the claim that the commandment of neighborly love marks an innovation of Christianity, he presents neighborly love as the soul of Mosaic Judaism, a Jewish principle of conduct that Jews began to disseminate among non-Jews a generation before the birth of Jesus. In this context, Jesus does not preach a religion of love that overcomes the coercive system of Mosaic law. The founder of Christianity figures here as but a latter-day Hillel; like Hillel, Jesus works within Mosaic law to teach the original essence of ancient Judaism.

In many ways, however, Mendelssohn's Jesus does more than echo Hillel. In *Jerusalem*, Jesus disseminates the doctrine of neighborly love in a particular historical context, one that underscores Mendelssohn's own concerns with fixing the boundaries between religion and politics and reconceptualizing Judaism as a religion devoid of all coercive power. For Mendelssohn, speaking of Judaism as a system of "ecclesiastical law" as Cranz does is blatantly anachronistic; in its inception, the "Mosaic constitution" was not "a hierocracy, an ecclesiastical government, a priestly state, [or] a theocracy," but a form of politics that has existed only once in the history of the world, a form of politics that did not yet even know the separation between church and state (*J* 131; *JubA* 8: 196). Like any politics, of course, the Mosaic constitution was not without coercive power, but following Mendelssohn's own political norms, it always punished actions alone; never did it seek to control the realm of conscience. Ancient Israel was thus not ruled by the brute force of ecclesiastical law; indeed, the "king" of the Mosaic commonwealth was God himself, who consistently showed not his wrath but his benevolence, love and grace to the ancient Israelites (*J* 122–23; *JubA* 8: 187–88). For Mendelssohn here, however, as in his preface to *Vindication of the Jews*, the political dimensions of ancient Judaism are of limited significance for modernity. What matters most about Judaism's original existence as a political commonwealth is its historical degeneration and, subsequently, its ability to be transformed and purified into a religion devoid of temporal power.

As early as the days of the prophet Samuel, Mendelssohn points out, the Israelites were demanding a human king, and this shift began to disrupt the original unity of state and religion. As a result, a conflict of duties between religion and politics gradually became possible, a situation that was subsequently exacerbated by the destruction of the Second Temple and the suspension of all those aspects of the law that were national in intent: "The civil bonds of the nation were dissolved; religious offenses were no longer crimes against the state; and the religion, as religion, knows of no punishment, no other penalty than the one the remorseful sinner *voluntarily* imposes on himself. It knows of no coercion, uses only the staff [called] *gentleness*, and affects only mind and heart" (*J* 130; *JubA* 8: 195–96). A Judaism that was no longer going to exist as a politics desperately needed to clarify its pristine essence as a religion, and it is here that Jesus enters on the scene, issuing a proclamation for religious reform:

> But let one follow history through all sorts of vicissitudes and changes, through many good and bad, God-fearing and godless regimes, down to that sad period in which the founder of the Christian religion gave this cautious advice: *Render unto Caesar that which is Caesar's and unto God what is God's.* Manifest opposition, a collision of duties! The state was under foreign dominion, and received its orders from foreign gods, as it were, while the native religion still survived, retaining a part of its influence on civil life. Here is demand against demand, claim against claim. "To whom shall we give? Whom shall we obey?" Bear both burdens—went the advice—as well as you can; serve two masters with patience and devotion. Give to Caesar, and give to God too! To each his own, since the unity of interests is now destroyed. (*J* 132–33; *JubA* 8: 197–98)

In citing Matthew 22: 32 here, Mendelssohn is not merely speaking the language of the dominant culture, choosing an example with which Christian authorities will be able to identify.[46] Echoing Spinoza, who presented Jesus's teachings as moral doctrines distinct from the laws of the state, Mendelssohn appropriates Jesus as a Jewish theorist of the separation of church and state. For Mendelssohn here, however—and this marks a departure from Spinoza—the "founder of the Christian religion" is a Jew who purifies the "native religion" of Roman Palestine into its religious aspects and sets it in a clear relationship to politics as something external to Judaism. Matthew 22: 32 represents thus not the beginning of a new religion but the crystallization of the religious elements of Judaism, the end of the degeneration of the original Mosaic constitution and the beginning of Jewish religious regeneration.

For Cranz, Jesus's abrogation of the law marked a primal moment of modernity, the very model for freedom of conscience. For Mendelssohn, Jesus also sets up political norms, but he does so working entirely within Judaism, and without ever releasing Jews from the law:

> Jesus of Nazareth was never heard to say that he had come to release the House of Jacob from the law. Indeed, he said, in express words, rather the opposite; and, what is still more, he himself did the opposite. Jesus of Nazareth himself observed not only the law of Moses but also the ordinances of the rabbis; and whatever seems to contradict this in the speeches and acts ascribed to him appears to do so only at first glance. Closely examined, everything is in complete agreement not only with Scripture, but also with the tradition. If he came to remedy entrenched hypocrisy and sanctimoniousness, he surely would not have given the

first example of sanctimoniousness and authorized, by example, a law which should be abrogated and abolished. Rather, the rabbinic principle evidently shines forth from his entire conduct as well as the conduct of his disciples in the early period. *He who is not born into the law need not bind himself to the law; but he who is born into the law must live according to the law, and die according to the law.* If his followers, in later times, thought differently and believed they could release from the law also those Jews who accepted their teaching, this surely happened without his authority. (*J* 134; *JubA* 8: 199)

Here, as in the Lavater affair, the figure of Jesus is deployed in order to authorize the continued existence of Judaism and challenge triumphant narratives of Christian supersessionism. In his review of *Jerusalem* in his *Oriental and Exegetical Library*, not surprisingly, Michaelis took issue with this passage, disagreeing with Mendelssohn's portrayal of Jesus as an exemplar of the Rabbinic principle and reinstating the scenario presented in his *Mosaic Law* of a clean break between Judaism and Christianity.[47] Challenging Michaelis's historical containment of Judaism and invoking a picture reminiscent of the Reimarus fragments, Mendelssohn presents both Jesus and his disciples as mere extensions of Jewish tradition. Christianity here is merely something added on to Jesus's Judaism, a revealed religion constructed after the fact that rewrites and betrays Jesus's essentially Jewish message.

What, then, is Jesus's message, and for whom is it ultimately intended? Cranz, we remember, juxtaposed Judaism's fixation on the Orient to Christians' ability to "see the essence of religion, in the words of our teacher, wherever the true adorers of God pray in spirit and in truth." Mendelssohn responds to this charge by appropriating the words of Jesus to legitimize the mission of Judaism to the nations and emphasize the continued relevance of Mosaic law apart from its Oriental culture and climate of origin. Jesus becomes here the spokesman for the Jewish Diaspora:

Give to Caesar, and give to God too! To each his own, since the unity of interests is now destroyed.

And even today, no wiser advice than this can be given to the House of Jacob. Adapt yourselves to the customs and the constitution of the land to which you have been removed; but hold fast to the religion of your fathers too. Bear both burdens as well as you can! It is true that, on the one hand, the burden of civil life is made heavier for you on account of the religion to which you remain faithful, and, on the other hand, the climate and the times make the observance of your religious laws in some respects more irksome than they are. Nevertheless, persevere; remain unflinchingly at the post which Providence has assigned to you, and endure everything that happens to you as your lawgiver foretold long ago.

In fact, I cannot see how those born into the House of Jacob can in any conscientious manner disencumber themselves of the law. We are permitted to reflect on the law, to inquire into its spirit, and, here and there, where the lawgiver gave no reason, to surmise a reason which, *perhaps*, depended upon time, place, and circumstances, and which, *perhaps*, may be liable to change in accordance with time, place, and circumstance—if it pleases the Supreme Lawgiver to make known to us His will on this matter, to make it known in as clear a voice, in as public a manner, and as far beyond all doubt and ambiguity as He did when He gave the law itself. As long as this has not happened, as long as we can point to no such authentic exemption from the law, no sophistry of ours can free us from the strict obedience we owe to the law. . . . (*J* 133; *JubA* 8: 199)

With his conception of the proper relationship between church and state, Jesus offers Jews the perfect ideology for the age of emancipation, one that upholds orthodox observance of Jewish ritual law at the same time as it encourages Jews to enter European cultural and political life. Challenging the vision of Judaism as an antiquated legal system inextricably bound to the ancient Near East, Mendelssohn claims a positive mission for the Jewish Diaspora here, and he does so with the authorization of Jesus himself. In this context, the significance of Mosaic law clearly cannot be explained in terms of the categories of Michaelis's biblical scholarship. For Mendelssohn, regarding Mosaic law solely as the product of its time, place and circumstance of origin fails to account for the ongoing significance ascribed to it by none less than Jesus himself; this amounts to little more than sophistry. In its purified form as articulated by Jesus, Judaism is anything but an "Oriental" legal system that can be juxtaposed to Christian universalism. Challenging the strategy by which modern biblical scholarship seeks to contain Judaism within its view of the ancient Orient, Mendelssohn de-Orientalizes Judaism, presenting it as a religion equally well suited for any place Jews happen to reside in the Diaspora, a religion perfectly compatible with the modern secular state. By doing so, Mendelssohn obviously calls for a certain degree of cultural and political assimilation. But Mendelssohn here hardly capitulates to the norms of the majority culture. He unsettles, rather, the very opposition between Orient and Occident; Judaism for Mendelssohn is neither strictly Oriental nor European but both—and thus also neither. When it comes to the realm of religion, Mendelssohn's vision of Judaism is hardly accommodating to its Christian environment. *Jerusalem* argues for Jewish emancipation by offering up a vision of the Jewish Jesus that is unsettling to contemporary Protestant theological discourse on Judaism *and* Christianity, a vision of the Jewish Jesus that seeks to discredit contemporary attempts to reinstate traditional narratives of Christianity's triumph over the Oriental religion of its alleged founder.

ROME AND JERUSALEM REVISITED

When Mendelssohn wrote to Dohm that Christians had become world conquerors, oppressors and slave traders despite the doctrine of their founder,
then, he was stressing the disparity between Christian actions and Christian
doctrine. But he was also setting the project of Christian imperialism in opposition to the universal, global tolerance he claimed as Jesus's Jewish legacy,
presenting Judaism as antithetical to colonial expansion. Judaism as it is
taught by Mendelssohn's Jesus, indeed, is incompatible with any form of
temporal power; nothing could be further from the spirit of true religion as
Mendelssohn envisions it than attempts to convert subject peoples and intervene into the realm of conscience. In expanding their domain to the East and
West Indies, Christian states betray rather than disseminate the teachings of
Jesus, using their political power in a manner that directly contradicts Jesus's
Jewish doctrine of neighborly love and mutual respect. Seen in this way,
Christianity's aspirations toward universality lead to the destruction of both
the universal truths of rational religion and religious diversity all over the
globe, legitimizing the twin projects of colonial expansion and the political
subjugation of European Jews.

Mendelssohn thus appropriates Jesus as an anti-colonial voice, a figure who
critiques Christianity's exclusive claim to universalism and authorizes the
unconditional emancipation of the Jews. The quotation from Matthew 22: 32
that he invokes over and over again in the final pages of *Jerusalem* does more
than articulate a directive for the separation of church and state. "Render unto
Caesar that which is Caesar's and unto God what is God's" also represents an
historically specific mode of accommodating empire, one that sets *Jerusalem*
in a very particular relationship to Dohm's treatise. Dohm structured his proposals around the symbolic opposition of Rome and Jerusalem, finding in the
Roman Empire a model for both Jewish civic virtue and his more general principles of political universalism. The ancient victory of Rome over Jerusalem
marked in this framework not a triumph of Roman imperialism that violently
destroyed Jewish identity but a primal moment of civic improvement, the
benevolent emancipation of the Jews from the theocratic politics of
Jerusalem. It was, for Dohm, under Roman rule that Jews finally became able
to participate in civic life and escape from the "national hatred" typical of the
ancient Jewish theocracy. Like Dohm, of course, Mendelssohn also valorizes
Diaspora and lacks interest in Jewish national restoration. The manner in
which he justifies his concept of Diaspora, however, blatantly challenges the
terms of civic improvement. Rather than participating in the debates on
"regeneration" and acquiescing in the power dynamics of such improvement,
Mendelssohn seeks to articulate an alternative mode of universalism, one that

would be grounded in an appreciation of cultural and religious difference. For Mendelssohn, it is not Rome but Jerusalem that offers a model for modernity, and it does so in explicit opposition to Roman imperial power.

Given Mendelssohn's frequent call for tolerance for the wide spectrum of human religions and his polemics against grand narratives of world-historical progress, it should not come as a surprise that *Jerusalem* is full of passages that argue against the denigration of non-European religions. When Mendelssohn speaks of the Roman destruction of Jerusalem, accordingly, he presents it not as a model for Jewish emancipation but as an event that exemplifies the violence of empire and the destruction of religious difference. He invokes the "conquerors of Jerusalem" who "plundered the Temple" and "saw everything with the eyes of barbarians" (*J* 114; *JubA* 8: 180) just once in *Jerusalem* but at a crucial juncture, at the culmination of a discussion of the difficulties of acquiring reliable knowledge about non-European peoples. Mendelssohn harshly criticizes travelers who, when "they report to us on the religion of distant peoples" fail to "acquaint themselves very intimately with the thoughts and opinions of a nation" and thus mistake the use of images and script in religious worship for simple idolatry (*J* 114; *JubA* 8: 180).[48] To make this point, he first uses the figure of Omai, the famous Tahitian brought back from the South Seas by Captain Cook, to invert the gaze of Enlightenment ethnography. Mendelssohn speculates that if a second Omai were to enter the Temple of Providence in Dessau, an image-free house of worship dedicated to rational religion, he would naturally conclude that the congregation gazing at the writing on the walls was engaging in idolatry. In regarding non-Christian religions as idolatrous, Mendelssohn implies, Europeans engage in similar strategies of self-legitimation, a phenomenon that is nowhere more prominent than at that other eighteenth-century colonial frontier, the East Indies. Lacking a proper appreciation of its symbolic language, Europeans typically deride Indian religion and reduce it to a source of amusement, "laugh[ing] at the Indian philosophers who say that this universe is borne by elephants, and place the elephants upon a large turtle, and maintain that the latter is upheld by an enormous bear, and that the bear rests on an immense serpent" (*J* 114; *JubA* 8: 180). In order to defend the Hindus and save them from both the conversion efforts of European missionaries and their misrepresentation by European Orientalists, Mendelssohn quotes liberally from John Zephaniah Holwell's *Interesting Historical Events, relative to the Provinces of Bengal* (1765–71), particularly the section on the "Religious Tenets of the Gentoos." The author of this work, Mendlessohn claims, viewed Indian religion "with the eyes of a native Brahmin" and was thus able to acquit the Hindus of the charge of idolatry and defend the compatibility of Indian religion with rational religion (*J* 114–15; *JubA* 8: 180).

As Arnold Eisen points out, Mendelssohn's sympathetic treatment of Hinduism and other purportedly "idolatrous" religions marks a revolutionary moment in the history of Jewish thought, and is one of the strategies by which Mendelssohn reworks Maimonides to present his own account of the function of Mosaic law and the tolerance Judaism shows other religions.[49] Along with his example from the South Seas, Mendelssohn's discussion of Indian religion also has a distinct polemical function within *Jerusalem*. Mendelssohn strives here to negotiate a form of cultural understanding that would be incompatible with both imperial domination and the manner in which Orientalists like Michaelis seek to contain and control their object of study. Mendelssohn here, to be sure, is not without his limitations. His "authoritative" British source for Indian religion, Holwell, was hardly in a position to present the religion of the "Gentoos" "with the eyes of a native Brahmin." Holwell lacked knowledge of Indian languages and relied for the most part on Persian sources; the section Mendelssohn cites that claimed to be an original translation of the ancient Hindu *Chartah Bhade Shastah* gave an English rendition of a text that no one else other than Holwell seems ever to have heard of.[50] As a real-life incarnation of the "noble savage," the historical Omai fulfilled functions for Europeans that similarly had little to do with Tahiti proper; this rings true for Mendelssohn's figure of a "second" Omai as well.[51] What matters here, however, is less whether Mendelssohn is successful in his effort at crosscultural understanding than the context in which he presents this project, the way he implicitly aligns Jews with Tahitians and the inhabitants of Hindustan to expose the link between political domination and discourse on religion:

> Our own travelers may very often make similar mistakes when they report to us on the religion of distant peoples. They must acquaint themselves very intimately with the thoughts and opinions of a nation before they can say with certainty whether its images still have the character of script, or whether they have already degenerated into idolatry. In plundering the Temple, the conquerors of Jerusalem found the cherubim on the Ark of the Covenant, and took them for idols of the Jews. They saw everything with the eyes of barbarians, and from their point of view. In accordance with their own customs, they took an image of divine providence and prevailing grace for an image of the Deity, for the Deity itself, and delighted in their discovery. (*J* 114; *JubA* 8: 180)

Aligning the destruction of Jerusalem with his two examples from the eighteenth-century colonial frontier, Mendelssohn redefines the Roman victory over Jerusalem as a cautionary tale about the perils of ethnography. In practice, Mendelssohn suggests, Enlightenment anthropology is often analogous to the Roman destruction of Jerusalem, an intellectual effort closely linked to the project of imperial rule. Mendelssohn here does not merely group Jews together with peoples at the margins of contemporary European rule. Focussing on the historical moment that gave Dohm his paradigm for civic improvement, he sees the Jews as the archetype for the misunderstood objects of ethnographic discourse and colonized peoples alike. Salvaging "Jerusalem" from its colonization by "Rome," Mendelssohn further revises Dohm's vision of emancipation, claiming for Judaism once again a paradigmatic status for modernity. Rome figures here not as the exemplar of civic virtue and religious tolerance but as an imperial power that misunderstands and destroys the religious traditions of those people it conquers. In this light, Mendelssohn's strategy of appropriating Matthew 22: 32 as a model for both modernity and Judaism does not just cast Judaism as a cornerstone of modernity. It makes modernity inherently anti-colonial, using Judaism as its prime exemplar to articulate a universalist vision grounded in an appreciation of cultural and religious difference that would relegate Christianity to its status as just one religion among others.

NEUTRALIZING OPPOSITION, OR THE AMBIVALENCE OF REFORM

Jerusalem sought to articulate an alternative mode of universalism for the Enlightenment, one that would have forced Mendelssohn's contemporaries to jettison Christianity's claim to universalism and recognize instead the seminal role Judaism had played in shaping the modern world. We shall see in subsequent chapters that Jewish writers frequently echoed this strategy in their contribution to the emancipation debates. Not surprisingly, Mendelssohn's Christian contemporaries hardly proved well disposed toward this critique of Christianity issued in the name of an alliance between Judaism and Enlightenment. Michaelis, as we noted above, immediately took Mendelssohn to task for his portrayal of Jesus, reinstating the scenario presented in *Mosaic Law* of a clean break between Judaism and Christianity, and he was not alone in reacting with such antipathy. Few of Mendelssohn's Christian peers were ready to accept his vision of the relationship between Judaism and modernity or his understanding of Jesus as a Jewish reformer entirely bound by Jewish tradition. In an anonymous tract published in 1799, for instance, a liberal theologian sympathetic to the Jews wrote that Mendelssohn's critique of Christianity derived simply from a basic "confusion" about the essence of faith; the only way to clear up this confusion would be acceptance of Jesus as Christ, which would also promote the more general aim of "purifying Christianity of those Jewish remains that have served as its scaffolding."[52] By 1799 this reading of *Jerusalem* had a substantial pedigree.

Kant offered a similar interpretation of Mendelssohn in *Religion within the Limits of Reason Alone* (1793), insisting that Mendelssohn's real intention in speaking about Judaism as the indispensable foundation for Christianity was to argue for a Christianity that would be purified of all traces of its Jewish heritage. Kant's Jesus was hardly an exemplar of the Rabbinic principle but an exemplary moral teacher who performed a fundamental break with Judaism to institute a pure, rational religion.

In other writings of the period, Mendelssohn's critique of Christianity came under even more intense attack. In a 1786 tract entitled *Moses Mendelssohn's Jerusalem, Insofar as This Writing is Opposed to Christianity*, the Protestant theologian Gotthelf Andreas Regenhorst argued that the primary intent of *Jerusalem* was to expose to Christians the philosophical inconsistencies of their faith and attack Christianity; Regenhorst responded to this assault by seeking to fortify Christian faith and demonstrate the philosophical contradictions in Mendelssohn's own thinking.[53] In *Golgatha and Scheblimini*, an influential 1784 polemic against Mendelssohn that was acclaimed not just by Lavater but by Herder, Goethe and Hegel, Johann Georg Hamann (1730–88) rallied against Mendelssohn's "distortion" of Judaism and its link to Christianity, reinstating the supersessionist narrative that Mendelssohn sought to challenge.[54] Hamann, a mystical philosopher known to his contemporaries as the "Magus of the North," complained that since Mendelssohn was disclaiming Jesus, the son, he clearly would not be reaching the father, and this Enlightenment figure who was born and circumcised a Jew was thus little more than a pagan, a Jew who had defiled Judaism in the name of an empty rationalist philosophy. The issue of the civil oppression of Jews, incidentally, was of no concern to Hamann, who felt simply that the time simply "had not come" for Jews—or blacks—to be emancipated.[55] Critiquing *Jerusalem* in this manner, moreover, was not the sole provenance of theologians. In the wave of antisemitic political pamphlets that took Berlin by storm in 1803, Mendelssohn's characterization of Christianity as a religion inextricable from its original Jewish foundation was frequently targeted for ridicule. Karl Wilhelm Friedrich Grattenauer, whom we will discuss in detail in Chapter 5, argued that Mendelssohn's position on Christianity was little more than "Rabbinic foolishness"; the history of religion, Grattenauer explained, simply "does not permit the opinion that Christianity was derived from Judaism," as Christianity is, in its universality, the "diametrical antithesis of all religions of the world."[56] Friedrich Buchholz, a contemporary of Grattenauer whom we will return to in Chapter 5 as well, denounced Mendelssohn in similar terms, presenting his claim for the continued relevance of Judaism in the modern world as a Rabbinic "web of dialectical hair-splitting and sentimental chatter" that basically reenacted the crucifixion.[57]

Like Michaelis, however, most of these authors were not in the least predisposed toward the project of civic improvement as Dohm had formulated it. For this reason, their wholesale rejection of *Jerusalem* is perhaps less interesting than the way proponents of civic improvement confronted Mendelssohn's critique of Christianity. Those of Mendelssohn's Christian peers who favored emancipation typically could not ignore the vision of Christianity and the insistence on Jesus's Jewishness that Regenhorst, Hamann, Grattenauer and Buchholz found so outrageous. They dealt with Mendelssohn's challenge to Christian universalism in a different manner, however, generally replacing it with grand narratives of Christian origins that once again rendered Judaism little more than an historical relic of the ancient Orient and that recentered political discussion on precisely that issue of moral "regeneration" Mendelssohn wanted to relegate to the sidelines of discussions over emancipation. Let us consider, for instance, a 1785 work that heralded Dohm's and Joseph II's efforts on behalf of the Jews and that was praised in the pages of Nicolai's *Universal German Library* for its "tolerant and genuine Christian sentiments": the *Addendum to the Suggestions and Means for Improving the Civic Culture and Religious Enlightenment of the Jewish Nation, With Notes on the Jews in Poland and the Russian Provinces*.[58] The author of this piece, Gottlieb Schlegel (1739–1810), at the time the leading theologian in Riga, later became a theology professor in Greifswald and general superintendent of all ecclesiastical and educational affairs in Pomerania.[59] Now largely forgotten, Schlegel was hardly a minor figure in his day. A former student of Kant in Königsberg and a one-time friend of Herder who had helped Herder land a job in Riga, he was the author of numerous popular theological works, a typical representative of the Protestant theology of his time, and it is for this reason that his intervention in the debates is important for us. In his *Addendum*, he presented himself as an expert on Judaism and Jewish law who was familiar with a part of the world—Poland—in which Jews were far more numerous than in Dohm and Mendelssohn's Prussia. He was thus keenly aware of the dangers of granting Jews rights without first ensuring their moral regeneration. Unlike Dohm, Schlegel did not suggest a secular program of civic improvement to achieve this end. He espoused an ideal of Christian–Jewish dialogue that would bring the Jews closer to Christianity and Christian morality. It is from this viewpoint that he dealt with Mendelssohn's appropriation of Jesus and his efforts to challenge Orientalist views of Judaism, ultimately enlisting both in the service of Christian universalism.

For Schlegel, Jews—who "often lack a secure dwelling place and can thus move around carrying their bags like Bedouins"[60]—occupy a liminal space between Orient and Occident. Unlike Christian Orientalists, he complains, these displaced Bedouins neither know nor have any interest in learning

Oriental languages other than Hebrew.[61] As a result, the religion they practice derives not from a proper historical understanding of the Old Testament
but from perversions performed on scripture by Rabbinic Judaism and the
Talmudists, more specifically, from word play, forced allegorical readings, literalism, strange comparisons and an "unseemly gesticulation reminiscent of
the action of the Orientals."[62] As a European Orientalist equipped with the
linguistic tools to understand scripture historically and appreciate the proper
function of Hebrew figurative language, Schlegel is thus in a position to
articulate the disjunction between the ancient Israelites and the gesticulating
Orientals who claim to be their heirs: "The [Jewish] nation is already too
Occidentalized for their souls to ascend to the high Orientalism."[63] Lacking
the proper understanding of their own Oriental origins and the figurative
language—the "high Orientalism"—of the poetry of the Hebrew Bible,
European Jews reside in a no man's land that is neither Orient nor Occident.
Schlegel himself, in contrast, can mediate effectively between these two
poles, and the result, not surprisingly, is a reading of the Old Testament that
points unequivocally toward its prefiguration of Jesus:

> You know that these holy men, as Orientals and as poets, speak in an
> elevated, lively and flowery language. They poured out their thoughts in
> images, the features of which they took from the sensual and physical
> things around them, and from things known at the time. One would
> make a mistake in these writings if one were to understand literally
> what was said figuratively and in images, or if one were to explicate
> Oriental texts in an Occidental sense and make what is poetic unpoetic.
> . . . Indeed, should the promised savior lead not just the Jews but all
> peoples of the earth: why is it that you appropriate all advantages for your
> nation?[64]

Schlegel, like Michaelis, presents modern Jews as the antithesis of the
European Orientalist. Jews read figurative language literally and misunderstand scripture by making its poetry prosaic, by explicating this ancient
Oriental text as if it were a modern Occidental one. With his sense of the difference between Orient and Occident, Schlegel is able to grasp the meaning
behind the flowery figures of Oriental poetry. In its highest form, it seems,
Orientalism prefigures its own supersession, the emergence of Jesus as the
savior of both the Jews and the entirety of humanity.

It is from this perspective that Schlegel calls for Christian–Jewish dialogue.
Quoting and paraphrasing *Jerusalem* extensively, he expresses his delight that
contemporary Jewish elites are beginning to show respect for Christianity,
Christian biblical scholarship and, most importantly, the person of Jesus
himself. Clearly, Schlegel acknowledges, Mendelssohn and other enlightened

Jews who regard Jesus as a great moral teacher do not understand Jesus entirely: in insisting on his Jewishness and his observance of the law, they are still blatantly challenging Christian doctrine, and this is a problem.[65] But the worst thing for Christians to do, he warns, would be to confront Jews like Mendelssohn outright, as this might put an end to the sort of religious dialogue necessary for the Jews' moral regeneration: "The Jews have often been reticent to pronounce their objections to our religion: let us take this fear from them and have them speak out!"[66] The agenda for this open dialogue, needless to say, is clearly set in advance. Schlegel wants to use the respect Mendelssohn shows for Jesus as a means of bringing Jews into the fold and encouraging if not their conversion, at least their moving closer toward Christianity.

Soon after stating his reluctance to challenge the author of *Jerusalem*, he proceeds to dismantle Mendelssohn's vision of the Jewish Jesus and his critique of Christianity. Blatantly undoing Mendelssohn's legitimation of Diaspora, he first argues that in the absence of the land, the Temple and their Oriental climate of origin, modern Jews are no longer Jews and simply cannot obey the law. Like so many other Jews, Mendelssohn fails to grasp the higher meaning of his Oriental religion; the "pure religion" which the religion of the patriarchs strives to realize is not Mosaic law but the religion of Jesus and his apostles. It is precisely this Jewish literalism that leads Jews like Mendelssohn to misunderstand Jesus's mission. This problem is exacerbated since the reports about Jesus "do not have the high Oriental form in which the older histories are written."[67] Jesus himself may have been Jewish, and even Oriental, but all accounts of him, written as they were in Greek, already belong to the Occident. The problem with Jews like Mendelssohn who read the New Testament, Schlegel suggests, is that they approach this text with the same unimaginative literalism as they use when reading the Hebrew Bible, so they fail to grasp that Jesus did not in fact remain contained by Judaism. He completed the law and preached a universal religion that far surpassed the religion of his fathers—just as one expected from the Jewish Messiah: "If Jesus did not abolish the law with explicit words, as he could not yet do at that time, he nevertheless taught a religion and ordained customs, and gave commands after his resurrection that the Jewish religion was useless and should be terminated. . . . God does not always make known his will through literal evidence; he also commands through Providence, which seems to have sufficiently abolished the binding political and religious constitution of Judaism by having its capital destroyed and its nation dispersed."[68] Like modern Jews, Jesus also occupies a liminal position between Occident and Orient, but he does so as the culmination of the high Orientalism of the Old Testament, as the figure who destroys the political and religious constitution of Judaism to replace it with the universality of Christianity. In Schlegel, as in Mendelssohn, Jesus becomes the spokesman for the Jewish Diaspora and for a de-Orientalized Judaism, but Schlegel's account of the relationship between Judaism and Christianity hardly challenges the opposition between Orient and Occident. It rehearses once again the paradigm of Christian supersessionism, the displacement of the Oriental laws of Moses by that form of Christianity which serves as both their negation and their highest fulfillment. For Schlegel, this is the framework in which one should debate the emancipation of the Jews.

The frustrations Mendelssohn encountered in his attempt to secure a position from which he might, as a Jew, speak authoritatively about Judaism and its relation to Christianity come into even sharper focus if we consider the contributions to the emancipation debates by an even more prominent Orientalist and one of Michaelis's most famous protégés: Johann Gottfried Eichhorn (1752–1827), a professor of Oriental studies at the University of Jena and the author of an extremely influential *Introduction to the Old Testament* (1780–83). In 1789, Eichhorn published in his *Universal Library of Biblical Literature*, a prominent journal of biblical criticism, a critique of Abbé Grégoire's *Essay on the Physical, Moral and Political Regeneration of the Jews* (1788) where he argued in similar terms against granting Jews rights without first ensuring their moral regeneration.[69] Pointing out to his German readers that this French treatise offered little that differed from the type of proposals for civic improvement that "have been echoing from one end of Germany to the other for the last eight years,"[70] Eichhorn insisted that Grégoire and Dohm were wrong to suggest that the "corruption" and "degeneration" of the Jews were the product of their treatment at the hands of Christian rulers. These problems ensued, rather, almost exclusively from their continued adherence to the Oriental laws of Moses. For Eichhorn, as for so many other Orientalists, modern Jews remain at a retarded level of cultural development, trapped in the primitive world of the ancient Orient: "[Mosaic law] was a legislation for the first weak political and moral education. As beneficial as it was for the early development of the nation, it nevertheless did not suffice and ultimately became harmful in the course of time. Consumed with the superiority and inalterability of their book of statutes, they have become trapped halfway along the path of moral education, since they only knew laws that sought to counter the most primitive wildness and put a halt to the crudest debauchery."[71] Other ancient peoples, Eichhorn concedes, did not measure up much better on the scale of morality; they have, however, "ennobled themselves through the acceptance of Christianity, which excels so marvelously in its pure and noble morality."[72]

Like Schlegel, Eichhorn does not lobby for conversion *per se*. Insisting that the political emancipation of the Jews needs to be contingent on their religious reform and moral regeneration, he simply wants Judaism to be de-Orientalized and be brought closer to the "pure and noble morality" of Christianity. In addition to education, Jews need "merely a reform of their religion, which for millennia has no longer been suited for the situation of the world," and indeed, he claims with an obvious reference to Mendelssohn, this is "what even their wiser men are now loudly recommending."[73] Like Schlegel, then, Eichhorn also coopts Mendelssohn's call for religious purification, using it to support precisely that view of Mosaic law as stagnant and in need of reform that Mendelssohn sought to combat. The notion that Mendelssohn exemplifies this type of reform is not Eichhorn's innovation. His critique of Grégoire borrows this view almost entirely from Justus Friedrich Runde (1741–1807), a professor of law in Cassel and then Göttingen and a prolific jurist who also called for a de-Orientalized Judaism as a precondition of emancipation. More than half of Eichhorn's critique of Grégoire and much of his argument, in fact, consist of a long quotation from a critique of Dohm Runde published in 1785.[74] Runde argued that Jews might become useful citizens only after a comprehensive "religious improvement . . . that would restore pure, original Judaism to its former standing and separate it out from all the addenda of tradition; and that would, in the wake of changes in circumstance and a political constitution that is now extinct, declare as nonbinding all elements of original Judaism that related to the circumstances of the time, political constitution and climate."[75] Runde did not just argue explicitly against Mendelssohn's insistence that Jews could not in any way disencumber themselves from the law. He managed to do so in such a way as to claim Mendelssohn for his case: "How, though, should this necessary reformation of the Jewish concept of religion be effected? . . . I know no better path than that the enlightened and praiseworthy human beings in the Jewish people—the Moses Mendelssohns—concern themselves with completing this great work through example and teachings and thereby become the true benefactors of their brothers."[76] For Runde, as for Eichhorn and Schlegel, Judaism needs to be assimilated to religious norms that are superior to its place of origin, and it is Mendelssohn who emerges—in spite of his explicit arguments to the contrary—as the bearer of the Christianizing reform that would sever Judaism from its Oriental roots and qualify Jews for emancipation.

From these examples—and in the next chapter we shall encounter a similar dynamic in Kant's interpretation of Mendelssohn as well—a clear pattern emerges. For all his efforts to reformulate the visions of universalism underwriting civic improvement, Mendelssohn was only able to provoke those hostile to emancipation to acknowledge his critique of Christianity for the subversive strategy that it was. Those willing to accommodate Jews or

Judaism in their vision of universalism tended to neutralize Mendelssohn's challenge, recasting his attempt to "purify" Judaism as precisely the sort of step toward Christian universalism it was Mendelssohn's goal to undermine. For these thinkers, reform inevitably meant a step toward Christianity. For all the grandeur of its polemics, Mendelssohn's Jewish vision of modernity thus failed to provide non-Jews with the alternative perspective for debating emancipation he so desperately wanted to insert into the public sphere. Indeed, even for his Jewish peers, as Michael Meyer noted more than thirty years ago, the actual terms of his defense of Judaism—his unflinching insistence on the observance of Mosaic law as a means of arriving at the universal truths of rational religion—represented little more than an "ephemeral solution" to the problems raised by the encounter between Judaism and the modern world.[77] Mendelssohn may indeed have presented a normative view of Judaism as a confession that lacked corporate autonomy. With his insistence on the eternal value of Mosaic law as a "revealed legislation," however, he obviously left little room for innovations in Jewish ritual practice or the related concept that Judaism had an "essence" distinct from the law that unfolded and might continue to unfold in the course of its history—both key elements of nineteenth-century Reform that began to be formulated by Saul Ascher and other of Mendelssohn's successors in the 1790s. In the nineteenth century, nearly all branches of German Jewry invoked both Mendelssohn's basic scheme of Judaism's compatibility with modernity and the figure of Mendelssohn as models for Jewish life in the modern world. Nevertheless, few nineteenth-century Jews, including the orthodox, found *Jerusalem* to be a viable religious platform.

However, Mendelssohn's more general vision of the political agency of reform—his insistence on religious purification as a means of both redefining the terms of the debates on civic improvement and challenging Protestant visions of the relationship between Judaism and Christianity—retained more than its share of normative power for his successors. Given the manner in which Schlegel, Eichhorn, Runde and other of his contemporaries could interpret his de-Orientalized model of Judaism, it makes sense that his heirs did not judge his particular vision of the relationship between religious reform and political emancipation to be a model worthy of emulation. In this sense, we might say, the importance of *Jerusalem* lies less in its success than in its failure. Mendelssohn was influential, that is, not because of his solution but because he articulated a religious-political *project* of normative value, a subversive attempt to link the purification of Judaism to political agency for Jews. It is this Mendelssohn—and not just the temperate mediator between Judaism and German culture—who provided an archetype for the next generation of Jewish intellectuals.

4

PHILOSOPHY, ANTISEMITISM AND THE POLITICS OF RELIGIOUS REFORM

Saul Ascher's Challenge to Kant and Fichte

ANTISEMITISM AND THE CLAIM TO MODERNITY

For modern scholars, the relationship between theological antagonism toward Jews and Judaism and secular, political antisemitism has typically been a contested issue. In 1951, Hannah Arendt could open *The Origins of Totalitarianism* by confidently presenting antisemitism as a distinctly modern ideology that had little if anything to do with medieval Jew-hatred.[1] Few today, indeed, would dispute that there are obvious differences between modern antisemitism and the Christian tradition's legacy of anti-Judaism. References to pre-Enlightenment theological literature hardly suffice to explain the prominence of the Jewish question in German political discourse, not to mention the various ways antisemitism functioned as a mobilizing force in politics in the 1870s and 1880s or the 1930s. For most recent scholars, nevertheless, the denial of *any* genealogical connection between modern antisemitism and religious antagonism toward Jews skirts an important issue, obscuring some of the reasons why Jews were able to become the targets of such sustained ideological assault in the modern era. So many of the grand narratives about the emergence of antisemitism that have circulated in the last thirty years or so, accordingly, have questioned the absolute modernity of modern anti-Jewish hostility, exposing moments of continuity where Arendt saw radical difference. In *The French Revolution and the Jews*, a 1968 book reissued in 1990 with the subtitle *The Origins of Modern Anti-Semitism*, Arthur Hertzberg traced how the Enlightenment secularized and modernized religious Jew-hatred, drawing on pagan writers from the classical tradition to revive and supplement medieval forms of Christian antagonism toward Jews.[2] Gavin Langmuir's *Toward a Definition of Antisemitism* (1990) located the shift from religious anti-Judaism to modern antisemitism much earlier, within medieval culture itself; for Langmuir, it was the emergence of irrational, chimerical fantasies about Jews in the twelfth and thirteenth centuries that inaugurated modern antisemitism.[3] Looking at a different tradition, Peter Schäfer has recently contended that antisemitism as Langmuir defines it actually predates Christian anti-Judaism and can be found in much of its modern form in the anti-Jewish literature of ancient Egypt, Greece and Rome—in that tradition whose eighteenth-century renaissance Hertzberg identified with the original moment of modern antisemitism.[4]

As even this quick constellation of examples demonstrates, the search for the definitive origins of antisemitism can often become a slippery enterprise, one that runs the risk of losing track of the claim to modernity that has been characteristic of so much Jew-hatred since the Enlightenment. For someone like Michaelis, we recall, the denigration of Jews and Judaism was anything but an unexamined prejudice inherited from an earlier era; it formed an integral part of an eighteenth-century colonial vision, part of an effort to imagine Germany's proper place in the modern world. Rather than seeking out the roots of antisemitism in earlier eras, it might thus be productive to affirm the ways in which antagonism toward Jews has frequently been a curious hybrid since the eighteenth century: often both secular and religious, both political and theological, both modern and premodern at once. Tracing the genealogy of antisemitism back to earlier traditions may not be the pressing task here; nor is it necessarily crucial to identify the exact historical juncture at which antisemitism surfaces in its pristine, full-fledged modernity and supersedes its precursor. Indeed, precisely what modern antisemitism *is* is a question that has clearly proven difficult to answer satisfactorily. If we concede that this elusiveness may even be a constitutive element of modern forms of Jew-hatred, then it may make sense to shift our attention from issues of derivation and definition to questions of form and function. We need to interrogate, in other words, the self-consciously modern strategies eighteenth- and early nineteenth-century thinkers used to legitimize their forms of Jew-hatred—and, conversely, the dynamic role such Jew-hatred played in framing certain visions of modernity. It is not the continuity or discontinuity between religious Jew-hatred and secular antisemitism that requires our attention here but the context in which hostility toward Jews came to present itself and be accepted as a modern phenomenon.

Contemporary Jewish reactions can serve as a crucial index of this process. For contrary to the cliché that German Jews consistently misread modern antisemitism as a lingering remnant of medieval prejudice, there were several prominent Jews who spoke out about the vigorous modernization of Jew-hatred they felt was accompanying the early discussions of Jewish emancipation. Mendelssohn in the early 1780s was already commenting on the emergence of secular biases against Jews among University of Göttingen luminaries who used their authority and position as scholars to challenge Dohm's argument that Jews could be regenerated and transformed into productive citizens. A decade later, a young Jewish bookseller in Berlin, Saul Ascher (1767–1822), offered a much more systematic analysis of Jew-hatred's novel claims to modernity. Ascher belonged to the second generation of Jewish intellectuals immersed in secular culture in the Prussian capital, a group of individuals that, as Shmuel Feiner has demonstrated, often called themselves Mendelssohn's disciples at the same time as they departed from both his particular vision of Judaism and his commitment to the rationalist metaphysics that dominated so much intellectual life in eighteenth-century Germany.[5] Like his friend Salomon Maimon (1754–1800) and his contemporary Lazarus Bendavid (1762–1832), Ascher had enthusiastically embraced the philosophical revolution unleashed by Kant's *Critique of Pure Reason* (1781), a work that Mendelssohn in his final years was not ashamed to admit he simply could not understand. By 1794, when Ascher offered his analysis of what he called an "entirely new species" of Jew-hatred in *Eisenmenger the Second*, he had already published a book on aesthetics indebted to Kant, as well as an anonymous pamphlet challenging Joseph II's decision to require Jews to perform military service without first granting them civil and political rights.[6] His most important contribution at the time, however, had been in the field of religion. Inspired by the ideal of individual moral autonomy Kant had expressed in his *Foundations of the Metaphysics of Morals* (1785) and his *Critique of Practical Reason* (1788), Ascher published in 1792 his *Leviathan, Or on Religion with Respect to Judaism*, a Kantian attempt to conceive of the "essence" of the Jewish religion as distinct from Mosaic law that moved decisively beyond Mendelssohn's defense of Judaism as a "revealed legislation" without religious dogma.[7] For Ascher, the essence of Judaism was not just distinct from the law, which he understood as just one of its possible historical manifestations; Judaism was, at its core, the perfect embodiment of Kant's ideal of moral autonomy and, as such, a religion ideally compatible with the modern age. Ascher today, not surprisingly, is widely hailed as the inaugural theorist of Reform Judaism, the first in a long line of German-Jewish thinkers who sought to reinterpret Judaism in Kantian terms and reconcile Jewish tradition with Kant's emphasis on individual moral responsibility and his demands for a rationally viable faith.[8]

In *Eisenmenger the Second*, Ascher traced how the debates over civic improvement had shown the religious Jew-hatred of earlier eras yielding to moral and political anti-Jewish sentiments much more sinister than Christian anti-Judaism, and the distinctive feature of this new Jew-hatred, he argued, was its characteristically modern claim to philosophical legitimation. Its disciples typically preached, he claimed, not from the pulpit but from the university lectern, and they did so using the state-of-the-art tools of Kant's critical philosophy, promoting Jew-hatred from the perspective of a secular universalism grounded in the Kantian philosophical revolution of the 1780s—the same philosophical system that supplied the parameters for Ascher's own vision of Jewish religious renewal.[9] Ascher did not argue in abstract terms. His reflections on the modernization of Jew-hatred had been provoked by a recent work that was, like Ascher's own writings, densely enmeshed in some of the most progressive philosophical and political concerns of the day: Johann Gottlieb Fichte's *Contribution to the Correction of the Judgments of the Public on the French Revolution* (1793).[10] It was Fichte (1762–1814), the rising Kantian philosopher, whom Ascher dubbed "Eisenmenger the Second," noting with irony the enormous "progress" the "science of hating Judaism and its followers" had made since Johann Andreas Eisenmenger's enormously influential theological tract of 1700, *Judaism Revealed*.[11] What made the *Contribution*'s brand of Jew-hatred so much more insidious than its theological precursors was that it did more than perpetuate premodern prejudice. Fichte offered the reading public what Ascher called, in Kantian terms, a "prolegomena" to a "critique of Jew-hatred," a distinctly modern philosophical grounding for antagonism toward Jews and Judaism articulated *within* a defense of the principles of the French Revolution.[12]

In the *Contribution*, Fichte sought to challenge the growing tide of conservative critics of the French Revolution inspired by Edmund Burke, August Wilhelm Rehberg and others by offering a philosophical defense of the Revolution based on the ethical universalism of Kant's categorical imperative and his ideal of moral autonomy. This grand defense made Fichte a figure of great notoriety at the time, causing some of his more conservative peers to view him, not entirely correctly, as a Jacobin radical. Fichte's interest in the *Contribution* was less in the actual events of the Revolution than in its potential philosophical appropriation, that is, the way it offered a "rich portrait" or a series of "instructive portrayals" one might use as an occasion to reason about universal human rights and duties;[13] his true position on the legitimacy of revolution was difficult to tease out from his philosophical reflections. Ascher's problem with Fichte, in any case, was not just that he failed to include Jews in his vision of republican renewal,[14] but that he portrayed Jews and Judaism as the symbolic antithesis of his idealist principles, presenting Judaism as the very opposite of a universalist politics. Judaism or Jewry (*Judenthum*), Fichte had written, was not just a clannish and dangerously exclusive "state within a state"; it was a "state grounded in the hatred of the entire human race," "a powerful, hostile state that lives with all others in constant warfare" and that "is spreading through almost all lands of Europe and terribly oppressing its citizens in many respects."[15] This basic denigration of Judaism as a misanthropic politics, of course, was hardly Fichte's innovation; the characterization of Judaism as a "state within a state" has parallels in other contemporary writers.[16] What was distinctive here is the role this negative vision of Judaism played in Fichte's universalism, the way he paired his enthusiasm for the French Revolution with a proposal for winning the "war" Jews were allegedly waging against the entirety of Europe. The *Contribution* intervened directly in the debates over the regeneration of the Jews, proposing a solution to the Jewish question that differed considerably from the decision of the French National Assembly to grant Jews equal rights: "I would see no other way to give the Jews civil rights than to cut off their heads in one night and put others on them in which there would not be a single Jewish idea."[17]

In this passage, which became legendary in subsequent years for its inflammatory rhetoric, Fichte clearly invoked the violence of the Revolution rather than its theoretical ideals, enlisting the guillotine in the service of a perverse recasting of Dohm's project of civic improvement. "Who would have thought," Ascher exclaimed in his comments on this passage, "that *decapitation* would have found followers in Germany who want an entire nation to be improved by such an experiment?"[18] In Fichte's scenario, Europe desperately needs to gain dominance over the international threat posed by Judaism's misanthropic politics, and the best way to do so is to subject Jews to the rhetorical threat of the guillotine. Better yet, Fichte suggested, would be to supplement this peculiar vision of civic regeneration with a concerted effort at imperial expansion: "If we want to protect ourselves from them, I see no other way than conquering the holy land for them and sending them all there."[19] Like Michaelis, Fichte also proposes a solution to the Jewish question in the realm of colonial fantasy, introducing the progress of empire as the best means to gain control over Judaism's international power. He argues for the French Revolution and against Jewish emancipation by pairing his invocation of revolutionary violence with a rhetorical call for a modern crusade, one that is less about conquering the ancient Jewish homeland for Christianity than it is about de-Judaizing Europe and protecting the interests of secular universalism at home.

By the time *Eisenmenger the Second* appeared in 1794, the author of the *Contribution* was a major target for a Jewish bookseller to attack so publicly. The history of philosophy as it is written today generally presents Fichte as a crucial figure in the development of German idealism from Kant to Hegel, and even before the publication of the first edition of what is now regarded as his most seminal work, the *Doctrine of Knowledge*, later in 1794, he had already emerged as one of the foremost idealist philosophers of his generation. His fame at this point was largely due to his *Attempt at a Critique of All Revelation* (1792), a work that, along with Ascher's *Leviathan*, was one of the earliest attempts to extend Kant's critical philosophy into the realm of religion. Fichte's approach to the question of revelation was so Kantian and his debt to Kantian ethics so explicit, in fact, that when the *Critique of All Revelation* was first published anonymously, it was widely held to be the long-awaited statement of Kant's own philosophy of religion; Kant's *Religion within the Limits of Reason Alone* did not appear until one year later, in 1793. Kant himself had played a role in arranging for the publication of *Critique of All Revelation*, and once Fichte's authorship became widely known, he quickly rose in the ranks of academic philosophy. Shortly before Ascher published *Eisenmenger the Second*, Fichte had assumed the coveted chair in philosophy at the University of Jena vacated by Karl Leonhard Reinhold, Kant's major popularizer of the 1780s. Keenly aware that he was taking on the philosophical vanguard of his day, Ascher strategically styled himself as an outsider to the academy, prefacing the text of *Eisenmenger* with an open letter full of false modesty from himself, the Jewish "autodidact," to "Herrn Professor Fichte in Jena."[20]

As Anthony La Vopa has noted, for all the debate it provoked in the 1790s, the *Contribution* never became the classic of Western political thought rivaling Burke's *Reflections on the Revolution in France* (1790) or Thomas Paine's *The Rights of Man* (1791) that Fichte sought to produce; it has lived on largely due to these anti-Jewish diatribes, which are invoked by historians of antisemitism—often along with Ascher's response—as routinely as they are ignored by philosophers studying Fichte's thought.[21] Fichte's own relationship to Jews and Judaism over the course of his career was clearly more complex and more ambivalent than his diatribes of 1793 might indicate.[22] In the years following its initial publication, however, the anti-Jewish polemics of the *Contribution* took on a life of their own in the debates over Jewish emancipation, where both they and Ascher's attempt at a rebuttal were frequently cited and discussed by friends and foes alike. Whatever their position might be in the development of Fichte's thought, these diatribes earned their author enormous respect among the anti-Jewish pamphleteers whose works flooded the book market in 1803; as we shall see in the following chapter, Fichte here was routinely hailed as a great philosopher of Jew-hatred, an authoritative voice in refusing Jews rights and seeking to contain their deleterious influence. Later critics, not surprisingly, have represented Fichte in a similar light. In his monumental *History of the Jews*, the renowned nineteenth-century Jewish historian Heinrich Graetz cast Fichte as "the father and apostle of national German hatred of the Jews, of a kind unknown before, or rather never before so clearly manifested."[23] Following in Graetz's footsteps, Paul Lawrence Rose has argued more recently that Fichte's *Contribution* announced the birth of a particularly German form of antisemitism that made national renewal contingent on the extermination of Jewishness; for Rose, Fichte's antisemitism represented the "formal debut" of an antagonism toward Jews and Judaism that ensued from "deep-rooted elements in German culture, German tradition, and the German psyche."[24]

For Fichte in 1793, however, it was not the German nation but the political principles of modernity that defined themselves in opposition to Judaism. The Fichte of the 1790s, indeed, was hardly a proto-nationalist. There is little in the *Contribution* or his other writings of this period that prefigure the concerns with nationhood in his influential 1807–08 *Addresses to the German Nation*, a work that has caused him to be classified as one of the great icons of modern German nationalism.[25] Seeing Fichte's Jew-hatred as a paradigmatic expression of the German national spirit fails to come to terms with the way the *Contribution* embedded its antisemitism in a vision of modernity and universalism that was not in any way tied to a vision of nationhood. For Ascher, who was the only contemporary sufficiently troubled by Fichte's anti-Jewish diatribes to attempt a full-fledged refutation, the problem was not that this antisemitism was designed to launch a vision of national renewal but that it helped ground a general theory of modernity. In his 1815 treatise *Germanomania*, Ascher later emerged as a significant critic of both German nationalism and nationalist Jew-hatred; *Germanomania*, in fact, clearly reveals how the antisemitism of the *Contribution* was appropriated in later years by a nationalist discourse made possible by texts such as Fichte's *Addresses to the German Nation*.[26] *Germanomania* issued a harsh indictment of the raging nationalism that had developed during the Napoleonic occupation, targeting not just Fichte and the budding nationalist Ernst Moritz Arndt but also the distinctly antisemitic nationalist pamphlets of the Berlin historian Friedrich Rühs, who issued, in 1815, the first major argument against emancipation that was couched in nationalist terms.[27] Ascher's *Germanomania* created quite an uproar, becoming one of the first books to be burned by groups of nationalist students at the infamous Wartburg Festival of 1817.[28] In *Eisenmenger*, however, Ascher targeted something much more subtle than a metaphysical opposition between German and Jew: the crucial function assigned to Jew-hatred in a vision of modernity that claimed to rise above the contingencies of national boundaries and defend the universalist principles of the French Revolution.

As well as calling attention to the anti-Jewish outburst in Fichte's book on the French Revolution, Ascher linked the secular form of Jew-hatred he found in Fichte's *Contribution* to both the *Critique of All Revelation* and Kant's *Religion within the Limits of Reason Alone*, a work that dedicated an inordinate amount of time and energy to denigrating Judaism and denying that it had any substantive link to the pure religion of reason introduced by Jesus. The rhetorical violence of Fichte's hypothetical solution to the Jewish question in the *Contribution* was thus not an exception to Kantian principles. To a certain extent—and on this point, Ascher proceeded carefully and also wavered a bit, due to his own philosophical allegiances—it was Kantian to the core, a crucial element of Kant's own vision of modernity. The same theoretical system that enabled Ascher to envision a "reform" of Judaism was also giving rise to a modernized Jew-hatred that would deny Jews emancipation as Jews and invalidate any talk of Jewish religious renewal. In this sense, Ascher's encounter with the anti-Judaism of Kant's *Religion* is a paradigmatic expression of the difficulties so many later reformers faced in rethinking Judaism from the perspective of Kant's philosophy.[29] It is no coincidence that Ascher was both a pioneering theorist of Reform Judaism and the first Jewish writer to offer up a systematic analysis of the modernization of antisemitism. *Eisenmenger* and *Leviathan* are linked, indeed, by a common effort to challenge, appropriate and reformulate the Kantian view of modernity. For Ascher, dismantling the self-consciously modern strategies antisemitism used to legitimize itself was inextricable from demonstrating the normative role of Judaism in the modern world; both represented efforts at political self-empowerment that are blatantly misunderstood if we read them as efforts at "assimilation." The fact that an analysis of antisemitism and the quest to gain equal rights lurk prominently in the background of Ascher's program for religious reform does not make Ascher an opportunist.[30] In presenting the "essence" of Judaism as distinct from Mosaic law in *Leviathan*, he left behind Mendelssohn's insistence on the binding nature of Jewish ritual practice, and along with it, Mendelssohn's particular rationale for the continued existence of Judaism in modernity. In no way, however, did he ever simply sacrifice tradition in an attempt to assimilate Judaism to a modern world hostile to things Jewish. In his proposals for a "purified" and "reformed" Judaism, indeed, he articulated a vision of religious regeneration that was radically unsettling to its non-Jewish environment, one that countered the modernization of Jew-hatred he found in Kant and Fichte with a model of Judaism as the ultimate prototype for modernity.

ASCHER VERSUS FICHTE: REASON, MODERNITY AND THE FATE OF HISTORY

Part of Ascher's goal in linking Fichte to Eisenmenger was to relativize Fichte's vision of modernity and expose the shortcomings of the particular version of Kantianism he found in Fichte. In the *Critique of Pure Reason* (1781), the text that first introduced his "Copernican" revolution, Kant characterized the present age as an "age of criticism" to which "everything must be subjected." "*Religion* through its *sanctity*, and *law-giving* through its *majesty*, may seek to exempt themselves from it," he wrote. "But they then awaken just suspicion, and cannot claim the sincere respect which reason accords only to that which has been able to sustain its test of free and public examination."[31] In "Answering the Question: What is Enlightenment?" (1784) and other publications of the 1780s and 1790s, Kant popularized this view of the distinctive role of the public in the modern age, setting up reason as the ultimate authority in matters of religion and politics and presenting the realm of print as that public forum in which reason might best rear its head and assert its critical power.[32] For this reason, Kant has typically earned a prominent position in attempts to trace the genealogy of the modern concept of the public; for Jürgen Habermas and others, it is Kant who first reflects in a systematic manner on the normative role of the public sphere in mediating between state and society and "rationalizing" politics.[33] In his celebrated definition of "enlightenment" as the "emergence of the human being from its self-incurred immaturity to use its understanding without the guidance of another," Kant delineated an individual process of gaining intellectual autonomy from the fetters of tradition and other forms of external authority. But enlightenment involved something else that it presented as distinctly modern: the emancipation of public reason, the construction of the realm of print as an arena for individuals to engage in a form of nonpartisan rational critique that would claim authority for itself in the worlds of religion and politics.

Fichte's *Contribution* drew heavily on the Kantian vision of the public sphere. Indeed, part of what made Kantianism so alluring for Fichte, La Vopa has argued, is that it gave him the conviction of having a transcendent perspective outside ideology that could help create an alternative public.[34] It was from this purportedly neutral vantage point that Fichte defended the Revolution against those who criticized it as the product of an unhealthy philosophical "enthusiasm" (*Schwärmerei*) dangerously estranged from the valued lessons of experience, tradition and history. Attacking Rehberg and other of the Revolution's empiricist critics for failing to abstract themselves from the limitations of the empirical world, Fichte mounted a spirited defense of the authority of reason in politics. Fichte was interested in the Revolution, as we commented earlier, as an occasion to reason about universal human rights and duties; his effort to "correct the judgments of the public" was as much about the German public as it was about the events in France. In its rhetorical form, as La Vopa demonstrates, the *Contribution* sought to "constitute an egalitarian rhetorical community, premised on a radically new relationship between speaker and interlocutor," a public grounded in the intimate encounter between moral equals in the medium of print.[35] The fact that Fichte published his work anonymously did not necessarily interfere with this ambition. In a roundabout way, anonymity helped promote Fichte's new public, as it bracketed his empirical identity to make way for a public sphere predicated on the abstract equality of moral individuals.[36] It was not the renowned author of the *Critique of All Revelation* who published the *Contribution* but simply a writer hoping to forge an egalitarian mode of public discourse in which reason could do its work and transcend the limitations of experience, tradition and history. By the time Ascher published *Eisenmenger*, incidentally, Fichte's authorship was no longer a well-kept secret, particularly in those circles of the reading public to which Berlin intellectuals like Ascher belonged.[37]

In publicly identifying Fichte as the author of the *Contribution* and dubbing him Eisenmenger the Second, Ascher obviously wanted to signal the extent to which the up-and-coming professor in Jena had failed to rise above the limitations of historical prejudice. In this sense, Fichte's diatribes against Jews and Judaism represented a blatant "inconsistency" for Ascher, an example of how his version of the critical philosophy remained limited by the sort of prejudice it should have been able to overcome.[38] But the Jew-hatred in the *Contribution* was ultimately more than an aberration from an otherwise solid philosophical program. It was, Ascher explained, the symptom of a systemic flaw in Fichte's philosophy, part of a fundamental problem with his self-consciously modern method of critique:

Philosophers, speaking in the most modern tone, call to their age: Human beings! You are at the greatest level of imperfection! What has happened before you is worthy of damnation. Arm yourselves with tools so that we may destroy the memory of the previous world and the monuments of great minds of the past, bury them in their rubble and build for us upon their oblivion a new world, entirely according to our own plan. . . . I turn now to the crew of speculative enthusiasts [*Schwärmer*] who are able to forget themselves in their consciousness so that they believe they do not exist at any place on the planet, who think their book cell [*Bücherzelle*] is the trail of a comet on which they are swarming over [*umherschwärmt*] our continent. These philosophers do not simply want to find shortcomings and ailments everywhere—for when were and should such problems ever be far from us? They attempt to make us distrustful of ourselves and advise us to suppress all our senses, to withdraw into ourselves and obtain the source of our salvation solely from ourselves.[39]

As Ascher explicates it here, modernity does not just seek to create a radically new world by turning inward and finding its salvation in itself. It does so quite explicitly at the expense of history and memory. It builds its vision of a rational future on a forced oblivion of the past, willfully destroying the legacies of earlier eras in its effort to clear the path for the establishment of its new self-legislated norms. In using the disembodied world of print to forge this new, rational public, Ascher suggests, Kantian philosophers like Fichte do not so much transcend as bypass the limitations of the empirical world. In its Fichtean adaptation, indeed, Kantianism is not the critical remedy to enthusiasm, *Schwärmerei* and historical prejudice but the highest imaginable form of enthusiasm, one that allows its followers to forget themselves and swarm through outer space while sitting comfortably in their *Bücherzellen*, believing they have achieved self-consciousness. Anything but a productive mode of critique, this sort of philosophical position confines its adherents to a self-enclosed world of print, alienating them from both themselves and the empirical world they ultimately seek to change.

To a certain extent, of course, Ascher here seems to echo the arguments of the conservative critics of the French Revolution whom Fichte sought to refute. But Ascher's goal is not naively to assert the claims of history and tradition and denigrate the enterprise of Kant's transcendental idealism. Elsewhere in *Eisenmenger* he explicitly counts himself among the "admirers" of Kant's work, lauding the "value of the spirit of the critical philosophy for our enthusiastic [*schwärmendes*] age," particularly when it comes to putting an end to "despotic" and "anarchic" forms of thinking and negotiating a truly impartial philosophical voice.[40] Ascher seeks in the passage above simply to call attention to the failure of speculative idealists to abstract themselves from reality in the way they claim to, to point out the disparity between the theory and practice of their mode of critique. Fichte's Jew-hatred represents in this sense more than a minor "inconsistency" in his philosophical position. It is in Fichte's anti-Jewish polemics that the contradictions in his practice of critique come most clearly to the foreground. "Do tell," Ascher asks Fichte in reference to his diatribes against Jews, "is it the plan of your guild [of philosophers] to see this new world . . . built, or is it already built? Is this your plan? If so, do tell me what your goal might be in pointing out to us particular blemishes and shortcomings of the current world which you or your guild have already consigned to eternal decay and oblivion."[41] If Fichte had remained faithful to the principles of Kantian critique, Ascher suggests, he might have seen the condition of contemporary Jews as a problem in need of critical attention and sought to reflect on the structural elements in society responsible for this unfortunate situation. Lacking a critical awareness of the world from which he wants to abstract himself, Fichte makes this particular "blemish" of society into the very foundation of his system.[42] For Fichte, Ascher complains, the Jew is "the first bone of contention in every society; he is the hydra that destroys everything in its path; just like Cerberus in hell, he lies in front of the gates of the temple of felicity, blocking access to all."[43] Fichte's quest to gain a neutral perspective from which he might pass critical judgment on the world hinges on universalizing the condition of the Jews, on misreading the shortcomings of the Jews' present position in society as the cause of all social disintegration. This move is not an exception to the logic of Fichtean critique. Consigning Jews and Judaism to "eternal decay and oblivion" is in a certain sense the fundamental gesture of Fichte's vision of a rational future, the focal point of his theory of modernity.

For Fichte here, modernity defines itself in opposition to Judaism, consigning Judaism to eternal oblivion as one of its key acts of self-constitution. If modernity secures its autonomy by destroying the legacies of history and memory, as Ascher argues, it does not do so simply on an abstract level. It sustains its myth of self-creation partly by performing a symbolic escape from the historical burdens of Judaism. This strategy, moreover, was not a Fichtean innovation on Kant but, as Ascher suggested in *Eisenmenger*, an essential element of Kant's own critical program. It was part of the legacy of Kant's *Religion within the Limits of Reason Alone*, a text that presented Judaism as a "collection of mere statutory laws" that did not deserve to be called a religion and that was incompatible with the Kantian ideal of moral autonomy.[44] As a worldly political commonwealth that "excluded from its communion the entire human race" and "which showed enmity toward all other people and which, therefore, evoked the enmity of all," Judaism for Kant was an historical faith utterly devoid of ethical impulse and virtually irreconcilable with humanity itself.[45] Jesus, in contrast, figures in the *Religion* as both the living "archetype of the moral disposition in all its purity" and the historical figure who first sought to disseminate the teachings of Kantian ethical principles.[46] The antithesis of all things Jewish, Kant's Jesus is "the first to expound publicly a pure and searching religion, comprehensible to the whole world," and he does so in explicit opposition to Judaism, the "dominant ecclesiastical faith which was onerous and not conducive to moral ends."[47]

For some modern apologists, the almost excessive attention Kant pays to Judaism in the *Religion* needs to be read as a strategic move. The *Religion*'s condemnation of Judaism's burdensome ceremonies and its blatant lack of rational ethics arguably stands in for criticism of the Protestant establishment that would never have passed government censors in the wake of the edicts on religion Frederick William II and his minister Johann Christoph Wöllner had introduced in order to keep the free-thinking "heresy" of the Enlightenment in check.[48] There is a certain logic to this position. Kant was engaged in battles with the authorities over his *Religion* and had to refrain from stressing the ways in which the Church fell short of his ideal of a rational religion; his criticism obviously had to be directed at targets other than the Protestant institutions of his day. Viewing "Judaism" solely as a cipher for

Christianity, however, ultimately does little to explain either the particulars of Kant's representation of Judaism or the way the *Religion* was received in the 1790s, especially by Jews like Ascher who were enthusiastic students of Kant's philosophy. Like subsequent generations of Jewish Kantians, Ascher perceived something onerous to contend with in Kant's disparagement of Judaism as the ultimate anti-religion.[49] The problem, again, is not just that nearly all the individual elements of Kant's vision of Judaism had precedents in earlier writers. Nor is it even that, given the debates raging over the ability of Judaism to produce moral citizens, it would have been strange, or at least somewhat difficult, for the reading public to identify this particular vision of Judaism with a contemporary Christianity in need of reform. For Judaism occupied, even more significantly, a position of *systemic* importance in the *Religion*'s recuperation of Christianity as a distinctly modern religion, and this is what Ascher found so problematic in Kant. Driven to salvage the purity of Christianity as a religion that in its inception owed its origins to reason alone, Kant presented Jesus as a disseminator of Kantian ethics only by willfully divorcing him from what Reimarus, Mendelssohn and other contemporaries had argued was his original Jewish context. Jesus's presciently modern moral religion represented the ultimate release from the burdens of both Judaism and history alike. It is this problem we need to address now, using Kant's reception of Mendelssohn's *Jerusalem* and his polemics against historical biblical criticism as a point of entry into the *Religion*'s contributions to launching a "new species" of Jew-hatred.

ASCHER VERSUS KANT: REASON, HISTORY AND THE FATE OF JUDAISM

Like the contemporaries of Mendelssohn whom we discussed in the previous chapter, Kant managed to read *Jerusalem* in such a way as to neutralize its challenge to Christianity's supersession of Judaism. In a 1783 letter to Mendelssohn, Kant expressed enthusiasm for *Jerusalem* yet completely ignored both the historical thrust of its argument and its defense of Judaism as a "revealed legislation." Kant welcomed Mendelssohn's text as "the proclamation of a great reform that is gradually becoming imminent, a reform that is in store not only for your own people but for other nations as well":

> You have managed to unite with your religion a degree of freedom of thought that one would hardly have thought possible and of which no other religion can boast. You have at the same time thoroughly and clearly shown it necessary that every religion have unrestricted freedom of thought, so that finally even the Church will have to consider how to rid itself of everything that burdens and oppresses man's conscience, and

mankind will finally be united with regard to the essential point of religion. For all religious propositions that burden our conscience are based
on history, that is, on making blessedness contingent on belief in the
truth of those historical propositions.[50]

What Kant admires about *Jerusalem* here is not its authentic presentation of
Judaism but its philosophical ingenuity, its surprising ability to overcome
all odds and reconceptualize Judaism to make it compatible with freedom
of conscience. *Jerusalem*, as Kant reads it, does not defend Judaism against
Christianity and reassess the legitimacy claims of the religion of the majority
culture. It elevates Judaism to a paradigmatic expression of rational religion,
the implication being that if Mendelssohn can recast Judaism in this manner,
then *any* historical religion can be made compatible with the claims of
reason in the present. Mendelssohn, for Kant, does not offer up an account
of Judaism and Christian origins that challenges Christian universalism
and defends "external" rituals against their denigration at the hands of
Protestant theologians. There is, indeed, nothing at all particularly Jewish—
or historically specific—about *Jerusalem*. What Mendelssohn does, Kant suggests, is offer an impressive example of the process by which one can move
beyond historical religions to arrive at the universalism of rational inquiry.
Rather than seeking to *reconcile* reason and historical religion, Mendelssohn
uses reason to overcome the burdens of Judaism and history alike, and it is
for this reason that *Jerusalem* offers such a propitious model for religious
reform.

The subordination of history to reason that Kant forces on Mendelssohn
represents an essential element of Kant's own thinking on religion and modernity. Like Fichte's *Critique of All Revelation*, *Religion within the Limits of Reason
Alone* defines its object as a corollary to Kant's rational ethics, and this move
hinges in crucial ways on a denigration of historical knowledge. Fichte's philosophical critique of revelation showed little interest in the historical world,
except for its concluding remark, duly noted by Ascher, that Christianity as a
revealed religion prescribed the same path as critical reason.[51] In his demonstration of the normative value of Jesus's Christianity, Kant spends much more
time squaring his view of rational religion with both the historical record and
contemporary historical scholarship. He intersperses his argument with frequent citations from the Bible, primarily the New Testament, and engages
explicitly with issues of historical biblical criticism, demonstrating his
familiarity with Reimarus's *Fragments* and works by Michaelis and other contemporary authors. For Kant, historical critics like Michaelis and Reimarus
practice a mode of exegesis that, in its overriding concern with empirical detail
and the historical past, travels decisively "beyond the limits of the domain of

bare reason" and frequently ends up being opposed to reason.[52] Kant proposes and practices thus an alternative biblical hermeneutics, one he defines both here and in the *Contest of the Faculties* (1798) as a "philosophical" as opposed to a "biblical" theology.[53] Unencumbered by the search for an authentic historical past, Kant's philosophical theologian deliberately seeks to *make* scripture compatible with the religion of reason, interpreting passages from the Bible in such a way as to assimilate them to the dictates of rational morality. The willfulness of this hermeneutics does not pose a problem for Kant. "Frequently," he concedes, "this interpretation may, in the light of the text (of the revelation), appear forced—it may often really be forced; and yet if the text can possibly support it, it must be preferred to a literal interpretation which either contains nothing at all [helpful] to morality or else actually works counter to moral incentives."[54] What reason needs to do in its encounter with historical religion is to obliterate all that which is merely historical so as to arrive at the rational morality that may (or may not) be embedded in scripture's "alleged revelations." For Kant, the sole purpose of reading the Bible is moral improvement, and the "historical element, which contributes nothing to this end, is something which is in itself quite indifferent, and we can do with it what we like."[55]

Kant was thus not just paying Mendelssohn a compliment by misrepresenting *Jerusalem* the way he did. By disposing of the historical dimension of Mendelssohn's account of Judaism, his recasting of *Jerusalem* also exemplified his own practice of interpretation. In this sense, the 1783 letter to Mendelssohn anticipates the peculiar discussion of *Jerusalem* in the *Religion*. In his effort to establish a radical opposition between the burdensome ceremonies and coercive laws of historical Judaism and the pure religion of reason introduced by Jesus, Kant clearly has to deal in some manner with Mendelssohn's account of Judaism serving as the indispensable foundation for the development of Christianity. When it comes to this aspect of *Jerusalem*, Kant initially finds himself unable to praise Mendelssohn for transcending the limitations of historical religion. As Kant sees it, however, Mendelssohn's problem is not his polemical stance *vis-à-vis* Christianity but his misunderstanding of the historical record, his failure to comprehend why Christianity originally represented itself as deriving from Judaism. Early Christians certainly did trace their genealogy to Judaism's textual tradition. In its inception, however, this was nothing more than a strategic move, a retrospective fiction invented as a means of introducing and disseminating their new faith. The reliance on such historical narratives is a "weak spot in the customary presentation of Christianity" that Mendelssohn ingeniously zoned in on so as to "reject every demand upon a son of Israel that he change his religion."[56] Lacking the proper understanding of the missionary tactics of the early followers of Jesus, Mendelssohn fell prey to an interpretive practice directly opposed to that of Kant's philosophical theologian: he misread this historical narrative as the foundational logic of Christianity, viewing Christianity solely as an historical religion rather than the pure rational faith that Kant takes it to be. Mendelssohn offered up a peculiarly "Jewish" version of Christianity: he refused to see it in form or content as anything more than an addendum to Judaism, remaking it in the image of Judaism as an historical faith.

For a philosophical theologian like Kant, however, it is also possible to read Mendelssohn against the grain, to tease out from his explicit pronouncements about Judaism and Christianity a call for the de-Judaization of Christianity that supports Kant's own program. Distancing himself once again from all that was merely historical in Mendelssohn, Kant is able to uncover for his readers the rational subtext apparently hidden in Mendelssohn's defense of historical Judaism. As in his letter to Mendelssohn, Kant here also hails *Jerusalem* as a model for universal religious reform, distinguishing Mendelssohn's apologetics for Judaism from what he insists was the Jewish philosopher's "real intention." What Mendelssohn really meant to say to his Protestant peers was the following: "First wholly remove Judaism itself out of your *religion* (it can always remain, as an antiquity, in the historical account of the faith); we can then take your proposal [for conversion] under advisement. (Actually nothing would then be left but pure moral religion unencumbered by statutes.) Our burden will not be lightened in the least by throwing off the yoke of outer observances if, in its place, another yoke, namely confession of faith in sacred history—a yoke which rests far more heavily upon the conscientious—is substituted in its place."[57] Read in this manner, Mendelssohn's *Jerusalem* does not defend Judaism as a revealed legislation that helps promote rational religion. It actively supports Kant's polemics against Judaism, celebrating rational religion over against Judaism's statutory laws, calling for a rejection of both historical religion and sacred history in order to embrace a pure moral religion free of statutes and the burdens of the past—which is, of course, Kant's vision of Christianity in its purest form. Judaism operates here as a paradigm for all revealed religion, gesturing toward a threat that can conveniently be contained as mere history. The "sacred books" of the Jews, he explains, will always be of value as a window into the history of antiquity, but "not for the benefit of religion."[58]

Arguing in this vein, Kant explicitly excludes Judaism from the history of religion proper. The lengthy section of the *Religion* dealing with the "historical account of the gradual establishment of the sovereignty of the good principle on earth" spends more time talking about Judaism than any other non-Christian faith, but it does so in order to deny it any role in the genesis of Christian universalism. Kant's interest here is not to write up an "historical account merely of the dogmas of diverse peoples" but to outline the "unity of principle" that helps one "construe the succession of different types of belief following one another as modifications of one and the same church."[59] Kant proposes a universal history of religious faith here that hinges on the same willful relation to the historical world as his philosophical biblical criticism; the empirical details of history need to be replaced by a philosophy of history here in much the same way as literal interpretations of the Bible needed to make way for the philosophical theologian's efforts to make scripture conform to the dictates of a rational morality.[60] In this context, Judaism becomes the ultimate embodiment of the opposition between reason and history, the historical faith that must by all means be excluded from Kant's universal history of rational religion. Judaism, Kant explains, may have immediately preceded Christianity and provided the "physical occasion" for the establishment of the Christian Church, but it has "no essential connection" to it.[61] In a move that secures the "unity of principle" he needs for his philosophy of history, Kant reduces Judaism to the historical faith *par excellence*, the merely physical occasion for the emergence of Christianity as a rational religion that towers above history. Representing the relationship between Judaism and Christianity as anything other than an instance of historical contingency both mistakenly perpetuates the missionary tactics of early Christians and runs the risk of unraveling the systematic intent behind the *Religion*'s entire philosophy of history: "We cannot, therefore, do otherwise than begin general church history, if it is to constitute a system, with the origin of Christianity, which, completely forsaking the Judaism from which it sprang, and grounded upon a wholly new principle, effected a thoroughgoing revolution in doctrines of faith."[62]

Kant's deliberate rewriting of *Jerusalem* is indicative of more general tensions in the *Religion*, a work that Ascher found to be grounded in serious anxieties over the role of Judaism in the genesis of Christianity. In *Eisenmenger*, Ascher reintroduced the historical aspect of Mendelssohn's writings that Kant had sought to dispose of, identifying a distinct power dynamic in the *Religion*'s denigration of Judaism and history alike: "It is the fate of Judaism, to which Christianity undoubtedly owes so much, that no champion of the latter can present his credentials without annihilating Judaism's lapsed right to the same with all the skills of a philosophical politics. And this is how Herr Kant begins."[63] The fact that champions of Christianity like Kant use a "philosophical politics" to denigrate Judaism results for Ascher directly from Christianity's lack of originality. It is apparently not enough that Christianity grew out of and allegedly surpassed Judaism at one point in history. It continually needs to disparage its Jewish origins in order to sustain itself in the present, pointing over and over again to Judaism's lapsed right to champion its own cause. Kant's insistence that there is no essential connection between Judaism and Christianity has to be seen in this framework as a self-conscious act of denial; his view of Christianity as a rational religion that produced itself out of itself is symptomatic of a much larger problem within Christianity, an antipathy toward the historical past grounded in Christianity's inability to give an adequate account of its own Jewish origins. Ascher thus reinstates the polemical thrust of Mendelssohn's *Jerusalem*, challenging Kant by offering up yet another Jewish account of the hybridity of Christian origins.

Ascher's goal in contesting Kant in this manner was not to jettison the *Religion* and assert the claims of history over against those of Kantian reason. As in his discussion of Fichte, here too he seeks to critique Kantianism from within, calling attention to the shortcomings of the critical philosophy in practice, the inability of philosophers like Kant to abstract themselves from history the way they claim to. Kant's problem, like Fichte's, is not that he aspires to establish rational norms of religion and morality that transcend history but that he fails to examine the extent to which his own position on Judaism—and history—may itself be the product of specific historical developments. Kant's relation to Judaism, like Fichte's, moreover, is more than an aberration from a philosophical system that is rigorous in all other respects. Anti-Judaism functions as a cornerstone of the *Religion*'s vision of modernity, a problem Ascher highlights by reflecting on Kant's peculiar account of Christianity as arising from Judaism in a manner that was "sudden, although not unprepared for."[64] For Ascher, it is in Kant's attempt to specify the exact nature of the historical contingency linking Judaism to Jesus's presciently modern Christianity that the full arbitrariness of his historiography reveals and unravels itself.

In the section of the *Religion* Ascher scrutinizes here, Kant explains that the Jewish political constitution and the power of the priesthood had degenerated by the time of Jesus, making it possible for "this otherwise ignorant people . . . to receive much foreign (Greek) wisdom. This wisdom presumably had the further effect of enlightening Judaism with concepts of virtue and, despite the pressing weight of its dogmatic faith, of preparing it for revolution."[65] If anything paved the way for Jesus's "sudden" revolution, that is, it must have been the liberating force of Greek philosophy, which Kant explicitly opposes to the oppressive spirit of Judaism's political constitution as "ethical doctrines of freedom" that were "staggering to the slavish [Jewish] mind."[66] In his unpublished *Reflections on Anthropology*, Kant takes these speculations one step further, speaking of a "Greek" Jesus whose genius consisted of cloaking Occidental wisdom in Oriental dress.[67] For Ascher, Kant's refusal to grant Judaism any normative role in the genesis of Christianity is more than an example of how Kant fails to rise above inherited prejudice.

This vision of the "sudden, though not unprepared for" emergence of Christianity constitutes a weakness that ultimately undermines his system:

> In the moment that he wrote this, Herr Kant entirely renounced his philosophy, that is, his calling as a thinker to investigate the causes and consequences of all phenomena. Imagine, my dear reader: Christianity arose suddenly. Suddenly, a principle developed (developed?—I have really no precise word for this) that could serve as the foundation for Christianity.—Suddenly, Jesus stood there and announced himself as having been sent from Heaven. What a philosophical *Deus ex machina!*— What a philosophical *Saltus mortalis!*
>
> We do not want to see the matter happening so *suddenly.*—Exactly what sort of political constitution did the Jews have at the time of the birth of Jesus of Nazareth? What culture did the nation have in itself, and what culture had it received from abroad? And what was the influence of all this on their religion and customs?—Whoever answers these questions with a critical spirit will not see Christianity arising suddenly. On the contrary, he will have to find the entire spirit of Christianity in the Judaism of the day.[68]

For Ascher, Kant's insistence on an absolute break between Judaism and Jesus's Greek-inspired version of Kantian ethics has little to do with a critical interrogation of the historical sources. It exposes like nothing else the willfulness of his historiography, his need to see a pure rational religion giving rise to itself within history yet apart from any and all historical contingency. Ascher obviously does not deny Hellenistic influences in ancient Palestine. In his *Leviathan*, in fact, he engaged explicitly with this issue, assigning Greek philosophy and the Septuagint a prominent role in preserving the fundamentals of Judaism in antiquity.[69] What Ascher calls for here is simply a more critical historiography than that governing Kant's historical "presumptions," one that would carefully study early Christianity against the diverse backdrop of first-century Judaism rather than view it as the static antithesis of a vilified Jewish anti-religion. In his effort to establish a priori norms of religion and morality, Kant, like Fichte, tends to sidestep rather than overcome the contingencies of the historical world. Kant presents Jesus's Christianity as a distinctly modern religion, that is, only by betraying his own philosophical principles, using a "philosophical *Deus ex machina*" and a "philosophical *Saltus mortalis*" that exemplify the sort of reliance on supernatural revelation that *Religion within the Limits of Reason Alone* and the *Critique of All Revelation* sought to displace. Ascher realizes in making this argument, of course, that nowhere in the *Religion* did Kant ever profess to be interested in the historical Jesus. The idea of Jesus is an idea of practical reason, the "archetype of the moral disposition in all its purity," a strictly rational idea that actually has no need of an empirical example.[70] The problem for Ascher is not that Kant elevates the historical Jesus to the status of an archetype or even that he rereads passages from scripture in order to present the religion of Jesus as the ultimate embodiment of Kantian ethics. What Ascher takes issue with is the byproduct of this method, the historical argument Kant presents in his effort to interpret Christianity in this manner. For the privilege Kant bestows on Christianity as a distinctly modern rational religion is inseparable from his account of Christian origins, and this historiography hinges on a denigration of Judaism that derives its legitimation from a *Deus ex machina* that contradicts the very spirit of Kant's critical philosophy.

Ascher's ambition in *Eisenmenger* is not just to expose this fundamental contradiction in the *Religion* but also to challenge Kant and Fichte by offering his own account of the relationship between Judaism and modernity. It is in this context, tellingly, that he calls attention to both the program for reform he issued two years earlier in *Leviathan* and to the political stakes of any such attempt to "purify" Judaism for modernity. Ascher seeks to do more in *Eisenmenger* than expose Fichte's and Kant's modernization of antisemitism. He endeavors to issue a distinct warning to his fellow Jews about the political implications of this novel species of "moral" Jew-hatred and to outline, for Jews and Gentiles alike, an alternative conception of modernity, one that would be grounded in a normative vision of Judaism.

THE POLITICS OF REFORM

By its very nature, the anti-Jewish arguments in Kant's *Religion* targeted Judaism *per se* rather than the political status of the Jews or their "national character." Kant's assumption, expressed in passing, of a radical opposition between Orient and Occident may indeed seem reminiscent of Michaelis's worldview. And elsewhere Kant did indulge in anti-Jewish comments of a more anthropological bent, casting serious doubts on the prospects of transforming this nation of "Palestinian swindlers" into productive citizens.[71] But nowhere in his *oeuvre*—and this includes his contributions to contemporary thinking on race—did he ever express anything resembling the racial grounding for Jewish identity we found in Michaelis. In this regard, Fichte's rhetorical suggestion that only guillotine-assisted head surgery might regenerate the Jews clearly marks a radicalization of Kant's anti-Judaism. Yet even in its strictly demarcated concern with Judaism rather than Jews, the *Religion* was obviously more than a treatise on religion. Given the atmosphere in which it was published, the contention that Judaism was incompatible with morality and incapable of producing moral human beings was a distinctly political argument about contemporary Jewry as well. The political import of the *Religion*, moreover, was not just apparent to Jews like Ascher. In *The Contest of the Faculties* (1798) Kant himself spelled out the ramifications of his argument for any consideration of Jewish emancipation, referring here with great enthusiasm to the proposals for reform put forth by another Jewish Kantian in Berlin, Lazarus Bendavid. In his 1793 pamphlet *On Jewish Characteristics*, Bendavid had encouraged Jews to renounce the "senseless" and "anachronistic" ceremonial law and return to the "pure teaching of Moses."[72] In *The Contest of the Faculties*, Kant equated Bendavid's reform project with an attempt to perform a "euthanasia of Judaism" and embrace the pure religion of Jesus. This, he argued—and not conversion to institutional Christianity—would be the best and only way to make the Jews an "educated, well-cultured people, capable of enjoying all the rights of civil society."[73] Jews can prove themselves worthy of civil rights, that is, only if they grant Judaism the natural death it should have experienced centuries earlier and reenact that inaugural moment of modernity Kant identified in the *Religion* with Jesus's introduction of rational religion in opposition to Jewish law.

When Prussian Jews such as Ascher began to call for religious reform in the 1790s, they did so against the background of this political and philosophical denigration of Judaism. Any effort to conceive of Judaism as distinct from Mosaic law here was potentially double-edged. Kantian reformers such as Bendavid and Ascher were in a particularly precarious situation, always in danger of appearing to participate in the modernized Jew-hatred Ascher identified as a hallmark of contemporary philosophy; Kant's representation of Jewish law as the antithesis of moral autonomy was practically predisposed to make any Jewish attempt to deemphasize the law appear as a step toward Kant's interpretation of Christianity. In the case of Bendavid, moreover, it is certainly possible to contend that Kant was not performing such an egregious misreading of his program for reform. Bendavid's *On Jewish Characteristics* was unrelenting in its critique of the degenerate state of contemporary Jewry and the "senselessness" of Mosaic law. Unlike Mendelssohn, Bendavid offered neither a significant challenge to the terms of emancipation nor a rigorous engagement with Jewish tradition. He simply equated the "pure teaching of Moses" with the "teachings of natural religion," declaring rather than arguing that a Judaism purged of the law would conform perfectly with Enlightenment ideals of rational religion and thus expedite civic improvement.[74] Jews less well versed in Kantian philosophy often trod on similar ground. The physician Sabattja Joseph Wolff (1757–1832) published an anonymous pamphlet in 1792 that also made emancipation contingent on rejection of the "burdensome" ceremonial law. Like Bendavid, Wolff defined reform in the vaguest possible terms, calling simply for the restoration of an essentially rational spirit of Judaism defined in strict opposition to the law.[75]

Particularly in the case of Ascher, whose 246-page *Leviathan* was by far the most substantial of these early reform proposals, it can be misleading to reduce religious reform to its political function or charge it with perpetuating Protestant attitudes toward Jewish legalism. Like Bendavid and Wolff, to be sure, Ascher also articulated his vision of reform in a distinctly political context; for all three writers, reform was part and parcel of the project of civic improvement, an effort to pave the way for the moral regeneration and eventual political emancipation of contemporary Jewry. Ascher's stated goal was as much to promote a practical "reformation" of Judaism for Jews as it was to demonstrate, for non-Jews, that Judaism as such was entirely capable of promoting morality and ensuring the development of a moral citizenry. His vision of religious regeneration, however, differed considerably from those of Bendavid and Wolff, not least of all because it was grounded in an explicit engagement with both Jewish tradition and the terms of the Kantian denigration of Judaism. Ascher published *Leviathan* one year before Kant's *Religion*, and thus without any awareness of the particulars of its presentation of Judaism. The *Religion*'s position on historical religion and Judaism in particular, however, derived almost entirely both from Kant's critical writings of the 1780s and from the general anti-Judaism of Enlightenment culture, and both of these were clearly in Ascher's mind as he set forth the terms of his Kantian vision of religious reform. It is not just in *Eisenmenger* that Ascher enlisted the arguments of *Leviathan* in his struggle against Kant and Fichte. In its very method, *Leviathan* was designed to undermine precisely that vision of history that would become the crux of Kant's modernized Jew-hatred.

In the opening section of *Leviathan*, Ascher insisted that the task of enlightenment was "not to forget and besmear all sacredness" but to translate the sacredness of previous ages into the medium of the present.[76] When it comes to the relationship between historical Judaism and the claims of reason in modernity, accordingly, *Leviathan* obviously takes a different tack than Kant's *Religion*. Complaining that nearly all contemporary writers view Judaism as inextricably rooted in the historical past, Ascher takes as his point of departure the notion that Judaism has an "essence" or an "inner spirit" distinct from any of its particular historical manifestations:

No one has attempt to develop Judaism in and for itself according to its supreme principles, to define and grapple with it as an object worthy of philosophical investigation. . . . [One needs, therefore,] to penetrate into the inner spirit of Judaism and show distinctly what constitutes its essence, insofar as one limits it from all sides and represents it entirely plainly and without all ornament. One must not show it as one perceives it at first glance, but as it can be under all circumstances, not insofar as it is influenced by culture, industry, change in customs and trade but insofar it is a fundamental need related to the necessary conditions of human thought, which is, after all, the proper purpose of every religion.[77]

Following the Kantian mode of critical inquiry whose imperfect application he censured in *Eisenmenger*, Ascher wants to abstract Judaism from all historical contingency. Ascher explicitly invokes the language of the *Critique of Pure Reason* here, making a distinction between Judaism as it appears and Judaism as it is in itself, between Judaism as "phenomenon" and Judaism as "noumenon." The very claim that Judaism has an essence, however, also mounts an obvious challenge to the typical position of Judaism in Enlightenment historiography—whether Michaelis's Orientalism, Lessing's vision of the education of humankind or Kant's opposition between historical Judaism and rational religion. Judaism for Ascher is a type of human religion related to the necessary conditions of human thought, and as such, it clearly cannot be viewed as the static antithesis of Jesus's Christianity or a primitive survival from the Oriental past. Like Kant's vision of Christianity, Judaism warrants and requires a philosophical investigation of its own, and it is by interrogating the essence of Judaism and translating it into the medium of the present that Ascher seeks to intervene in the debates over emancipation.

Ascher unfolds this argument about Judaism within a broader theory of religion. Part I of *Leviathan* treats "religion in general" at great length, arguing that all religions are products of the human spirit that help promote individual and collective felicity. In vague (and not always consistent) anticipation of Romantic views on religion, Ascher contends that religious faith is an experience *sui generis* that cannot be assimilated to reason, and it is this move that allows him to defend revelation, rendering it a function of religious faith.[78] For the most part, however, *Leviathan* remains indebted to Enlightenment views of rational religion infused with a heavy dose of Kantian ethics. Ascher's argument hinges on a distinction he draws, using Kantian terminology, between "regulative" and "constitutive" religion. In "regulative" religion— and nearly all religions are regulative in their inception—the essence or spirit of a religion is always present and continually in flux, lacking the external trappings of church, dogma or ecclesiastical laws. When a religion organizes itself and gives itself an external form, a "constitution," it becomes "constitutive" for Ascher. It is in the light of this distinction that he deals, in part II, with Judaism, foraying into Jewish history in search of the doctrinal essence of Judaism as a regulative religion. Ascher concentrates here, not surprisingly, on pre-Mosaic Judaism, presenting Mosaic law as but one possible "constitution" for Judaism, and one that Mendelssohn and Spinoza mistakenly confused with Judaism's supreme purpose. It is, Ascher demonstrates, not the law but a "true autonomy of the will" that characterizes Judaism in its regulative form.[79] Part III of *Leviathan* sets out the terms of Ascher's proposed "purification" or "reformation" of Judaism, calling for a new religious "constitution" that would clearly lay forth Judaism's doctrinal core and demonstrate, for Jews and non-Jews alike, the timeless value of their ancient faith.

Ascher's interest here is not liturgical or ritual reform. In this sense, *Leviathan*'s immediate ambition differs considerably from that of the Reform movement that began to develop in the early decades of the nineteenth century. In later years, in fact, Ascher spoke disdainfully of the practically oriented reform efforts of his Jewish contemporaries, insisting that the first task of religious regeneration had to be to clarify and codify Judaism's dogmatic teachings, not to engage in "superficial" modifications of the prayer service or succumb to Christian influences and put choirs and organs in Jewish houses of worship.[80] *Leviathan* engages specifically with this task, proposing that Jews adopt a series of "articles of faith" as the basis for their new religious constitution. Ascher himself suggests fourteen such articles of faith, all of which seek to strike a balance between the universality of Judaism's ethical monotheism and the particularity of Jewish identity. Calling on his fellow "children of Israel" to "remain on the path of our parents," Ascher begins here by delineating the Jewish belief in one God who revealed himself to the Jews' forefathers and gave them laws at Mount Sinai. The God of Judaism, he stresses, is a God of love, who will reward the good and punish the bad and who governs the world through his care and omnipotence. Claiming that Jews now have a secure faith in God and his prophets, Ascher insists that the laws that were holy to his forefathers are no longer necessary. By no means, however, does he simply substitute clearly formulated religious doctrine for Jewish law. Ascher's new constitution expressly perpetuates rituals such as circumcision and the observance of the Sabbath and the festivals. Unlike Mendelssohn, moreover, he includes an explicit commitment to the idea of messianic redemption in his normative vision of modern Judaism.[81]

Delineating a new constitution for contemporary Jewry is not just about religious regeneration for Ascher. It is also a political move, and not only because it is intended to help pave the way for emancipation. In the chapter at the center of the book that lays forth the "essence of Judaism," Ascher makes clear that recuperating the spirit of Judaism in its regulative form has major consequences for how contemporary thinkers view Christianity.

Without any knowledge of the particulars of Kant's *Religion*, Ascher expresses a fundamental critique of the dynamic underlying Kant's recuperation of Christianity as a distinctly modern religion:

> According to the purpose that the most profound thinkers ascribe to the Christian religion, Christ is supposed to have come to teach moral truths to humans. I honestly admit I cannot accept this notion, but let me hypostatize this purpose, not to degrade it but to view it in a much more sublime light. If I do so, I must ask whether it would not be far preferable, from a methodological perspective, to give the human being the basis of all his concepts, letting him independently prescribe a norm for his own behavior by himself—just as every revealed religion must do if it is supposed to be universally applicable?
>
> One says that Christ's principles are for all human beings. Yet would not a foundation that supplies the sources of all these principles be more excellent? And does not Judaism actually supply such a foundation?
>
> Judaism, as we have seen, merely gives a rule for the understanding; Christianity gives also a rule for the will. Should thus primitive Judaism not be able to supply a universal religion much more easily than Christianity, if one regards it as a rule for the will? A rule of the will gains its determination only through a form of reason, and for this reason, Judaism alone should be sufficient. Why would we need objective rules that do not elevate the human being above his dignity, as religion should, but simply leave him as human as he is to begin with?[82]

Mendelssohn, we remember, challenged his contemporaries' views of the coercive nature of Mosaic law by arguing that Judaism was not a revealed religion but a revealed legislation that lacked doctrine or religious dogma. For Mendelssohn, Judaism only prescribed laws governing conduct and thus never sought to control the realm of conscience in the same manner as did Christianity. Mosaic law had the function of leading Jews toward the truths of rational religion, and it did so in an entirely noncoercive fashion, without ever forcing Jews to accept the type of dogma he found typical of Christianity. In his account of the relationship between Judaism and Christianity here, Ascher obviously rejects the position that Judaism lacks all dogmatic content; in its regulative form, Judaism is indeed a revealed religion for Ascher. It is, however, precisely in his departure from Mendelssohn that Ascher perpetuates Mendelssohn's polemical defense of Judaism, updating it with the tools of Kantian ethics. For as Ascher explicates it here, the difference between Judaism and Christianity is again one of freedom versus coercion, autonomy versus heteronomy. The image of Jesus as a moral teacher—and Kant was the last in a long line of Enlightenment thinkers who put forth this view—

involves for Ascher a form of pedagogy that is diametrically opposed to the type of free rational inquiry one encounters in Judaism. Judaism does not merely supply the historical foundation for Christianity. It also gives Christianity its philosophical groundwork, guiding the individual toward the type of intellectual and moral autonomy Kant had foregrounded in his writings of the 1780s. In *Leviathan*, as in *Jerusalem*, Christianity blatantly betrays its Jewish foundations, giving rules to the will in a manner that is antithetical to the spirit of Kantian ethics. As a revealed religion, Judaism supplies the individual with the basis for independent rational and moral development, and it is for this reason that it—and not Christianity—figures in *Leviathan* as the ideal prototype for a universal religion.

As one might expect, it is this section of *Leviathan* that Ascher references in his arguments against Kant and Fichte in *Eisenmenger*. One of the crucial problems with Kant's *Religion*, he writes, is that it fails to consider the extent to which Judaism "originally had no constitutive institution; it was, as I have demonstrated at greater length elsewhere, *regulative*."[83] Ascher here censures Kant for failing to read *Leviathan*, a work that was reviewed in prominent journals and that certainly would have been available to Kant had he been interested in following Ascher's thought.[84] Rather than considering the essence of Judaism and recognizing that it contains the germ of a universal church, Kant mistakes a caricature of Judaism's constitution for its essence and thus perpetuates all sorts of prejudices about it—that it lacks a belief in the afterlife; that it only forms a political rather than an ethical commonwealth; that it excludes the entire human race from its congregation; that although it envisions its ineffable God as the ruler of the world, it only borrowed this notion from the polytheistic ideas of other peoples, etc.[85] Retrospectively, then, Ascher explicitly casts his *Leviathan* as a corrective to the *Religion*, calling attention to the manner in which his earlier vision of Judaism's fundamental compatibility with—and anticipation of—the Kantian vision of modernity blatantly challenges the denigration of Judaism so central to Kant's *Religion*.

In developing this argument in *Eisenmenger*, Ascher revisits Kant's account of the historical relationship between Judaism and Christianity, expanding on the point he made earlier that the "entire spirit" of Christianity was present in first-century Judaism. Ascher zones in here on one crucial aspect of the *Religion*, Kant's insistence that the abolition of circumcision by later Christians somehow offers solid proof of the radical disjunction between Christian universalism and the Jews' this-worldly national politics. Kant had argued, as part of his discussion of Christianity's "sudden" emergence, that "dispensing with the corporal sign" was sufficient evidence that Christianity was not bound to the "statutes" of Judaism but was intended instead to "comprise a religion valid for the world."[86] The discontinuation of this sign of Jewish difference among early Christians, then, offers proof of Jesus's ultimate intents; Kant gives Christianity an historical grounding only by making its origins once again exempt from the forces of historical development. Ascher's response, not surprisingly, is to open up for investigation precisely this historical gap between Jesus's intentions and the development of early Christianity. For Ascher, Jesus was not just a Jew preaching to his fellow Jews but a circumcised Jew with little interest in abolishing this ancient Jewish rite:

> I am gladly willing to admit that the divinity was helpful to the founder of Christianity in insisting that Judaism be given a different direction by the purer moral doctrine that his apostles ascribed to Jesus. I will, however, never admit that Jesus invented this moral doctrine so that it might be communicated to the world. This does prove, however, that Judaism was merely transformed into Christianity rather than that Christianity was in and for itself supposed to be opposed to Judaism. . . .
>
> The apostles saw that the words of their teacher were finding few followers among the Jews and that these few were not able to speak out. They thus felt it necessary to leave Palestine. Much of what Jesus had said were truths spoken to the Jews, and in this context he always took the cornerstones of their religious constitution into consideration. I am convinced that the apostles were not so shortsighted as to go abroad and recite these truths along with these expressed limitations. I believe much more that they sought to disseminate these truths naked of all caviling. Jesus in preaching to the Jews neither wanted to nor could have begun by abolishing circumcision. The apostles, however, neither wanted to nor could have made this rite a condition of their faith abroad. Only eventually, as the faith of the apostles gained many followers abroad, did the Jewish-Christians venture to abolish circumcision. The subsequent abolition of circumcision thus does not license Herr Kant to claim that Jesus's intent was to establish a world religion.[87]

Anything but the bodily inscription of the difference between Judaism and Christianity, circumcision is here identified as the corporal sign of their fundamental connection. Judaism is no longer the merely "physical occasion" for the emergence of Christianity as a rational universal religion that towers above history. Circumcised Jews, rather, played a crucial role in the early dissemination of Christianity, preaching a moral doctrine to Gentiles that had its spiritual origins entirely within the Jewish world of Jesus and his early followers. Christianity is thus not a world religion that can be defined as the negation of Judaism. It has to be understood instead as an outgrowth of Judaism's regulative spirit. Anything but a corporal sign that marks the antithesis of the form of modernity Kant found in Christianity, circumcision serves as the sign of Judaism's universalist potential and historical mission.

In *Leviathan* and *Eisenmenger* Ascher does much more than claim a central historical and philosophical role for Judaism in the genesis of both Christianity and modernity. By foregrounding this aspect of Jewish identity in both his critique of Kant and the articles of faith he proposes for Judaism's new constitution, he unsettles the rigid oppositions between reason and history, Christianity and Judaism, spirit and body that were so crucial to Kant's vision of modernity and its denigration of Judaism. In seeking to lay bare the doctrinal essence of Judaism, Ascher's program for a "reformed" Judaism calls attention to what has traditionally been Jewish men's most noted sign of self-imposed difference, granting circumcision a symbolic function for contemporary Jewry and underlining its crucial role in the genesis of Christianity. As Ascher presents it, a reformed Judaism would not merely ensure a moral citizenry and enable the political emancipation of Jews. In translating Judaism into the medium of the present, he also calls attention to the presence of the past, as it were, ensuring the perpetuation of that religion that Kant wanted to dispose of as a merely "physical" occasion for the genesis of Christianity. If Kant characterizes modernity as the triumph of reason over Judaism and history alike, Ascher counters Kant by claiming for Judaism an historical and philosophical role in the genesis of modernity, a role Jews should commemorate in the present by following a religious constitution that perpetuates precisely that bodily Jewish rite whose abolition signals for Kant the onset of modernity.

ASCHER'S GHOST

For a book with such ambitious goals, *Eisenmenger* did not shake up the philosophical world of its day. There were, to be sure, individual expressions of sympathy—if not overwhelming solidarity—with Ascher's critique of Kant and Fichte. When the poet and translator Karl Ludwig von Knebel (1744–1834), a close friend of Goethe, sent Johann Gottfried Herder a copy of *Eisenmenger* in 1794, he did so with the comment that "the Jew" presented a good argument against Fichte, one that was perhaps more consistent than Fichte's own.[88] An anonymous reviewer in a prominent journal similarly remarked that Ascher illuminated significant "improprieties" in Fichte's text and was correct in his critique of Kant as well, even though the author qualified his praise by introducing Ascher as "nothing less than a blind and passionate apologist for Judaism."[89] Yet these restrained words of appreciation were not typical of the more general reaction to *Eisenmenger*. Modern critics, as mentioned earlier, routinely reference Ascher when discussing Kant's and

Fichte's anti-Jewish polemics, using the voice of a Jewish contemporary to bolster their own arguments about the problematic nature of Kant's and Fichte's statements about Jews and Judaism. Participants in the debates over Jewish emancipation in following years, moreover, frequently invoked Fichte's polemics and Ascher's response. In the 1790s, however—and this is the crucial issue—not a single Kantian felt the need to respond to Ascher's challenge in any formal manner whatsoever. There is no evidence that Kant or Fichte even took notice of Ascher's book. Ascher's contention that Kantian universalism was marred in practice by its legitimation of Jew-hatred indicated a problem that clearly did not trouble—or even interest—most of his contemporaries in the philosophical world. In a roundabout way, the reception of *Eisenmenger* thus serves as indirect testimony to the power of the "new species of Jew-hatred" it sought to combat. Kantianism did not merely provide the semblance of a philosophical grounding for a distinctly modern form of moral and political antagonism toward Jews and Judaism. It apparently did so with enormous ease, provoking apart from Ascher's critique no noteworthy rebuttals of any kind.

Eisenmenger was not the only of Ascher's works to meet this fate. *Leviathan* also ended up being largely ignored by those contemporaries whom it sought to provoke into dialogue. In 1815, in *Germanomania*, Ascher still spoke of the "undivided approval" *Leviathan* met with in the Christian theological world, noting that Jews probably ignored his seminal vision of religious reform because it broke so prominently with Mendelssohn's defense of Judaism as a revealed legislation.[90] In the 1790s, indeed, *Leviathan* was reviewed rather widely, and at times favorably, in journals read by German Protestants, and while Ascher obviously exaggerates its positive reception in these circles, his account of the failure of his program for a "purified" Judaism to effect widespread change or even provoke much serious discussion in the Jewish community is right on target. Like Ascher himself, German-Jewish historians routinely invoke Ascher as the inaugural theorist of Reform Judaism. The main echo *Leviathan* left among Jewish intellectuals of the day, however, was Bendavid's derogatory comment, in his own reform proposals, that Ascher's work was a *Stockfisch*—a dried cod, or a stick-in-the-mud—acting as it if were a Leviathan.[91] *Leviathan* left no direct traces on the Reform movement that began to develop in the early nineteenth century. Unlike Bendavid or Friedländer, whom we will discuss in the next chapter, Ascher was somewhat of an outsider and not an active participant in Jewish community life. Unlike Mendelssohn, not surprisingly, Ascher has earned his place in German-Jewish historiography less for his direct influence than for his work as a speculative thinker, his articulation of theoretical positions and possibilities that strayed at times considerably from the mainstream.[92]

It is largely in the form of a ghost that Ascher has survived in the realm of German letters. In the German-Jewish poet Heinrich Heine's *Harz Journey* (1826), published four years after Ascher's death, Ascher appeared quite literally as an apparition, paying a nighttime visit to his former acquaintance Heine in Goslar. Heine portrayed Ascher as a caricature of Enlightenment rationalism with a "special malice" against Christianity, a "doctor of reason" who cites Kant's *Critique of Pure Reason* to dispute his own existence as a ghost.[93] Heine's mockery of Ascher was not atypical of the judgments nineteenth-century intellectuals passed on their Enlightenment precursors. There may be more—or less—at stake here than the anxiety of influence. As Walter Grab has noted, there is an obvious parallel between this characterization of Ascher and Heine's later polemics against his contemporary Ludwig Börne (1786–1837), a prominent German-Jewish political writer for whom one can justifiably claim Ascher as a precursor.[94]

What is most important for us about Heine's caricature of Ascher is the way it conceals nearly all the tensions in Enlightenment thought we have been exploring in this chapter. Characterizing Ascher as a figure who exemplifies Enlightenment rationalism obscures precisely the limitations of Enlightenment thought Ascher sought to expose and overcome. In both *Leviathan* and *Eisenmenger* Ascher was anything but a simple representative of Kantianism. He issued in these works a significant challenge to Kantian thought, charging it with failing to apply its mode of critique to the situation of contemporary Jews and with actively contributing to the modernization of Jew-hatred. Ascher, to be sure, may have been a polemicist without wide influence, but it is precisely the grand gestures of his polemics that are of interest to us, his vain effort to put forth a Jewish discourse on modernity that would challenge the philosophical vanguard of his day. Equating this position with a "special malice" against Christianity trivializes the powerful critique of Enlightenment universalism Ascher sought to express in his polemics against Kant and Fichte. The fact that Ascher's works from the 1790s did not provoke the reactions Ascher hoped for should not detract from their historical value. Indeed, particularly if we are concerned with appreciating the efforts of Jews to claim agency for themselves in the debates over their civic improvement, we should be careful not to equate lack of perceptible influence with lack of historical importance. What matters here is that Ascher *did* issue a challenge to the regnant discourse on Judaism and modernity, and that this challenge was overlooked by precisely those whom it sought to provoke into dialogue. Continuing the tradition of oppositional writing inaugurated by Mendelssohn, Ascher sought to radically reformulate the dominant discourse on modernity by the very act of securing a place for Jews and Judaism within it. The fact that Ascher's writings from this period fell on deaf ears may indeed have made it possible for Ascher to live on as a ghost haunting his nineteenth-century German-Jewish heirs. For us today, however, it may make sense to memorialize Ascher as a different sort of specter, as the author of a self-consciously modern—and self-consciously Jewish—critique of modernity that modernity seems not to have been able to accommodate.

DAVID FRIEDLÄNDER.

Fig. 8. Portrait of David Friedländer.
Courtesy of the Leo Baeck Institute, New York, with thanks to the Bildarchiv der
Österreichischen Nationalbibliothek.

5

JEWISH BAPTISM AND THE QUEST FOR
WORLD RULE

Perceptions of Jewish Power around 1800

FRIEDLÄNDER, GRATTENAUER AND THE SPECTER OF JEWISH POWER

For all their best efforts, neither Mendelssohn nor Ascher succeeded in articulating a Jewish vision of modernity forceful enough to provoke their non-Jewish contemporaries into a dialogue about the power dynamic by which they consigned Judaism to the irrevocable past. It is a fact of enormous importance that the one work from this period that was able to launch sustained debate among non-Jews about Judaism's claim to modernity is a text that Jewish historiography has traditionally had great difficulties viewing in any sort of positive terms. Indeed, the work in question, the *Open Letter to His Reverend, Provost Teller, Councilor of the Upper Consistory in Berlin* that David Friedländer published anonymously in 1799 in the name of "Several Family Heads of the Jewish Religion," hardly presented a religious or political platform any of its heirs could view as viable.[1] Friedländer (1750–1834), a member of Berlin Jewry's economic elite and a wealthy businessman, was a disciple of Mendelssohn who became his successor as the intellectual leader of the Berlin community after Mendelssohn's death in 1786. A collaborator on Mendelssohn's translation of the Pentateuch in the 1780s, Friedländer was a cofounder of the first modern Jewish school in Berlin, the Jüdische Freyschule, and had, like his mentor, published widely in journals targeting both Jews and the general public of Enlightenment intellectuals. In his *Open Letter* of 1799, he presented Wilhelm Abraham Teller, a liberal proponent of rational religion with a leading role in the governing body of the Protestant Church, with a proposal that has often been regarded as the ultimate example of opportunist assimilationism. Arguing that the essence of all religions was basically identical, Friedländer contended that the Jewish ceremonial law so important to Mendelssohn was but an outdated "shell" for the truths of rational religion. For this reason, he suggested that a group of enlightened

Jews like himself undergo baptism and convert to Christianity. The goal of Friedländer's Jewish family heads in writing to Teller was to inquire into the possibilities of joining the Church under these conditions and, if this inquiry should meet Teller's approval, to ask this prominent member of the upper consistory to suggest a form of baptism appropriate for a group of Jews willing to embrace the ritual forms of Protestant Christianity as mere containers for rational religion.

Unlike Mendelssohn's *Jerusalem* or Ascher's *Leviathan*, Friedländer's *Open Letter* has earned its place in German-Jewish historiography less as an honest attempt at Jewish religious renewal than as an act of political opportunism. In his enormously influential *History of the Jews*, the nineteenth-century historian Heinrich Graetz helped entrench this view of Friedländer, whose letter to Teller he denounced as a "cowardly," "silly," "dishonorable" and "foolish" scheme that attracted much more attention than it deserved at the time. Graetz accused Friedländer and his Jewish family heads of undermining the possibilities of sustaining Jewish identity in the modern era, lumping them together with the "sinful" and "morally depraved" Jewish women of the period whose eventual conversion to Christianity, he claimed, actually did Judaism a great service. For Graetz, both Friedländer and the prominent Jewish salonières of turn-of-the century Berlin such as Rahel Varnhagen and Henriette Herz essentially performed the work of the enemies of the Jews and broke the "power of Israel."[2] In her biography of Rahel Varnhagen, Hannah Arendt offered quite a different appraisal of the German-Jewish women of the period, stressing, among other things, the challenges Rahel issued to the logic of assimilation in acting as a "conscious pariah." For all her obvious differences from Graetz, however, Arendt retained his judgment of Friedländer, seeing the blatant opportunism of the letter to Teller as the antithesis of Rahel's grand act of resistance. In setting the stage for her discussion of Rahel, Arendt wrote that a political struggle for equal rights for Jews as Jews was "wholly unknown to this generation of Jews whose representatives even offered to accept mass baptism (David Friedländer). Jews did not even want to be emancipated as a whole; all they wanted was to escape from Jewishness, as individuals if possible."[3]

This verdict is not entirely off the mark. It was clear to many readers at the time that Friedländer's letter drew its motivation from despair over the fading possibilities of Jewish emancipation. Friedländer had been a passionate advocate of emancipation in the years leading up to the publication of the letter. He played a leading role in an unsuccessful campaign for increased Jewish rights from 1787 to 1793, writing a series of petitions and memoranda to the government that echoed Dohm's plea for emancipation; when these efforts finally failed, he presented the public with the documentation of this struggle, expressing once again his hope for rights that would not be contingent on the Jews' first proving themselves worthy of citizenship.[4] It was in the light of this impasse in the struggle for rights that his letter to Teller appeared, making concessions to the majority culture that would never have occurred to Mendelssohn or Ascher, or to subsequent generations of religious reformers and political activists. Like his labors of 1787–93, Friedländer's proposed baptism of 1799 failed to usher in any changes in the political status of the Jews. Ignored by those government officials it would have needed to draw into the debate, the anonymous letter had no direct consequences for the group of Jewish family heads who were its alleged authors. Teller himself chose to respond not as a church official but as a private individual, and even writing in this capacity, he found himself unable to accept in good conscience the conditions under which these enlightened Jews proposed baptism.[5] Friedländer, whose authorship was widely suspected from the beginning, quickly gave up the effort and subsequently remained a respected and active figure in the Jewish community, his reputation apparently untarnished. Elected as an elder of the community in 1808, he continued to lobby for Jewish emancipation, religious reform and communal welfare by more traditional routes, ultimately playing a decisive role in campaigning for the Prussian emancipation decrees of 1812. The legislation of 1812 crowned Friedländer with the success that had eluded him in earlier years, extending to Prussian Jews nearly all the same rights and duties as Prussian Christians.

A failure as a political program, Friedländer's letter to Teller is important because of the phenomenon that Graetz was at a loss to explain: the responses it provoked in the intellectual community. From the moment of their publication in April 1799, Friedländer's proposals unleashed heated debate. Friedländer's letter and Teller's reply each appeared in three editions and were reviewed extremely widely in the press, and the next two years produced no fewer than forty pamphlets, books and periodical articles dealing with the issue of Jewish baptism.[6] There were certainly Christians who celebrated Friedländer's act as a welcome sign of Jews moving toward Christianity. And while the letter did not cause Friedländer to lose respectability among Berlin Jews, there were voices within the community that anticipated Graetz's and Arendt's judgment that the letter represented an effort of elite Jews to abandon solidarity with Jewry as a whole.[7] The general tenor of debate, however, moved in a different direction. When the Göttingen philosophy and geology professor Jean André de Luc lambasted the Jewish family heads for daring to attack Christianity so publicly, he underscored a crucial dimension of the controversy.[8] Indeed, for many non-Jews participating in the discussions—Friedländer's letter provoked only one published

Jewish critique late in 1800, and a fairly tame one at that[9]—it was clear that the Jewish family heads' proposed conversion went hand in hand with a heavy dose of criticism of Christianity and a passionate commitment to the superiority of Judaism. Few contemporaries found the letter to Teller to be the specimen of assimilationism that German-Jewish historiography has often taken it to be. It was often viewed as a subversive document that threatened the foundations of both Christianity and the modern state. For the budding young theologian Friedrich Schleiermacher (1768–1834), whose now classic *On Religion* had appeared at roughly the same time as Friedländer's proposals, the letter was a dangerous text that threatened to spread the "disease" of a "Judaizing Christianity."[10] Heinrich Eberhard Gottlob Paulus (1761–1851), yet another figure who would emerge in the years to come as a major theologian, warned that conversion as Friedländer set it forth might create a Jewish "caste" within the state, a privileged power base that would stand in the way of the state's promotion of equality for all citizens.[11] Christian Ludwig Paalzow (1753–1824), a criminal lawyer with the supreme court (*Kammergericht*) in Berlin, deplored the Jewish family heads' great "condescension" toward Christianity and explained this superciliousness by entering into an historical investigation that uncovered a Jewish quest to dominate others and gain world rule that apparently had its origins in ancient times.[12]

These objections to Friedländer's proposals obviously differ in tone, argument and audience. In this sense, they were typical of the controversy; to a certain extent, of course, it was the lack of consensus on the meaning of the letter that enabled the debates over Jewish baptism to go on for so long. But it was equally the general perception of Jewish agency articulated by these writers that propelled the discussions. For so many of the participants in these debates, Jews were no longer well suited to be passive objects of a government program of civic improvement; the Jewish family heads were hardly malleable material out of which the state might craft productive and useful citizens. They were perceived as political agents seeking to better their lot and enter the modern world on their own terms, and it was overwhelmingly clear to many contemporaries that despite their willingness to submit to a nominal baptism in exchange for rights, the Jewish family heads very much wanted to enter the modern world *as Jews*. Exactly how Friedländer defined Jewishness in this context, needless to say, is an issue we will need to explore. For many in the non-Jewish world, at any rate, the Jewish family heads were mounting, in the name of Enlightenment, a defense of Jewishness and a challenge to Christianity and Christian universalism—a Jewish claim to the modern world much like that which they easily ignored in the works of Mendelssohn and Ascher. It was, it seems, only when the Jewish entry into modernity was coupled with an entry into the Protestant Church that Jewish challenges to Christianity's exclusive purchase on universalism came to be recognized as potentially subversive. It was apparently one thing for Mendelssohn, writing as an orthodox Jew, to appropriate Jesus for Judaism and question the foundations of Christianity; challenges like this could be easily contained within traditional accounts of Christianity's supersession of Judaism. But when a group of elite Jewish family heads proposed to revive Mendelssohn's challenge to Christianity *from within the Church itself*, things took a different turn, yielding a discourse on Jewish economic and political power that significantly reshaped the emancipation debates.

The widespread perception of Jewish power that arose in response to Friedländer's letter was in some ways not a new development. Indeed, in his piece on the French Revolution, we remember, Fichte also invoked visions of an international Jewish conspiracy, and Michaelis had speculated that extending rights to Jews would put rich Jews in a position to buy up land and create a "defenseless, despicable Jewish state" on German soil (D 2: 46). Ernst Traugott von Kortum, an Austrian government official whom Dohm singled out as one of his major critics, argued along similar lines in 1795, claiming that emancipation would enable the Jews—the "most extensive trading company in the world"—to become universal oppressors and gain world rule.[13] And on one level these visions of Jewish power had important antecedents in medieval traditions as well.[14] In the period up until 1799, however, such visions of Jewish power never became a dominant force shaping discussions about emancipation. In this sense, Friedländer's letter to Teller marks a decisive turning point. Friedländer's non-Jewish contemporaries certainly recognized the subversive elements of his Jewish appropriation of Enlightenment universalism, finding in the letter to Teller a clear link between the Jews' pursuit of political equality and the intellectual authority they claimed over both Judaism and Christianity. Readers of the letter often extrapolated from this quest for intellectual authority and political agency a Jewish desire for political and economic power, and this gave rise to a vision of the contemporary world under siege that did not disappear once the reading public began to lose interest in the particular issue of Jewish conversion.

Barely three years after the debates subsided, a colleague of Paalzow at the supreme court, the thirty-year-old commissioner of justice Karl Wilhelm Friedrich Grattenauer (1773–1838), published a brochure *Against the Jews* that unleashed a vociferous pamphlet war in Berlin and throughout the German lands.[15] Focussing his attention on seemingly assimilated Jewish elites, on both men like Friedländer and the Jewish women he perceived to be dominating the world of high culture in Berlin, Grattenauer promoted widespread anxiety over Jewish power and Jewish money. His goal in issuing this "word of warning to his Christian fellow-citizens"—this was the subtitle of his work—was to alert his contemporaries to the Jews' designs for world domination, a warning that was necessary particularly in the case of a Jewish population that was shedding what had been their familiar signs of difference. Characterizing the Jews as an "Oriental foreign people" that historians and anthropologists alike agreed were a distinct "race,"[16] Grattenauer unmasked a Jewish will to power slowly gaining ascendancy in Prussia and elsewhere. Grattenauer's writings drew their power from both their apparent wit—his contemporary, the respected political writer Friedrich Gentz (1764–1832), hailed him as a great social critic whose polemical style was reminiscent of Lessing[17]—and the veneer of scholarly authority under which he presented his anti-Jewish diatribes. Quoting liberally from Fichte, Paalzow and Eisenmenger, Grattenauer enlisted an impressive repertoire of German and Roman legal records, excerpts from Talmudic and Rabbinic writings, and the usual citations from classical writers, all of which he documented with an extensive bibliography. With 13,000 copies printed in six editions in 1803 followed up by an "explanation" and a "supplement" written by Grattenauer himself, not to mention a planned Polish translation, *Against the Jews* was one of the best-selling titles of its era, provoking a level of debate—sixty contributions in 1803 alone—that could only be stopped by the institution of censorship on the part of Prussian authorities fearing public unrest.[18]

For many historians, Grattenauer's pamphlets represent a pivotal transitional moment in the development of modern racial and economic antisemitism.[19] Indeed, the visions of Jewish power we will encounter in this chapter do seem to foreshadow the images of international Jewish conspiracy that became such a staple of late nineteenth- and early twentieth-century forms of antisemitism. It should not be surprising that German historians during the Third Reich often acclaimed Grattenauer as the heroic voice of reason in an era in which Jewish power had reached unacceptable levels.[20] This view of Jewish imperial designs is also important, however, because it was not the sole property of writers whose names routinely appear in histories of antisemitism. In different forms, it found its way into the writings of a wide variety of figures, including some—Schleiermacher, for instance—who favored granting Jews rights and rejected the racial-anthropological visions of Jewish identity espoused by writers like Grattenauer. In exploring how visions of Jewish power develop from Friedländer's letter to the debates set off by *Against the Jews*, this chapter traces a major shift in public perceptions of the Jews' relation to state power. Jews begin to be seen no longer simply as potential subjects of a program of internal expansion but as a unique power base threatening to put Prussia in a position of intellectual and economic subjugation.

The main question that arises here is how to explain these novel visions of Jewish power, particularly given the links, implicit and explicit, between the debates set off by Friedländer's letter to Teller and the pamphlet wars of 1803. To a certain extent, of course, these fantasies of Jewish domination have to be understood in relation to the increasingly prominent position of Jews in the cultural and economic landscape of turn-of-the-century Berlin. While Jews in Berlin were for the most part subject to the same legal restrictions as all other Jews in Prussia, all in all, this was not a group perceived to be mere victims of persecution and prejudice. Unlike both Ascher and Mendelssohn, Friedländer himself belonged to the upper crust of patrician Jewish families that had risen to prominence in the aftermath of the Seven Years War (1756–63).[21] The son of the wealthiest Jew in his native Königsberg, he was married to the daughter of Daniel Itzig, a leader of the Berlin Jewish community and the wealthiest Jew in the city. Active in both the silk industry and as a private banker—Wilhelm von Humboldt was one of his clients— Friedländer was one of the twenty most affluent Jews in the Prussian capital, and his position near the top of the social ladder was not entirely atypical. Indeed, in marked contrast to German Jewry as a whole, the Berlin Jewish community at the turn of the century was wealthy and prominent in the economy; the committee set up in 1803 to create the Berlin stock exchange, for instance, had an equal number of Jewish and non-Jewish representatives, a staggering figure considering Jews made up no more than 2 percent of the population of Berlin at the time.[22] As a sort of substitute bourgeoisie in a city that had come of age extremely quickly—the population of Berlin grew from 24,000 to 172,000 over the course of the eighteenth century[23]—this Jewish merchant and banking class played a leading role in Berlin's cultural life as well. Occupying palatial homes alongside those of the nobility on prominent boulevards such as Unter den Linden, elite Jews helped set taste in fashion and in high society and were highly visible at the theater and other cultural institutions, far more integrated into non-Jewish cultural and intellectual life than Jews anywhere else in Europe. Salons hosted by prominent Jewish women such as Henriette Herz, Rahel Varnhagen and Friedländer's sister-in-law Sara Levy were pivotal for the literary and intellectual life of Berlin at the time, and indeed, of Germany as a whole. These salons served as an important meeting ground for Jews, intellectuals, literati, diplomats, government officials and members of the nobility, bringing together guests as diverse as the theologian Schleiermacher, the grand theorists of Romanticism August Wilhelm and Friedrich Schlegel, the writer Heinrich von Kleist, the statesman-philosopher Wilhelm von Humboldt and his scientist brother Alexander, the sculptor Johann Gottfried Schadow, Friedrich Gentz and many others.

In her book *Jewish High Society in Old Regime Berlin*, Deborah Hertz portrayed Grattenauer's antisemitism as the expression of a dormant resentment of Jewish economic and cultural power in Berlin; for Hertz, the popular anti-Jewish sentiments of 1803 were largely a reaction to the prominence of Jews in the Prussian capital, one that eventually helped bring an end to this era of Jewish involvement in Berlin high society.[24] Arguing in a slightly different register, Peter Erspamer has read the debates of 1803 as a symptom of more general fears about the accelerating pace of economic modernization that were subsequently projected onto Jews; part of what makes Grattenauer so insidious for Erspamer is the way he played on his readers' economic anxieties to present the Jews as the symbolic representatives of a rising capitalist order.[25] Particularly when we consider the extent to which the pamphlet wars of 1803 grew out of the debates set off by Friedländer's proposals in 1799, however, we shall see that the phantasm of Jewish intellectual and political domination did not come into the public eye solely as a response to actual Jewish power or even as an immediate reaction to actual Jewish involvement in Prussian cultural and economic life. Clearly, the visions of Jewish power at stake here were not *caused* by Friedländer's Jewish critique of Christianity and his proposal that Jewish elites use an insincere act of baptism to gain political rights. But they did come into the public eye very much as reactions to concrete efforts of Jews to claim political agency for themselves. These visions of Jewish power are important for understanding the nature of modern forms of antisemitism not simply because they emerged in response to actual or imagined Jewish domination. In part they were a response to a group of Jews who sought to pair political rights for Jews with a Jewish critique of Christianity's claim to universalism, rationality and modernity. There is more at stake here than resentment of Jews or fears about economic modernization. These fantasies of Jewish power offer us a crucial window into the various ways the dominant culture managed the attempt of Jews to refashion themselves as active players in the process of their own emancipation. They offer a crucial commentary on the way the Protestant majority accommodated an explicit challenge to its traditional power over Judaism on the part of a group of Jewish elites whose emancipation it deliberated in the name of Enlightenment, secularism and progress.

FRIEDLÄNDER'S CHALLENGE: THE JEWISH REFORMATION

The last decades of the eighteenth century witnessed a rise in the number of conversions among Berlin Jews, and while the actual figures do not support the vision of a "baptismal epidemic" that was once standard in German-Jewish historiography, the phenomenon of Jews converting to Christianity to gain citizenship did provoke public attention at the time.[26] Indeed, just weeks before Friedländer's letter appeared, a prominent Berlin journal published an anonymous "Political-Theological Exercise on the Treatment of Jewish Converts" that grappled with the difficult question of the political status the state should grant apostates from Judaism.[27] This article, which was republished in pamphlet form in 1799, was often discussed alongside Friedländer's proposals. The author of the piece proposed that Jews undergoing baptism be subjected to a six-year waiting period before being granted citizenship, and his rationale for dissociating conversion and citizenship in this manner was an anthropological vision of Jewish national character reminiscent of Michaelis's concept of a degenerate Jewish race. The only reasonable explanation why Jews have hitherto been excluded from the rights and privileges of citizenship, he hypothesized, is a

> certain disharmony, wrongness and uselessness of their bodily and intellectual capabilities. . . . One has to assume that an inherited mixture of fluids has lamed or slackened their bodily powers; that the forms of education and learning propagated by their ancestors have mutilated the higher faculties of their soul and given them an adverse direction; that both inherited opinions, maxims sucked in with their mother's milk, and intercourse with each other have altered and corrupted their inclinations and feelings, particularly their social ones, and made them detrimental to society as a whole. . . .[28]

The Jews emerge here as an anthropological aberration, a people whose minds and bodies have been deformed, disfigured and mutilated by both racial degeneration and their own dubious intellectual culture. Clearly, the mere act of baptism will not produce the physiological and cultural transformation necessary to make Jews worthy of citizenship, and it is for this reason that the state would do well to treat converts as "convalescents" in need of "medical care" before granting them equal rights.[29] Countering Michaelis's vision of the permanence of Jewish national character with what seems almost a parody of Blumenbach's belief in the possibility of racial regeneration, the "political-theological exercise" concludes by suggesting that just six years will suffice to make converts ready for citizenship.

Despite the seemingly bizarre solution to the problem it addressed, this piece provided an important perspective in deliberating the issue of Jewish emancipation in the years to follow. Its anthropological vision of Jewish identity reemerged in authors like Grattenauer, who invoked contemporary scientific discourse to protest against the Jews' characteristic "odor," their innate inability to feel compassion, and other physical deficiencies of this "Oriental foreign people;"[30] arguing along these lines, Grattenauer had little use for a belief in regeneration. More importantly, though, the essay accompanied Friedländer's proposals for baptism into the public eye from the beginning, voicing anxieties about insincere conversion and an unsupervised entry of Jews into non-Jewish religious and political life that remained concerns for many contributors to the debates. Friedländer himself never mentions this other piece—and indeed, it is unclear whether he was even aware of it while composing his letter to Teller[31]—but he does engage with its basic assumptions. He plainly criticizes the arrogance of those in power who claim the right to pronounce others like Jews or "Negroes" as innately inferior on a moral level, discrediting the anxiety voiced by the "Political-theological Exercise" that Jewish converts would spread immorality.[32] He completely ignores discussion on the inferiority of the Jewish body, opening his piece instead by adopting the rhetoric of Kant's definition of Enlightenment and invoking the emancipatory potential of Enlightenment rationality—a strategy that implicitly challenges those who view Jews and Judaism as an anthropological problem. Friedländer uses Kant, moreover, not just to argue for the belated inclusion of Jews in the universalist project of modernity but also to claim a very particular role for Jews and Judaism within this project.

In his 1784 essay "What is Enlightenment?" Kant presented Enlightenment as the "emergence of the human being from its self-incurred immaturity to use its understanding without the guidance of another."[33] Defined as a process of learning to think for oneself, Enlightenment for Kant was both an individual affair and a collective one. In practice, Kant conceded, most individuals need to be encouraged by others to think for themselves; if left to their own devices, they might continue to rely on "statutes" and other "mechanical tools" for abusing their "natural gift" of reason and thus remain "immature" for life. It is thus essential that there be a free realm for public discourse in society, a space in which individuals who have cast off the mechanical statutes that are the "foot shackles of permanent immaturity" might encourage others to do the same. Kant's model here, we remember from the previous chapter, is the realm of print, which both facilitates the dissemination of the spirit of Enlightenment and makes possible a collective form of rational critique that claims authority for itself in the realms of religion and politics.

Friedländer's letter to Teller painstakingly adopts Kant's rhetoric, arguing that Judaism as it is practiced actively impedes Enlightenment, making Jews into "tools" and "machines" and putting them into an "eternal condition of immaturity" marked by the reliance on the external authority of their statutory law.[34] In a move that perpetuates the anti-Judaism we found in Kant's *Religion*, Friedländer sees Judaism in its current form as the antithesis of Enlightenment, and initially he uses Kant's language to outline the necessary reform, the necessary Enlightenment, of Judaism as well. It is in this context, ironically, that he defines his relationship to Mendelssohn, explicitly claiming Mendelssohn's principles and doctrines as his own at the same time as he presents his former mentor as the broker for a reform project that renders Mendelssohn's own commitment to Jewish ceremonial law an anachronism:

> Who portrays the emergence from slavery of the intellect to freedom! Who calculates the charms, the strengthened power of the soul of those human beings who ascend from the feeling that they wear chains to the decision to cast them off! Let one not say that this ascension of culture is so improbable and unbelievable. No, in a state such as Prussia, all the conditions have been met. . . . The mild constitution, the more purified concepts of the period, a level of humanity that is a fine custom, knowledge disseminated in writings and schools—in such a state, everything, indeed, everything invites the youth who has been otherwise cast out and neglected to participate in and enjoy the world.[35]

Assuming the pose of the grateful subject of Prussian benevolence, Friedländer here highlights the political conditions that have produced a Mendelssohn, a figure who sets the tone for the Jewish Enlightenment by offering his fellow Jews an example of how they might decide to liberate themselves from the slavery and chains of Jewish law. Rejecting Mendelssohn's insistence on Mosaic Judaism's compatibility with modernity, Friedländer stresses at this point in his letter the *external* basis for Jewish reform, the way contact with Protestants in eighteenth-century Prussia has enabled open-minded Jews to escape from the "drawstrings"—yet another reference to Kant—of habit and Jewish legalism to examine the true "essence of our religion."[36] He stresses that the "Jewish family heads" approaching Teller are only relying on the view held by the heads of Protestant churches that all religions are identical in their essence and the "historical" element of religions is always incidental.[37] Jews have benefited enormously from the liberal spirit and freedom of religious inquiry typical of Protestant Prussia, and Friedländer explicitly presents the Protestant Reformation and its continuing echoes in the Prussian religious Enlightenment as the model for his own Jewish reform project. Arguing in this manner, he views the Jewish Enlightenment as a side effect of its Prussian elder sibling, a belated opportunity for Jews to participate in the exhilarating intellectual liberation that is both the universal destiny of the human being and the particular product of Prussian culture.

Given this expression of overwhelming subservience to the state and its institutions at the beginning of Friedländer's letter, it makes sense that later generations of Jews often dismissed his proposals as an example of opportunist assimilationism. Friedländer's invocation of Kant's definition of Enlightenment may indeed have the effect of challenging anthropological views of Jewish difference, but it does so in such a way as to perpetuate the denigration of Judaism central to Kant's universalist project; Jews are salvaged, as it were, ostensibly only at the expense of Judaism. In this sense, Friedländer may have been influenced by Kant's own call for a "euthanasia of Judaism" one year earlier in the *Contest of the Faculties*.[38] When considered alongside the rest of Friedländer's letter, however, the pose of subservience struck at the beginning has to be seen as a strategic move, part of an attempt to appropriate the Kantian project so as to offer a Jewish challenge to it from within. Friedländer ultimately conceptualizes the relationship between the Jewish Enlightenment and its Protestant environment in a subversive manner, claiming a privileged role for Jews that is difficult to subsume within a concept of assimilation.

It may well be the influence of Protestants that has encouraged Jews to interrogate the essence of their religion, but what Jews like Friedländer actually define as the essence of Judaism mounts a challenge to the ruling Protestant discourse on Judaism and its relation to Christianity. Paraphrasing Mendelssohn's *Jerusalem*, Friedländer foregrounds the original function of Mosaic law to lead Jews toward the truths of rational religion. Unlike Mendelssohn, however, he casts Moses as a legislator, emphasizing thus the human and historical dimension of those laws Mendelssohn insisted derived directly from divine revelation. Robbing Mosaic law of its divine origin and eternally binding claims, Friedländer echoes the arguments of Protestant Orientalists to stress the law's historically specific nature, its appropriateness to the relatively primitive condition of the ancient Israelites. But Friedländer parts company with his Protestant peers in two important ways. He refuses to equate Judaism with the law and he insists that the abrogation of the law he wishes to perform in the present is a development entirely *internal* to Judaism, an essential aspect of Judaism as articulated by both the Hebrew scriptures and the Talmud.[39] Indeed, Moses, he claims, would himself command the abolition of Jewish ritual law if he were alive today, and Friedländer distinguishes sharply between giving up the law in this sense and any type of conversion to Christianity.[40] Particularly given Kant's interpretation of Lazarus Bendavid's reform proposals as an effort to perform the "euthanasia of Judaism" to revive the pure religion of Jesus, this claim that the abrogation of the law actually falls entirely within the spirit of the Mosaic system undermines the way contemporary thinkers such as Kant celebrated Jesus's Christianity in opposition to the oppressive burdens of Jewish legalism. Friedländer does more than insist that the Jewish family heads are not prepared to accept Jesus as the son of God, or any other aspects of Christian dogma, for that matter.[41] He never once so much as draws a parallel between his Jewish reform project and the question of Jesus's relation to the law. Friedländer's proposals for institutional conversion to Christianity render both Jesus and Christianity's supersession of Judaism superfluous.

Friedländer continues his challenge to Protestant anti-Judaism in his account of the role the Jewish family heads would play should they be granted entry into the Church. He may indeed take the Protestant Reformation as the model for his purification of Judaism, but he does so in such a way as to grant reformed Jews a unique position in the Protestant Church. Clearly, he wants the Church to become the institutional home for his reformed Judaism, but this is a home that Jews will need to remake in their own image. The Church is not merely supposed to take in Jews. Friedländer also expects it to embrace wholeheartedly the enlightened Jews' unwillingness to accept Christian dogma or profess faith in Christianity's historical truths. "We have striven, to the best of our abilities," he writes, "to clearly present what we recognize as the foundation of every religion, and particularly the religion of Moses. The individual propositions this consists of have the highest evidence for us; and we do not doubt that the Christian teacher to whom we would give our public confession would accept this as the proclamation of an aggregate of truths not in which we *believe* but of which we are *convinced*. The *words* of our profession will differ from the customary ecclesiastical confession of faith, but its *meaning* agrees with it."[42] Friedländer here proposes a Jewish confession of rational religious conviction that would stand in for, and ultimately be superior to, the customary Christian declaration of faith. He and his fellow enlightened Jews are not prepared to accept the "ceremonies" of the Protestant Church as "signs" that they accept church dogma; they will subject themselves to these ceremonies, to be sure, but only as "merely formal acts required for acceptance in a society."[43] Combining Mendelssohn's notion of Judaism's superiority to Christianity with Christian accounts of the limitations of Mosaic law, Friedländer negotiates a curious middle ground between the two, a purified Judaism that is institutionally linked to—and politically legitimized by—a church whose dogma and rituals it would nevertheless continually critique. In a sense, then, the Jews emerge here as the proper heirs to the critical spirit of the Protestant Reformation, the religious thinkers Christianity desperately needs if it is ever going to justify itself before the court of reason, the critical voices Protestantism needs if it is ever going to move beyond the Lutheran emphasis on faith to enter into the world of pure rational religion. His epistle radically rewrites the views on religion and history that Teller himself had articulated in previous writings, claiming for Judaism the historical position Teller reserved for what he called "pure Christianity."[44]

Like Ascher, then, Friedländer appropriates Kant in such a way as to argue for Judaism's seminal role in the modern world. He presents Judaism not as the superseded other of Jesus's Christianity but as the religion of the future, the pure rational religion that, once admitted into the structure of the Church, will be able to supplant Christianity with its relatively primitive reliance on faith and dogma. It is from this position that he finally salvages the specificity of Judaism, claiming for Jews a privileged position as the exegetes of the Hebrew Bible. Echoing arguments made in his earlier writings, Friedländer links the purification of Judaism to the project of developing a specifically Jewish form of Orientalist scholarship that would draw on modern historical, philological and exegetical works to defend the Hebrew Bible and challenge the anti-Judaism typical of Protestant Orientalism.[45] With its overabundance of signs, tropes and figures, the Hebrew scriptures are continually open to misinterpretation, he comments, particularly since the "Oriental" did not have a language to explicitly recognize the direct and indirect workings of God in nature. As a result, the Hebrew Bible often speaks of the "invisible, incorporeal ruler of the world" as if he were visible and corporal, as if he were human, even though the clear intent behind scripture is to invoke an invisible, incorporeal God.[46] The new Orientalist scholarship Friedländer calls for would read for the spiritual concepts behind the physical figures and thereby defend the Hebrew scriptures against their customary denigration at the hands of Protestant scholars.

Friedländer's vision of a specifically Jewish mode of exegesis does more than seek to displace Protestant Orientalists and stake out the Jews' interpretive authority over the Jewish past. In his claim that the figures of the Hebrew Bible signify both the spiritual content of Judaism and the truths of rational religion, he challenges any Christian understanding of the Old Testament as a prefiguration of the New, rendering both Jesus and Christianity once again superfluous in the history of world religion. Entirely self-sufficient as a manual for rational religion, the Hebrew scriptures apparently contain the supersession of Mosaic law entirely within themselves, and the task of modern Jews, as Friedländer defines it, is to help Christians come to appreciate both the intrinsic value and the autonomy of historical Judaism. Anything but zealous converts to Christianity, Jews like Friedländer who seek to enter the Protestant Church ultimately take on the function of missionaries, preaching the rational spirit of Judaism to Protestants not yet enlightened enough to move beyond the limitations of faith—Christians whose dogmatic insistence on Jesus being the "son of God" actually perpetuates the crude sort of "Oriental" literalism with which they commonly charge Judaism.

THE PROTESTANT COUNTEROFFENSIVE

Naturally, some of Friedländer's Protestant contemporaries charged the letter to Teller with putting forth a "Judaized" version of Christianity and harboring a condescending attitude toward the Church in which these Jewish family heads were allegedly seeking refuge. On one level these appear understandable responses to Friedländer's anticipation of Judaism's supersession of Christianity, mere reactions to the letter's strategy of presenting Judaism as the religion of the future. Focusing on Friedländer's vision of the self-sufficiency of Judaism, the earliest reviewer of the letter speculated that Teller would be likely to require that Jews accept Jesus as the figure who abolished the law and demand that they subsequently submit to baptism in the name of the father, the son and the holy spirit.[47] As it turned out, Teller saw no need for the Jewish family heads to accept the doctrine of the trinity or any other aspects of Christian dogma. He did insist, however, that they frame their conversion explicitly in relation to Jesus's supersession of Judaism. Unsatisfied with Friedländer's proposals for a confession of rational religious conviction, Teller wanted the Jews to profess their faith in one simple historical truth: the truth that "Christ was the founder of the better moral religion . . . chosen and sent by God to create a better religion than your entire ceremonial service was and could ever be."[48]

What Teller contested was not the Jews' rejection of the ceremonial law in favor of the universal truths of rational religion but the symbolic significance Friedländer attributed to this move, the challenge the Jewish family heads mounted to Christianity's exclusive purchase on the truths of rational religion and its claim to be the beacon of universalism. Teller dealt with this problem in his presentation of the issue by completing de-Judaizing Friedländer's proposals, severing all ties between his vision of reform and the Jewish tradition whose essence it professed to be expressing. Claiming that this reform project actually derived entirely from the spirit of the Gospels, Teller stressed that Jews entering the Church would need to acknowledge the extent to which their efforts to reform and abolish the law ensued directly from Jesus's example. Since the Jewish family heads were in essence already thinking like Christians, that is, it was only logical that their confession of faith include an explicit commitment to "Christ as the founder of a more spiritual and more gratifying religion than that of the congregation to which you have hitherto belonged."[49] If Friedländer sought to overturn Christian supersessionism by making the "letter" of Judaism anticipate Judaism's own spiritual essence, Teller responded by reinstating the Pauline opposition between the dead letter of Jewish law and the living spirit of the Gospels, calling on Jews to reenact early Christianity's negation and completion of the law and embrace the truth of Christianity.[50] The move from the limitations of Judaism to the liberating spirit of Christian universalism, moreover, would need to be reflected in a particular baptismal practice reserved for the Jewish converts. Jews would have to be baptized, that is, not merely in the name of Christ but also in the name of a God whom they, "coming from Judaism," have finally now come to recognize as the "father of all human beings."[51]

Teller's response reveals the problems with a Jewish reform project that defined itself so closely in relation to Protestant attacks on Judaism—a reform project that seemed at times concerned more with usurping Protestant claims to universalism and modernity than with defending Judaism on its own terms. For all its efforts to topple Protestant hegemony over Judaism and claim Judaism as a universal rational religion, Friedländer's letter could easily be appropriated by its recipient as essentially Christian in spirit; with relatively minor effort on Teller's part, the Jewish family heads' challenge to Christianity lent itself to being recast as a Christian critique of Judaism. The dialogue between Friedländer and Teller illustrates the double bind in which the Jewish intellectuals found themselves in relation to Enlightenment culture, demonstrating once again the enduring power of master-narratives of Christian supersessionism to neutralize and coopt Jewish claims to universalism.

In this sense, Teller, with all his reservations about Friedländer's proposals, does not differ tremendously from those who welcomed the letter as an unequivocal sign of the Jews moving closer to Christianity. In a review published soon after the letter appeared, the philosopher, economist and publicist August Hennings (1746–1826), who had been a friend and frequent correspondent of Mendelssohn, expressed unreserved enthusiasm for Friedländer's proposals and called on Christians to do everything possible to invite *all* Jews to follow Christ's example and renounce the burden of Mosaic law.[52] An anonymously published *Dialogue between a Christian Theologian and an Elderly Jew* (1799) similarly celebrated Friedländer's letter as a step toward the universal brotherhood made possible by Jesus's negation and completion of the law. In an astonishing but hardly unusual act of misreading, both the elderly Jew and the theologian in this fictional dialogue claimed that the Jewish family heads explicitly identified Jesus as the purifier of Judaism and expressed their readiness to accept the historical truths of Christianity. The *Dialogue* made this argument, moreover, in an effort to put to rest the preposterous claim advanced by a Berlin minister that the letter to Teller was actually the work of opportunists who saw Judaism as superior to Christianity.[53] The liberal theologian Gottlob Benjamin Gerlach argued in a comparable fashion in *Moses and Christ*, a 1799 book that opened by complaining about the ways philosophical concepts of race were increasingly providing a rationale for states to refuse Jews rights rather than facilitate their conversion and integration.[54] Enthusiastic about the prospects of conversion, Gerlach acknowledged Friedländer's critique of Christianity but claimed it derived from a confusion inherited from Mendelssohn; for Gerlach, a simple acceptance of Christ would clear up all confusion and help promote the more general project of "purifying Christianity of those Jewish remains that have served as its scaffolding."[55] The anonymously published sentimental novel *Charlotte Sampson: History of a Jewish Family Head Who with His Family Renounced the Faith of His Fathers* (1800)—to cite just one final example—also assimilated Friedländer's proposals to the tradition of Christian supersessionism they sought to challenge.[56] A mechanical grafting of the familial conflict in Lessing's *Miss Sara Sampson* (1755) onto the situation of Jews in turn-of-the-century Berlin, *Charlotte Sampson* told the story of Samuel Sampson and his daughter Charlotte, who in the aftermath of Teller's rejection of Friedländer's proposals ran off with the Protestant boy next door. Unlike Lessing's drama, which is generally regarded as the inaugural German "bourgeois tragedy," *Charlotte Sampson* ends on a happy note. Father and daughter reconcile and convert to the pure teachings of Jesus, while Samuel's old friend, a Rabbi, converts along with his daughter, who ends up marrying the young and energetic Protestant minister whose long discourses on religion motivated everyone's conversion and reconciliation in the first place. A reviewer noted that *Charlotte Sampson* differed little from Friedländer's letter to Teller in its intent; the views that the Jewish family heads claimed as their own derived, after all, less from Judaism than from Jesus's Christianity.[57]

It is against this background that Schleiermacher's interventions in the debates stand out so prominently. Just two days after publishing his now seminal text *On Religion*, a work generally credited with heralding the Romantic appreciation of the unique nature of religious experience, the thirty-one-year-old theologian began work on his *Letters Occasioned by the Political-Theological Exercise and the Open Letter of Jewish Family Heads.*[58] A major presence at the Jewish salons of the 1790s, Schleiermacher was not unfamiliar with the political conditions that drove Friedländer to make his proposals to Teller. He knew both men personally; they probably made each other's acquaintance at the Herz salon where Schleiermacher was such a frequent guest, and he seems to have been distinctly aware of Friedländer's authorship of the letter.[59] For Schleiermacher, it was clear that enlightened Jews such as Friedländer were simply using Christianity to gain entry into civil society.[60] Considerably less enthusiastic than Teller, Gerlach and the other authors discussed above, Schleiermacher found in Friedländer's letter a passionate defense of Judaism and a distinctly Jewish critique of Christianity. Pointing out that the Jewish family heads remained committed to the spirit of Abrahamite Judaism and harbored a bitter antagonism toward Christianity, he rejected Friedländer's proposals for conversion as plainly "anti-Christian."[61] At the same time, however—and this is what makes his text one of the most radical of the period—he also insisted on extending citizenship to Jews as Jews, claiming that reason dictates "that all people should be citizens but knows nothing of the notion that all people should be Christians."[62] Echoing arguments by Dohm rarely invoked at the turn of the century, Schleiermacher charged those who wanted to deny citizenship to Jews with falling prey to the "lazy political reasoning according to which the remnants of barbaric times are indestructible."[63] A truly modern and rational state should be able to emancipate Jews without regard to their Judaism. As Peter Foley has argued, the overarching intent of Schleiermacher's *Letters* is to make religion irrelevant to consideration of granting Jews civil rights.[64] He argued in *On Religion* that Judaism is "long since a dead religion, and those who at present still bear its colors are actually sitting and mourning beside the undecaying mummy and weeping over its demise and its sad legacy" but this denigration of Judaism only underscores his political position here.[65]

The motivation for this unusual statement of tolerance toward Judaism, however, derives less from a deep-seated commitment to political liberalism than from Schleiermacher's interest in safeguarding the Church against what he calls the "disease" of a "Judaizing Christianity."[66] He lobbies for granting Jews rights not as a lay intellectual but as a theologian encouraging the state to remove the political conditions that impel Jews with such impure motives to seek conversion and infiltrate the Church. Schleiermacher, who was in Potsdam at the time, published his text anonymously, assuming the persona of an unnamed member of the Prussian royal cabinet publishing his correspondence with an anonymous "preacher outside of Berlin." This correspondence, importantly, offers little in way of epistolary dialogue. Indeed, the politician figure never finds his own writings significant enough to include in the published collection of letters, all of which involve the preacher anticipating and correcting the views of his politician correspondent. Even at the level of their formal structure, then, the *Letters* support the coordination of church and state under the supervision of the theologian rather than any strict separation of temporal and ecclesiastical powers. It is from this position that the *Letters* reclaim and ultimately rewrite Dohm's vision of civic improvement, making citizenship explicitly contingent on the Jews' adoption of a reform program of Schleiermacher's own making. As an alternative to Friedländer's Jewish attack on Christianity, Schleiermacher proposes a reform of Judaism under the close supervision of the state, which he claims is in the spirit of Friedländer's letter. Exactly what would be positive—or Jewish—about this program for religious renewal is unclear and of minimal interest to him. He delineates only those political aspects of Judaism that will need to be eradicated in order to make Judaism compatible with modern citizenship and prevent the current situation in which Jews like Friedländer might infiltrate the ranks of the Church and usurp Christianity's claim to universalism. Schleiermacher's reform program is quite simple: Jews who desire citizenship must explicitly subordinate Jewish law—"the laws of their proper fatherland"—to the laws of the Prussian state and formally and publicly renounce all hopes of messianic restoration.[67] If Jews meet these conditions, he proposes, the state should allow for the creation of a new "religious society" for them; it goes without saying that the political authorities will need to supervise this process carefully and not automatically grant citizenship, for instance, to the descendants of such Reform Jews.[68]

Theologians like Schleiermacher, then, do not merely write off Judaism as a dead religion. By advising the state on how best to contain its power, they seek to defend the Church against an onslaught by those who endeavor to grant it renewed life. Schleiermacher goes much further than Teller. As well as insisting on his intellectual authority over Judaism, he calls attention to the state's *political power* over Jews, entreating the political authorities to put an end to Jewish conversions and set up a controlled experiment by which Jewish readiness for citizenship might be measured and Judaism's efforts at external expansion might be kept in check. Importantly, Schleiermacher has little interest in traditional formulations of Christianity's supersession of Judaism. He claims in *On Religion*, indeed, to "hate that type of historical reference in religion" that casts Judaism as "somehow the forerunner of Christianity."[69] Speaking as a theologian, he shifts the focus of the debate away from historical theology toward the question of the power of contemporary Jews. He may revive Dohm's call for emancipation, but he does so largely for the sake of the Church, introducing his program of "civic improvement" as an antidote to a vision of Jewish power that was nowhere to be found in Dohm's treatise.

One on level, Schleiermacher's strategy here is obviously part of his larger theological project to define religion as a mode of subjective experience *sui generis*, a form of prereflexive "feeling" that cannot be reduced to rationality or morality or exhausted by codification of its essential universal truths. His *Letters* contain polemics not just against Friedländer but against Kantians and other proponents of Enlightenment who Schleiermacher claims are essentially indifferent to religion as such; indeed, he wishes to ban from the Church not just Jewish converts but all Christians who are Christian in name alone.[70] His *Letters* join *On Religion* in challenging the Enlightenment vision of rational religion that made Friedländer's proposals possible. Part of Schleiermacher's argument, certainly, aims simply to expose the superficiality of Friedländer's vision of religion. Complaining of an age where "one exchanges one's religion at market rate," he claims that "it is impossible that someone who has really had one religion could ever take on another."[71] But there is more at stake in the *Letters* than the formulation of a Romantic view of religion. For in responding to Friedländer's proposals, Schleiermacher also involves himself in a discussion of Jewish agency, invoking a scenario in which Judaism is both a dead religion and an uncannily powerful living force to contend with, a scenario in which Jews are claiming Christianity as their own in such a way as to destroy the very integrity of the Church.

Schleiermacher frames his vision of Jewish power in relation to models of colonization that have little to do with his novel views on religion. Echoing arguments common in the 1780s, he defends the project of civic improvement by claiming that it is just as "strange to be out to make conquests when we still have wastelands to reclaim and swamps to dry out within our borders" as it is "to fetch foreigners from abroad as citizens when we still have a large mass of human beings who are really not yet citizens."[72] Like the writers we considered in Chapter 1, Schleiermacher compares the emancipation of Jews to a state-engineered cultivation of domestic resources that is analogous to colonialism. Yet he no longer sees Jews as the malleable human mass for internal colonization that they represented for Dohm. Jews have agency of their own for Schleiermacher, apparent, for instance, in the overwhelming "hatred" of Christianity that leads elite Jewish family heads to contend that a "half conversion" to Christianity would be "the most one could expect from a rational and educated man."[73] A state-controlled internal Jewish reform program, of course, would be able to combat this Jewish claim of intellectual superiority; removing the political conditions that cause Jews to seek conversion will ostensibly lessen Jewish elites' unfounded arrogance toward Christianity. But the battle to discredit the Jews' attempts to claim agency for themselves has to be fought on a different front as well. Schleiermacher himself inaugurates the necessary counteroffensive by exposing the Jews' pretense to intellectual authority as the product of ignorance and by explaining the Jews' antagonism toward Christianity by symbolically aligning them with a very specific colonial power base. Writing in 1799, during the heyday of Napoleonic expansionism, he equates the Jewish challenge to Christianity with the specter of French cultural and political hegemony over Germany: "I have often read in published essays how these enlightened and educated Jews all expect us to know something about Judaism, and expect us to find taste in Chaldaic wisdom and beauty, as much as this is contrary to our European spirit. Do these Jews all know so damn little about Christianity? They seem to me to be like the Frenchmen who have been living among us for ten years and yet still do not want to learn a word of proper German; of course, the Jews carry this off in a much grander style."[74] Schleiermacher here does much more than set up an opposition between Christians and Jews that is staked out along the axis of Europe and the Orient. He aligns both of these oppositions with one between Germany and France, casting Germans and Christians as the people under siege by Jews and Frenchmen alike. European Christians are familiar with and can even appreciate the Jews' "Oriental" tradition in much the same way as educated Germans know and speak French. Like the French, however, Jews are completely unacquainted with the language, culture and religion they are threatening to dominate, and it is for this reason that the reform of Judaism needs to be so closely supervised by the political authorities. Clearly, it will not be enough to *trust* the Jews to subordinate "the laws of their proper fatherland" to the laws of their new Prussian homeland and voluntarily renounce all hopes of messianic restoration in the Orient. The state needs to make the subordination of Orient to Occident the first condition of emancipation, ensuring that Jews will not colonize the Church in the same manner as Napoleonic forces are threatening to occupy Prussia.

The alignment of Jewish power with the potential threat of French imperialism is of course merely a rhetorical move here, an analogy Schleiermacher invokes at just this one juncture in his *Letters*. Coming on the heels of a distinct vision of Jewish power, however, it is important because it appears in a text that both Schleiermacher's contemporaries and modern historians have seen as pivotal to the debates unleashed by Friedländer's proposals. Unlike, say, Christian Ludwig Paalzow's *The Jews*, a 1799 book which the *Allgemeine Literatur-Zeitung*, a prominent and respected review journal, claimed was fundamentally lacking in proof for its anti-Jewish tirades, Schleiermacher's solution to the problems raised by Friedländer's proposals was well received at the time; the *Allgemeine Literatur-Zeitung* celebrated the *Letters* in 1800 as the most thorough and balanced examination of the issues to date.[75] The chimera of Jewish power the *Letters* invokes here is also important, however, because it converges with the arguments of writers who were much more easily written off as marginal. Before we consider the contribution by Paalzow, a figure who became a major player in the debates opened up by Grattenauer in 1803, let us consider the views of yet another writer who emerged as a major theologian in the years to follow, Heinrich Eberhard Gottlob Paulus (1761–1851), the liberal rationalist theologian remembered today both for his 1828 *Life of Jesus* and for his antisemitic polemics against Gabriel Riesser in the aftermath of the 1830 revolution.[76] Paulus claimed in a lengthy article in 1799 that conversion as the Jewish family heads set it forth would create a new Jewish power base in the state. Like Schleiermacher, Paulus too claimed for

theology the right to supervise political affairs where Jews were concerned—
he published his critique in a theological review journal—but his concern
was directed less at the Jews' power to infiltrate the Church than what he
speculated were their political ambitions. Similarly suspicious of the Jewish
family heads' religious convictions, Paulus conjectured that the collective
conversion of a group of elite Jews would promote Jewish particularism,
enabling the Jews to maintain their "national bonds" and traditional exclusiveness and eventually to form a privileged "caste" in the state that would
stand in the way of the modern goals of the consolidation of the state and the
equality of all citizens.[77] Justice, after all, dictates that those who are already
citizens should have nothing to fear from Jewish converts, and the modern
state has every right to supervise the social and political conversion of
Jews to make sure that they really do reject their "nationalism and social
particularism."[78]

In voicing the need for the state to control the Jews' potential power as
Jews, both Schleiermacher and Paulus anticipate aspects of Paalzow's *The
Jews*, the first of a series of works by Paalzow that portrayed the contempo-
rary world as threatened by a Jewish will to power and contended that the
Jewish character and religion were incompatible with citizenship. As marginal
as Paalzow was to the debates of 1799, even then it was difficult to write him
off as a crackpot or an irrationalist. Indeed, as the German translator of
Voltaire's commentary on Montesquieu, Paalzow was a criminal lawyer and
writer with impressive credentials.[79] Paalzow (1753–1824) had studied law in
Halle and assumed a position as *Kriminalrath* at the supreme court in Berlin
in 1787, the same year as he published, along with Julius Friedrich Knüppeln
and Karl Christoph Nencke, an influential volume, *Busts of Berlin Scholars,
Writers and Artists*.[80] Starting in the early 1780s, Paalzow emerged as a frequent
translator from the French and a prolific author in his own right in both Latin
and German, producing treatises on a variety of theological and legal issues.
His authoritative multivolume *Handbook for Practical Legal Scholars in the
Prussian States*, published in 1802–03 and reissued in 1816–19, reinforced his
professional stature.[81] It is certainly important, as we noted above, that the
Allgemeine Literatur-Zeitung discredited his anti-Jewish polemic in 1799. It is
just as important, however, that it judged it worthy of such serious refutation,
dedicating a full eight pages to discussing *The Jews*—considerably more space
than it reserved for nearly all the other responses to Friedländer's proposals.
Schleiermacher's *Letters* received only one quarter as much press. And it was
not merely Paalzow's reputation that made *The Jews* and his subsequent writings difficult to dismiss out of hand. He also wrote in a manner that commanded authority. Well versed in Enlightenment political theory, Paalzow
introduced his anti-Jewish polemic within a larger argument *for* freedom of

conscience and separation of church and state. This translator of Voltaire and Montesquieu could cite Kant's *Religion* to his benefit, and he supported his argument that the Jews' character and religion made them unfit for citizenship by drawing on an immense repertoire of classical sources—Tacitus, Juvenal, Julian, Plutarch, Josephus, Horace, and many more.

In *The Jews*, Paalzow portrayed Friedländer's letter to Teller, with its characteristic "denigration" of Christianity, as but the last in a long sequence of events exemplifying the Jews' quest for world domination.[82] Like Schleiermacher, but with much more animosity, Paalzow saw contemporary Jews' attempt to claim intellectual authority over Judaism and Christianity as a sign of Jews' arrogance and scramble for power. The Jewish view of Christianity as a "heretic" branch of Judaism that "ruined" its mother religion derives for Paalzow from the same dream of world rule that is the very essence of Jewish messianism. "The Jews," he claims, "never give up the hope that they will someday be redeemed from their current misery to become the happiest and most powerful people in the world and that all other peoples who have not been exterminated will become their slaves."[83] The Jewish emphasis on Judaism's seminal role in world history amounts here to little more than a smokescreen for designs at world domination. This threat of Jewish rule, moreover, is not merely hypothetical. Indeed, if any state were to give the Jews the same rights and freedoms it grants its other citizens, the Jews, aided by their character and their notorious clannishness, would quickly take control of all trade and industry, making Christians their slaves, and transforming all native industry into a "monopoly of their nation."[84] In this respect, Paalzow contends, modernity would be wise to take a cue from ancient Rome, the "most tolerant people in the world" who knew that if they had not destroyed Jerusalem and sent the Jews into Diaspora, the Jews would have gained ascendancy over the entire ancient world.[85] The solution he proposes is thus a radical destruction of both Judaism and the Jews' character, and he suggests the state accomplish this by eradicating Judaism and integrating the Jews via a program of complete assimilation and forced intermarriage.[86]

In the debates of 1799–1800, Paalzow still appeared as a somewhat marginal voice, a writer who pushed Schleiermacher's reservations about Jewish power to extremes that were out of sync with both Schleiermacher's basic support for granting Jews rights and the various doubts other writers held about extending citizenship to Jewish converts. But it is noteworthy that apart from its hyperbole and rhetorical excess, the solution Paalzow actually proposed was not entirely alien to the spirit of the debates. Aside from a small number of orthodox Christian voices, few contributors to the debates were willing to attach any intrinsic value to Judaism.[87] Paalzow's proposals for a

complete annihilation of Judaism arguably offered only an extreme formulation of the hostility toward Jewish agency shared by other participants in the
debates. With its proposals for a cultural and physiological transformation of
Jewish character, after all, the "Political-Theological Exercise" also attested
to an unfettered belief in the infinite ability of the state to reshape human
character, a problem that the case of Jews seeking to use baptism as a means
to gain political rights had simply brought into clear focus. Indeed, apart from
the specter of world domination it invokes, Paalzow's call for a revival of
Roman "tolerance" seems in many ways lifted directly from the pages of
Dohm's treatise. From the beginning, the debates over civic improvement
had been about the potential power of the state to remold Jewish character.
Appearing in response to a clear attempt by Jews to claim agency for themselves as Jews, Paalzow's vision of a Jewish will to power registers a significant threat to the logic of civic improvement. Paalzow, to be sure, goes much
further than simply acknowledging that Jews may be much more than passive
material for governmental programs of civic improvement and internal colonization. He radically inflates his perception of the Jews' attempt to subvert
the project of regeneration, producing a vision of Jewish imperial power that
eventually came to take on a life of its own.

Once the public began to lose interest in an issue that was clearly of merely
theoretical concern, discussions over the merits of Friedländer's proposals lost
steam. Friedländer presented his overture to the Church, after all, as a
concrete political proposal, a means to gain rights, and apart from Teller and
Paalzow, no other government officials publicly spoke out about the Jewish
family heads' proposed entry into the Church. Both Teller and Paalzow, moreover, responded as private citizens, as writers, and not in their official capacities, as member of the upper consistory or court lawyer, respectively. As
Friedländer's efforts quickly became known as an apparent failure, the seriousness with which the intellectual community entertained his proposals
proved difficult to sustain, and by late 1800, debate on the issue had petered
out. The core ideas of Paalzow's response, on the other hand, did not fade
into oblivion. Early in 1803 Paalzow published a Latin-language *Tractatus historico-politicus de civitate Judaeorum* (Historical-Political Tractate on the State
of the Jews) that rehashed many of his ideas in *The Jews*, offering a history of
the Jews from Egypt to the present that demonstrated once again that their
character and religion were incompatible with citizenship.[88] Thanks to his colleague at the supreme court Karl Wilhelm Friedrich Grattenauer, this work
did not go unnoticed. In the opening section of *Against the Jews*, Grattenauer
extolled the *Tractatus* as the much-needed counterpart to Fichte's merely
speculative unmasking of the "evil spirit of Judaism" and the "Jewish national
character" in his 1793 *Contribution to the Correction of the Judgments of the Public*

on the French Revolution.[89] Fichte was, to be sure, a "great philosopher," and Grattenauer quoted extensively from him as well, but Paalzow's *Tractatus* had the advantage of offering a *historical* demonstration of the extreme dangers "the nature and essence of Judaism" have always posed to both the state and the common good.[90] Discussing Paalzow alongside the theological anti-Judaism of Eisenmenger's *Judaism Revealed*, a text he also cited copiously, Grattenauer called for both an immediate German translation of Paalzow's *Tractatus* and a modern edition of Eisenmenger's classic of 1700. The plea for a reissue of *Judaism Revealed* fell on deaf ears, but Grattenauer's colleague quickly obliged and did his part, producing a German edition of the *Tractatus* dedicated to Grattenauer, whom he now hailed as the "new Eisenmenger."[91] In a roundabout way, then, Friedländer's attempts to secure a position for Judaism within modernity had led to a revival of the distinctly modern form of Jew-hatred we saw Ascher diagnose in *Eisenmenger the Second*. The *Allgemeine Literatur-Zeitung* commented in early 1804, just over six months after the pamphlet wars started by Grattenauer had come to an end, that Ascher's best efforts of the previous decade had apparently done little to prevent Eisenmenger from making a comeback.[92] As a Jewish critic of Grattenauer argued, the public now was clearly being presented with "Eisenmenger the Third."[93]

EISENMENGER THE THIRD

Far more than the intellectual interchanges of 1799–1800, the pamphlet wars of 1803 were very much a market-driven enterprise, with a much more popular readership than the relatively elite group of intellectuals and theologians who discussed Friedländer's proposals. Berlin newspapers such as the *Vossische Zeitung* took out enormous advertisements for Grattenauer's pamphlets, promoting his writings in a manner that well-situated members of society like Friedrich Gentz felt was in poor taste and typical of their author's questionable reputation.[94] Grattenauer, whose only connection to the world of the salons was through the duties he performed as Gentz's lawyer, lacked the stature of the intellectuals participating in the debates of 1799. He was a notary and commissioner of justice at the court in Berlin and an alumnus of both the celebrated pietist orphanage in Halle and the University of Halle's theology and law faculties.[95] At the time he published *Against the Jews*, however, he was already being prosecuted on larceny charges, and larceny does not seem to have been his only alleged act of indiscretion.[96] When Gentz left Berlin to escape his debts, he left his financial affairs in Grattenauer's hands, and once Grattenauer went bankrupt late in 1803, after the end of the pamphlet wars, he promptly disappeared with the money he was supposed to use to pay off his client's creditors.[97] All this is not to imply that Grattenauer lacked a deep commitment to his anti-Jewish sentiments; indeed, in 1791, at the age of eighteen, he made his writerly début with an anonymous treatise *On the Physical and Moral Constitution of Jews Today* that anticipated his later tirades against the Jews, and he also claimed in official correspondence to have been personally wronged by Jews.[98] The immediate motivation for the 1803 pamphlets, however, seems to have been largely a financial one. In a declaration to Chancellor von Goldbeck in which he sought to defend his writings against the impending threat of censorship, he conceded that his goals in seeking to curb the enormous "power of Jewish money" were not merely about public service; he was also a father of four simply trying to make an honest income for his family.[99] The money and fame earned from his pamphlets of 1803 did help Grattenauer out of his financial predicament for a bit. As a result of his newfound celebrity status, the Frankfurt bookseller Varrentrapp und Wenner, the publisher of the *German Encyclopedia* and other highly respected works, offered him an attractive honorarium to assume the editorship of a new journal *Against the Jews*.[100] With the institution of censorship on all writings "for" or "against" the Jews in late September 1803, however, the journal never materialized, and Grattenauer fell on hard times once again. Ultimately dismissed from his position at the court, he eventually landed on his feet, emerging in Breslau as the editor of a newspaper and the author of various legal handbooks and reference works.[101] Never again, though, did he regain the notoriety he enjoyed for a brief period in 1803. Even a later antisemitic work of 1817 published under his own name seems to have left little echo.[102]

The pamphlet wars of 1803, then, were as much about invoking and confronting the specter of Jewish money as they were about mining the book market for potential profits. For both Grattenauer and the Prussian authorities who finally intervened to impose censorship, it was not just Jewish power but the ability of the book trade to disseminate the phantom of the power of Jewish money that was at stake. Grattenauer's rise to fame had transpired extremely quickly; it was only on August 1 that he received permission from the censors to print *Against the Jews*, 13,000 copies of which had been sold by the time censorship was instituted less than two months later, on September 27.[103] As the privy councilor of finance Borgstede wrote to Minister von Hardenberg in a memorandum encouraging close state control of the media in early September, public writings on the Jews were degenerating into "unpolitical," "immoral" and near-illegal actions, riling the lower classes of Christians against a "colony that is protected by the state."[104] Borgstede contended that the continuation of public insults against Jews would eventually lead to more riotous acts, and for this reason it would not be enough to institute a ban on new publications; the newspapers, too, would have to be forbidden from advertising any existing anti-Jewish writings in the manner in which they had been doing.[105] The state disseminated its decision to use censorship to prevent verbal assault from turning into real violence, appropriately, in the pages of the *Vossische Zeitung*, the newspaper whose advertisements for Grattenauer's pamphlets Gentz had found so distasteful.[106] As Minister von Hardenberg commented in his final decision on this matter on September 19, freedom of the press was certainly important, but it would simply not do to sacrifice civil law and the constitution of the state to the "partisan spirit and the financial speculation of a guild of writers."[107] Much more than a conflict between Grattenauer and the Jews, the pamphlet wars brought to light the tensions between the economic forces of the book market and the state's desire to maintain its hold on public order. Given the way the debates were brought to an end, it should not be surprising that when Grattenauer finally disappeared from the scene in 1803, the rumor was that he had been paid off by the Jewish community.[108] The decision to institute censorship may have restored public order and brought an end to an era of debate on Jewish emancipation, but this mandate to protect Jews from further print attacks only helped further the perception of Berlin Jewry's special privileges. Indeed, for at least one author, the imposition of censorship that the Jews had apparently engineered was yet another symptom of Jewish domination; the ban on all writings "for" and "against" the Jews represented nothing less than a "Jewish" desecration of the cherished Prussian principles of Enlightenment and freedom of the press.[109]

To some extent, as mentioned earlier, the resonance Grattenauer's polemics met with in the reading public has to be understood in relation to the actual power Jews wielded in Berlin at the time. Particularly his defamatory comments in his second and third pamphlets about the disgusting smell, bodily impurities and physical lure of upper-class Jewish women who strive in vain to achieve the appearance of being cultivated seem rather direct attacks on prominent Jewish salonières such as Rahel Varnhagen and Henriette Herz.[110] The tone that runs through all three pamphlets was geared at provoking the resentments of non-elites excluded from high society. Grattenauer cast himself as an outsider, the struggling jurist and writer whose lifestyle contrasted so strikingly with that of the Jews, who lived lives of leisure and had ample time to dedicate themselves to high culture and partake so ostentatiously in public forms of entertainment.[111] Clearly, the stated goal of *Against the Jews* and Grattenauer's other pamphlets was to create a public forum for airing resentment of the Jews. Interpreting the pamphlet wars of 1803 solely as a popular protest against actual Jewish power, however, misses some crucial aspects of the debates. This explanation runs dangerously close to reproducing the arguments of the openly antisemitic Nazi historians who worked on this era.[112] It also overlooks the discursive context for Grattenauer's best-selling pamphlets of 1803, the close relation of this print phenomenon to both the emancipation debates that had been raging since 1781 and the specific issues brought into the public sphere by Friedländer just four years earlier.

Grattenauer opened his first pamphlet by directly inserting himself in the debates over emancipation, invoking the danger of Jews lobbying for future political rights and warning his contemporaries that political equality would allow the "chosen people" to enslave all Gentiles and gain complete political power.[113] He closed the last pamphlet by entreating the state to reassert its power and clarify both the particular conditions under which Jews were to be "tolerated" and the "legal border" between "us" and the "foreigners"—issues he himself promised to deal with in yet another future work.[114] In the 1820s, Friedländer would still complain of the "trials and tribulations, scorn and mockery" both he himself and the Jewish community were subjected to in the period following the publication of his letter to Teller.[115] It should thus hardly come as a surprise that Friedländer's proposals to Teller lurked prominently in the background of all three of Grattenauer's pamphlets. Grattenauer openly scorned Friedländer as his major opponent, quoting the letter to Teller and rallying against the notion of a union of Jews and Christians as a "foolish" and "sinful" effort to "Judaize Christianity."[116] If Grattenauer here echoes (and twists) the rhetoric that Schleiermacher used to critique Friedländer, elsewhere in his pamphlets he sought to surpass Schleiermacher's *Letters* and style himself as the ideal respondent to Friedländer's proposals for conversion: in his second pamphlet, he advertised a future work that would finally deal with the open letter of the Jewish family heads—and all the responses to it—to everyone's satisfaction.[117] It was, of course, not just the unresolved issues raised by Friedländer's letter that helped set the stage for the pamphlet wars of 1803. The mere fact that a group of elite Berlin Jews had been at the center of debate four years earlier undoubtedly paved the way for the emergence of Grattenauer's bestseller, making a reading public that had been deliberating emancipation since 1781 even more receptive to the hysteria and paranoia promoted by Grattenauer, Paalzow and others.

In his pamphlets, moreover, Grattenauer directly challenged the efforts of Jews like Friedländer to stress Judaism's seminal role in shaping the modern world. Like Paalzow in his response to Friedländer, Grattenauer too recognized the way Jews introduced distinctly Jewish accounts of the origins of Christianity to bolster their polemics for the emancipation of Jews and stake out a Jewish claim to the modern world. Grattenauer directly quoted Mendelssohn's characterization of Christianity in *Jerusalem* as a religion inextricable from its original Jewish foundation, claiming that this towering figurehead of the Enlightenment did little more here than put "Rabbinic foolishness" in the dress of popular philosophy; the history of religion, Grattenauer explained, simply "does not permit the opinion that Christianity was derived from Judaism," as Christianity is, in its universality, the "diametrical antithesis of all religions of the world."[118] For Grattenauer, Judaism simply had no legitimate role to play in the modern world, and he elaborated this argument by revitalizing the Orientalist position articulated by Michaelis in the 1780s, supplementing it with a heavy dose of citations from Eisenmenger's *Judaism Revealed*. Indeed, the authority Grattenauer claimed for himself throughout the pamphlets derived from his alleged training in church history and Oriental studies with Semler and others in Halle, and he interspersed his polemics with frequent quotes—in the original—from Talmudic and Rabbinic writings.[119] Many of Grattenauer's contemporaries, and not just the Jewish ones, recognized his flawed discussion of Jewish sources.[120] Clearly, though, many others did not. Gentz, no great fan of his lawyer's character, commented that Grattenauer's pamphlets were thorough and knowledgeable. The Jews, he claimed, had never yet been attacked with such "superiority, and if Grattenauer had a better reputation, this attack would be lethal for them."[121] Posing as a certified Orientalist, Grattenauer did not merely portray Judaism in historically specific terms as a religion well suited to the climate and culture of ancient Israel. He gave what he called the "spirit of Judaism" almost metaphysical, ahistorical status. Denying any link between Judaism and Christianity, he ultimately characterized the Jews as an "Oriental foreign people" who historians and anthropologists alike agreed were a distinct "race."[122] These were the people seeking to dominate the entire world, and Grattenauer thus closed his third and final pamphlet with an open declaration of "war" against this "Asiatic foreign people."[123]

In contrast to Friedländer's proposals, Grattenauer's pamphlets tended not to produce sustained, serious debate. Apart from Lazarus Bendavid, who speculated that Grattenauer's first pamphlet, which was initially published anonymously, was the work of a convert from Judaism, no prominent members of the Jewish community spoke out.[124] Much to Grattenauer's chagrin, Friedländer remained silent. The main attempt to refute *Against the Jews*, a work by the state official Johann Wilhelm Andreas Kosmann entitled *For the Jews: A Heartening Word to the Friends of Humanity and the True Admirers of Jesus*, did go through three editions but did little to change the direction of the debates.[125] Speaking as a Christian advocate of Enlightenment visions of civic improvement, Kosmann argued less for the Jews than for the possibility and necessity of their regeneration, doing little more than echo arguments that had been circulating two decades earlier. The Jewish physician Sabbatja Joseph Wolff, whose reform project we discussed briefly in the previous chapter, published an anonymous *Open Letter of a Christian to a Local Jew* that similarly offered a fairly lackluster defense of tolerance and humanity.[126] Other writers registered that the public was being presented with a distinctly modern form of Jew-hatred and sought to challenge Grattenauer's claim to scholarly expertise, but they too failed to redefine the terms of debate.

Much more typical of the pamphlet wars were the writers who jumped on the bandwagon and joined in with Grattenauer. One rather sensational anonymous pamphlet, which went through three editions in 1803 and was widely discussed, echoed Grattenauer's visions of Jewish power and suggested the state control the Jewish population by substituting ceremonial castration for the Jewish ritual of circumcision.[127] Another work, by a "practical businessman who had experienced remarkable Jewish swindling," elaborated on Grattenauer's visions of the Jews' plans to dominate Christians and establish a Jewish state in all of Europe; claiming to be more grounded in experience than Grattenauer, he suggested containing Jewish power by setting up a closely controlled Jewish colonial settlement on desolate land in Europe.[128] And once censorship on writings for and against the Jews was instituted in 1803, the tide of authors seeking to ride on Grattenauer's coattails did not die down entirely; debate in Berlin was simply transferred to the literary realm, which produced in 1804 alone two distinctly antisemitic dramas as well as an almanac "for the children of Israel" full of anti-Jewish prose and anecdotes.[129]

There were exceptions to the blunt opportunism with which these authors sought to turn the new trend of Jew-hatred into financial profits. Distancing himself from the pamphleteering of his contemporaries, the writer Friedrich Buchholz produced a 266-page book that sought to bring to the debates a level of philosophical and historical clarity that this author claimed was simply not possible to achieve in pamphlet form. Entitled *Moses and Jesus, Or On the Intellectual and Moral Relation of Jews and Christians: An Historico-Political Treatise*, Buchholz's book was nevertheless not entirely the product of a disinterested quest for knowledge.[130] At the time, and indeed, throughout much of his life, Buchholz (1768–1843) was a struggling and prolific writer seeking to make a name for himself and obtain a government appointment. After having to curtail his studies at the University of Halle prematurely for financial reasons in 1787, he spent twelve years as a tutor at an academy for children of the nobility in Brandenburg before coming to Berlin in the hope of securing a job as a civil servant. Buchholz's subsequent publication record demonstrates his commitment to the anti-Jewish sentiments expressed in *Moses and Jesus*.[131]

His "philosophical" intervention in the pamphlet wars of 1803, however, was obviously an attempt to take advantage of the current popularity of anti-Jewish tracts to stage his own emergence as a nonpartisan, authoritative political voice who would, he insisted, regard the issue at hand from a perspective that was neither Jewish nor Christian but simply that of the good of the state.[132] While Buchholz for the most part never achieved the fame or the career he strove for most of his life, *Moses and Jesus* did provoke attention and had the longest shelf life of all the contributions of 1803. In 1804, after the debates had subsided, it generated both a book-length refutation and a lengthy review in a prominent journal, and the *Allgemeine Literatur-Zeitung* still thought it worthwhile in 1808 to publish a seventeen-page review, listing the title as still for sale.[133] In 1813, a publishing house in Copenhagen produced a Danish translation.[134] Buchholz's peers, to be sure, took him to task for many an historical inaccuracy and for being simply too prejudiced against the Jews to write the necessary historico-political treatise on the "intellectual and moral relation of Jews and Christians," but *Moses and Jesus* was taken seriously as a work of scholarship. In the eyes of his contemporaries, Buchholz was attempting to grant the issues brought into the public by Grattenauer the serious attention they deserved, and it is for this reason that a discussion of *Moses and Jesus* offers a fitting conclusion to this chapter's reflections on perceptions of Jewish power around 1800.

Like Grattenauer's and Paalzow's pamphlets, Buchholz's book reacted directly to the Jewish claim to modernity typical of Jewish elites' arguments for emancipation. Referring to Friedländer's proposals, he spoke mockingly of Jewish plans for mass conversion, which, he said, would only desecrate the sacrament of baptism and do nothing to heal the "cancer of state" afflicting all the states of Northern Europe.[135] Like Grattenauer, he quoted Mendelssohn's account of the relationship between Judaism and Christianity in *Jerusalem*. His response was to denounce Mendelssohn's claim for the continued relevance of Judaism in the modern world as a Rabbinic "web of dialectical hairsplitting and sentimental chatter" that basically reenacted the crucifixion.[136] Christianity for Buchholz was not just radically opposed to Judaism but predicated historically on the destruction of Judaism, and for this reason, any Jewish claim to the universalism that rightfully belonged only to Christianity had to be regarded as an act of great violence, a direct assault on Jesus himself. It was not just in his diatribes against Mendelssohn and Friedländer that Buchholz zoned in on the subversive manner in which Jews often claimed agency for themselves. The vision of Jewish power conjured up by the treatise as a whole read as if it had been engineered to undermine any possible attempt by Jews to stake out a claim to the modern world. In many ways, *Moses and Jesus* did indeed bring a level of clarity to the discussions of the previous four years, for it confronted precisely the link between knowledge and power, between intellectual authority and political agency, permeating so many of the contributions to the debates.

Buchholz offered his "historico-political" analysis of Jewish power in the vocabularies of both empire and historical theology, using the question of Jesus's relation to Judaism so crucial to Jewish polemics for emancipation as a foil for his vision of the contemporary world as under siege by the power of Jewish money. For Buchholz, the "cancer of state" besetting modern Europe had a precursor in the ancient world, in the "struggle for world domination" between Rome and the Jews.[137] The progress of Roman imperialism, he explained, depended entirely on the industry of its subject peoples, on a politics of appropriating the "subsistence basis of other nations" by force.[138] Aided by their close ties, the "terrorism" of Mosaic law, their belief in a "national god" and their practices of usury and haggling, the Jews dispersed throughout the Roman world in an effort to undermine the power base of Roman imperialism and "establish the type of world rule that the English have realized in our times."[139] In Alexandria Jews helped found a trade network that lasted more than 1,700 years, until Vasco da Gama discovered the route to India around the Cape of Good Hope, and Jews elsewhere in the empire sought to bring the Romans down by accumulating all the money in the Roman world in the Temple treasury in Jerusalem.[140] It is against this backdrop that Jesus emerges, not as the Jewish Messiah but as a prophet of a universalist morality of brotherly love intended to destroy the Jews' "national character," their national God and their "dreams of future world domination."[141] Buchholz's Jesus is thus both an anti-Jewish and an anti-imperial voice who destroys Jewish law and the Jews' national bonds to replace them with a new sort of "world spirit" that resuscitates the life of the half-dead "body" of the human race.[142] In its original form, Christianity is a universalist morality that figures as the antithesis of both the Jews' and the Romans' quests for world domination. Indeed, the Romans themselves degrade Christianity, transforming its pure morality into a coercive institutional religion, and it is only the Germanic tribes who conquer Rome who perform the necessary "revolution" that brings Christianity back to its original purity.[143]

Arguing in this manner, Buchholz grounded his tirades against Jewish money in a world-historical scheme designed to discredit any Jewish claim to modernity. Clearly, any attempt to appropriate Jesus as a Jew or claim a role for Judaism in the modern world amounts to an act of violence against Christianity and its universalism, yet another attempt to realize the Jewish dream of world domination. For Buchholz, importantly, antiquity offers no model for how to deal with the Jews' scramble for power. Holding onto their

dreams of complete independence and world rule, Jews in the first century—
like Mendelssohn in the eighteenth—simply could not understand Christian
morality and sought to persecute Jesus as a criminal, and Christianity could
do little to defend itself.[144] The Romans, who mistakenly thought that
destroying the Jews' political existence would suffice to produce what
Buchholz terms their "identification with other peoples," similarly failed to
eradicate Judaism.[145] The best solution at the time, Buchholz points out,
would have been to deport all Jews to North America, which would have
forced them to "identify" with native Americans and lose all traces of their
previous identity.[146] In the absence of the possibility of assimilation into native
American life, the Jews conquered by Rome entered an economic world that
was based more and more on money, and this only gave them more power,
eventually enabling them to bring down the Roman Empire by indirectly
facilitating the barbarian conquests.[147] It is in this way that the Jewish threat
has continued unabated into the present. As modern society has grown
increasingly complex, it has become increasingly based on money, and
the Jews have, without exception, persistently refused the necessary
"identification" with other peoples.[148]

As one would expect for a sober-minded historico-political treatise, *Moses
and Jesus* was not without a solution to the problem it diagnosed. Like
Paalzow, Buchholz endorsed a secular program of civic improvement, and he
made no secret of the coercion and violence that would be necessary to regenerate the Jews.[149] The problem with Dohm, Buchholz claimed, was that he
simply lacked the knowledge to devise an effective means of getting the Jews
to "identify" with others, and Buchholz concludes his treatise by suggesting
military service as the ideal means of transforming the Jews into moral human
beings able to be assimilated by the non-Jewish world. Claiming that the
"spirit of the military stands in the most decisive opposition to the spirit of
the Jews and will suppress it," he lauds the transformative power of military
discipline: Jews entering the military will perish as Jews but survive as human
beings ready to participate in modern society. *Moses and Jesus* ends on a
friendly note of sorts, welcoming Jews into modernity and calling on them to
celebrate the destruction of their "national existence" and find "their
Palestine among us." Buchholz thus counters Jewish designs for world domination with the perfect exercise in social engineering, a recasting of Dohm's
project of regeneration that foregrounds the coercive elements of civic
improvement in a manner that far surpasses anything in Dohm. Like Paalzow,
Buchholz seeks to offer a practical solution to combat Jewish power, and he
closes his work not with the rhetorical excess of Grattenauer's "war against
Asia" but with a program for assimilating this "Asiatic nation" into the
universalist community of the modern European state.[150]

1803 AND THE SHAPE OF MODERN ANTISEMITISM

If the texts by Paalzow, Grattenauer and Buchholz represent a pivotal moment in the development of modern antisemitism, it is not solely because they conjured up the phantom of Jewish economic world rule and stressed the otherness of the Jews in a manner that surpasses anything we encountered in previous chapters. Nor it is simply because of the modern scholarly garb in which they presented their arguments. For very much like Teller, Schleiermacher and others responding to Friedländer, these writers issued their anti-Jewish polemics very much as a reaction to Jews attempting to claim an intellectual role for themselves, as Jews, in shaping the modern world. Of all the Jewish interventions in the discussions of civic improvement since 1781, Friedländer's letter provoked the most intense debate. The antisemitism we encounter around 1800 did more than react to the cultural and economic prominence of Berlin Jewry or register anxieties over economic modernization. It also constituted a defensive strategy *vis-à-vis* the efforts of Jewish elites to stress the importance of Judaism in generating modern norms of rationalism and universalism. If Jews typically accompanied their pleas for emancipation with an emphasis on the normative value of Jewish tradition, however understood, for modernity, non-Jewish writers hostile to Judaism reduced this insistence on the world-historical role of Judaism as an *intellectual* force to a Jewish quest for power plain and simple. In this sense, the form of Jew-hatred we have encountered in Paalzow, Grattenauer and Buchholz is clearly not anti-modern in its basic sensibilities. It is marked not by nostalgia for earlier forms of social and political collective life but by an attempt to defend the project of modernity from its subversive appropriation at the hands of Jewish elites. Grattenauer may have declared a rhetorical war against Asia, but the fact that Paalzow, Buchholz and other antisemitic authors writing in 1803 still came out in favor of state-sponsored programs of civic improvement—however coercive their particular proposals may have been—underscores their basic commitment to Enlightenment models of the malleability of human character: their antisemitism tended to bolster rather than undermine a faith in Enlightenment universalism. Clearly, the openly coercive manner in which Paalzow and Buchholz proposed remaking the Jews' character was hardly compatible with Dohm's vision of emancipation or his tolerance of Judaism as a religion. But the invocation of the project of civic regeneration even alongside such harsh polemics against Jews and Jewish power does seem to indicate that this discourse may be less a rejection of Enlightenment universalism than one of its possible permutations.

It is crucial that the debates of 1803 did not frame their Jew-hatred in nationalist terms. Grattenauer, to be sure, saw the idea of granting Jews rights as a "Jacobin blasphemy" and "sanscullotism"; criticizing the decision of the French revolutionaries to emancipate the Jews, he voiced anti-French sentiments that were frequently echoed in the debates and that were hardly unusual in the first decades of the nineteenth century.[151] Indeed, a parody of Grattenauer published in 1804 claimed that "all Jacobism and terrorism" was a Jewish invention, and that Moses was simply a demagogue in the tradition of Robespierre.[152] Yet nowhere in his pamphlets did Grattenauer ever seek to demarcate a "German nation," either positively, on its own terms, or negatively, in opposition to either the Jews or the French.[153] His work, we recall, was subtitled a "word of warning to all our Christian fellow citizens," and for nearly all the participants in the pamphlet wars of 1803—and the same claim is valid for the debates of 1799–1800—it was still the issue of citizenship in the modern state that was at stake, not the claims of German or even Prussian nationalism. Indeed, Grattenauer's word of warning was targeted not just at Prussians but as the French as well, and when censorship was imposed, we remember, a Polish translation was already in the works; Buchholz too, while speaking in a different tone, was also seeking to address Europe in general. As the parodist cited above made clear in the title of his work, it was not the claims of particular nations that were at stake here but "the world, humanity, Christendom and all states"—all of which would perish if "all Jewish men were not promptly slaughtered and all Jewish women sold into slavery." The specter of Jewish power this text parodies cannot be written off simply as an irrational, reactionary rejection of Enlightenment universalism. In 1803, unlike in the period following the Napoleonic era, it is inappropriate to talk about the Romantic, nationalist Jew-hatred Ascher later diagnoses in his *Germanomania*. It would be senseless, to be sure, to classify Grattenauer as a representative of the Enlightenment, but the phenomenon his works gave rise to is important because it was, to a certain extent, a byproduct of Enlightenment concepts of modernity, the attempt of a group of writers to reclaim modernity from its subversive appropriations by Jewish elites.

CONCLUDING REMARKS

In *The Origins of Totalitarianism*, a work first published in 1951, just six years after the end of the war, Hannah Arendt offered an analysis of antisemitism that, much to the dismay of some of her critics, focused its attention on the role of Jews in creating the conditions for the rise of the distinctly modern forms of Jew-hatred that had helped mobilize Hitler's *Reich*.[1] In his influential *Reflections on the Jewish Question*, published in 1946, Jean-Paul Sartre had argued that the Jew was essentially a product of the antisemite, that modern forms of Jewish self-consciousness were largely if not entirely the result of antisemitism.[2] Arendt, in contrast, offering an explicit critique of Sartre, sought to explore antisemitism as a phenomenon grounded in the historical realities of Jewish–Gentile relations since the eighteenth century. She refused to see Jews as mere victims without political agency of their own—outsiders to history who just happened to become the targets of totalitarian ideology. For Arendt, theories of an "eternal antisemitism," like both Sartre's "existentialist" interpretation of the Jew and "scapegoat" theories of antisemitism, had the problematic effect of denying all Jewish responsibility, of effacing all Jewish agency. Indeed, regarding Jews as arbitrary targets, she claimed, ultimately reproduced the logic of totalitarianism, whose primary goal was to "liquidate the very possibility of human activity," to destroy the very dignity of human action.[3] Jews for Arendt, certainly, did not *cause* antisemitism. But writing the history of antisemitism without viewing the Jews as agents in their own right ran the risk of perpetuating the dream of Jews as powerless victims that Nazi totalitarianism sought to make a reality.

The history of antisemitism that Arendt wrote following this theoretical injunction was not without its problems. Overemphasizing the importance of court Jews as financiers for Europe's emergent nation-states—they played no significant role in France, for instance[4]—she sketched an account of the power of Jewish banking families that seemed uncannily close to antisemitic myths of an international Jewish conspiracy. But Arendt's goal was not to produce a traditional historical narrative. She sought, as a political theorist, to argue that the prominence and economic influence of families like the Rothschilds should have opened up the doors to a Jewish entry into politics that would have fought the rise of imperialism and antisemitism. On a similar note, Arendt's infamous strategy in *Eichmann in Jerusalem* (1963) of focusing not on Jewish victims but on the way in which the Jewish Councils helped facilitate Nazi genocide was not meant to blame the victims, although her rhetoric at times provoked her critics to make precisely this claim.[5] She tried, here again, to center on missed moments of Jewish political agency, and to delineate how Nazi totalitarianism systematically liquidated the possibility of political agency. Rather than casting Eichmann as a diabolical monster out to kill the Jews, Arendt examined the totalitarian system that made possible this mass liquidation of human agency and human beings, and how Eichmann was, in a sense, the embodiment of this system.

My goal in bringing up Arendt in these concluding remarks is not to engage in extensive dialogue with the analysis of antisemitism and totalitarianism she offered more than fifty years ago. Indeed, so much of Arendt's *oeuvre*, with its overwhelming lack of interest in religion, completely obscures the issues that have been under exploration in this book. The operating assumption of *The Origins of Totalitarianism* of a radical disjunction between religious Jew-hatred and modern, secular political antisemitism hardly provides a productive framework for studying the hybrid forms of antagonism toward Jews and Judaism we have seen develop from Michaelis's *Mosaic Law* and the Lavater affair in the 1770s to the pamphlet wars of 1803. *The Origins of Totalitarianism*, like Arendt's *Rahel Varnhagen* or Bauman's *Modernity and Ambivalence*, more-over, is wedded to a vision of assimilation that deflects our attention from the radical nature of so much German-Jewish thought of this period, blinding us to the particular ways in which Jews in this period actually sought to claim agency for themselves. Indeed, what made the writings of a Mendelssohn, an Ascher or a Friedländer politically subversive were precisely their visions of Jewish religious renewal. Anything but the assimilators one encounters in Arendt's *oeuvre*, these Jewish thinkers challenged both nascent antisemitism and dominant visions of universalism by the act of issuing proposals for Jewish reform, and contrary to Gerschom Scholem's insistence that all German-Jewish dialogue amounted to a "cry into the void" on the part of Jews, these writings did elicit responses. For the participants in the debates over Jewish emancipation, the universalist vision of modernity was not a monolithic, abstract force to contend with but a project whose terms were very much up for debate, and a project that was intensely debated between Germans and Jews.

Arendt is useful here less for the details of her analysis than for her provocative suggestion that we focus our attention on those moments when Jews have in fact wielded power, for her suggestion that we do not study the history of modern antisemitism apart from a consideration of how Jews have sought to claim agency for themselves in the modern era. To risk stating the obvious, it is entirely possible to have antisemitism without Jews, and it has not been the goal of this book to put forth a comprehensive theory about the rise of modern antisemitism. Indeed, my investigation of the Jewish attempt to intervene in debates over the terms of universalism begs for a study of the shifts that this Jewish endeavor to appropriate and redefine modernity underwent with the rise of nationalism in the wake of the Napoleonic occupations— a crucial topic that lies beyond the scope of this book. In themselves, nevertheless, the developments I have been tracing in German political discourse of the late eighteenth and early nineteenth centuries do indicate a clear relationship between the Jews' attempt to claim political agency and the rise of forms of Jew-hatred that issued a claim to modernity geared at invalidating the vision of Judaism's compatibility with modernity so central to the efforts of Jews to redefine the terms of emancipation. The antisemitic writers such as Grattenauer, Buchholz and Paalzow whose pamphlets dominated the political debates of 1803 did not merely invoke the phantom of a Jewish quest for power that only Nazi historians have felt accurately reflected the state of affairs. They openly challenged the attempt by Jews to stake out a valid claim to the modern world.

Now clearly—and this harks back to the dynamic of Arendt's analysis— none of these attacks on Jews was caused by Jews, and any argument to this effect would only legitimize the position of Grattenauer, Paalzow and Buchholz that Jews were undermining the very fabric of the modern world. But the novel forms of antisemitism that culminated in the pamphlet wars of 1803 did arise in part as a reaction to the roles Jews sought to claim for themselves in setting forth novel visions of both Judaism and the proper role Judaism had played and should continue to play in determining the shape of the modern world. In 1781, Dohm could speak of Jewry as a mass of malleable material for crafting productive and useful citizens for a modern, secular state. For all his opposition to civic improvement, Michaelis too hardly perceived any unmanageable tension between the power of the state and the claims of its Jewish inhabitants. But by 1803, and even by 1799, the stakes of the debates had changed considerably. When Grattenauer, Paalzow and Buchholz made their harsh indictments of Jewish power, they were offering less a rejection of modernity and its universalist claims than a *defense* of modernity against the perceived threat of being appropriated for the cause of Judaism. Obviously, the fact that this anxiety-ridden defense was issued rhetorically in the name of a sober-minded rationality does not mean that it was either sober minded or rational. But it was very much a reaction to Jewish critiques of modernity like those we have encountered in Mendelssohn, Ascher and Fichte, and this novel form of antisemitism thus needs to be grouped together with the responses of much more liberal thinkers to the visions of modern Judaism circulating during this period. Grattenauer's *Against the Jews*, to be sure, differs tremendously from Kant's misreading of Mendelssohn's *Jerusalem* in his *Religion within the Limits of Reason Alone*, from Gottlieb Schlegel's or Johann Gottfried Eichhorn's misreadings of Mendelssohn, from Schleiermacher's response to Friedländer or from the ways Ascher's contemporaries disregarded his vision of Judaism's claim to modernity. But all these authors together voiced a clear aversion to any form of agency for Jews as Jews—however this was to be defined—and in this sense, they were part of the same broad cultural development, a common response to the subversive, distinctly Jewish appropriations of Enlightenment universalism we have been studying here.

This book has shown how distinctly modern forms of antisemitism emerged not as a reaction to the Enlightenment but as an integral part of it, a byproduct of the Enlightenment's effort to envision a self-consciously modern political order grounded in the principles of secular universalism. The goal of opening up this dimension of Enlightenment thought, needless to say, has not been to indict the Enlightenment for promoting a vision of universalism antagonistic to all forms of difference and hostile to alternative truth claims. For, indeed, if any distinct vision of the Enlightenment legacy emerges from this book, it should be a richly ambivalent one, one full of contradictions and opposing tendencies. For the Jews intervening in the debates over emancipation, the Enlightenment's promise of emancipation was by its very nature a double-edged affair. Precisely the vision of universalism that made it thinkable to grant Jews rights and political equality also tended to legitimize novel forms of denigrating Jews and Judaism. The self-consciously modern discourse that sought to liberate Jews from their civic misery did so at the same time as it typically marked Judaism as irretrievably out of sync with the modern era. Political principles that seemed so inclusive could be used in practice to exclude Jews, as Jews, from the project of modernity, and secular ideals that claimed to supersede Christianity and its traditional denigration of Judaism tended only to reinstate and modernize traditional forms of antagonism to Judaism—and the list goes on. The point here is not just that all these tensions have been so clearly manifest to *us* in our examination of the controversies over Jewish emancipation. They were also apparent to the Jews who sought to enter these debates, and indeed our own ability to reflect on these contradictions in the visions of modernity that the Enlightenment has bequeathed to us is arguably a product of those like Mendelssohn, Ascher and Friedländer who sought to reconfigure the terms of debate—those who sought to promote, from within the Enlightenment, a critique of the Enlightenment that is as much a legacy of this era as are the dominant ideas it sought to reformulate.

Modernity, in this sense, may be less a mode of envisioning the present that is hopelessly dated and the property of a past era than, to invoke Jürgen Habermas's term, an "unfinished project" that retains its share of normative power today.[6] It is certainly possible, even today, to write the history of Enlightenment in such a way as to isolate the formulations of those ideas that ultimately emerged as triumphant. Following in the traditions of liberal historiography wedded to the Enlightenment's own ideals, we can choose to overlook the contradictions attending the initial articulation of these ideas and disregard the alternative visions of modernity that never gained the same sort of hegemony and influence as the ideas of more central figures. Following certain trends in postmodern thinking, alternatively, we can focus singularly on those elements of the Enlightenment legacy that threaten to undermine its emancipatory rhetoric, thus stressing the repressive dimensions of the Enlightenment's dreams of secular universalism. This latter form of critique, however, is hardly a postmodern innovation. Probing the limits of the Enlightenment's dream of secular modernity and political emancipation is itself part of the legacy of these initial stirrings of modernity that we have been examining in this book, part of the challenge that the debates over Jewish emancipation should still elicit in us today.

NOTES

INTRODUCTION: MODERNITY AND THE
LEGACY OF ENGLIGHTENMENT

1. Dohm's meeting with Frederick the
Great is related in the biography
written by his son-in-law, W. Gronau,
*Christian Wilhelm von Dohm nach seinem
Wollen und Handeln* (Lemgo:
Meyersche Hof-Buchhandlung, 1824),
54–55. The other important source
for Dohm's biography is Ilsegret
Dambacher, *Christian Wilhelm von
Dohm: Ein Beitrag zur Geschichte des
preußischen aufgeklärten Beamtentums
und seiner Reformbestrebungen am
Ausgang des 18. Jahrhunderts* (Bern:
Lang, 1974).
2. Dohm, *Geschichte der Engländer und
Franzosen im östlichen Indien* (Leipzig:
Weygand, 1776); Dohm elaborated
his plans for a work on India that
would echo de Pauw's *Recherches sur
les Chinois* in a 1774 letter to Johann
Wilhelm Ludwig Gleim, cited in
Gronau, *Christian Wilhelm von Dohm*,
33.
3. Dohm, "Probe einer kurzen Charakter-
istick einiger der berühmtesten Völker
Asiens," *Lippische Intelligenzblätter* 41
(1774), reprinted in Dohm, *Ausgewählte
Schriften*, ed. Heinrich Detering
(Lemgo: Naturwissenschaftlicher und

historischer Verein für das Land Lippe,
1988), 31–36.
4. See Robert Liberles, "From *Toleration*
to *Verbesserung*: German and English
Debates on the Jews in the Eighteenth
Century," *Central European History*
22 (1989): 3–32, also Jacob Toury,
"Toleranz und Judenrecht in der
öffentlichen Meinung vor 1783,"
Wolfenbütteler Studien zur Aufklärung 4
(1977): 55–73.
5. Jeffrey A. Grossman, *The Discourse on
Yiddish in Germany: From the Enlightenment to the Second Empire* (Columbia,
SC: Camden House, 2000).
6. Eichhorn makes these comments in a
review of one of the French treatises
indebted to Dohm, Abbé Grégoire's
*Essai sur la régéneration physique, morale
et politique des Juifs*, in his *Allgemeine
Bibliothek der biblischen Litteratur* 2
(1789), 293.
7. Dohm, *De la réforme politique des Juifs*,
trans. Johann Bernouilli (Dessau,
1782). On the French reception of
Dohm, see Leonore Loft, "Mirabeau
and Brissot Review Christian Wilhelm
Dohm and the 'Jewish Question,'"
History of European Ideas 13 (1991):
605–22.
8. Volkmar Eichstädt, *Bibliographie
zur Geschichte der Judenfrage I:*

1750–1848 (Hamburg: Hanseatische Verlagsanstalt, 1938).

9. Schechter, "The Jewish Question in Eighteenth-Century France," *Eighteenth-Century Studies* 32 (1998): 84–91. Schechter draws on and seeks to correct an essay with a similar approach to the same topic, Gary Kates's "Jews into Frenchmen: Nationality and Representation during the French Revolution," in *The French Revolution and the Birth of Modernity*, ed. Ferenc Fehér (Berkeley: University of California Press, 1990).

10. Hans Martin Blitz, *Aus Liebe zum Vaterland. Die deutsche Nation im 18. Jahrhundert* (Hamburg: Hamburger Edition, 2000), also Hans Peter Herrmann, Hans Martin Blitz and Susanna Moßmann, eds, *Machtphantasie Deutschland. Nationalismus, Männlichkeit und Fremdenhaß im Vaterlandsdiskurs deutscher Schriftsteller des 18. Jahrhunderts* (Frankfurt am Main: Suhrkamp, 1996).

11. Hertzberg, *The French Enlightenment and the Jews* (New York: Columbia University Press, 1968).

12. Rose, *Revolutionary Antisemitism in Germany from Kant to Wagner* (Princeton: Princeton University Press, 1990), Goldhagen, *Hitler's Willing Executioners: Ordinary Germans and the Holocaust* (New York: Knopf, 1996).

13. Bauman, *Modernity and Ambivalence* (Ithaca, NY: Cornell University Press, 1991), 102–59, here 154.

14. Ibid., 158.

15. Arendt, *The Origins of Totalitarianism* (New York: Harcourt Brace Jovanovich, 1973), *Rahel Varnhagen: The Life of a Jewess*, ed. Liliane Weissberg, trans. Richard and Clara Winston (Baltimore: The Johns Hopkins University Press, 1997). See also the essays collected in Arendt, *The Jew as Pariah: Jewish Identity and Politics in the*

Modern Age, ed. Ron H. Feldman (New York: Grove Press, 1978).

16. David Sorkin, "Emancipation and Assimilation: Two Concepts and Their Application to German-Jewish History," *LBIYB* 35 (1990): 17–33.

17. Sorkin, *The Transformation of German Jewry, 1780–1840* (New York: Oxford University Press, 1987).

18. *German-Jewish History in Modern Times*, ed. Michael Meyer et al. (New York: Columbia University Press, 1996–98), 4 vols.

19. Mendes-Flohr, *German Jews: A Dual Identity* (New Haven and London: Yale University Press, 1999).

20. Compare here Klaus Berghahn, *Die Grenzen der Toleranz: Juden und Christen im Zeitalter der Aufklärung* (Cologne: Böhlau, 2000) and Peter R. Erspamer, *The Elusiveness of Tolerance: The "Jewish Question" from Lessing to the Napoleonic Wars* (Chapel Hill: University of North Carolina Press, 1997). Both Berghahn and Erspamer do stress the historical limits and failures of tolerance, but it is still the Enlightenment concept of tolerance in its ideal form that provides the organizing focus of their work. For a productive critique of the Enlightenment notion of toleration in relation to the Jews, see Adam Sutcliffe's essays, "Enlightenment and Exclusion: Judaism and Toleration in Spinoza, Locke and Bayle," *Jewish Culture and History* 2 (1999): 26–43, and "Myth, Origins, Identity: Voltaire, the Jews and the Enlightenment Notion of Toleration," *The Eighteenth Century: Theory and Interpretation* 39 (1998): 107–26. For an alternative approach, see Jeffrey S. Librett, *The Rhetoric of Cultural Dialogue: Jews and Germans from Moses Mendelssohn to Richard Wagner and Beyond* (Stanford: Stanford University Press, 2000).

21. Scholem, "Against the Myth of the German-Jewish Dialogue" and "Once

More: The German-Jewish Dialogue," in *On Jews and Judaism in Crisis: Selected Essays*, ed. Werner J. Dannhauser (New York: Schocken, 1976), 61–70, here 62.

22. Scholem, "Once More: The German–Jewish Dialogue," 68.

23. Bauman, *Modernity and Ambivalence*, 138.

24. Peter Hanns Reill, *The German Enlightenment and the Rise of Historicism* (Berkeley: University of California Press, 1975).

25. *Reflexionen Kants zur Anthropologie. Aus Kants handschriftlichen Aufzeichnungen*, ed. Benno Erdmann (Leipzig: Fues's Verlag, 1882), 213–14.

26. Heschel, *Abraham Geiger and the Jewish Jesus* (Chicago: University of Chicago Press, 1998).

27. Said, *Orientalism* (New York: Vintage, 1979).

28. Pollock, "Deep Orientalism? Notes on Sanskrit and Power Beyond the Raj," in *Orientalism and the Postcolonial Predicament: Perspectives on South Asia*, ed. Carol A. Breckenridge and Peter van der Veer (Philadelphia: University of Pennsylvania Press, 1993), Pasto, "Islam's 'Strange Secret Sharer': Orientalism, Judaism, and the Jewish Question," *Comparative Studies of Society and History* 40 (1998): 437–74, Hess, "Johann David Michaelis and the Colonial Imaginary: Orientalism and the Emergence of Racial Antisemitism in Eighteenth-Century Germany," *Jewish Social Studies* 6 (2000): 56–101.

29. See here, for instance, Dominique Bourel, "Die deutsche Orientalistik im 18. Jahrhundert. Von der Mission zur Wissenschaft," in *Historische Kritik und biblischer Kanon in der deutschen Aufklärung*, ed. Henning Graf Reventlow, Walter Sparn and John Woodbridge (Wiesbaden: Harrassowitz, 1988).

30. Zantop, *Colonial Fantasies: Conquest, Family, and Nation in Precolonial Germany, 1770–1870* (Durham, NC: Duke University Press, 1997).

31. See here, for instance, Ann Laura Stoler, *Race and the Education of Desire: Foucault's History of Sexuality and the Colonial Order of Things* (Durham, NC: Duke University Press, 1995).

32. There is a growing body of important literature on race thinking in the eighteenth and early nineteenth centuries. See here, in addition to Zantop, *Colonial Fantasies*, Nicholas Hudson, "From 'Nation' to 'Race': The Origins of Racial Classification in Eighteenth-Century Thought," *Eighteenth-Century Studies* 29 (1996): 247–64, Robert Bernasconi, "Who Invented the Concept of Race? Kant's Role in the Enlightenment Construction of Race," in Bernasconi, ed., *Race* (Oxford: Blackwell, 2001), and the essays in Mark Larrimore and Sara Paulson Eigen, eds., *The German Invention of Race* (submitted for publication), proceedings of a conference held at Harvard in May 2001 on *The German Invention of Race*.

33. Michael A. Meyer, *Response to Modernity: A History of the Reform Movement in Judaism* (Detroit: Wayne State University Press, 1988), also Steven M. Lowenstein, *The Berlin Jewish Community: Enlightenment, Family, and Crisis, 1770–1830* (New York: Oxford University Press, 1994), 134–47.

34. Meyer, *Response to Modernity*, 17.

35. Sorkin, "Religious Reforms and Secular Trends in German-Jewish Life—An Agenda for Research," *LBIYB* 40 (1995): 170–85, here 172–73.

36. See Meyer, *Response to Modernity*, also Sorkin, *The Transformation of German Jewry*.

37. See here, for instance, Michael A. Meyer, *The Origins of the Modern Jew: Jewish Identity and European Culture in*

Germany, 1749–1824 (Detroit: Wayne State University Press, 1967), Jacob Katz, *Out of the Ghetto: The Social Background of Jewish Emancipation, 1770–1870* (Cambridge, Mass.: Harvard University Press, 1973), Heinz Moshe Graupe, *The Rise of Modern Judaism: An Intellectual History of German Jewry 1650–1942*, trans. John Robinson (Huntington, NY: Krieger, 1978) and Katz, ed., *Toward Modernity: The European Jewish Model* (New Brunswick: Transaction Books, 1987).

38. Cohen, "German Jewry as Mirror of Modernity," *LBIYB* 20 (1975): ix–xxxi, here xiii.

39. See Sorkin, *The Transformation of German Jewry*, and Lois C. Dubin, *The Port Jews of Habsburg Trieste: Absolutist Politics and Enlightenment Culture* (Stanford: Stanford University Press, 1999).

40. Volkov, ed., *Deutsche Juden und die Moderne* (Munich: Oldenbourg, 1994), and Volkov, *Das jüdische Projekt der Moderne* (Munich: Beck, 2001).

41. Blackbourn and Eley, *The Peculiarities of German History: Bourgeois Society and Politics in Nineteenth-Century Germany* (Oxford: Oxford University Press, 1984).

42. Ibid., 292.

43. Jürgen Habermas, *The Philosophical Discourse of Modernity*, trans. Frederick Lawrence (Cambridge, Mass.: MIT Press, 1987), Hans Robert Jauss, "Literarische Tradition und gegenwärtiges Bewußtsein der Modernität," in *Literaturgeschichte als Provokation* (Frankfurt: Suhrkamp, 1970), Hans Ulrich Gumbrecht, "Modern," in Otto Brunner, Werner Conze and Reinhart Koselleck, eds, *Geschichtliche Grundbegriffe* (Stuttgart: Klett-Cotta, 1972ff.) 4: 93–131.

44. Peter Szondi, *Antike und Moderne in der Ästhetik der Goethezeit*, in *Poetik und Geschichtsphilosophie I. Studienausgabe der Vorlesungen 2*, ed. Senta Metz and Hans-Hagen Hildebrandt (Frankfurt: Suhrkamp, 1974).

45. See here, for instance, Herder, "Ueber die neuere deutsche Literatur" (1766–68), also "Shakespear" (1773), in *Herders Sämmtliche Werke*, ed. Bernhard Suphan (Berlin: Weidmannsche Buchhandlung, 1877), 1: 131–531, and 5: 208–31.

46. See Jonathan M. Hess, *Reconstituting the Body Politic: Enlightenment, Public Culture and the Invention of Aesthetic Autonomy* (Detroit: Wayne State University Press, 1999).

47. Hans Blumenberg, *The Legitimacy of the Modern Age*, trans. Robert M. Wallace (Cambridge, Mass.: MIT Press, 1983).

48. Reinhart Koselleck, *Futures Past: On the Semantics of Historical Time*, trans. Keith Tribe (Cambridge, Mass.: MIT Press, 1985), here 235, 243

49. Ibid., 250.

50. Habermas, "The German Idealism of the Jewish Philosophers," in *Philosophical-Political Profiles* (Cambridge, Mass.: MIT Press, 1983), 26.

I   ROME, JERUSALEM AND
THE TRIUMPH OF MODERNITY:
CHRISTIAN WILHELM DOHM AND
THE REGENERATION OF THE JEWS

1. Dohm, "Ueber die Kaffeegesezgebung," *Deutsches Museum* 2 (1777): 123–45, here 126, 143–44.

2. Dohm, "Vorerinnerung," *Deutsches Museum* 1 (1777): 1–6, here 4–5, also the January 29, 1776 letter Dohm sent Johann Wilhelm Ludwig Gleim along with the first issue of the journal, quoted in W. Gronau, *Christian Wilhelm von Dohm nach seinem Wollen und Handeln* (Lemgo: Meyersche Hof-Buchhandlung, 1824), 39–40.

3. Dohm, "Briefe nordamerikanischen Inhalts," *Deutsches Museum* 1 (1777): 159–85.

4. Wolfgang Schivelbusch, *Tastes of Paradise: A Social History of Spices, Stimulants, and Intoxicants*, trans. David Jacobson (New York: Pantheon, 1992), 15–84.

5. Ibid., 72.

6. See here, for instance, Schlözer, *Briefwechsel meist historischen und politischen Inhalts* 44 (1781): 123–29; 46 (1781): 210–15, here *Briefwechsel* 44 (1781): 121.

7. Dohm, "Ueber die Kaffeegesezgebung," 123, 126.

8. Ibid., 126.

9. Ibid., 144–45.

10. Susanne Zantop, *Colonial Fantasies: Conquest, Family, and Nation in Precolonial Germany, 1770–1870* (Durham, NC: Duke University Press, 1997).

11. On Dohm's economic thinking, see Ilsegret Dambacher, *Christian Wilhelm von Dohm: Ein Beitrag zur Geschichte des preußischen aufgeklärten Beamtentums und seiner Reformbestrebungen am Ausgang des 18. Jahrhunderts* (Bern: Lang, 1974), 97–140.

12. See here, for instance, W.O. Henderson, *Studies in the Economic Policy of Frederick the Great* (London: Frank Cass, 1963): here 126, but also the chapter on "Die preußische Einwanderung und ländliche Kolonisation des 17. und 18. Jahrhunderts" in Gustav von Schmoller, *Umrisse und Untersuchungen zur Verfassungs-, Verwaltungs- und Wirtschaftsgeschichte besonders des Preußischen Staates im 17. und 18. Jahrhundert* (Hildesheim: Olms, 1974).

13. Von Schmoller, *Umrisse*, 593.

14. See the review of the first volume of Dohm's work in the *Allgemeine Deutsche Bibliothek* 50 (1782): 301–11, here 309, and Heinrich F. Diez, "Ueber Juden. An Herrn Kriegsrath Dohm zu Berlin," *Berichte der allgemeinen Buchhandlung der Gelehrten* 1 (1783): 320–47, here 336.

15. Büsching, review of *Ueber die bürgerliche Verbesserung der Juden, Wöchentliche Nachrichten von neuen Landcharten, geographischen, statitischen und historischen Büchern und Sachen* 9 (1781): 299–302, 319–20, 331–35.

16. August Wilhelm [Friedrich] Crome, review of *Ueber die bürgerliche Verbesserung der Juden, Berichte der allgemeinen Buchhandlung der Gelehrten* 1 (1782): 460–75.

17. Mendelssohn, *JubA* 8: 4, Gronau, *Dohm*, 88.

18. See here Franz Reuss, *Christian Wilhelm Dohms Schrift "Über die bürgerliche Verbesserung der Juden" und deren Einwirkung auf die gebildeten Stände Deutschlands* (Kaiserslauten: Blenk, 1891), Horst Möller, "Auklärung, Judenemanzipation und Staat: Ursprung und Wirkung von Dohms Schrift über die bürgerliche Verbesserung der Juden," in *Deutsche Aufklärung und Judenemanzipation*, ed. Walter Grab, *Jahrbuch des Instituts für deutsche Geschichte* Beiheft 3 (1980): 119–49, and most recently, Robert Liberles, "Dohm's Treatise on the Jews: A Defense of the Enlightenment," *LBIYB* 33 (1988): 29–42.

19. See here Reuven Michael, "Die antijudaistische Tendenz in Christian Wilhelm Dohms Buch Ueber die bürgerliche Verbesserung der Juden," *Bulletin des Leo Baeck Instituts* 77 (1987): 11–48, and Paul Lawrence Rose, *Revolutionary Antisemitism in Germany from Kant to Wagner* (Princeton: Princeton University Press, 1990), 70–79.

20. Jacob Katz, "The Term 'Jewish Emancipation': Its Origin and Historical Impact," in Katz, *Emancipation and Assimilation: Studies in Modern Jewish History* (Farnborough: Gregg, 1972), 21–45, esp. 34–35.

21. [Saul Ascher,] *Bemerkungen über die bürgerliche Verbesserung der Juden veranlaßt bei der Frage: Soll der Jude Soldat*

werden? (Frankfurt an der Oder: Kunze, 1788).

22. See here, for instance, von Schmoller, *Umrisse*, 562–66.

23. One cannot help but note the formal similarity here between Dohm's historiographical maneuvers and the commemorative narratives that have been so central to the implementation of Zionist ideology. Indeed, if Dohm's attempt to incorporate the Jews into a non-Jewish body politic hinges on a historiography that reenacts the victory of Rome over Jerusalem, Zionist historiography has typically done the exact opposite. Eager to stress its continuity with the ancient Jewish state, much Zionist historiography has viewed the entire period of exile as empty time, as a period of suppressed Jewish nationhood. The only historical moments in Jewish exile that gain prominence in this schema are typically events like the fall of Masada or the Bar Kokhba rebellion, events conceived of—in the case of Masada often with great difficulty—as expressions of Jewish political resistance to the Romans. See on this issue Yael Zerubavel, *Recovered Roots: Collective Memory and the Making of Israeli National Tradition* (Chicago: University of Chicago Press, 1995).

24. On this question see Marc Shell, "Marranos (Pigs), or From Coexistence to Toleration," *Critical Inquiry* 17 (1991): 306–35, also Daniel Boyarin, *A Radical Jew: Paul and the Politics of Identity* (Berkeley: University of California Press, 1994), 246ff.

25. Diez, "Ueber Juden," quoted above.

26. See on this point Edward Breuer, "Politics, Tradition, History: Rabbinic Judaism and the Eighteenth-Century Struggle for Civil Equality," *Harvard Theological Review* 85 (1992): 357–83.

27. Lessing, "The Education of the Human Race," in Lessing, *Nathan the Wise, Minna von Barnhelm, and Other Plays and Writings*, ed. Peter Demetz (New York: Continuum, 1991), 328. German in Lessing, *Werke und Briefe*, ed. Wilfried Barner (Frankfurt am Main: Deutscher Klassiker Verlag, 1985), 10: 88.

28. The implicit differences between Mendelssohn and Dohm I illuminate in this particular passage should be understood as relative differences, not as a clear-cut opposition. As I noted in my introduction, Dohm wrote his treatise at Mendelssohn's request and closely cooperated with Mendelssohn during its composition; Mendelssohn also helped supervise Johann Bernouilli's French translation. See Alexander Altmann, "Letters from Dohm to Mendelssohn," in *Salo Wittmayer Baron: Jubilee Volume on the Occasion of his 80th Birthday*, ed. Saul Lieberman, Arthur Hyman and Jeanette Meisel Baron (Jerusalem: American Academy for Jewish Research, 1974), 1: 39–64, also Breuer, "Politics, Tradition, History."

29. For a discussion of the role Jewish memory plays in the ideology of emancipation, see my essay, "Memory, History and the Jewish Question: Universal Citizenship and the Colonization of Jewish Memory," in *The Work of Memory: New Directions in the Study of German Society and Culture*, ed. Alon Confino and Peter Fritzsche (Champaign: University of Illinois Press, 2002).

30. Herder, "Bekehrung der Juden," *Adrastea* 4 (1802): 142–66. See my discussion in "Memory, History and the Jewish Question."

31. See here, in addition to my further comments on this issue in Chapters 2 and 3: "Des Hrn. Prediger Schwager Gedanken, bey Lesung dieser Schrift," in D 2: 89–111; Dohm's own discussion of his critics on these points

in D 2: 222–46; O. E Kling, *Soll der Jude Soldat werden?* (Vienna, 1788); and [Ascher,] *Bemerkungen*. Dohm's concern with the degenerate Jewish body is of course not atypical of Western attitudes toward Jews; see Sander L. Gilman, *The Jew's Body* (New York: Routledge, 1991).

32. Note the similarity to Michel Foucault, *Discipline and Punish*, trans. Alan Sheridan (New York: Vintage, 1979), esp. 135–36.

33. Karl Philipp Moritz, *Reisen eines Deutschen in England im Jahr 1782, in Briefen an Herrn Direktor Gedike*, in *Werke*, ed. Horst Günther (Frankfurt am Main: Insel, 1981). On Moritz's travelogue and his views on the Prussian military, see Jonathan M. Hess, *Reconstituting the Body Politic: Enlightenment, Public Culture and the Invention of Aesthetic Autonomy* (Detroit: Wayne State University Press, 1999), 121–54.

34. Reinhard Rürup, "The Torturous and Thorny Path to Legal Equality—'Jew Laws' and Emancipatory Legislation in Germany from the Late Eighteenth Century," *LBIYB* 31 (1986): 3–34, also Rürup, *Emanzipation und Antisemitismus: Studien zur "Judenfrage" der bürgerlichen Gesellschaft* (Göttingen: Vandenhoeck & Ruprecht, 1975), 37–74, and Sucher B. Weinryb, *Der Kampf um die Berufsumschichtung: Ein Ausschnitt aus der Geschichte der Juden in Deutschland* (Berlin: Schocken, 1936).

35. David Sorkin, *The Transformation of German Jewry, 1780–1840* (New York: Oxford University Press, 1987), 13–40.

36. Michaelis, review of Dohm, *Orientalische und exegetische Bibliothek* 19 (1782): 1–40, reprinted in D 2: 40–41.

37. Review of Dohm, *Ephemeriden der Menschheit* 1 (1782): 404–25, esp. 407–08.

38. Review of Mendelssohn's edition of Manasseh Ben Israel's *Rettung der Juden, Ephemeriden der Menschheit* 10 (1782): 418–32, 426–27. I thank Jonathan Sheehan for these references.

39. Fichte, *Beitrag zur Berichtigung der Urtheile des Publikums über die französische Revolution*, in Fichte, *Gesamtausgabe der Bayerischen Akademie der Wissenschaften*, ed. Reinhard Lauth and Hans Jacob (Stuttgart-Bad Canstatt: Frommann, 1964), 1: 293n.

40. Herder, "Bekehrung der Juden," 152. Herder here invoked a plan for mass repatriation by David Hartley but gave it a new twist by alluding to the French debates surrounding Napoleon's 1799 expedition to Palestine. For context, see Jeremy Popkin, "Zionism and the Enlightenment: The 'Letter of a Jew to his Brethren,'" *Jewish Social Studies* 43 (1981): 113–20.

41. *Gedanken eines Land-Geistlichen über eine an dem Ohio-Fluss in Amerika entdeckte Juden-Kolonie* (Frankfurt am Main, 1774), quoted and discussed in Don Heinrich Tolzmann, "The German Image of Cincinnati before 1830," *Queen City Heritage* 42.3 (1984): 31–38. On proposals for Jewish colonies, see Jacob Toury, "Emanzipation und Judenkolonien in der öffentlichen Meinung Deutschlands (1775–1819)," *Jahrbuch des Instituts für deutsche Geschichte* 11 (1982): 17–53, and Rainer Erb and Werner Bergmann, *Die Nachtseite der Judenemanzipation: Der Widerstand gegen die Integration der Juden in Deutschland 1780–1860* (Berlin: Metropol, 1989), 97–135.

42. See here, for instance, Karl Wilhelm Friedrich Grattenauer, *Ueber die physische und moralische Verbesserung der heutigen Juden* (Leipzig, 1791).

43. Friedrich von Schuckmann, "Ueber Judenkolonien. An Herrn Geheimen-Rath Dohm," *Berlinische Monatsschrift* 5 (1785): 50–58; Weinryb, *Der Kampf um die Berufsumschichtung*, 14–17.

44. Dohm, "Ueber die Juden-Toleranz," *Briefwechsel meist historischen und politischen Inhalts* 10 (1782): 279–83, responding to a proposal for a Jewish colony on pp. 250–55.

45. Maurycy Lewin, "Geschichte der Juden in Galizien unter Kaiser Joseph II. Ein Beitrag zur Geschichte der Juden in Oesterreich" (dissertation, University of Vienna, 1933), 80–104, also Josef Karniel, *Die Toleranzpolitik Kaiser Josephs II*, trans. Leo Koppel (Gerlingen: Bleicher, 1985), 469.

46. "Schreiben eines deutschen Juden, an den Präsidenten des Kongresses der vereinigten Staaten von Amerika," *Deutsches Museum* 1.6 (1783): 558–66. See, for background, Hans Lamm, "The So-Called 'Letter of a German Jew to the President of the Congress of the United States of America' of 1783," *Publications of the American Jewish Historical Society* 37 (1947): 171–77.

47. Fritz Kasch, *Leopold F. G. von Goeckingk* (Marburg: Elwert, 1909).

48. Albert A. Bruer, *Geschichte der Juden in Preußen* (Frankfurt am Main: Campus, 1991), 84. These figures do not include the large numbers of Jews residing in the areas gained in the 1772 Polish partition.

49. Mendelssohn refers to this bill as a potential danger in the closing of his 1783 *Jerusalem, JubA* 8: 203; *J* 139.

50. "Schreiben eines deutschen Juden," 566.

51. See Lamm, "The So-Called 'Letter of a German Jew,'" 173.

52. *Schreiben eines deutschen Juden an den amerikanischen Präsidenten O.*, ed. Moses Mendelsohn [*sic*] (Frankfurt and Leipzig, 1787).

53. See Lamm, "The So-Called 'Letter of a German Jew.'" Neither the literature on Goeckingk nor Goeckingk's own correspondence with Johann Heinrich Voß from this period makes mention of the letter. Johann Heinrich Voß, *Breife an Goeckingk, 1755–1786*, ed. Gerhard Hay (Munich: Beck, 1976).

54. "Schreiben eines deutschen Juden," 558–59.

55. Ibid., 565–66.

56. See Ludwig Geiger, "Aus Briefen Dohms an Nicolai," *Zeitschrift für die Geschichte der Juden in Deutschland* 5 (1892): 75–91, here 79.

57. Hißmann, [Review of Dohm, *Ueber Je bürgeliche Verbesserung der Juden*] *Zugabe zu den Göttingischen gelehrten Anzeigen*, 48. Stück, den 1. December 1781, pp. 753–63. Hißmann's essay was reprinted as "Anmerkungen über Dohms bürgerliche Verbesserung der Juden. Aus den Göttingischen gelehrten Anzeigen" (Vienna, 1782). See also Hißmann's review of the second volume of Dohm's treatise, *Göttingische Anzeigen* 1 (1784): 489–91.

58. See Robert Bernasconi, "Who Invented the Concept of Race? Kant's Role in the Enlightenment Construction of Race," in Bernasconi, ed., *Race* (Oxford: Blackwell, 2001).

59. See D 1: 19, 97n, 136–37.

2   ORIENTALISM AND THE COLONIAL IMAGINARY: JOHANN DAVID MICHAELIS AND THE SPECTER OF RACIAL ANTISEMITISM

1. On the history of the term "antisemitism," see Reinhard Rürup and Thomas Nipperdey, "Antisemitismus—Entstehung, Funktion und Geschichte eines Begriffs," in Rürup, *Emanzipation und Antisemitismus: Studien zur "Judenfrage" der bürgerlichen Gesellschaft* (Göttingen: Vandenhoeck & Ruprecht, 1975), 95–114.

2. August Ludwig von Schlözer, *Fortsetzung der Allgemeinen Welthistorie* (Halle, 1771), 31: 281, also Schlözer,

"Von den Chaldäern," *Repertorium für biblische und morgenländische Litteratur* 8 (1781): 131–76, esp. 161.

3. Eichhorn, *Einleitung in das Alte Testament*, second edition (Leipzig, 1787), 1: 45ff, Herder, *Vom Geist der Ebräischen Poesie*, in *Herders Sämmtliche Werke*, ed. Bernhard Suphan (Berlin: Weidmannsche Buchhandlung, 1879), 9: 429–44.

4. Maurice Olender, *The Languages of Paradise: Race, Religion, and Philology in the Nineteenth Century*, trans. Arthur Goldhammer (Cambridge, Mass.: Harvard University Press, 1992), also Léon Poliakov, *The Aryan Myth: A History of Racist and Nationalist Ideas in Europe*, trans. Edmund Howard (New York: Basic Books, 1974).

5. Michaelis, *Orientalische und exegetische Bibliothek* 19 (1782): 1–40, reprinted in D 2, here 40–41. Compare Michaelis, *Mosaisches Recht*, third edition (Frankfurt am Main, 1793), 1: 229–34, also vol. 4 (1778, second edition), 185ff.

6. See Sander Gilman, *The Jew's Body* (New York: Routledge, 1991). For a productive comparative analysis of the political uses of such bodily differences, see Yosef Hayim Yerushalmi, "Assimilation and Racial Anti-Semitism: The Iberian and the German Models," *Leo Baeck Memorial Lecture* 26 (New York: Leo Baeck Institute, 1982).

7. See here, for instance, Anna-Ruth Löwenbrück, *Judenfeindschaft im Zeitalter der Aufklärung. Eine Studie zur Vorgeschichte des modernen Antisemitismus am Beispiel des Göttinger Theologen und Orientalisten Johann David Michaelis (1717–1791)* (Frankfurt am Main: Peter Lang, 1995), also Barbara Fischer, "Residues of Otherness: On Jewish Emancipation during the Age of German Enlightenment," in *Insiders and Outsiders: Jewish and Gentile Culture in Germany and Austria*, ed. Dagmar

C. G. Lorenz and Gabriele Weinberger (Detroit: Wayne State University Press, 1994), 30–38.

8. *Allgemeine Deutsche Bibliothek* 59 (1784), 19–43.

9. Geiger, "Der Kampf christlicher Theologen gegen die bürgerliche Gleichstellung der Juden," *Wissenschaftliche Zeitschrift für jüdische Theologie* 1 (1835): 52–67, 340–57, and 2 (1836): 78–92, 446–73.

10. There is extensive literature on Michaelis's contributions to the rise of modern biblical scholarship: Anna-Ruth Löwenbrück, "Johann David Michaelis' Verdienst um die philologisch-historische Bibelkritik," in *Historische Kritik und biblischer Kanon in der deutschen Aufklärung*, ed. Henning Graf Reventlow, Walter Sparn and John Woodbridge (Wiesbaden: Harrassowitz, 1988), 157–70; Löwenbrück, "Johann David Michaelis et les débuts de la critique biblique," in *Le siècle des Lumières et la Bible*, ed. Yvon Belaval and Dominique Bourel (Paris: Beauchesne, 1986), 113–28; Rudolf Smend, "Aufgeklärte Bemühung um das Gesetz: Johann David Michaelis' 'Mosaisches Recht,'" in *"Wenn nicht jetzt, wann dann?"*, ed. Hans-Georg Geyer, Johann Michael Schmidt, Werner Schneider and Michael Weinrich (Neukirchen-Vluyn: Neukirchener Verlag, 1983), 129–42; Rudoph Smend, "Johann David Michaelis und Johann Gottfried Eichhorn—zwei Orientalisten am Rande der Theologie," in *Theologie in Göttingen: Eine Vorlesungsreihe*, ed. Bernd Moeller (Göttingen: Vandenhoeck & Ruprecht, 1987); Walter Schmithals, "Wisenschaftliches Verstehen und existenzielles Verstehen im Geiste," in *Theologie des Geistes*, ed. Otto Dilschneider (Gütersloh: Mohn, 1980), 109–20; and Hans-Joachim Kraus, *Geschichte der historisch-*

kritischen Erforschung des Alten Testaments, third edition (Neukirchen-Vluyn: Neukirchener Verlag, 1982), 97–102. On the status of "Oriental studies" in the eighteenth century, see Dominique Bourel, "Die deutsche Orientalistik im 18. Jahrhundert. Von der Mission zur Wissenschaft," in *Historische Kritik und biblischer Kanon in der deutschen Aufklärung*, ed. Reventlow et al., 113–26. On Michaelis's career, see his autobiography, *Lebensbeschreibung von ihm selbst abgefaßt* (Leipzig, 1793), also Michaelis, *Literarischer Briefwechsel*, ed. Joh. Gottlieb Bulhe (Leipzig, 1794–96), 3 vols.

11. Löwenbrück, *Judenfeindschaft*, offers the best available introduction to Michaelis's thought. Frank E. Manuel has also stressed the relationship between Michaelis's antisemitism and his *Mosaic Law*, noting the inverse relation between Michaelis's admiration of ancient Judaism and his polemics against the emancipation of contemporary Jews; see Manuel, *The Broken Staff: Judaism through Christian Eyes* (Cambridge, Mass.: Harvard University Press, 1992), 252–62.

12. Löwenbrück, *Judenfeinschaft*, esp. 162, 208.

13. Poliakov argues that modern antisemitism simply expressses "the ineradicable feelings and resentments of the Christian West . . . in a new vocabulary" (*The Aryan Myth*, 194).

14. Edward W. Said, *Orientalism* (New York: Vintage, 1979).

15. *Abulsedae Descriptio Aegypti, arabice et latine. Ex codice parisiensi edidit, latine vertit, notas adiecit, Ioannes David Michaelis* (Göttingen, 1776).

16. Carsten Niebuhr, *Beschreibung von Arabien. Aus eigenen Beobachtungen und im Lande selbst gesammleten Nachrichten* (Copenhagen, 1772), *Reisebeschreibung nach Arabien und andern umliegenden Ländern* (Copenhagen, 1774 [vol. 1], 1778 [vol. 2]). A third volume of the

1774–78 *Reisebeschreibung* was published posthumously in 1837; selections from all three volumes are available in a contemporary German edition, Carsten Niebuhr, *Entdeckungen im Orient: Reise nach Arabien und anderen Ländern, 1761–1767*, ed. Robert and Evamaria Grün (Stuttgart: Erdmann, 1983). The English translation, *Travels through Arabia, and other Countries in the East*, trans. Robert Heron (Edinburgh, 1792), includes excerpts from Niebuhr's 1774–78 *Reisebeschreibung* (in volume 1) and selections from the 1772 *Beschreibung von Arabien* (in volume 2).

17. Mary Louise Pratt, *Imperial Eyes: Travel Writing and Transculturation* (London: Routledge, 1992).

18. Goethe, *From My Life: Poetry and Truth*, trans. Robert R. Heitner, introduction and notes by Thomas P. Saine, *Goethe: Suhrkamp Edition in 12 Volumes*, vol. 4 (New York: Suhrkamp, 1987), 209.

19. *Herders Sämmtliche Werke* 5: 423–4, 425. Herder's review was originally published in the *Frankfurter Gelehrte Anzeigen* 34 (April 28, 1772): 265–69.

20. Compare here, for instance, "Auch eine Philosophie der Geschichte zur Bildung der Menschheit" (1774), *Herders Sämmtliche Werke* 5: 502ff.

21. Johann David Michaelis, *Mosaisches Recht* 1: 2. All further references will be indicated in the body of the text by volume and page number.

22. See here especially *Mosaisches Recht* 6: 1–190.

23. Friedrich Schaffstein, "Johann David Michaelis als Kriminalpolitiker. Ein Orientalist am Rande der Strafrechtswissenschaft," *Nachrichten der Akademie der Wissenschaft in Göttingen* Jahrgang 1988, Nr. 3 (Göttingen: Vandenhoeck & Ruprecht, 1988): 93–117.

24. Letter from John Pringle to Michaelis of May 2, 1774, in Michaelis, *Literarischer Briefwechsel*, 2: 381–86; see also *Mosaisches Recht* 2: 388.

25. Assmann, *Moses the Egyptian: The Memory of Egypt in Western Monotheism* (Cambridge, Mass.: Harvard University Press, 1997).

26. Herder, *Ideen zur Philosophie der Geschichte der Menschheit, Herders Sämmtliche Werke* 16: 58, Eichhorn *Einleitung in das Alte Testament*, fourth edition (Göttingen, 1823), 1: 3–8, 3: 349–50.

27. Michaelis does admit that it would be better "to know the customs of the Arabs from their own writers," particularly those "before Mohammed, before the victories over so many foreign peoples, and contact with these, was able to bring about some change in the customs of the Arabs" (1: 13). And elsewhere, giving credence to common eighteenth-century prejudices, he speaks of the "crude and barbarian law" that the "very uncultivated Mohammed" gave to his "savage people," aspects of which, interestingly enough, are "not Oriental, not Hebrew or ancient Arab, but entirely Mohammedan" (2: 92). These occasional concessions of the importance of Islam prove to be of little consequence for his vision of the goals and methods of Oriental studies. Michaelis's views of the "savage" and "uncultivated" religion of Islam do nothing to disturb his attempt to find ancient Israelite customs alive and well among contemporary Arabs. Islam represents little more than a hurdle to jump over, something the Orientalist in search of ancient Israelite customs should be vaguely aware of, at most.

28. See the letter of January 27, 1770, reprinted in *JubA* 12: 1, 213.

29. Herder, "Bekehrung der Juden," *Adrastea* 4 (1802): 142–66, here 145.

30. Michaelis, *Lebensbeschreibung*, 74–75.

31. In this passage, Michaelis does cite scripture (Exodus 1: 10) to support his claim that the Egyptians were suspicious of the Israelites. What ultimately matters here, however, is Michaelis's basic emphasis, the way in which his Egyptian-identified account of the Exodus "liberates" the Israelites only to subject them once again to Egyptian rule.

32. Niebuhr, *Travels through Arabia* 2: 2–3.

33. The best sources of information on the expedition are Michaelis, *Lebensbeschreibung*, 66–76, Michaelis, *Literarischer Briefwechsel*, Niebuhr's two travelogues, cited above, and Michaelis, *Fragen an eine Gesellschaft gelehrter Männer, die auf Befehl ihro Majestät des Königes von Dännemark nach Arabien reisen* (Frankfurt am Main, 1762). The only substantial twentieth-century discussion of the expedition is geared toward the general public and reads at times like an adventure novel; see Thorkild Hansen, *Arabia Felix: The Danish Expedition, 1761–67*, trans. James and Kathleen McFarlane (London: Collins, 1964).

34. Letter from Michaelis to Baron von Bernstorff of August 30, 1756, *Literarischer Briefwechsel* 1: 299–324, here 299–305.

35. Ibid. 1: 310.

36. Michaelis, *Lebensbeschreibung*, 66.

37. *Descriptiones animalium, avium, amphibiorum, piscium, insectorum, vermium; quae in itinere orientali observavit Petrus Forskål. Post mortem auctoris edidit Carsten Niebuhr* (Copenhagen, 1775), *Flora aegyptiaco-arabica, sive, Descriptiones plantarum, quas per Egyptum inferiorem et Arabiam felicem detexit, illustravit Petrus Forskål. Post mortem auctoris edidit Carsten Niebuhr* (Copenhagen, 1775).

38. Hansen, *Arabia Felix*, 318–24.

39. Michaelis, *Literarischer Briefwechsel* 2: 223–24.

40. Immanuel Kant, "Von den verschiedenen Racen der Menschen" (1775), *AA* 2: 429–43, here 432; Johann Friedrich Blumenbach, *De generis*

humani varietate nativa, 1775 and 1795 editions, *On the Natural Varieties of Mankind* (1865; New York: Bergman, 1969), 122, 126, 128, 129, 245, 307; and Herder, *Ideen zur Philosophie der Geschichte der Menschheit, Herders Sämmtliche Werke* 13: 225, 250; 14: 27, 46, 58.

41. Niebuhr, *Travels through Arabia* 2: 253–54.

42. Michaelis, *Lebensbeschreibung,* 73–74.

43. This tendency, interestingly enough, characterizes much of the twentieth-century literature on the expedition as well. See Hansen, *Arabia Felix,* also the preface to the anthology, *Reisen im Orient: Berichte deutscher Forscher aus dem 18. und 19. Jahrhundert,* ed. Herbert Scurla (Berlin: Verlag der Nation, 1966).

44. Letter from [Gerhard Anton] von Halem to Michaelis, February 27, 1760, Michaelis, *Literarischer Briefwechsel* 1: 423–24.

45. Letter from Pringle to Michaelis, March 23, 1772, ibid., 2: 317.

46. Hansen, *Arabia Felix,* 56.

47. Niebuhr, *Travels through Arabia* 2: 3–5.

48. Pratt traces, in *Imperial Eyes,* how scientific voyages promoted by Linnaeus and his students like Forsskål served to construct a distinctly Euro-centered form of global consciousness. The classificatory project of Linnaean natural history, Pratt argues, unfolded in explicit relation to older imperial rhetorics of conquest, promoting "strategies of representation whereby European bourgeois subjects seek to secure their innocence in the same moment as they assert European hegemony" (7). Rather than reflecting on their own implication, however indirect, in the power dynamics of imperialist expansion, such scientific voyages typically cast the European as but a passive, disinterested observer with a "harmless hegemonic vision that

installs no apparatus of domination" (34).

49. Niebuhr, *Travels through Arabia* 2: 15.

50. Ibid. 2: 20.

51. Ibid. 2: 22–23, 158.

52. Letter from von Haven to Grand-Maréchal Comte de Moltke, July 5, 1762, included in letter from von Bernstorff to Michaelis, July 2, 1763, Michaelis, *Literarischer Briefwechsel* 2: 69–70.

53. Niebuhr, *Travels through Arabia* 1: 86, 94–97, translation modified; *Reisebeschreibung nach Arabien und andern umliegenden Ländern* 1: 141–43.

54. See here, for instance, Schlözer, *Briefwechsel meist historischen und politischen Inhalts* 44 (1781): 123–29; 46 (1781): 210–15.

55. Ibid. 44 (1781): 121.

56. Robert Louis Stein, *The French Sugar Business in the Eighteenth Century* (Baton Rouge: Louisiana State University Press, 1988), also Sidney W. Mintz, *Sweetness and Power: The Place of Sugar in Modern History* (New York: Viking, 1985).

57. Stein, *The French Sugar Business.*

58. "Der Zukker," *Neueste Mannigfaltigkeiten: Eine gemeinnützige Wochenschrift* 1.10 (1778): 145–47.

59. "Revolutionen in der Diät von Europa seit 300 Jaren," *Briefwechsel meist historischen und politischen Inhalts* 44 (1781): 93–120, esp. 98–99. Schlözer here reprints sections of an essay by a Professor Leidensfrost that had appeared in the *Wöchentliche Duisburgische Anzeigen* in 1768 but that apparently did not receive the attention Schlözer believes it should have.

60. "Revolutionen in der Diät," 93n.

61. "Von Jamaica. Eingesandt aus NAmerika, im Decemb. 1780," *Briefwechsel meist historischen und politischen Inhalts* 40 (1781): 143–45. Compare Edward Long, *The History of Jamaica* (London, 1774), 2: 229.

62. "Vertrauliche Briefe aus Jamaika, vom 31 Okt.–23 Dec. 1778," *Briefwechsel meist historischen und politischen Inhalts* 29 (1779): 313–30, here 316.

63. "Natürliche Merkwürdigkeiten von Jamaica," *Neues Hamburgisches Magazin* 114 (1780): 551–55, here 551–52.

64. As a result of Dohm's queries, the leaders of the Sephardic community published an *Essai historique sur la colonie de Surinam* (Paramaribo, 1788), which included their correspondence with Dohm. This text is available in a modern English-language edition: *Historical Essay on the Colony of Surinam 1788*, trans. Simon Cohen, ed. Jacob R. Marcus and Stanley F. Chyet (Cincinnati: American Jewish Archives, 1974). See also W. Gronau, *Christian Wilhelm von Dohm nach seinem Wollen und Handeln* (Lemgo: Meyersche Hof-Buchhandlung, 1824), 88.

65. Karl Wilhelm Friedrich Grattenauer, *Ueber die physische und moralische Verfassung der heutigen Juden. Stimme eines Kosmopoliten* (Leipzig, 1791), 114–15, 56f. The trope Grattenauer uses—"washing a blackamoor white"—has of course a long history that predates modern thinking about race. What matters here, however, is less the genealogy of this term than the way in which the modern period witnesses a transformation in its use. See Jean-Michel Massing, "From Greek Proverb to Soap Adverts: Washing the Ethiopian," *Journal of the Warburg and Courtauld Institutes* 58 (1995): 180–201.

66. Grattenauer, *Wider die Juden* (Berlin: Schmidt, 1803), *Erklärung an das Publikum über meine Schrift: Wider die Juden* (Berlin: Schmidt, 1803), 36–37, and *Erster Nachtrag zu seiner Erklärung über seine Schrift: Wider die Juden* (Berlin: Schmidt, 1803), 29–30.

67. Christoph Meiners, "Ueber die Natur der Afrikanischen Neger," *Göttingisches Historisches Magazin* 6 (1790): 385–456.

68. Gerlach, *Moses und Christus, Oder über den innern Werth und die wahrscheinlichen Folgen des Sendschreibens einiger Hausväter jüdischer Religion an Herrn Probst Teller und dessen darauf ertheilte Antwort* (Berlin: Maurer, 1799), 3–20.

69. For helpful overviews of eighteenth-century race theory, see Nicholas Hudson, "From 'Nation' to 'Race': The Origins of Racial Classification in Eighteenth-Century Thought," *Eighteenth-Century Studies* 29 (1996): 247–64, also, dealing more specifically with Germany, Susanne Zantop, *Colonial Fantasies: Conquest, Family, and Nation in Precolonial Germany, 1770–1870* (Durham, NC: Duke University Press, 1997), 66–80, and Robert Bernasconi, "Who Invented the Concept of Race? Kant's Role in the Enlightenment Construction of Race," in Bernasconi, ed., *Race* (Oxford: Blackwell, 2001).

70. The five-part division does not appear in the 1775 edition. It is only after Captain Cook's voyages in the South Seas that Blumenbach integrates the category "Malay" into his typologies.

71. Blumenbach, *On the Natural Varieties of Mankind* (1795), 269.

72. Ibid., 265. On the link between categories of aesthetic evaluation and anthropological typologies, see George L. Mosse, *Toward the Final Solution: A History of European Racism* (New York: Fertig, 1978), 17–34, also Zantop, *Colonial Fantasies*, 66–80.

73. On this issue, see Hudson, "From 'Nation' to 'Race,'" and Zantop, *Colonial Fantasies*, 66–80.

74. Blumenbach, *On the Natural Varieties of Mankind*, 157.

75. Ibid., 122.

76. Ibid., 234.

77. Said, *Orientalism*, 17–19.

78. Susannah Heschel, *Abraham Geiger and the Jewish Jesus* (Chicago: University of Chicago Press, 1998), 19–21, 50–75.

79. On this issue—and and for a further argument that parallels my conclusions here—see James Pasto, "Islam's 'Strange Secret Sharer': Orientalism, Judaism, and the Jewish Question," *Comparative Studies of Society and History* 40 (1998): 437–74.
80. Said, *Orientalism*, 27.

3   MENDELSSOHN'S JESUS: THE
FRUSTRATIONS OF JEWISH RESISTANCE

1. Anonymous review of vol. 2 of *On the Civic Improvement of the Jews, Allgemeine Deutsche Bibliothek* 59 (1784), 19–43, here 22.
2. See, on Linnaeus, Mary Louise Pratt, *Imperial Eyes: Travel Writing and Transculturation* (London: Routledge, 1992), 32–33. Bougainville's physician Commerçon published a "Lettre sur un Peuple Nain de l'Isle de Madagascar" in the *Journal des Scavans*, a piece that was translated and published in German as "Nachricht von den Pygmäen," *Mannigfaltigkeiten: Eine gemeinnützige Wochenschrift* 3 (1771): 765–67.
3. Georg Forster, "Ueber die Pygmäen," *Hessische Beiträge zur Gelehrsamkeit und Kunst* 1.1 (1785): 1–17.
4. Alexander Altmann's *Moses Mendelssohn: A Biographical Study* (Philadelphia: Jewish Publication Society, 1973) remains the most comprehensive study of Mendelssohn to date. Altmann's work, however, has been supplemented in recent years by two important monographs: Allan Arkush, *Moses Mendelssohn and the Enlightenment* (Albany: SUNY Press, 1994), and David Sorkin, *Moses Mendelssohn and the Religious Enlightenment* (Berkeley: University of California Press, 1996). The section on Mendelssohn in Michael A. Meyer's *The Origins of the Modern Jew: Jewish*

Identity and European Culture in Germany, 1749–1824 (Detroit: Wayne State University Press, 1967), 11–56, remains of value as well.
5. Sorkin, *Mendelssohn*, 148–55, also, for constrast, Alexander Altmann, "Moses Mendelssohn as the Archetypal German Jew," in *The Jewish Response to German Culture: From the Enlightenment to the Second World War*, ed. Jehuda Reinharz and Walter Schatzberg (Hanover, NH: University Press of New England, 1985), 17–31.
6. Mendelssohn, "Schreiben an den Herrn Diaconus Lavater zu Zürich," *JubA* 7: 5–17.
7. "Mendelssohns Nacherinnerung," *JubA* 7: 41, also the February 9, 1770 letter to Bonnet, ibid. 7: 318.
8. November 16, 1770 letter to Elkan Herz, ibid. 7: 352.
9. *Manasseh Ben Israel Rettung der Juden. Aus dem Englischen übersetzt. Nebst einer Vorrede von Moses Mendelssohn. Als ein Anhang zu des Hrn. Kriegsraths Dohm Abhandlung: Ueber die bürgerliche Verbesserung der Juden, JubA* 8: 1–72.
10. "Das Forschen nach Licht und Recht in einem Schreiben an Herrn Moses Mendelssohn auf Veranlassung seiner merkwürdigen Vorrede zu Manasseh Ben Israel" (Berlin, 1782), reprinted in *JubA* 8: 73–87.
11. Sorkin, *Mendelssohn*, 120–46.
12. Arkush, *Mendelssohn*.
13. Note here the difference from Sorkin, *Mendelssohn*. Sorkin persuasively positions Mendelssohn within the religious Enlightenment, presenting his use of rationalist philosophy to uphold revealed religion as the heir to early eighteenth-century Wolffian theology. Sorkin's primary interest is Mendelssohn's thought, and by looking at his German writings alongside his Hebrew works he demonstrates that his views on Judaism never underwent fundamental change. My

emphasis is less on the inner unity of Mendelssohn's thought than on the emergence of his polemical voice *vis-à-vis* his German public; in this context it becomes necessary to highlight his engagement with his more immediate contemporaries. Sorkin, to be sure, touches on this problem as well, but his presentation of Mendelssohn's particular mode of fusing Enlightenment philosophy and Judaism tends to obscure some of the sites of conflict I explore in this chapter.

14. Heschel, "Revolt of the Colonized: Abraham Geiger's *Wissenschaft des Judentums* as a Challenge to Christian Hegemony in the Academy," *New German Critique* 77 (1999): 61–86.

15. Arnold Eisen, *Galut: Modern Jewish Reflection on Homelessness and Homecoming* (Bloomington: Indiana University Press, 1986), 59–64.

16. Heschel, "Revolt of the Colonized," also Heschel, *Abraham Geiger and the Jewish Jesus* (Chicago: University of Chicago Press, 1998).

17. See Anna-Ruth Löwenbrück, "Johann David Michaelis und Moses Mendelssohn: Judenfeindschaft im Zeitalter der Aufklärung," in *Moses Mendelssohn und die Kreise seiner Wirksamkeit*, ed. Michael Albrecht, Eva J. Engel and Norbert Hinske (Tübingen: Niemeyer, 1994).

18. Lavater, in *JubA* 7: 3. For an extensive discussion of the background of the Lavater affair, see Altmann, *Mendelssohn*, 194–263.

19. Bonnet, June 24, 1770 letter to Mendelssohn, quoted verbatim also in Bonnet's January 29, 1771 letter to Lavater, *JubA* 7: 349, 365–66.

20. See on this question David Sorkin, "Jews, the Enlightenment and Religious Toleration—Some Reflections," *LBIYB* 37 (1992): 3–16.

21. On Mendelssohn's fears of censorship during the Lavater affair, see Altmann, *Mendelssohn*, 223.

22. In some cases, as Moshe Pelli points out, Mendelssohn practically adopts Toland's phrasing verbatim. See Pelli, "The Impact of Deism on the Hebrew Literature of the Enlightenment in Germany," *Eighteenth-Century Studies* 6 (1972): 35–59, here 49–50.

23. See Blu Greenberg, "Rabbi Jacob Emden: The Views of an Enlightened Traditionalist on Christianity," *Judaism* 107 (1978): 351–63.

24. Mendelssohn, January 15, 1771 letter to Lavater, *JubA* 7: 361–63.

25. On Mendelssohn's Bible translations, see, in addition to Sorkin, *Mendelssohn*, 53–94, especially Edward Breuer, *The Limits of Enlightenment: Jews, Germans, and the Eighteenth-Century Study of Scripture* (Cambridge, Mass.: Harvard University Press, 1996), Steven M. Lowenstein, "The Readership of Mendelssohn's Bible Translation," *Hebrew Union College Annual* 53 (1982): 179–213, and Werner Weinberg, "Language Questions Relating to Moses Mendelssohn's Pentateuch Translation," *Hebrew Union College Annual* 55 (1984): 197–242.

26. February 8, 1782 letter to Nicolai, *JubA* 13: 31.

27. See here Jacob Katz, "The Term 'Jewish Emancipation': Its Origin and Historical Impact," in Katz, *Emancipation and Assimilation: Studies in Modern Jewish History* (Farnborough: Gregg, 1972), 21–45, esp.34–35.

28. *Zugabe zu den Göttingischen gelehrten Anzeigen*, 48. Stück, den 1. December 1781, pp. 753–63, 755–57.

29. Michaelis, review of Lessing's *Die Juden, Göttingische Anzeigen von gelehrten Sachen*, 40. Stück, den 13. Junius 1754, pp. 620–22. Lessing included Mendelssohn's letter as part of his essay "über das Lustspiel 'Die

Juden'" in the 1754 edition of his works; Lessing, *Werke und Briefe*, ed. Wilfried Barner (Frankfurt am Main: Deutscher Klassiker Verlag, 1985) 1: 492–96. English in Lessing, *Nathan the Wise, Minna von Barnhelm and Other Plays and Writings* (New York: Continuum, 1991), 166–72.

30. Mendelssohn quotes this passage verbatim, with one small omission, in *Jerusalem* (*J* 86–87, *JubA* 8: 153–54); translation here according to Arkush, except for the passage not reproduced in *Jerusalem*.

31. German in Lessing, *Werke und Briefe*, vols. 8–9; English in *Reimarus: Fragments*, ed. Charles H. Talbert, trans. Ralph S. Fraser (Philadelphia: Fortress Press, 1970). On the role of the fragments in initiating historical-critical approaches to the New Testament, see Albert Schweitzer, *The Quest of the Historical Jesus: A Critical Study of its Progress from Reimarus to Wrede*, trans. William Montgomery (New York: Macmillan, 1959); Colin Brown, *Jesus in European Protestant Thought, 1778–1860* (Durham, NC: Labyrinth Press, 1985), 1–55; and Heschel, *Abraham Geiger and the Jewish Jesus*, 127–61. On Reimarus in relation to eighteenth-century theological thought, see Henry E. Allison, *Lessing and the Enlightenment: His Philosophy of Religion and its Relation to Eighteenth-Century Thought* (Ann Arbor: University of Michigan Press, 1966) and Thomas P. Saine, *The Problem of Being Modern, or, The German Pursuit of Enlightenment from Leibniz to the French Revolution* (Detroit: Wayne State University Press, 1997).

32. Reimarus, *Die vornehmsten Wahrheiten der natürlichen Religion*, ed. Günter Gawlick, intro. Michael Emsbach and Winfried Schröder (Göttingen: Vandenhoeck & Ruprecht, 1985).

33. See on this question Schweitzer, *The Quest of the Historical Jesus*, Brown, *Jesus in European Protestant Thought*, and Heschel, *Abraham Geiger and the Jewish Jesus*.

34. See, on Semler, Brown, *Jesus in European Protestant Thought*, 10–16, Peter Hanns Reill, *The German Enlightenment and the Rise of Historicism* (Berkeley: University of California Press, 1975), 168–72, and Heschel, *Abraham Geiger and the Jewish Jesus*, 139–40.

35. Lessing, *Die Erziehung des Menschengeschlechts*, in Lessing, *Werke und Briefe* 10: 75; English in Lessing, *Nathan the Wise, etc.*, 320.

36. Lessing, *Werke und Briefe* 10: 89–90; *Nathan the Wise, etc.*, 328–29.

37. Lessing, *Werke und Briefe* 10: 89; *Nathan the Wise, etc.*, 328.

38. Edward Breuer, "Of Miracles and Events Past: Mendelssohn and History," *Jewish History* 9 (1995): 27–52, here 45, also Willi Goetschel, "Moses Mendelssohn und das Projekt der Aufklärung," *Germanic Review* 71 (1996): 163–75.

39. Arkush, *Mendelssohn*, 194–99.

40. Sorkin, *Mendelssohn*, 85.

41. See ibid., 78–87.

42. Altmann, *Mendelssohn*, 333.

43. Heinrich Graetz, *History of the Jews* (Philadelphia: JPS, 1895) 5: 322.

44. Quoted according to Altmann, *Mendelssohn*, 562.

45. See ibid., 565–66, also Graetz, *History of the Jews* 5: 322.

46. Note the contrast to Altmann, who argues that Mendelssohn here is merely using an "example . . . which Christian rulers will respect" (*J* 235n).

47. *Orientalische und exegetische Bibliothek* 22 (1783): 92f.

48. The role that "script" plays in Mendelssohn's conception of Judaism's mission of combating

idolatry and spreading the spirit of monotheism to is a crucial aspect of *Jerusalem* that has been explored elsewhere. See here especially Arnold Eisen, "Divine Legislation as 'Ceremonial Script': Mendelssohn on the Commandments," *Association for Jewish Studies Review* 15.2 (1990): 239–67, and Amos Funkenstein, *Perceptions of Jewish History* (Berkeley: University of California Press, 1993), 222–29.

49. Eisen, "Divine Legislation as 'Ceremonial Script,'" 247.

50. Thomas R. Trautmann, *Aryans and British India* (Berkeley: University of California Press, 1997), 30–34.

51. See Michael Alexander, *Omai: "Noble Savage"* (London: Collins & Harvill, 1977).

52. [Gottlob Benjamin Gerlach,] *Moses und Christus, oder über den innern Werth und die wahrscheinlichen Folgen des Sendschreibens einiger Hausväter jüdischer Religion an Hern. Probst Teller, und dessen darauf ertheilte Antwort* (Berlin: Maurer, 1799), 29–33, 62.

53. [Gotthelf Andreas Regenhorst,] *Gedanken über Mosis Mendelssohn Jerusalem, in so fern diese Schrift dem Christenthum entgegen gesetzet ist* (Bremen, 1786), quoted and discussed in Altmann's notes on *Jerusalem, JubA* 8: lxxx–lxxxi.

54. Hamann, *Golgatha und Scheblimini* (Riga, 1784). See Ze'ev Levy, "Johann Georg Hamann's Concept of Judaism and Controversy with Mendelssohn's 'Jerusalem,'" *LBIYB* 29 (1984): 295–329.

55. Hamann, *Briefwechsel mit Friedrich Heinrich Jacobi*, ed. C.H. Gildemeister (Gotha, 1868), 645, quoted according to Levy, "Johann Georg Hamann's Concept of Judaism," 296.

56. Grattenauer, *Wider die Juden. Ein Wort der Warnung an alle unsere christliche*

Mitbürger (Berlin: Schmidt, 1803), 47–48, *Erklärung an das Publikum über meine Schrift: Wider die Juden* (Berlin: Schmidt, 1803), 15.

57. Friedrich Buchholz, *Moses und Jesus, oder über das intellectuelle und moralische Verhältniß der Juden und Christen. Eine historisch-politische Abhandlung* (Berlin: Unger, 1803), 87–90.

58. *Zusatz zu den Vorschlägen und Mitteln über die bürgerliche Cultur und Religionsaufklärung der Jüdischen Nation, mit einigen Nachrichten von den Juden in Polen und den rußischen Provinzen* (Königsberg, 1785), reviewed in *Allgemeine Deutsche Bibliothek* 77 (1787): 187–89, here 187.

59. The review cited lists Schlegel as author. On Schlegel, see Günther Ott, "Gottlieb Schlegel, der Greifswalder Lehrer Ernst Moritz Arndts, und die Aufklärungstheologie seiner Zeit," *Wissenschaftliche Zeitschrift der Ernst-Moritz-Arndt Universität Greifswald* 24 (1975): 219–29.

60. Schlegel, *Zusatz*, 4.

61. Ibid., 20.

62. Ibid., 22.

63. Ibid., 55.

64. Ibid., 60–62.

65. Ibid., 41–51.

66. Ibid., 51.

67. Ibid., 63–64.

68. Ibid., 64.

69. Eichhorn, *Allgemeine Bibliothek der biblischen Litteratur* 2 (1789): 293–302.

70. Ibid., 294.

71. Ibid., 300.

72. Ibid., 301.

73. Ibid., 301–02.

74. Runde, "Ueber die bürgerliche Verbesserung der Juden: an Herrn Geheimen Rath Dohm in Berlin," *Hessische Beiträge* 1.1 (1785): 56–67.

75. Ibid., 61.

76. Ibid., 65–66.

77. Meyer, *The Origins of the Modern Jew*, 11–56.

4 PHILOSOPHY, ANTISEMITISM AND
THE POLITICS OF RELIGIOUS REFORM:
SAUL ASCHER'S CHALLENGE TO KANT
AND FICHTE

1. Hannah Arendt, *The Origins of Totalitarianism*, new edition with added prefaces (New York: Harcourt, Brace & World, 1973), xi.
2. Arthur Hertzberg, *The French Enlightenment and the Jews* (New York: Columbia University Press, 1968).
3. Gavin I. Langmuir, *Toward a Definition of Antisemitism* (Berkeley: University of California Press, 1990).
4. Peter Schäfer, *Judeophobia: Attitudes toward the Jews in the Ancient World* (Cambridge, Mass.: Harvard University Press, 1997).
5. Shmuel Feiner, "Mendelssohn and 'Mendelssohn's Disciples'—A Reexamination," *LBIYB* 40 (1995): 129–67.
6. Ascher, *Eisenmenger der Zweite. Nebst einem vorangesetzten Sendschreiben an den Herrn Professor Fichte in Jena* (Berlin, 1794), 35; Ascher, *Scolien, oder Fragmente der Philosophie und Kunst* (Berlin, 1790), reprinted three years later as *Philosophische Betrachtungen über Empfindungs- und Erkenntniskraft* (Berlin, 1793); and *Bemerkungen über die bürgerliche Verbesserung der Juden veranlaßt bei der Frage: Soll der Jude Soldat werden?* (Frankfurt an der Oder, 1788).
7. *Leviathan oder Ueber Religion in Rücksicht des Judenthums. Herausgegeben von S. Ascher* (Berlin, 1792).
8. See Ellen Littmann, "Saul Ascher: First Theorist of Progressive Judaism," *LBIYB* 5 (1960): 107–21, also Jacob Katz, *Out of the Ghetto: The Social Background of Jewish Emancipation, 1770–1870* (Cambridge, Mass.: Harvard University Press, 1973), 133–36, and Michael A. Meyer, *Response to Modernity: A History of the Reform Movement in Judaism* (Detroit: Wayne State University Press, 1995), 21–23. The most comprehensive study of Ascher to date is Walter Grab, "Saul Ascher: Ein jüdisch-deutscher Spätaufklärer zwischen Revolution und Restauration," *Jahrbuch des Instituts für deutsche Geschichte* 6 (1977): 131–79. Christoph Schulte's article, "Saul Ascher's *Leviathan*, or the Invention of Jewish Orthodoxy in 1792," *LBIYB* 25 (2000), unfortunately came to my attention after the current chapter was completed.
9. Ascher, *Eisenmenger der Zweite*, 51.
10. Fichte, *Beitrag zur Berichtigung der Urtheile des Publikums über die französische Revolution*, in Fichte, *Gesamtausgabe der Bayerischen Akademie der Wissenschaften*, ed. Reinhard Lauth and Hans Jacob (Stuttgart-Bad Canstatt: Frommann, 1964), vol. 1. On Fichte's *Contribution*, see Anthony J. La Vopa, "The Revelatory Moment: Fichte and the French Revolution," *Central European History* 22.2 (1989): 130–59, also La Vopa, *Fichte: The Self and the Calling of Philosophy, 1762–1799* (Cambridge: Cambridge University Press, 2001), 100–30.
11. *Eisenmenger der Zweite*, 32–33. On Eisenmenger, see Jacob Katz, *From Prejudice to Destruction: Anti-Semitism, 1700–1833* (Cambridge, Mass.: Harvard University Press, 1980), 13–22, also Klaus Berghahn, *Die Grenzen der Toleranz: Juden und Christen im Zeitalter der Aufklärung* (Cologne: Böhlau, 2000), 12–22.
12. Ascher, *Eisenmenger der Zweite*, xviii.
13. Fichte, *Beitrag, Gesamtausgabe* 1: 203.
14. Ascher, *Eisenmenger der Zweite*, xiv–xvi.
15. Fichte, *Beitrag, Gesamtausgabe* 1: 292.

16. See Jacob Katz, "A State within a State: The History of an Anti-Semitic Slogan," in Katz, *Emancipation and Assimilation: Studies in Modern Jewish History* (Farnborough: Gregg, 1972), 47–76.

17. Fichte, *Beitrag, Gesamtausgabe* 1: 293n.

18. Ascher, *Eisenmenger der Zweite*, 25.

19. Fichte, *Beitrag Gesamtausgabe* 1: 293n.

20. Ascher, *Eisenmenger der Zweite*, viii.

21. La Vopa, *Fichte*, 131–49, Paul Lawrence Rose, *Revolutionary Antisemitism in Germany from Kant to Wagner* (Princeton: Princeton University Press, 1990), 117–32, Erich Fuchs, "Fichtes Stellung zum Judentum," *Fichte-Studien* 2 (1990): 160–77; and Walter Grab, "Fichtes Judenfeindschaft," *Zeitschrift für Religions- und Geistesgeschichte* 44 (1992): 70–75.

22. See here, in addition to La Vopa, *Fichte*, Paul R. Sweet, "Fichte and the Jews: A Case of Tension between Civil Rights and Human Rights," *German Studies Review* 16 (1993): 37–48, also Richard Schottky, "Fichtes Nationalstaatsgedanke auf der Grundlage unveröffentlichter Manukripte von 1807," *Fichte Studien* 2 (1990): 160–77.

23. Graetz, *History of the Jews*, trans. Bella Löwy (Philadelphia: JPS, 1895), 5: 462.

24. Rose, *Revolutionary Antisemitism*, 117–32, also 17, 67.

25. See, on this point, La Vopa, *Fichte*, 11–12, 427, n2.

26. Ascher, *Die Germanomanie. Skizze zu einem Zeitgemälde* (Berlin, 1815).

27. Rühs, "Ueber die Ansprüche der Juden an das deutsche Bürgerrecht" *Zeitschrift für die neueste Geschichte, d. Staaten- u. Völkerkunde* 3 (1815): 129–61.

28. See Ascher, *Die Warthburgs-Feier. Mit Hinsicht auf Deutschlands religiöse und politische Stimmung* (Leipzig: Achenwall, 1818).

29. Meyer, *Response to Modernity*, 64–66.

30. Compare Max Wiener, *Jüdische Religion im Zeitalter der Emanzipation* (Berlin: Philo, 1933), 40–41.

31. Kant, *Critique of Pure Reason*, trans. Norman Kemp Smith (New York: St. Martin's Press, 1965), 9n, translation modified according to *AA* 4: 9n.

32. On Kant's view of the public, see Jonathan M. Hess, *Reconstituting the Body Politic: Enlightenment, Public Culture and the Invention of Aesthetic Autonomy* (Detroit: Wayne State University Press, 1999).

33. See here Jürgen Habermas, *The Structural Transformation of the Public Sphere: An Inquiry into a Category of Bourgeois Society*, trans. Thomas Bürger with Frederick Lawrence (Cambridge, Mass.: MIT Press, 1989).

34. La Vopa, "The Revelatory Moment," also La Vopa, *Fichte*, 100–30.

35. La Vopa, "The Revelatory Moment," 148.

36. Ibid., 152–53.

37. Ascher begins the preface to *Eisenmenger the Second*, in fact, by expressing his outrage at learning of Fichte's authorship of the *Contribution* in a gathering of Enlightenment intellectuals in Berlin; see *Eisenmenger der Zweite*, v–vii.

38. Ascher, *Eisenmenger der Zweite*, xviii–xii.

39. Ibid., 3–4, 6–7.

40. Ibid., 36.

41. Ibid., 7–8.

42. Ibid., 9.

43. Ibid., xv.

44. Kant, *Religion within the Limits of Reason Alone*, trans. Theodore M. Greene and Hoyt H. Hudson (New York: Harper & Row, 1960), 116–17; German in *AA* 6: 125–26.

45. Kant, *Religion*, 117; *AA* 6: 127.

46. Kant, *Religion*, 54; *AA* 6: 57.

47. Kant, *Religion*, 146; *AA* 6: 158.

48. See, for instance, Heinz Moshe Graupe, "Kant und das Judentum,"

Zeitschrift für Religion und Geistes-geschichte 13 (1961): 308–33, esp. 317.

49. On Jewish responses to Kant's legacy, see Meyer, *Response to Modernity*, 64–66, Nathan Rotenstreich, *Jews and German Philosophy: The Polemics of Emancipation* (New York: Schocken, 1984), also, on a more general level, Arnold M. Eisen, *Rethinking Modern Judaism: Ritual, Commandment, Community* (Chicago: University of Chicago Press, 1998).

50. Kant, August 16, 1783 letter to Mendelssohn, in *Kant: Philosophical Correspondence, 1759–99*, edited and translated by Arnulf Zweig (Chicago: University of Chicago Press, 1967), 107–08; *AA* 20: 347.

51. Fichte, *Attempt at a Critique of All Revelation*, trans. Garrett Green (Cambridge: Cambridge University Press, 1978), 172; German in Fichte, *Gesamtausgabe* 1: 122. See Ascher, *Eisenmenger der Zweite*, 49–51.

52. Kant, *Religion*, 39n, also 9–10 and 100–02; *AA* 6: 43n, 10–11, 110–11.

53. For a more extensive discussion of Kant's biblical criticism than I can offer here, see Yirmiahu Yovel, *Kant and the Philosophy of History* (Princeton: Princeton University Press, 1980), 201–23. At times, Yovel's emphasis on the "process whereby reason explicates its latent potential" (222) in confrontation with history tends to underplay the tensions he also notes surrounding Kant's subordination of history to reason.

54. Kant, *Religion*, 100–01; *AA* 6: 110.

55. Kant, *Religion*, 102; *AA* 6: 111. This mode of interpretation is not unique to Kant's *Religion*. The *Critique of Judgment* describes an analogous procedure in its analysis of the "intellectual interest in the beautiful" in §42; see my discussion in *Reconstituting the Body Politic*, 234–35.

56. Kant, *Religion*, 154n; *AA* 6: 166n.

57. Kant, *Religion*, 154n; *AA* 6: 166n.
58. Kant, *Religion*, 154n; *AA* 6: 166n.
59. Kant, *Religion* 115–16; *AA* 6: 124–25.
60. See Hess, *Reconstituting the Body Politic*, 202–10, for an analysis of a parallel mode of historiography in Kant.
61. Kant, *Religion*, 116; *AA* 6: 125.
62. Kant, *Religion*, 118; *AA* 6: 127.
63. Ascher, *Eisenmenger der Zweite*, 57.
64. Kant, *Religion*, 118; *AA* 6: 128.
65. Kant, *Religion*, 118; *AA* 6: 128.
66. Kant, *Religion*, 74; *AA* 6: 79–80.
67. See *Reflexionen Kants zur Anthropologie. Aus Kants handschriftlichen Aufzeichnungen*, ed. Benno Erdmann (Leipzig: Fues's Verlag, 1882), 213–14.
68. Ascher, *Eisenmenger der Zweite*, 66–68.
69. Ascher, *Leviathan*, 131–37.
70. Kant, *Religion*, 56; *AA* 6: 62.
71. *Anthopologie in pragmatischer Hinsicht*, *AA* 7: 205–06n.
72. Bendavid, *Etwas zur Charakteristik der Juden* (Leipzig, 1793).
73. See *Der Streit der Fakultäten*, *AA* 7: 53. Compare Bendavid, *Etwas zur Charakteristik*, 45, 64–65.
74. Bendavid, *Etwas zur Charakteristik*, 65. On this point, see Meyer, *Response to Modernity*, 20–21, also, particularly on the proximity of Bendavid's and Kant's positions, Ephraim Navon, "The Encounter of German Idealists and Jewish Enlighteners—1760–1800," *Deutsche Aufklärung und Judenemanzipation, Jahrbuch des Instituts für deutsche Geschichte*, Beiheft 3 (1980): 225–41.
75. [Sabattja Joseph Wolff], *Freymüthige Gedanken über die vorgeschlagene Verbesserung der Juden in den Preußischen Staaten von einem Juden mit Zusätzen eines Christen* (Halle, 1792). On Wolff, see Michael A. Meyer, "The Orthodox and the Enlightened—An Unpublished Contemporary Analysis of Berlin Jewry's Spiritual Condition in the Early Nineteenth Century," *LBIYB* 25 (1980): 101–30, esp. 104–10.

76. Ascher, *Leviathan*, "Vorerinnerung des Herausgebers," not paginated.
77. Ascher, *Leviathan*, 8–9.
78. Ibid., 50–56.
79. Ibid., 229.
80. See Ascher, *Germanomanie*, 62, also *Die Warthburgs-Feier*, 28.
81. Ascher, *Leviathan*, 232, 237–38.
82. Ibid., 108–09.
83. Ascher, *Eisenmenger der Zweite*, 58.
84. See the reviews of *Leviathan* in *Annalen der neuesten Theologischen Litteratur und Kirchengeschichte* 5.23 (1793): 358–63, *Neue allgemeine deutsche Bibliothek* 5.2 (1793): 365–68, and *Allgemeine Literatur-Zeitung* 133 (1794): 185–92. Valentin Heinrich Schmidt and Daniel Gottlieb Gebhard Mehring's *Neuestes gelehrtes Berlin; oder literarische Nachrichten von jetztlebenden Berlinischen Schriftstellern und Schriftstellerinnen* (Berlin: Maurer, 1795) lists two additional reviews that were not at my disposal, one in the *Leipziger Anzeiger* 47 (1793), the other in the *Erfurter Zeitung* 30 (1793). All these reviews, I should note, appeared in 1793 and 1794 and thus would not necessarily have been available to Kant's during the composition of the *Religion*. But the fact that *Leviathan* was reviewed at least five times in 1793–94 in theological and philosophical journals targeting non-Jews does suggest that Ascher's work had a substantial readership. Ascher's assumption that Kant might have been familiar with his work is thus not entirely far-fetched.
85. Ascher, *Eisenmenger der Zweite*, 58–62.
86. Kant, *Religion*, 118; *AA* 6: 127.
87. Ascher, *Eisenmenger der Zweite*, 69–71.
88. Letter from Knebel to Herder, Jena, October 10, 1794, in *J.G. Fichte im Gespräch. Berichte der Zeitgenossen*, ed. Erich Fuchs with Reinhard Lauth and Walter Schieche (Stuttgart-Bad Canstatt: frommann-holzboog, 1978), 1: 156.

89. Je—, review of *Eisenmenger der Zweite*, *Neue allgemeine deutsche Bibliothek* 21 (1796): 339–40.
90. Ascher, *Germanomanie*, 58–59.
91. Bendavid, *Etwas zur Charakteristik*, 32.
92. See here, for instance, Katz, *Out of the Ghetto*, 133.
93. Heinrich Heine, *The Harz Journey*, trans. Charles G. Leland (New York: Marsilio, 1995), 55–61. The text Heine refers to in speaking of Ascher's "special malice" against Christianity is Ascher's *Ansicht vom künftigen Schicksal des Christenthums* (Leipzig, 1819).
94. See Grab, "Saul Ascher," 134. Ascher and Börne took fundamentally different approaches to the questions of religion and assimilation, however; see Jonathan M. Hess, "Ludwig Börne's Visit to the Anatomical Cabinet: The Writing of Jewish Emancipation," *New German Critique* 55 (1992): 105–26.

5   JEWISH BAPTISM AND THE QUEST FOR WORLD RULE: PERCEPTIONS OF JEWISH POWER AROUND 1800

1. Friedländer, *Sendschreiben an Seine Hochwürden, Herrn Oberconsistorialrath und Probst Teller zu Berlin, von einigen Hausvätern jüdischer Religion* (Berlin: Mylius, 1799). In later years, Friedländer confessed his authorship, claiming that the *Sendschreiben* represented, as its title indicated, the views of a group of like-minded Jews. See Friedländer, *Ueber die Verbesserung der Israeliten im Königreich Pohlen* (Berlin: Nicolai, 1819), ix, also Friedländer, *An die Verehrer, Freunde und Schüler Jerusalem's, Spalding's, Teller's, Herder's und Löffler's* (Leipzig: Hartmann, 1823), 15. On Friedländer and his *Sendschreiben*, see Ellen Littmann, "David Friedländers Sendschreiben an Probst Teller und sein Echo," *Zeitschrift für die Geschichte der Juden in*

Deutschland 6 (1935): 92–112; Michael A. Meyer, *The Origins of the Modern Jew: Jewish Identity and European Culture in Germany, 1749–1824* (Detroit: Wayne State University Press, 1967), 57–84; Steven M. Lowenstein, *The Jewishness of David Friedländer and the Crisis of Berlin Jewry* (Ramat-Gan: Bar-Ilan University, 1994); and David Charles Smith, "Protestant Anti-Judaism in the German Emancipation Era," *Jewish Social Studies* 36 (1974): 203–19, esp. 210–14.

2. Graetz, *History of the Jews*, trans. Bella Löwy (Philadelphia: JPS, 1895), 5: 421–28.

3. Arendt, *Rahel Varnhagen: The Life of a Jewess*, ed. Liliane Weissberg, trans. Richard and Clara Winston (Baltimore: The Johns Hopkins University Press, 1997), 88. The common equation of Friedländer's letter with assimilationist opportunism is qualified in the most important recent literature, cited above, none of which, however, stresses the subversive aspects of this act in the way I do in this chapter.

4. Friedländer, *Akten-Stücke, die Reform der Jüdischen Kolonien in den Preußischen Staaten betreffend* (Berlin: Vossische Buchhandlung, 1793), here 27. On Friedländer's campaign for emancipation, see Ismar Freund, *Die Emanzipation der Juden in Preußen, unter besonderer Berücksichtigung des Gesetzes vom 11. März 1812* (Berlin: Poppelauer, 1912), 33–65, and Steven M. Lowenstein, *The Berlin Jewish Community: Enlightenment, Family, and Crisis, 1770–1830* (New York: Oxford University Press, 1994), 75–83.

5. Teller, *Beantwortung des Sendschreibens einiger Hausväter jüdischer Religion an mich, den Probst Teller* (Berlin: Mylius, 1799).

6. See the bibliography compiled by Littmann, "David Friedländer's Sendschreiben," also the listings in Volkmar Eichstädt, *Bibliographie zur Geschichte der Judenfrage* (Hamburg: Hanseatische Verlagsanstalt, 1938), 27–30. Friedländer's letter appeared in three editions in 1799; Teller's response was published once more in 1799 and then again in a third edition in 1801.

7. [F. L.] Schönemann, "An die Herrn. Verfasser des Sendschreibens an Herrn O.K. Rath Teller," *Neue Berlinische Monatsschrift* 4 (1800): 208–25. Schönemann, the son of an Eastern European Jewish Enlightener who settled in Berlin, authored several Enlightenment works in both Hebrew and German; see Lowenstein, *The Berlin Jewish Community*, 34.

8. De Luc, *Lettre aux auteurs juifs d'un mémoire adressé à Mr. Teller* (Berlin, 1799), promptly published in German translation: *An die Hausväter jüdischer Religion, Verfasser eines an den Herrn Ober-Consistorialrath und Probst Teller zu Berlin gerichteten Sendschreibens* (Berlin: 1799).

9. Schönemann, "An die Herrn. Verfasser."

10. [Friedrich Schleiermacher,] *Briefe bei Gelegenheit der politisch theologischen Aufgabe und des Sendschreibens jüdischer Hausväter. Von einem Prediger außerhalb Berlin* (Berlin: Friedrich Franke, 1799), 36–37.

11. Paulus, Review of *Sendschreiben*, *Allgemeine Bibliothek der neuesten theologischen Literatur* 2 (1799): 314–44.

12. Paalzow, *Die Juden. Nebst einigen Bemerkungen über das Sendschreiben an Herrn Obersonsistorialrath und Probst Teller zu Berlin von einigen Hausvätern jüdischer Religion und die darauf erfolgte Tellersche Antwort* (Berlin: Schöne, 1799).

13. [Ernst Traugott von Kortum,] *Ueber Judenthum und Juden, hauptsächlich in Rüksicht ihres Einflusses auf bürgerlichen Wohlstand* (Nuremberg: Raspesche Buchhandlung, 1795), 64–94. Dohm

notes the importance of Kortum and names him as author of this book in his *Denkwürdigkeiten meiner Zeit* (Lemgo: Meyer, 1814–19), 2: 284n.

14. See Steven E. Aschheim, "'The Jew Within': The Myth of 'Judaization' in Germany," in *The Jewish Response to German Culture: From the Enlightenment to the Second World War*, ed. Jehuda Reinharz and Walter Schatzberg (Hanover: University Press of New England, 1985).

15. Grattenauer, *Wider die Juden. Ein Wort der Warnung an alle unsere christliche Mitbürger* (Berlin: Schmidt, 1803).

16. See ibid., also Grattenauer, *Erklärung an das Publikum über meine Schrift: Wider die Juden* (Berlin: Schmidt, 1803), 36–37, and Grattenauer, *Erster Nachtrag zu seiner Erklärung über seine Schrift: Wider die Juden* (Berlin: Schmidt, 1803), 29–30.

17. See Gentz's letter of October 8, 1803 to Karl Gustav von Brinkmann, in *Briefe von und an Friedrich von Gentz*, ed. Friedrich Carl Wittichen (Munich: R. Oldenbourg, 1910) 2: 163–68, esp. 164–66.

18. Grattenauer's *Erklärung*, cited above, was published in four editions in 1803. The *Erster Nachtrag* only appeared once before censorship was instituted. On the reception and offical reactions to *Wider die Juden*, see Ludwig Geiger, *Geschichte der Juden in Berlin* (Berlin: Guttentag, 1871) 2: 301–19. Geiger reprints archival documents that are no longer available. For bibliography, see Eichstädt, *Bibliographie zur Geschichte der Judenfrage*, 30–35.

19. Arendt speaks of *Against the Jews* as the "first modern hate-sheet" (*Rahel Varnhagen*, 148). For more elaborate arguments linking Grattenauer to the rise of modern antisemitism, see Deborah Hertz, *Jewish High Society in Old Regime Berlin* (New Haven: Yale University Press, 1988), 260–64, also Peter R. Erspamer, *The Elusiveness of Tolerance: The "Jewish Question" from Lessing to the Napoleonic Wars* (Chapel Hill: University of North Carolina Press, 1997), 113–20.

20. See Kurt Fervers, *Berliner Salons: Die Geschichte einer großen Verschwörung* (Munich: Deutscher Volksverlag, 1940), 204–10, also Hans Karl Krüger, *Berliner Romantik und Berliner Judentum* (Bonn: Ludwig Röhrscheid Verlag, 1939), 40–48.

21. Lowenstein, *The Jewishness of David Friedländer*. On Berlin Jewry at the time, see Lowenstein, *The Berlin Jewish Community*, and Hertz, *Jewish High Society*, also Geiger, *Geschichte der Juden in Berlin*. It is not insignificant here that Daniel Itzig's family was able to secure citizenship for itself in 1791, as part of a special deal with the Prussian government. Friedländer, who was included in this provision as his son-in-law, had no success in gaining rights for the members of his extended family. It was during this period—and this is telling for gauging Friedländer's commitment to Jews and Judaism—that Friedländer emerged as an advocate for the emancipation of the *entirety* of Prussian Jewry. On Friedländer's biography and standing in the Jewish community, see Lowenstein, *The Jewishness of David Friedländer*.

22. Lowenstein, *The Berlin Jewish Community*, 29.

23. Hertz, *Jewish High Society*, 26. Hertz speaks of Berlin Jewry as a surrogate bourgeoisie.

24. Ibid., 260–64.

25. Erspamer, *The Elusiveness of Tolerance*, 113–20.

26. See Lowenstein, *The Berlin Jewish Community*, 120–33, for an exemplary statistical analysis of the social-historical phenomenon of Jewish baptisms.

27. "Politisch-theologische Aufgabe über die Behandlung der jüdischen Täuflinge," *Berlinisches Archiv der Zeit und ihres Geschmacks* 1 (1799), 228–39, reprinted in pamphlet form as well (Berlin: Maurer, 1799).

28. "Politisch-theologische Aufgabe," 230–31.

29. Ibid., 238.

30. Grattenauer, *Wider die Juden*, 12–14; *Erklärung*, 12–13, 16–19, 36–37; *Erster Nachtrag*, 29–30.

31. Littmann's speculation that Friedländer played a role in arranging for the earlier essay to be put before the public in an attempt to generate interest in his later proposals seems unfounded, particularly given the central role that racial thinking plays in the *Berlinisches Archiv* essay. See Littmann, "David Friedländers Sendschreiben," 97–98.

32. Friedländer, *Sendschreiben*, 46. Compare "Politisch-theologische Aufgabe," 233–36.

33. See Kant, *AA* 8: 34–36, also my discussion in *Reconstituting the Body Politic: Enlightenment, Public Culture and the Invention of Aesthetic Autonomy* (Detroit: Wayne State University Press, 1999), 19–22, 194–202.

34. Friedländer, *Sendschreiben*, 7–10.

35. Ibid, 11–12.

36. Ibid., 14.

37. Ibid., 17–18.

38. See my discussion of Kant in the previous chapter. Ephraim Navon has speculated that Friedländer was directly influenced by Kant here; see Navon, "The Encounter of German Idealists and Jewish Enlighteners—1760–1800," *Deutsche Aufklärung und Judenemanzipation, Jahrbuch des Instituts für deutsche Geschichte* Beiheft 3 (1980): 225–41.

39. Friedländer, *Sendschreiben*, 26–27.

40. Ibid., 48–49.

41. Ibid., 61.

42. Ibid., 51.

43. Ibid., 67–68.

44. In his earlier work, Teller charted the development from a "Christianity of faith" based on belief alone to a "Christianity of reason" based on critical questioning to a "pure Christianity" based on clearly recognized truths. See Teller, *Die Religion der Vollkommeneren* (Berlin, 1792), also Martin Bollacher, "Wilhelm Abraham Teller. Ein Aufklärer der Theologie," *Über den Prozeß der Aufklärung in Deutschland im 18. Jahrhundert. Personen, Institutionen und Medien*, ed. Hans Erich Bödeker and Ulrich Herrmann (Göttingen 1987).

45. See *Der Prediger. Aus dem Hebräischen von David Friedländer. Nebst einer vorangeschickten Abhandlung: Ueber den besten Gebrauch der h. Schrift in pädagogischer Rücksicht* (Berlin, 1788).

46. Friedländer, *Sendschreiben*, 55–57.

47. Review of *Sendschreiben*, *Allgemeine Literatur-Zeitung* 2 (1799): 329–33, published on May 7, 1799.

48. Teller, *Beantwortung*, 35–36, 39.

49. Ibid., 45–46.

50. Ibid., 58.

51. Ibid., 45–46.

52. August Hennings, review of Friedländer's *Sendschreiben* and Teller's *Beantwortung*, *Der Genius der Zeit* 18.3 (1799): 30–50, esp. 42.

53. *Gespräch über das Sendschreiben von einigen jüdischen Hausvätern an den Probst Teller, zwischen einem christlichen Theologen und einem alten Juden* (Berlin: Rottmann, 1799), 29–33. The work critiqued is *An einige Hausväter jüdischer Religion, über die vorgeschlagene Verbindung mit den protestantischen Christen. Von einem Prediger in Berlin* (Berlin: Dieterici, 1799).

54. [Benjamin Gottlob Gerlach,] *Moses und Christus, oder über den innern Werth und die wahrscheinlichen Folgen des Sendschreibens einiger Hausväter jüdischer*

Religion an Hern. Probst Teller, und dessen darauf ertheilte Antwort (Berlin: Maurer, 1799), 3–20.

55. Ibid., 29–33, 62.

56. *Charlotte Sampson oder Geschichte eines jüdischen Hausvaters, der mit seiner Familie dem Glauben seiner Väter entsagte. Eine Geschichte der neuesten Zeit* (Berlin: Johann Friedrich Unger, 1800).

57. Review of *Charlotte Sampson* in *Allgemeine Literatur-Zeitung* 1 (1800): 659–61.

58. [Schleiermacher,] *Briefe bei Gelegenheit der politisch theologischen Aufgabe und des Sendschreibens jüdischer Hausväter,* cited in note 10 above.

59. Hertz, *Jewish High Society,* 121; Schleiermacher, *Briefe bei Gelegenheit,* 11–12.

60. Schleiermacher, *Briefe bei Gelegenheit,* 10.

61. Ibid., 25, 36–37.

62. Ibid., 12–13.

63. Ibid., 15.

64. Peter W. Foley, "Der Jude als moralisch zurechnungsfähiger Bürger: Schleiermachers philosophische Erwiderung auf die Frage der Bürgerrechte für Juden," *Theologische Literaturzeitung* 126 (2001): 721–34. Foley's piece offers a crucial revision of Gunter Scholtz's important essay, "Friedrich Schleiermacher über das Sendschreiber jüdischer Hausväter," *Wolfenbütteler Studien zur Aufklärung* 4 (1977): 297–352.

65. Schleiermacher, *On Religion: Speeches to its Cultured Despisers,* trans. Richard Crouter (Cambridge: Cambridge Univeristy Press, 1988), 113–14. For Scholz, unlike for Foley, this disparagment of Judaism contradicts the tolerance of Schleiermacher's letters on Friedländer's *Sendschreiben.*

66. Schleiermacher, *Briefe bei Gelegenheit,* 36–37.

67. Ibid., 46–49.

68. Ibid., 50–51.

69. Schleiermacher, *On Religion,* 114.

70. Schleiermacher, *Briefe bei Gelegenheit,* 36–37.

71. Ibid., 20, 36.

72. Ibid., 15.

73. Ibid., 26.

74. Ibid., 27–28.

75. The review of Paalzow's *Die Juden* appeared in *Allgemeine Literatur-Zeitung* 3 (1799): 513–20; the review of Schleiermacher appeared in *Allgemeine Literatur-Zeitung* 2 (1800): 79–80.

76. Paulus, *Allgemeine Bibliothek der neuesten theologischen Literatur* 2 (1799): 314–44. On Paulus's subsequent career, see Albert Schweitzer, *The Quest of the Historical Jesus: A Critical Study of Its Progress from Reimarus to Wrede,* trans. William Montgomery (New York: Macmillan, 1959), 48–57, and Jacob Katz, *From Prejudice to Destruction: Anti-Semitism, 1700–1933* (Cambridge, Mass.: Harvard University Press, 1980), 155–58.

77. Paulus, 330–35.

78. Ibid., 330–31, 337.

79. *Voltaire Commentar über Montesquieus Werk von den Gesetzen,* trans. Christian Ludwig Paalzow (Berlin, 1780). For bibliography until 1795, see the entry on Paalzow in Valentin Heinrich Schmidt and Daniel Gottlieb Gebhard Mehring, *Neuestes gelehrtes Berlin; oder literarische Nachrichten von jetztlebenden Berlinischen Schriftstellern und Schriftstellerinnen* (Berlin: Maurer, 1795) 2: 96–98. The frequently cited biography of Paalzow in the *Allgemeine Deutsche Biographie* indicates incorrectly that Paalzow left Berlin in 1798; even his writings from 1803 still present him as a *Kriminalrath* with the *Kammergericht* in Berlin.

80. Paalzow, Knüppeln and Nencke, *Büsten Berliner Gelehrten, Schriftsteller und Künstler* (Stendal, 1787).

81. Paalzow, *Handbuch für practische Rechtsgelehrte in den Preussischen Staaten*

(Berlin: Nauck, 1802–03), second, enlarged edition, 1816–19.

82. Paalzow, *Die Juden*, 59.

83. Ibid., 31–34.

84. Ibid., 46. Paalzow here echoes and cites Kortum, *Ueber Judenthum und Juden*, quoted in note 13 above.

85. Paalzow, *Die Juden*, 26.

86. Ibid., 56–57.

87. See here, for instance, Daniel Joachim Köppen, *Wer ist ein Christ? Oder über den Begriff von einem Christen. Nebst Bemerkungen über das Sendschreiben der jüdischen Hausväter an den Herrn Ober-Consist.-Rath Teller und Dessen Beantwortung* (Leipzig: Christian Gottlob Hilscher, 1800). In this work, Köppen, a pastor in Zettemin and the author of a widely read 1797 work defending the Bible as a "work of divine wisdom" (*Die Bibel, ein Werk der göttlichen Weisheit* [Rostock, Leipzig: K.C. Stiller, 1797]), mounted a sustained attack on the way in which deists have deformed the true essence of Christianity and denigrated Judaism in their effort to recast Jesus's Christianity as a prototype of pure rational religion. Arguing against both Teller's and Friedländer's "atheism," he defended the continued survival of Judaism as part of a divine plan to heal the Jews through the spirit of Christ. Jean André de Luc argued in a somewhat similar manner in his *Lettre aux auteurs juifs*. Critiquing Friedländer's attack on Christianity, he defended the text of revelation and encouraged Jews to remain Jews and hold fast to the divine ceremonial law.

88. Paalzow, *Tractatus historico-politicus de civitate Judaeorum* (Berlin: Schöne, 1803).

89. Grattenauer, *Wider die Juden*, 7–18.

90. Ibid., 8, 17.

91. *Ueber das Bürgerrecht der Juden von C. L. Paalzow, übersetz von einem Juden* (Berlin: in allen Buchhandlungen, September 1803).

92. Review of Paalzow, Grattenauer, etc., in *Allgemeine Literatur-Zeitung* 2 (1804): 58–64, here 64.

93. [Sabbatja Joseph Wolff,] *Sendschreiben eines Christen an einen hiesigen Juden, über den Verfasser der Schrift: Wider die Juden* (Berlin: Schöne, 1803), 7.

94. Gentz, letter of September 10, 1803 to von Brinkmann, in *Briefe* 2: 152.

95. Grattenauer's pamphlets of 1803 refer to his student days in Halle, where he claims to have studied Oriental languages with Johann Salomo Semler and others (*Wider die Juden*, 54–55). His claim to have been an alumnus of the famous pietist orphanage in Halle in the same passage is substantiated by the *Schülerverzeichnis der Lateinischen Schule* in the archives of the *Franckesche Stiftungen*, online at http://www.franckesche-stiftungen. uni halle.de/latina/grod13%7E1.html.

96. The reference to Grattenauer's larceny charge is in Eleonore Sterling, *Judenhaß: Die Anfänge des politischen Antisemitismus in Deutschland (1815–1850)* (Frankfurt am Main: Europäische Verlagsanstalt, 1969), 153, based on archival materials in Merseburg. The article in the November 17, 1803 edition of the *Zeitung für die elegante Welt* also seems to allude to the larceny charges; see "Nachtrag zu Hrn. Grattenauer's Beschuldigungen wider die Juden," *Zeitung für die elegante Welt* 138 (1803): 1095–99, esp. 1098–99.

97. See Gentz, *Briefe* 2: 152–53, 162–66, also Paul Sweet, *Friedrich von Gentz: Defender of the Old Order* (Madison: University of Wisconsin Press, 1941), 73–74.

98. See *Ueber die physische und moralische Verfassung der heutigen Juden. Stimme eines Kosmopoliten* (Leipzig, 1791), a fairly uninfluential work that was given extremely negative reviews in both the *Allgemeine Deutsche Bibliothek* 112 (1792): 292–96, and the *Allgemeine*

Literatur-Zeitung 2 (1794): 553–56. Grattenauer claimed that Jews had "deceived" and "pillaged" him in 1796 in his petition to Chancellor von Goldbeck of September 14, 1803, reprinted in Geiger, *Geschichte der Juden in Berlin*, 2: 315.

99. See the petition from Grattenauer to von Goldbeck of September 14, 1803, in Geiger, *Geschichte der Juden in Berlin*, 2: 314–16.

100. Grattenauer, *Erklärung*, 44–45, also Geiger, *Geschichte der Juden in Berlin*, 2: 315.

101. The title page to the second volume of Grattenauer's *Repertorium aller die Kriegslasten, Kriegsschäden und Kriegseinquartierungen betreffenden neuern Gesetze und Verordnungen, nebst vollständiger Litteratur: Ein Handbuch für Juristen, Kammeralisten, Einquartierungs- Munizipal-Servis- und Polizeibeamte* (Breslau: Korn, 1810), lists Grattenauer as the editor of the *Königlich-Preußisch-Schlesisches Intelligenzblatt*. Grattenauer also published frequently in the *Schlesische Provinzialblätter* in the years after he left Berlin.

102. Grattenauer, *Von Stamme Aaron und dessen angeblichen Vorrechten: Ein Beytrag zum Judenwesen* (Jerusalem: David, 1817).

103. See the memorandum of the official censor, reprinted in Geiger, *Geschichte der Juden in Berlin*, 2: 316.

104. See Borgstede's report to Minister von Hardenberg, ibid., 313.

105. Borgstede, cited according to Geiger, ibid.

106. Ibid., 318.

107. See Hardenberg's memorandum to Goldbeck, ibid., 317.

108. "Nachtrag zu Hrn. Grattenauer's Beschuldigungen," 1099.

109. *Können die Juden, ohne Nachtheil für den Staat, bei ihrer jetzigen Verfassung bleiben?* (Berlin: Hayn, 1803), here 9–10, 18–19. This anonymous work,

which went through three editions in 1803, proposed substituting ceremonial castration for the Jewish practice of circumcision. Not surprisingly, its claim that Jews actively lobbied for censorship finds no support in the official documents reprinted in Geiger. Contemporaries too were reluctant to grant this piece any credibility; see here, for instance, the preface to the *Schreiben eines Lords an seinen Correspondenten zu Paris. Zur Vertheidigung der Juden. Aus dem Französischen übersetzt, und mit einer Vorrede nebst Anmerkungen begleitet von B.*** (Breslau: Barth, 1804), xxiii.

110. See Grattenauer, *Erklärung*, 10–11, also *Erster Nachtrag*, 49–56.

111. Grattenauer, *Erster Nachtrag*, 71.

112. Fervers, *Berliner Salons*, 204–10, Krüger, *Berliner Romantik*, 40–48.

113. Grattenauer, *Wider die Juden*, 5–6, also *Erklärung*, 30–32.

114. Grattenauer, *Erster Nachtrag*, 78.

115. Friedländer, *An die Verehrer*, 16.

116. Grattenauer, *Erklärung*, 40, 29–30; *Erster Nachtrag*, 23.

117. Grattenauer, *Erklärung*, 43. Grattenauer elaborated his plans for a "review of all writings about the Open Letter of the Jewish Family Heads" in a petition to the authorities, reprinted in Geiger, *Geschichte der Juden in Berlin*, 2: 318.

118. Grattenauer, *Erklärung*, 15, *Wider die Juden*, 47–48.

119. Grattenauer, *Wider die Juden*, 54–55.

120. See here, for instance, Johann Wilhelm Andreas Kosmann, *Für die Juden. Ein Wort zu Berherzignug [sic] an die Freunde der Menschheit und die wahren Verehrer Jesu* (Berlin: Schöne, 1803), 29; *Der Pseudo-Haman, oder kurze Widerlegung der Schrift: wider die Juden* (Berlin: Schöne, 1803); and Aaron Wolfssohn, *Jeschurun, oder unparteyische Beleuchtung der dem Judenthume neurdings gemachten Vorwürfe. In Briefen von Aaron Wolfs-*

sohn, Oberlehrer und Inspektor an der königl. Wilhelmsschule zu Breslau (Breslau: Adolf Gehr, 1804).

121. Gentz, *Briefe* 2: 164–65.

122. *Wider die Juden,* 12–14, *Erklärung* 36–37, and *Erster Nachtrag,* 29–30.

123. Grattenauer, *Erster Nachtrag,* 78.

124. In his second pamphlet, Grattenauer attacked Bendavid for daring to speak out, referring to a piece apparently published by Bendavid in the *Spenersche Zeitung* 99 (*Erklärung,* 11).

125. Kosmann, *Für die Juden,* cited in note 99 above.

126. Sabbatja Joseph Wolff, *Sendschreiben eines Christen an einen hiesigen Juden, über den Verfasser der Schrift: Wider die Juden* (Berlin: Schöne, 1803).

127. *Können die Juden, ohne Nachtheil für den Staat, bei ihrer jetzigen Verfassung bleiben?,* cited in note 87 above.

128. *Auch ein Wort wider die Juden. Veranlaßt durch des Herrn Justiz-Commisarii Grattenauer Schrift: Wider die Juden. Von einem praktischen Geschäftsmann, der merkwürdige jüdische Schwindeleien erfahren hat* (Berlin, 1803).

129. See here, in addition to Julius Voss's well-known *Der travestirte Nathan der Weise* (Berlin, 1804), also *Der wucherde Jude am Prange*r (Berlin, 1804), and *Taschenbuch für die Kinder Israels oder Almanach für unsre Leute* (Berlin, 1804), all quoted according to Gunnar Och, *Imago judaica: Juden und Judentum im Spiegel der deutschen Literatur, 1750–1812* (Würzburg: Königshausen & Neumann, 1995), 42. On antisemitic literature of the period see, in addition to Och, Erspamer, *The Elusiveness of Tolerance,* 127–50.

130. Friedrich Buchholz, *Moses und Jesus, oder über das intellectuelle und moralische Verhältniß der Juden und Christen. Eine historisch-politische Abhandlung* (Berlin: Unger, 1803). See, on Buchholz in general, Rütger Schäfer, *Friedrich Buchholz—ein vergessener Vorläufer der Soziologie* (Göppingen: Kümmerle, 1972), also Kurt Bahrs, *Friedrich Buchholz. Ein preußischer Publizist 1768–1843* (Berlin: E. Ebering, 1907). Neither of these works—both of which claim Buchholz was free of all chauvinism—sufficiently integrates Buchholz's anti-Jewish writing into their analysis.

131. See here, for instance, Buchholz's postscript to Igance Chauffour, *Betrachtungen über die Anwendung des Kaiserlichen Dekrets vom 17ten März 1808 in Betreff der Schuldforderungen der Juden,* trans. with a postscript by Friedrich Buchholz (Berlin: Ameland, 1809), also Buchholz, *Gemälde des gesellschaftlichen Zustandes im Königreiche Preußen, bis zum 14ten Oktober des Jahres 1806* (Berlin: Historisch-politisch-militärisches Institut, 1808), 176–99.

132. Buchholz, *Moses und Jesus,* 2, also 201–02.

133. See Peter Villaume, *Vereinbarkeit der Juden mit andern Nationen; mit Rücksicht auf die Buchholzische Schrift: Moses und Jesus* (Hamburg: Villaume, 1804), *Neue allgemeine deutsche Bibliothek* 92 (1804), 504–13, *Allgemeine Literatur-Zeitung* 2 (1808), 89–93, 98–102, 106–10.

134. *Moses og Jesus, eller, Om Jødernes og de Christnes intellektuelle og moralske forhold: en historisk-politisk afhandling,* trans. Thomas Thaarup (Copenhagen: Brummer, 1813).

135. Buchholz, *Moses und Jesus,* 203.

136. Ibid., 87–90.

137. Ibid., 105.

138. Ibid., 49–50.

139. Ibid., 55–56.

140. Buchholz's account of the role of Jews in Alexandria is lifted from Paalzow's 1803 work; see *Ueber das Bürgerrecht der Juden,* 57. Buchholz, *Moses und Jesus,* 47, 55–56.

141. Buchholz, *Moses und Jesus,* 56–67.

142. Ibid, 68.

143. Ibid., 70–71.

144. Ibid., 61–62, 65–66.
145. Ibid., 107.
146. Ibid., 122–23.
147. Ibid., 57.
148. Ibid., 122–57.
149. Ibid., 244.
150. Ibid., 206, 201–54, 228–38, 262, 242.
151. Grattenauer, *Erklärung*, 5, 38; *Wider die Juden*, 52–54.
152. *Unumstößlicher Beweis, daß ohne die schleunige Niedermetzlung aller Juden, und den Verkauf aller Jüdinnen zur Sclaverei, die Welt, die Menschheit, das Christenthum und alle Staaten nothwendig untergehen müssen, von Dominikus Hamann Epi-phanes, dem Judenfeinde* (Königsberg, 1804), 16–19.
153. Note the difference from Erspamer, who asserts that Grattenauer sought to "promote the monologic hegemony of a mystical Christian-based nationalism" (*Elusiveness of Tolerance*, 119).

CONCLUDING REMARKS

1. Arendt, *The Origins of Totalitarianism* (New York: Harcourt Brace Jovanovich, 1973).
2. Sartre, *Réflexions sur la question juive* (Paris: P. Morihien, 1946), translated into English as *Anti-Semite and Jew*, by George J. Becker (New York: Schocken, 1948).
3. Arendt, *Origins of Totalitarianism*, xv, 8.
4. Arthur Hertzberg, *The French Enlightenment and the Jews* (New York: Columbia University Press, 1968), 6.
5. Arendt, *Eichmann in Jerusalem: A Report on the Banality of Evil* (New York: Viking Press, 1963).
6. Jürgen Habermas, *The Philosophical Discourse of Modernity*, trans. Frederick Lawrence (Cambridge, Mass.: MIT Press, 1987).

SELECT BIBLIOGRAPHY

This bibliography lists only the most important secondary sources for this study. The notes contain full references for all secondary sources cited, as well as full citations for all primary literature.

Altmann, Alexander. "Letters from Dohm to Mendelssohn." *Salo Wittmayer Baron: Jubilee Volume on the Occasion of His 80th Birthday.* Ed. Saul Lieberman, Arthur Hyman and Jeanette Meisel Baron. Jerusalem: American Academy for Jewish Research, 1974.

——. *Moses Mendelssohn: A Biographical Study.* Philadelphia: Jewish Publication Society, 1973.

Arendt, Hannah. *The Jew as Pariah: Jewish Identity and Politics in the Modern Age.* Ed. Ron H. Feldman. New York: Grove Press, 1978.

——. *The Origins of Totalitarianism.* New York: Harcourt Brace Jovanovich, 1973.

——. *Rahel Varnhagen: The Life of a Jewess.* Ed. Liliane Weissberg. Trans. Richard and Clara Winston. Baltimore: The Johns Hopkins University Press, 1997.

Arkush, Allan. *Moses Mendelssohn and the Enlightenment.* Albany: SUNY Press, 1994.

Assmann, Jan. *Moses the Egyptian: The Memory of Egypt in Western Monotheism.* Cambridge, Mass.: Harvard University Press, 1997.

Bauman, Zygmunt. *Modernity and Ambivalence.* Ithaca, NY: Cornell University Press, 1991.

Berghahn, Klaus. *Die Grenzen der Toleranz: Juden und Christen im Zeitalter der Aufklärung.* Cologne: Böhlau, 2000.

Bernasconi, Robert. "Who Invented the Concept of Race? Kant's Role in the Enlightenment Construction of Race." *Race.* Ed. Bernasconi. Oxford: Blackwell, 2001.

Blackbourn, David and Geoff Eley. *The Peculiarities of German History: Bourgeois Society and Politics in Nineteenth-Century Germany.* Oxford: Oxford University Press, 1984.

Blumenberg, Hans. *The Legitimacy of the Modern Age.* Trans. Robert M. Wallace. Cambridge, Mass.: MIT Press, 1983.

Bourel, Dominique. "Die deutsche Orientalistik im 18. Jahrhundert. Von der Mission zur Wissenschaft." *Historische Kritik und biblischer Kanon in der deutschen Aufklärung.* Ed. Henning Graf Reventlow, Walter Sparn and John Woodbridge. Wiesbaden: Harrassowitz, 1988.

Breuer, Edward. *The Limits of Enlightenment: Jews, Germans, and the Eighteenth-Century Study of Scripture.* Cambridge, Mass.: Harvard University Press, 1996.

——. "Of Miracles and Events Past: Mendelssohn and History." *Jewish History* 9 (1995): 27–52.

——. "Politics, Tradition, History: Rabbinic Judaism and the Eighteenth-Century Struggle for Civil Equality." *Harvard Theological Review* 85 (1992): 357–83.

Brown, Colin. *Jesus in European Protestant Thought, 1778–1860.* Durham, NC: Labyrinth Press, 1985.

Bruer, Albert A. *Geschichte der Juden in Preußen.* Frankfurt am Main: Campus, 1991.

Cohen, Gerson. "German Jewry as Mirror of Modernity." *LBIYB* 20 (1975): ix–xxxi.

Dambacher, Ilsegret. *Christian Wilhelm von Dohm: Ein Beitrag zur Geschichte des preußischen aufgeklärten Beamtentums und seiner Reformbestrebungen am Ausgang des 18. Jahrhunderts.* Bern: Lang, 1974.

Eichstädt, Volkmar. *Bibliographie zur Geschichte der Judenfrage I: 1750–1848.* Hamburg: Hanseatische Verlagsanstalt, 1938.

Eisen, Arnold. "Divine Legislation as 'Ceremonial Script': Mendelssohn on the Commandments." *AJS Review* 15.2 (1990): 239–67.

——. *Galut: Modern Jewish Reflection on Homelessness and Homecoming.* Bloomington: Indiana University Press, 1986.

——. *Rethinking Modern Judaism: Ritual, Commandment, Community.* Chicago: University of Chicago Press, 1998.

Erb, Rainer and Werner Bergmann. *Die Nachtseite der Judenemanzipation: Der Widerstand gegen die Integration der Juden in Deutschland 1780–1860.* Berlin: Metropol, 1989.

Erspamer, Peter R. *The Elusiveness of Tolerance: The "Jewish Question" from Lessing to the Napoleonic Wars.* Chapel Hill: University of North Carolina Press, 1997.

Feiner, Shmuel. "Mendelssohn and 'Mendelssohn's Disciples'—A Re-examination." *LBIYB* 40 (1995): 129–67.

Fervers, Kurt. *Berliner Salons: Die Geschichte einer großen Verschwörung.* Munich: Deutscher Volksverlag, 1940.

Foley, Peter W. "Der Jude als moralisch zurechnungsfähiger Bürger: Schleiermachers philosophische Erwiderung auf die Frage der Bürgerrechte für Juden." *Theologische Literaturzeitung* 126 (2001): 721–34.

Funkenstein, Amos. *Perceptions of Jewish History.* Berkeley: University of California Press, 1993.

Geiger, Abraham. "Der Kampf christlicher Theologen gegen die bürgerliche Gleichstellung der Juden." *Wissenschaftliche Zeitschrift für jüdische Theologie* 1 (1835): 52–67, 340–57, and 2 (1836): 78–92, 446–73.

Geiger, Ludwig. "Aus Briefen Dohms an Nicolai." *Zeitschrift für die Geschichte der Juden in Deutschland* 5 (1892): 75–91.

——. *Geschichte der Juden in Berlin*. Berlin: Guttentag, 1871.

Gilman, Sander L. *The Jew's Body*. New York: Routledge, 1991.

Goetschel, Willi. "Moses Mendelssohn und das Projekt der Aufklärung." *Germanic Review* 71 (1996): 163–75.

Goldhagen, Daniel J. *Hitler's Willing Executioners: Ordinary Germans and the Holocaust*. New York: Knopf, 1996.

Grab, Walter. "Saul Ascher: Ein jüdisch-deutscher Spätaufklärer zwischen Revolution und Restauration." *Jahrbuch des Instituts für deutsche Geschichte* 6 (1977): 131–79.

Graetz, Heinrich. *History of the Jews*. Trans. Bella Löwy. Philadelphia: Jewish Publication Society, 1895.

Graupe, Heinz Moshe. *The Rise of Modern Jewry: An Intellectual History of German Jewry, 1650–1942*. Trans. John Robinson. Hurtington, NY: Krieger, 1978.

Greenberg, Blu. "Rabbi Jacob Emden: The Views of An Enlightened Traditionalist on Christianity." *Judaism* 107 (1978): 351–63.

Gronau, W. *Christian Wilhelm von Dohm nach seinem Wollen und Handeln*. Lemgo: Meyersche Hof-Buchhandlung, 1824.

Gumbrecht, Hans Ulrich. "Modern." *Geschichtliche Grundbegriffe*. Ed. Otto Brunner, Werner Conze and Reinhart Koselleck. Stuttgart: Klett-Cotta, 1972ff. Vol. 4: 93–131.

Habermas, Jürgen. *The Philosophical Discourse of Modernity*. Trans. Frederick Lawrence. Cambridge, Mass.: MIT Press, 1987.

——. *The Structural Transformation of the Public Sphere: An Inquiry into a Category of Bourgeois Society*. Trans. Thomas Bürger with Frederick Lawrence. Cambridge, Mass.: MIT Press, 1989.

Hansen, Thorkild. *Arabia Felix: The Danish Expedition, 1761–67*. Trans. James and Kathleen McFarlane. London: Collins, 1964.

Hertz, Deborah. *Jewish High Society in Old Regime Berlin*. New Haven: Yale University Press, 1988.

Hertzberg, Arthur. *The French Enlightenment and the Jews*. New York: Columbia University Press, 1968.

Heschel, Susannah. *Abraham Geiger and the Jewish Jesus*. Chicago: University of Chicago Press, 1998.

Hess, Jonathan M. *Reconstituting the Body Politic: Enlightenment, Public Culture and the Invention of Aesthetic Autonomy*. Detroit: Wayne State University Press, 1999.

Hudson, Nicholas. "From 'Nation' to 'Race': The Origins of Racial Classification in Eighteenth-Century Thought." *Eighteenth-Century Studies* 29 (1996): 247–64.

Jauss, Hans Robert. *Literaturgeschichte als Provokation*. Frankfurt am Main: Suhrkamp, 1970.

Katz, Jacob. *Emancipation and Assimilation: Studies in Modern Jewish History*. Farnborough: Gregg, 1972.

——. *From Prejudice to Destruction: Anti-Semitism, 1700–1833*. Cambridge, Mass.: Harvard University Press, 1980.

——. *Out of the Ghetto: The Social Background of Jewish Emancipation, 1770–1870*. Cambridge, Mass.: Harvard University Press, 1973.

Katz, Jacob, ed. *Toward Modernity: The European Jewish Model.* New Brunswick: Transaction Books, 1987.

Koselleck, Reinhart. *Futures Past: On the Semantics of Historical Time.* Trans. Keith Tribe. Cambridge, Mass.: MIT Press, 1985.

Krüger, Hans Karl. *Berliner Romantik und Berliner Judentum.* Bonn: Ludwig Röhrscheid Verlag, 1939.

Langmuir, Gavin I. *Toward a Definition of Antisemitism.* Berkeley: University of California Press, 1990.

La Vopa, Anthony J. *Fichte: The Self and the Calling of Philosophy, 1762–1799.* Cambridge: Cambridge University Press, 2001.

———. "The Revelatory Moment: Fichte and the French Revolution." *Central European History* 22.2 (1989): 130–59.

Levy, Ze'ev. "Johann Georg Hamann's Concept of Judaism and Controversy with Mendelssohn's 'Jerusalem.'" *LBIYB* 29 (1984): 295–329.

Liberles, Robert. "Dohm's Treatise on the Jews: A Defense of the Enlightenment." *LBIYB* 33 (1988): 29–42.

———. "From Toleration to *Verbesserung*: German and English Debates on the Jews in the Eighteenth Century." *Central European History* 22 (1989): 3–32.

Librett, Jeffrey. *The Rhetoric of Cultural Dialogue: Jews and Germans from Moses Mendelssohn to Richard Wagner and Beyond.* Stanford: Stanford University Press, 2000.

Littmann, Ellen. "David Friedländers Sendschreiben an Probst Teller und sein Echo." *Zeitschrift für die Geschichte der Juden in Deutschland* 6 (1935): 92–112.

———. "Saul Ascher: First Theorist of Progressive Judaism." *LBIYB* 5 (1960): 107–21.

Löwenbrück, Anna-Ruth. *Judenfeindschaft im Zeitalter der Aufklärung. Eine Studie zur Vorgeschichte des modernen Antisemitismus am Beispiel des Göttinger Theologen und Orientalisten Johann David Michaelis (1717–1791).* Frankfurt am Main: Peter Lang, 1995.

Lowenstein, Steven M. *The Berlin Jewish Community: Enlightenment, Family, and Crisis, 1770–1830.* New York: Oxford University Press, 1994.

———. *The Jewishness of David Friedländer and the Crisis of Berlin Jewry*, Ramat-Gan: Bar-Ilan University, 1994.

Mendes-Flohr, Paul. *German Jews: A Dual Identity.* New Haven and London: Yale University Press, 1999.

Meyer, Michael A. *The Origins of the Modern Jew: Jewish Identity and European Culture in Germany, 1749–1824.* Detroit: Wayne State University Press, 1967.

———. *Response to Modernity: A History of the Reform Movement in Judaism.* Detroit: Wayne State University Press, 1988.

Meyer, Michael A. et al., eds. *German-Jewish History in Modern Times.* New York: Columbia University Press, 1996–98. 4 vols.

Möller, Horst. "Auklärung, Judenemanzipation und Staat: Ursprung und Wirkung von Dohms Schrift über die bürgerliche Verbesserung der Juden." *Deutsche Aufklärung und Judenemanzipation.* Ed. Walter Grab. *Jahrbuch des Instituts für deutsche Geschichte* Beiheft 3 (1980): 119–49.

Navon, Ephraim. "The Encounter of German Idealists and Jewish Enlighteners—
1760–1800." *Deutsche Aufklärung und Judenemanzipation.* Ed. Walter Grab. *Jahrbuch
des Instituts für deutsche Geschichte,* Beiheft 3 (1980): 225–41.

Och, Gunnar. *Imago judaica: Juden und Judentum im Spiegel der deutschen Literatur,
1750–1812.* Würzburg: Königshausen und Neumann, 1995.

Olender, Maurice. *The Languages of Paradise: Race, Religion, and Philology in the
Nineteenth Century.* Trans. Arthur Goldhammer. Cambridge, Mass.: Harvard
University Press, 1992.

Pasto, James. "Islam's 'Strange Secret Sharer': Orientalism, Judaism, and the Jewish
Question." *Comparative Studies of Society and History* 40 (1998): 437–74.

Poliakov, Léon. *The Aryan Myth: A History of Racist and Nationalist Ideas in Europe.*
Trans. Edmund Howard. New York: Basic Books, 1974.

Pollock, Sheldon. "Deep Orientalism? Notes on Sanskrit and Power Beyond the Raj."
Orientalism and the Postcolonial Predicament: Perspectives on South Asia. Ed. Carol A.
Breckenridge and Peter van der Veer. Philadelphia: University of Pennsylvania
Press, 1993.

Pratt, Mary Louise. *Imperial Eyes: Travel Writing and Transculturation.* London:
Routledge, 1992.

Reill, Peter Hanns. *The German Enlightenment and the Rise of Historicism.* Berkeley:
University of California Press, 1975.

Reinharz, Jehuda and Walter Schatzberg, eds. *The Jewish Response to German Culture:
From the Enlightenment to the Second World War.* Hanover: University Press of New
England, 1985.

Rose, Paul Lawrence. *Revolutionary Antisemitism in Germany from Kant to Wagner.*
Princeton: Princeton University Press, 1990.

Rotenstreich, Nathan. *Jews and German Philosophy: The Polemics of Emancipation.* New
York: Schocken, 1984.

Rürup, Reinhard. *Emanzipation und Antisemitismus: Studien zur "Judenfrage" der
bürgerlichen Gesellschaft.* Göttingen: Vandenhoeck & Ruprecht, 1975.

——. "The Torturous and Thorny Path to Legal Equality—'Jew Laws' and
Emancipatory Legislation in Germany from the Late Eighteenth Century."
LBIYB 31 (1986): 3–34.

Said, Edward. *Orientalism.* New York: Vintage, 1979.

Schechter, Ronald B. "The Jewish Question in Eighteenth-Century France."
Eighteenth-Century Studies 32 (1998): 84–91.

Schivelbusch, Wolfgang. *Tastes of Paradise: A Social History of Spices, Stimulants, and
Intoxicants.* Trans. David Jacobson. New York: Pantheon, 1992.

Scholem, Gerschom. *On Jews and Judaism in Crisis: Selected Essays.* Ed. Werner J.
Dannhauser. New York: Schocken, 1976.

Scholtz, Gunter. "Friedrich Schleiermacher über das Sendschreiben jüdischer
Hausväter." *Wolfenbütteler Studien zur Aufklärung* 4 (1977): 297–352.

Schweitzer, Albert. *The Quest of the Historical Jesus: A Critical Study of Its Progress
from Reimarus to Wrede.* Trans. William Montgomery. New York: Macmillan,
1959.

Smith, David Charles. "Protestant Anti-Judaism in the German Emancipation Era." *Jewish Social Studies* 36 (1974): 203–19.

Sorkin, David. "Emancipation and Assimilation: Two Concepts and Their Application to German-Jewish History." *LBIYB* 35 (1990): 17–33.

———. "Jews, the Enlightenment and Religious Toleration—Some Reflections." *LBIYB* 37 (1992): 3–16.

———. *Moses Mendelssohn and the Religious Enlightenment.* Berkeley: University of California Press, 1996.

———. "Religious Reforms and Secular Trends in German-Jewish Life—An Agenda for Research." *LBIYB* 40 (1995): 170–85.

———. *The Transformation of German Jewry, 1780–1840.* New York: Oxford University Press, 1987.

Sterling, Eleonore. *Judenhaß: Die Anfänge des politischen Antisemitismus in Deutschland (1815–1850).* Frankfurt am Main: Europäische Verlagsanstalt, 1969.

Sutcliffe, Adam. "Enlightenment and Exclusion: Judaism and Toleration in Spinoza, Locke and Bayle." *Jewish Culture and History* 2 (1999): 26–43.

———. "Myth, Origins, Identity: Voltaire, the Jews and the Enlightenment Notion of Toleration." *The Eighteenth Century: Theory and Interpretation* 39 (1998): 107–26.

Toury, Jacob. "Emanzipation und Judenkolonien in der öffentlichen Meinung Deutschlands (1775–1819)." *Jahrbuch des Instituts für deutsche Geschichte* 11 (1982): 17–53.

Volkov, Shulamit. *Das jüdische Projekt der Moderne.* Munich: Beck, 2001.

Volkov, Shulamit, ed. *Deutsche Juden und die Moderne.* Munich: Oldenbourg, 1994.

Zantop, Susanne. *Colonial Fantasies: Conquest, Family, and Nation in Precolonial Germany, 1770–1870.* Durham, NC: Duke University Press, 1997.

INDEX